BEFORE THE MUSES

AN ANTHOLOGY
OF AKKADIAN LITERATURE

Benjamin R. Foster

VOLUME II: MATURE, LATE

CDL Press
Bethesda, Maryland

Library of Congress Cataloging-in-Publication Data

Foster, Benjamin R. (Benjamin Read)
   Before the muses : an anthology of Akkadian literature /
   Benjamin R. Foster
      p.   cm.
   Includes bibliographical references.
   Contents: v. 1. Archaic, classical, mature — v. 2. Mature, late.
   ISBN 0-9620013-4-1
      1. Akkadian literature — Translations into English.   I. Title.
PJ3951.F67 1993
892'.1—dc20   92-42779
                                                       CIP

The preparation of the contents of this volume was made possible
by a grant from the Translations Program of the National Endowment for the Humanities, an independent Federal agency. The
publication of this volume was made possible by a grant from the
Publication Subvention Program of the National Endowment for
the Humanities, an independent Federal agency.

Designed by Karen Polinger Foster and Elizabeth Duncan Lyons.

Printed in Ann Arbor, MI by Cushing-Malloy, Inc.

SBN 0-9620013-5-x

Contents

VOLUME I

GENERAL INTRODUCTION
IN SEARCH OF AKKADIAN LITERATURE

CHAPTER I

THE ARCHAIC PERIOD
(2300 - 2000 B.C.)

CHAPTER II

THE CLASSICAL PERIOD
(2000 - 1500 B.C.)

CHAPTER III

THE MATURE PERIOD
(1500–1000 B.C.)

CHAPTER IV

THE LATE PERIOD

(1000–100 B.C.)

D. GREAT HYMNS AND PRAYERS

III.25 GULA HYMN OF BULLUTSA-RABI

This hymn extols in alternating stanzas Gula, goddess of healing, and her spouse, using different names (see also III.42a). The text is unusual because of the author's "signature" in the concluding lines. It is a work of great learning; rare and dialectal words abound. The hymn makes numerous allusions to mythology and may quote directly other compositions. It was popular in learned circles and was quoted in an ancient commentary. It is also attested in an ancient list of famous authors of the past and their putative literary works.

The frame of the composition is a third-person prayer by Bullutsa-rabi. He introduces the goddess in the first stanza and concludes the whole composition with a prayer that she intercede for him. The goddess speaks her own praises, a well-attested mode in Akkadian.[1] She discourses upon her astral character, her elevation to a position of authority, her interest in agriculture, her unalterable word, her healing abilities, her control of destinies, her sexual attractiveness, her upbringing and education, marriage, and scholarship.

The poet thereby proceeds from her general attributes of divinity, her role, function, and physical attributes to her major "rites of passage" and concludes with praise of her medical learning. Perhaps this aspect of her persona was of particular appeal to the poet, who says he is sick and in need of her ministrations. By contrast, her spouse is consistently portrayed as a fierce and terrible warrior, without developing a theme. Gula's personality is more complex; she has more names than her husband. Despite the dual structure of the hymn, the goddess is clearly the author's primary interest.

i

The goddess is the most capable of all deities who sit on daises,   (1)
"I am noble, I am lordly, I am splendid and sublime.
"My station is on high, I am a woman of dignity.
"I excel among goddesses,
"Great is my star in heaven, my name in the netherworld.   (5)

---

1. Von Soden (RA 52 [1958], 132) suggests possible cultic significance for first-person texts of this type; this genre may be restricted to goddesses. Whatever the literary background, the goddess's self-predication seems to lend her praises extra authority. Compare the self-praise of Ishtar II.4 and IV.53.

"Fair it is to hold me in mind, (it is) good health and life.
"People discourse of me (in) sickness (and in) health,
"My great name is Nintinugga.[1]

ii

"My spouse is the warrior, son of Enlil, the mighty,
"Valorous one, trampler of the foe,   (10)
"Who crushes the enemy, (but) who makes the righteous stand,
"Who fulfilled Enlil's wishes, whose strength is sublime,
"The strong lord who slew Anzu,
"[   ] the responsibility of (Enlil's) supremacy.[2]
"[   ] to whom Ninlil listens,   (15)
"Ninurta, the merciful offspring of heaven,
"Pure progeny, heir of Esharra.[3]

iii

"I was sought out, for E[nli]l chose me among goddesses,
"He looked up [   ], he fell in love with me.
"He wed me [for the ...] his supremacy,   (20)
"He allotted the management of Esharra [ ] into my hands.
"He added [   ] procedures,
"He [   ] me,
"He made fair my name [   ] among goddesses.
"He called [me   ] Nin-[   ], I have no rival.   (25)

iv

"[(My spouse is)] the great master of portions,
"Pure light of heaven, the one who calls for the work song,
"Resettler of devastated agricultural lands,
"Pursuer, wild bull with head held high,
"Who seized ..., who split stones[4] and begot grains,   (30)

1. Sumerian healing deity, "Lady Who Revives the Dead."
2. Allusion to the Anzu poem, see III.22.
3. A temple of Enlil in Nippur, hence the author is saying "son of Enlil."
4. Allusion to the Sumerian poem of "Ninurta and the Stones," for which see J. J. A. van Dijk, *LUGAL-UD ME-LÁM-BI NIR-GÁL* (Leiden, 1983), 37–44, with this passage alluded to 42 note 139.

"Heaper up of grain piles,
> who performed the great festival for Enlil,

"Who makes teeming mankind live in abundance,
> who resettles abandoned mounds,

"Stately, tall of form, pure shining son of Anu,

"Mightiest of the gods, great Ningirsu.

v

"Opener of the furrow, director of daybreak,   (35)

"Who drives out the (plow) ox, mistress of (its) track,

"Beloved of the stars which are the signs for plowing,

"Who silos fodder for the oxen,

"Who grants good work to the plowman,

"Mistress of basket, seed grain, plow, plowfield, share,
> and field hand(?),   (40)

"Who stretches out the measuring cord, cubits,
> and measuring rod,

"Who carries a stylus as she works, doing the accounts,

"Mother Nanshe,[1] mistress of the field boundary am I.

vi

"My towering husband is an honored noble of heaven,

"Clad in awesomeness and divine splendor,   (45)

"Who makes heaven and netherworld quake,
> lofty one among the Igigi-gods,

"Who charges through canebrakes, who dances in battle,

"Who examines the heights of heaven,
> who investigates the bottom of the netherworld,

"Who implements wise counsel, master of decisions,

"Who gathers to himself wisdom, of profound intelligence,   (50)

"Reared by the depths, splendid one, offspring of Mami,

"Rider of all the winds, lord of battle and warfare,

"Great storm, brilliant of feature, lord of lords, Ninazu.[2]

---

1. A goddess at home in the Lagash region, not usually equated with Gula, but perhaps through Ningirsu (Lagashite god) = Ninurta (see Anzu [III.22]); see also line 34.
2. "Lord Physician," a Sumerian deity (usually a brother of Ninurta).

vii

"I am sublime in heaven, I am queen in the netherworld,
"Among the gods I have no peer,   (55)
"Among goddesses I have no equal.
"I am mistress of the depths, Ea's place,
"Lofty and great are my responsibilities.
"The limits I (set) cannot be changed,
"(My) command cannot be altered.   (60)
"My name is great, I am sublime,
"I tower in my stance, I am enormous in form.
"I grant portions to all the gods.
"I am daughter, I am bride, I am spouse,
     I, indeed, manage the household,   (65)
"Wife of the foremost one, Pabilsag,[1]
"Ninkarrak,[2] mistress of counsel, am I.

viii

"The lofty one, favorite of the gods, Anu's son,
"He is the foremost one, surpassing all lords.
"The Igigi-gods consult with him,
     the shining breastplate(?)* of heaven.   (70)
"Great is fear of him among the gods,
     every one of them is in awe of his name,
"They await his command.
"He is the foremost one, towering hero, noble,
     virile one, bastion,
"He is firm of foot in heaven, powerful in the depths,
"Great in the netherworld, sublime in Ekur,   (75)
"Cherished son of Enlil,[3]
"Pure offspring of Nin<lil>,
"Double of Anu, the warrior Ninurta.

---

1. Sumerian deity, husband of Nininsina, a healing goddess.
2. Healing goddess.
3. Variant omits Enlil.

ix

"I am the physician, I can save life,
"I carry every herb, I banish illness.   (80)
"I gird on the sack with life-giving incantations,
"I carry the texts which make (one) well.
"I give health to mankind.
"(My) clean dressing salves the wound,
"(My) soft bandage relieves the pain.   (85)
"At my examination, the moribund revives,
"At a word from me, the feeble one arises.
"I am merciful, [I am] kindly [ ]
"The mighty man [   ]
"I am she who gives [   ]   (90)
"Ninigiziba[ra   am I].

x

"My beloved is the young man ... [   ]
"The mighty one, endowed with strength [   ]
"Overpowering lord whose vigor cannot be equalled,
"Towering, with stately physique,
       always ready to charge mountains,   (95)
"Lovely, adorned with allure, and gorgeous all over,
"Who dances in the pride of young manhood, adorned with joy,
"First fruits of the harvest song, whose look is abundance,
"Fierce, irresistible, overcoming foes,
"Crusher of stones,¹ Zababa.²   (100)

xi

"I am a warrior and am skilled through experience,*
"I am the spouse of the mighty one, light of the gods.
"I make decisions, I give commands,
"In Esharra (my) way is sublime,
"In Ekur, dwelling of the gods, (my) dwelling is on high.   (105)

1. See p. 492 note 4.
2. A warrior god often equated with Ninurta; see, for example, Anzu (III.22) Tablet III line 142.

"I have mercy on the weak, I enrich the destitute,
"I bestow life on the one who reveres me.
"I make straight the path of the one who seeks after my ways,
"I am the great one, daughter of Anu, mother Ba'u,[1]
      life of the people.

xii

"My beloved is the warrior, foremost one, king of kings,   (110)
"Furious one, slayer who tangles (in) battle,
"Launcher of the deluge,
"Who loves [   ] and bride.
"Being merciful, he heeds prayers,
"He turns the wicked and enemies into clay.   (115)
"He burns the roots of all disobedient like reeds,
"Ninurta, foremost of the vanguard, mighty son of Enlil.

xiii

"I am fairest voiced among goddesses,
"I am the most beautiful among queens,
"I am the most attractive among young women,   (120)
"I am the most seemly among fine ladies.
"I have been given to his divinity,
"I am led to the foremost one, lord of the gods.
"My face is attractive,
"I am seductive to the mighty one, son of the lord of the gods. (125)
"I have come into his pure place,
"Into awe-inspiring Eshumesha,[2]
"Into (its) Ekashbar, house of destinies, place of commands,
"I am Ungalnibru,[3] the pure princess.

xiv

"Lofty one, lord who is the very greatest in heaven,   (130)
"Terror of whom makes all lands quake(?),[4]

---

1. Sumerian goddess, wife of Ningirsu (see p. 493 note 1).
2. Temple of Ninurta and spouse at Nippur.
3. Sumerian epithet, "Queen of Nippur."
4. See p. 492 note 4.

"Fear of whom envelops the mountain[s],
"He wears the heavens on his head, like a tiara,
"He is shod with the netherworld, as with [san]dals.
"He holds in his grasp commands that no [god kn]ows of,   (135)
"At his glance ... [   ]
"Swift [   ], multiplying prosperity,
"[   ], trampler, lofty Uta'ulu.[1]

xv

"Antu bore me, cherished me steadfastly,
"She taught me fair counsel, adorned me with charm,   (140)
"She gave me to the fullest the joys of young girls.
"Anu my father named me according to his own name,*
"He made me excel among my brothers.
"Ea in the depths gave me in full of his wisdom,
"He gave me the tablet stylus from his own hand,   (145)
"He entrusted to me the physician's craft,
          a secret of the gods,
"Enlil chose me as bride for the mighty one, his son.
"I am Gula, mistress of heaven and netherworld.

xvi

"Foremost one, slayer, mountain, overwhelmer of the sea,
"Irresistible storm, battle deluge,   (150)
"Instigator of discord, declarer of war,
"Who brings opponents to submission, mastering the foe,
"Mighty one who relies on his own strength,
"Savage, pitiless, who musters the ill wind, who grants victory,
"Esharra's trust, sublime son, who takes his own high rank,   (155)
"Avenger of the father who begot him,
"Pure god, deserving of kingship,
"My fair spouse, Lugalbanda.[2]

1. Another name for Ninurta; compare the hymn to Ninurta III.47b, line 4.
2. Legendary Sumerian king of Uruk, who, like Ninurta, contested with Anzu. For the equation of Lugalbanda and Ninurta, compare Anzu (III.22) Tablet III line 142.

xvii

"...

"My allure is compelling ... [ ]   (160)

"I am adorned with ... [   ]

"My [   ] are ...

"My [   ] are piping,

"I wear(?) a ...

"When I go in procession, charm falls like the dew,   (165)

"When I come in there is splendor,

"In my bed ...

"There is no one like me,

"I am Ninsun,[1] the merciful goddess.

xviii

"My beloved is the favorite among goddesses,   (170)

"He wears on his head a tiara with superb horns,

"He wields sharp weapons,

"He leads about fierce storm demons,

"Conqueror of all mountains,

"Who overthrew hard stones, as many as there were,[2]   (175)

"He forced to submit those

            who were insubmissive to Enlil,

"Strongest of the strong, slayer of slayers, Lugalbanda.

xix

"I am merciful, I hear (prayer) from afar off,

"I fetch up the dead from the netherworld,

"I am girded with the leather bag,

            I ... the scalpel and knife.   (180)

"I examine the weary, I watch over the sick,

            I open(?) the sore,

"I am mistress of life.

"I am physician, I am diviner, I am exorcist,

"I, who am expert in calculations,

1. "Wild Cow," mother of Gilgamesh.
2. See p. 492 note 4.

no one has explained (to me) a single wedge,[1]
"I ... every one of them.   (185)
"There is life in my [   ],
"I am Ninlil, the merciful [goddess]."

xx

[   ] bo[th] gods [   ],
Have mercy on the servant who fears your divinity [   ]!
Heed what he says, stand by him when he prays,   (190)
Accept his entreaty, listen to his words,
Take your seats (of judgment) and administer his case,
Set right his confusion, illumine his darkness.
Let him strip his mourning weeds,
        let him put on (normal) clothes.
That servant, meek and lowly,   (195)
May his life be prolonged at the unalterable command
        of your great divinity.
O Gula, great lady, whose help is Ninurta,
Intercede for him with the mighty one,
        your splendid spouse,
That he bring forth recovery for Bullutsa-rabi,
That he may kneel before you daily.   (200)

Text: W. G. Lambert, OrNS 36 (1967), pl. VIII-XXIII.
Edition: W. G. Lambert, OrNS 36 (1967), 105-132, to which this translation is greatly indebted.
Translation: Hecker, TUAT II/5, 759-764 (partial).
Notes to Text: (70) CAD N/1, 149a, "pectoral," though see Lambert, OrNS 36 (1967), 131 *ad loc.* (101) CAD L, 154a suggests that this line is a faulty adaptation of Creation Epic Tablet I line 59; however, the same expression occurs in KAR 321.10': *ṭu-ub-ba et-pe-šu i-le-'a-a*, so one need not seek a parallel in the Creation Epic. (142) Not clear. The first person referent -*anni* occurs eight times in nine successive lines; an etymological play may lie there (W. G. Lambert, OrNS 36 [1967], 132).

---

1. This may refer to calculation of propitious times or the time suffering could be expected to last; compare Poem of the Righteous Sufferer (III.14) Tablet II line 1.

III.26 ISHTAR QUEEN OF HEAVEN

As W. G. Lambert has shown, this hymn is a conflation and reworking of various texts about Ishtar. The basic components were three or four hymns of varying styles and subject matter sewn together with a penitential psalm.

One of these hymns, portions of which are found in i 1-26, iii 39-92, and iv 16-53, is characterized by learned etymological speculations, archaizing grammatical forms, and repeated use of certain words (e.g., the word rendered below as "cherish"). The psalm portion speaks of a sufferer in the third person who is understood to be the speaker, and who unfolds his sad fate in the style usual for the genre (compare II.7, III.14, 15, 28 etc.). A hymn with refrain, a well-known Sumerian style (see III.2, III.38c) but rare in Akkadian, is preserved in iii 1-38.

Column iv 1-15 preserves a hymn in honor of Nippur and the sanctuary there called E-bardurgarra, considered to be Ishtar's. Column iv 54-87 is a hymn dealing with Ishtar's festivity and relaxation in her favorite abode; this could originally have been an independent composition. The end of the text may contain either a further blessing on the Ebardurgarra or a blessing on the author or ruling king.

The text is therefore a celebration of the goddess, her residence, cult, and aspects. She is honored as a celestial phenomenon, compared to the moon and sun. One section deals with her names (compare III.17).

This composition is typical of one kind of creativity in the Mature period. Novelty was not always an end in itself in Mesopotamian creative process. Successful adaptation and reuse of earlier material was esteemed highly. While this composition may seem like an extreme case of creative reuse, resembling a pastiche, it offers a unity of purpose that makes its varying styles seem symphonic rather than disconcerting. The very choice of materials suggests that the compiler was a person of unusual talents. Perhaps one or more segments of the composition were original with the compiler, though this is impossible to tell.

(first part of text, consisting of praises for Ishtar, too fragmentary for translation)

ii

There was a man, he made no provision for the Capable Lady,
I was th(at) [man], who did not speak to Ishtar!
She [thun]dered at him like a storm, she grew full of anger at him,
[She ...] his dignity, she drove off his protective spirit.[1]
His [god forsook him], his goddess threw him over.   (10)
[   ] family, kept away and did not come near.
His lofty stature he bent to a crook,
He leaned his head beside his feet.
His city avoided him, his people were afraid of him,
He was always walking, hunched over,
          in the outskirts of his city,   (15)
Nor did hair and beard(?) remain.*
He had not sought her sanctuary,
          indeed, he did not wait upon her!
One of furious strength, her established envoy,
The Owl Demon, who peers into bedrooms,
Leaned malignantly through the window, heard that man.   (20)
She cast a chill of fear upon him, so he fell silent ...
She set the Dusk Demon to spy on him,
She drove him out of his mind [   ]
[   ] terrified him [   ]
He knew [no] dignity, (his) [sought] another,   (25)
He kept walking about [na]ked [   ].
Her [merciless ...] were clustered around.
[Mother?], infant, spouse, [father?],
[   ] chamber, abode of [   ]
[   ] her chamber, her storehouse [   ]   (30)

(fragmentary lines, then breaks off)

1. For this motif, compare the Poem of the Righteous Sufferer (III.14) Tablet I lines 42ff.

iii

(hymn with refrain, names of Ishtar)

No one but she can   (1)
[Hold the lead]rope[1] of heaven
No one but she can
[   ] mountains and seas [   ]
No one but she can   (5)
Grant kingship, lordship [   ]
No one but she can
[   ] the inhabited world [   ]
No one but she can
... the staff of [   ]   (10)
No one but she can
[Sur]round the main street of [ ] with excellence
No one but she can
Make fairest all that exists [   ]
No one but she can   (15)
Make the voice [of the people?] heard
No one but she can
Complete their pure governance [   ]
No one but she can
Become enraged, relent, have mercy [ ]   (20)
No one but she can
Punish, take pity, forgive, [   ]
No one but she can
[   ] where there is anger
No one but she can   (25)
[Lead by the han]d out of danger
No one but she can
Bring back the one who reveres her from the grave
No one but she can
Revive the dead, restore [   ]   (30)
No one but she can
Grant long life to him who heeds her

---

1. For the leadrope of heaven, compare II.14a, line 10.

No one but she can
Do without ... [   ]
No one but she can!   (35)
Ishtar is mistress of the [   ] designs of land and peoples,
She has made everything perfect,
Completed the rites and gathered to herself everything.

Which god brought forth her sign?

(eleven lines fragmentary)

[   ], her names are [sur]passing:

Anu, Enlil, and Ea made her important,
        the Igigi-gods cherished her.
Her very first name, her great appellation
Which her father Anu, whom she adores, named her of old,
Is Ninanna "Queen of Heaven" (= An),   (55)
Mistress of the inhabited world, who loves the peoples,
        companion to the sun,
Fierce in terror, Minu-anni,[1]
Exalted (in) the awesome strength of a young bull, Minu-ulla.
Her second great appellation,
By which her begetter, divine Duranki,[2] made her great,   (60)
Is Ne'anna, "She whose Strength is Sublime,"
[   ] of mankind, goddess who is the strength of Anshar,
[   ] of Anu, she bears terror,
[   ] of heaven, impetuous, goddess of pity.

[For a third] did Ninshiku, the warrior Ea,   (65)
[In his art]ful wisdom distinguish her as a name:
Zannaru "The Capable One,"
[Mistress? of] the four world regions, cherished of Dagan,
[A]nunu,[3] creatress of subject peoples,

---

1. This and the by-name in the next line are of unknown meaning.
2. A name for Enlil; compare, for example, Anzu (III.22a), Old Babylonian Version, Tablet II line 21, and below, iv 1.
3. A by-name.

[Who can tu]rn man to woman and woman to man.[1]   (70)
... Namrasit, "Brilliant-Rising God,"[2]
            father of [her] favorite brother,[3]
[   ] for a fourth [name] did cherish her,
[   ] totality [   ]
[bo]nd of the peoples, life of [the land],
[   ] light of mankind,   (75)
[   ] she glows awesomely, she overwhelms [   ],
[   ] discord, ter[rifying aura]
[   ] she is a woman, she is a man [   ].

                (thirteen fragmentary lines)

                            iv

                    (Ishtar and Nippur)

[Nippu]r, bond of heaven and earth,[4]
            li[nkage] of the four world regions,   (1)
Growing on the [fla]nk of an unapproachable mountain,
[The city Ni]ppur, surrounded by splendor,
            having coming forth within it,
Enlil built (it) for himself to live in.
[He ap]proached her and bestowed it upon her for her queenship, (5)
He ordained her Ebardurgarra as its sanctuary,
"Let the house be a shrine just like his dwelling!"[5]
The [   ] of supremacy lies within it,
High indeed is its head, it is the double of Ekur.
Brilliant is its light, covering the whole inhabited world,   (10)
Its radiance is found in the heart of the mountain.
It adores(?) her and looks after her,
Its inside is always filled with gladness,

---

1. A reference to sexual deviation, one of Ishtar's domains.
2. Sin, the moon.
3. Possibly a reference to Ishtar's pairing with the moon in the evening sky, as opposed to her pairing with the sun in the morning sky (56); on the other hand, WGL suggests to me that Tammuz is meant.
4. Translation of Duranki; see above, p. 503 note 2.
5. Lambert (*Studies Kraus*, 216) suggests that this is an Akkadian etymological explanation of the Sumerian name.

Ebardurgarra adores(?) the mistress.
The four world regions of one accord bring it their yield.   (15)
She ordains destiny foremost with Enlil,
She sets out regulations for the great gods, as Anu does.
Daily the gods assemble around her, the great gods for counsel,
The great Igigi-gods gods keep running towards her,
To fix their portions, to receive their com[mands].   (20)
All the goddesses of the peoples kneel down before her,
They supplicate her together, they kneel at her feet.
She examines their sanctuaries, she inspects their chambers,
She fixes the portions of the gods of holy places.
She is the very greatest, the most important of goddesses,   (25)
Mighty daughter of the luminary of the night sky,
      the heart's delight of Enlil,
Cherished goddess, princess of her brothers.[1]

Living handiwork of Dagan, female double of Anu,
Beloved of Ea, who is master of wisdom,
Cherished of the Mother Goddess, the omnipotent, princess,   (30)
She is princess, cherished, goddess, and mistress,
Spouse, mistress, beloved, ...,[2]
Bride of the "Fierce Lion,"[3] mistress of Eridu,
The Ishtar of Anu, who dwells in the sanctuary Eanna,[4]
She is the most lofty one, supreme, sublime, and queen.   (35)
Sweet are songs of her praise, great her cherishing,
The Queen of Nippur is sublime and queen,
Sweet are songs of her praise, magnificent her cherishing,
Who is cherished like the goddess, Queen of Nippur, their deity?
The Seven Gods have proclaimed her seven names.*   (40)

May this song be pleasing to you, O Ishtar,
May it never cease before you, may it abide at your command.
Where there is lamentation, may there be a dirge for you,

1. Sun and moon (both male); see iii 56, 71.
2. The parallelism calls for an epithet like "Divine Mother of Eridu."
3. Reference uncertain.
4. Word plays on the proper names Ishtar, Anu, and Eanna.

Where there is happiness, may there be cherishing of you.
In the chamber of your rites may they hail you,   (45)
Where your rituals are performed, may they address you,
In the chambers of the monthly festival, rejoicing and festivity.
Listen, O Mistress, may your mood be joyous,
May your heart gladly demand festivi[ty],
May the day bring you gladness, the night repose,   (50)
May Inimanizida[1] bring you [   ]
May the goddesses of beer [   ]

(about ten lines lost or fragmentary)

Take your seat in the immensities, O Ishtar,
May Anu, Enlil, and Ea be seated with you.
In a [   ], sweet drink in a lapis [   ]   (65)
Let them drink wine, "Drink, drink wine!"
[   ] ...
May your features beam and [   ]
May your hearts be glad and be full of rejoicing!
Rejoice, O Ishtar, may [   ] be joyous,   (70)
Be at ease, O Daughter of Sin, [   ]
They have given you the destiny of divine Duranki,
        your begetter,
Be at ease in Ebardurgarra,
        take up residence in your [dwel]ling.
When you decree destinies with Anu, Enlil, and Ea,
Make the destiny of Duranki surpassing [   ]   (75)
[Command] the well-being of Uruk,[2]
[Command] a favorable lot for Akkad,
May Larsa [raise high its head?] to heaven,
May [   ] shine,
May Bad-Tibira [   ] repose,   (80)
As for the Ekur of Bad-Tibira [   ]
May Kish [   ]
May Hursagkalamma be(?) a sanctuary(?) [   ]
May Ur be renewed [   ]

1. "His-Word-is-True," here a personification.
2. The proper names which follow are cities and sanctuaries in Sumer and Babylonia.

May Edilmunna [   ]   (85)

(seven fragmentary lines)

The invocation of its name [   ] forever.

Text: W. G. Lambert, *Studies Kraus*, 182-191.
Edition: W. G. Lambert, *Studies Kraus*, 173-218.
Translation: Seux, *Hymnes*, 93-98.
Notes to Text: (16) Very doubtful; emending text to *zi-iq-na!-su*. (iv 32) Perhaps DINGIR. AMA.NUN.ME(?), WGL: Amazilla. (iv 40) Following CAD I/J, 321f. against AHw, 411a; see Lambert, *Studies Kraus*, 217.

III.27 GREAT PRAYER TO ISHTAR

This composition is of particular interest for its literary history, as one can discern definite stages in the evolution of its text. An older version, dating to the latter part of the second millennium, is known from a learner's tablet from Hattusha, the capital of the Hittites in Anatolia, while the later one is known from a Neo-Babylonian manuscript from Mesopotamia. There is also a Hittite translation from a lost Akkadian original that was apparently superior to the Akkadian version now preserved from Hattusha.

Comparison of the two versions will show that the prototype text was enlarged, although the structure and organization of the original were not greatly affected. Ideas and patterns already in the text were expanded and elaborated. Some of the variants between the older and later versions given here are the results of mistakes in the earlier manuscript, as shown by the Hittite version, which agrees in some instances with the later version against the older one.

Comparison of the two versions provides an excellent case study in how a Mesopotamian literary text could evolve or expand and still remain true in its essentials to the intentions of the original author.

(a) OLDER VERSION (from Hattusha)

I implore you, lady of ladies, goddess [of goddesses],   (1)
Ishtar, lady of all the inhabited world,
     who governs the four world regions,
Innana, noble one, greatest of the Igigi-gods,
You are exalted, you are queen, exalted in your name,
You are the luminary of heaven, daughter of Sin, capable lady,   (5)
Who brandishes weapons and sets up [   ],
Fierce one, the most capable of the Igigi-gods,
Most valiant among [the gods] her brethren,
Who gathers to herself all rites, who takes nobility for her own.
O Mistress, splendid is your greatness, exalted over all the gods,   (10)
Planet for the warcry, who can make harmonious brothers
     set at one another,
Who can make the wives of kings afraid(?),*

Strong mistress of the winds(?), who gores mountains,
[Gus]hea[1] of combat, clothed in chilling fear,
You render final judgment and decision,
    the command for heaven and netherworld,   (15)
Chapels, sanctuaries, altars, [and daises are attentive] to you.
Where is not your name, where are not your daises?
Where are not your rites,
    where are your designs not put into effect?
[   ] have exalted you,
    they have made your authority the greatest,
[They exalt you] among all the gods,
    they have made your position highest of all.   (20)
At mention of your name, the [gods] totter,
    the great gods tremble,
The countries extol [your awe-inspiring name],
    you are the great one, the exalted [one].
[All   ] living creatures, mankind praise [your valor],
[Have mercy, O mis]tress of heaven and earth,
    shepherd of the human [race],
[Have mercy, O mis]tress of holy Ayakku, the pure [treasury],   (25)
[Have mercy, O mistress] whose feet weary not,
    [whose legs are strong to ru]n,
[Have mercy], O mistress of combat [and of every melee],
[O splendid lioness] of the Igigi-gods,
    who makes [furious gods submissive],
[   ] ... [   ]
[   ]   (30)
G[reat is your valor], O [vali]ant mistress,
[   ] who goes to the fight.
Fiery glow [that blazes against the enemy, that wr]eaks
    destruction on [the fierce],
[who] masses the multitude,
[   ] which [no one] can learn,   (35)
[   ] ... the evil one perishes,
[   ] joy

1. By-name of Ishtar; compare the Agushaya Poem (II.6) Tablet II vii 16.

[   ] may your heart be calmed,
[Furious] wild bull, [may your feelings be] eased,
May your benevolent eyes rest [upon me],   (40)
[   ] ... me,
[May my angry god and goddess be reconci]led with me,
    my entreaty [   ].
How long, my mistress, will imbeciles
    [and weaklings surpass me]?

(possibly one or two lines missing)

[   ] night and day [   ]
Look steadfastly upon me!
Your sweet [wind] wafted upon me
[With] my eyes, I will see your light,   (5')
[   ], preserve me!

(b) LATER VERSION

I implore you, lady of ladies, goddess of goddesses,   (1)
Ishtar, queen of all the inhabited world,
    who governs the peoples,
Irnini, you are noble, the greatest of the Igigi-gods,
You are powerful, you are queen, exalted is your name.[1]
You are the luminary of heaven and earth,
    the valiant daughter of Sin,   (5)
Who brandishes weapons, who prepares for battle,
Who gathers to herself all rites, who dons the lordly tiara.
O Mistress, splendid is your greatness, exalted over all the gods.
Planet for the warcry, who can make harmonious
    brothers set at one another,
Who can always grant a comrade,   (10)
Strong(?) one, mistress of the tilt, who gores mountains,
Gushea, whose mail is combat, clothed in chilling fear.
You render final judgment and decision,

---

1. Or: "are your names."

the command for heaven and netherworld,
Chapels, sanctuaries, altars, and daises are attentive to you.
Where is not your name, where are not your rites?   (15)
Where are your designs not put into effect,
        where are your daises not set up?
Where are you not great, where are you not exalted?
Anu, Enlil, and Ea have lifted you high, they have made
        your authority greatest among the gods,
They have given you the highest rank among all the Igigi-gods,
        they have made your (heavenly) station highest of all.
At the thought of your name, heaven and netherworld quake,   (20)
The gods totter, the Anunna-gods tremble.
Mankind extols your awe-inspiring name,
You are the great one, the exalted one.
All the black-headed[1] folk, living creatures, mankind,
        praise your valor.
You are the one who renders verdicts
        for subject peoples in truth and justice,   (25)
You look upon the oppressed and abused
        and always set them right.
Have mercy, mistress of heaven and earth,
        shepherdess of the human race!
Have mercy, mistress of holy Eanna, the pure treasury!
Have mercy, mistress whose feet weary not,
        whose legs are strong to run!
Have mercy, mistress of combat and of every melee!   (30)

O splendid lioness of the Igigi-gods,
        who renders furious gods submissive,
Most capable of all sovereigns,
        who grasps the leadrope of kings,
Who opens the veils of all young women,
You rise up, bring yourself down,*
        great is your valor, O valiant Ishtar,
Shining torch of heaven and earth,

1. The Mesopotamians.

brilliance of all inhabited lands.   (35)
Furious in irresistible onslaught, hero to the fight,
Fiery glow that blazes against the enemy,
    who wreaks destruction on the fierce,
Dancing one, Ishtar, who masses the multitude,
Goddess of men, Ishtar of women,
    whose intentions no one can learn,
Wherever you look the dead come to life, the sick arise,   (40)
The unjustly treated prosper at the sight of you.
I myself call upon you, your exhausted, desperate,
    most stricken servant,
Look upon me, mistress, accept my entreaty!
Look steadfastly upon me, hear my prayer!
Speak a word of mercy for me, let your feelings be eased.   (45)
Have mercy on my wretched person,
    which is full of confusion and perturbation!
Have mercy on my most stricken heart,
    which is full of tears and sighing!
Have mercy on my wretched omens,
    confused and perturbed!
Have mercy on my anguished household,
    which moans for grief!
Have mercy on my feelings,
    which abide in tears and sighing!   (50)
Irninitum, raging lion, may your heart be calmed.
Furious wild bull, may your feelings be eased.
May your benevolent eyes rest upon me,
Look upon me with your beaming features!
Drive off the evil witchcraft from my person,
    let me see your shining light!   (55)
How long, my mistress, will my opponents glower at me,
And with lies and falsehood plot evil against me?
My harassers and ill-wishers are raging against me,
How long, my mistress, will imbeciles and weaklings surpass me?
The feeble has gone on ahead, I have lagged behind,   (60)
The weak have grown strong, I have grown weak.
I churn like a wave which an adverse wind masses,

My heart soars and flutters like a bird of heaven.
I moan like a dove, night and day,
I am ..., I cry bitterly. (65)
My feelings are most stricken from crying "Woe!" and "Alas!"
I, O my god, O my goddess, what have I done?
I am dealt with as if I did not revere my god and my goddess.
Disease, headpains, decline, and ruin beset me,
Constraints, averted faces, and anger beset me, (70)
Wrath, rage and fury of gods and men.
I have experienced, O my mistress, days of darkness,
       months of gloom, years of grief,
I have experienced, O my mistress,
       a judgment of upset and turmoil.
Death and misery have a hold on me,
My chapel is deathly still, my sanctuary is deathly still, (75)
A ghastly stillness has fallen upon my household,
       my courtyard, and my fields,
My god's face is turned some other place,
My relations are scattered, my fold dispersed.
I am attending you, my mistress, waiting for you,
I implore you, absolve my debt! (80)
Absolve my crime, misdeed, sin, and wrong-doing!
Forget my sin, accept my plea,
Loose my fetters, set me free!
Make straight my path, let me pass through the street,
       proud and radiant among the living.
Speak, that from your speaking the angry god be reconciled, (85)
That the goddess who became furious relent!
May my dark and smoky hearth burn clear,
May my snuffed-out torch burst to flames,
May my scattered relations regroup themselves,
May my paddock enlarge and my fold expand, (90)
Accept my supplication, hear my prayer!
Look steadfastly upon me, ...
How long, my mistress, will you be angry and your face averted?
How long, my mistress,
       will you be enraged and your feelings in a fury?

Turn around your cast-down head,
    resolve on a favorable word!   (95)
Like water, the standing pool(?)* of a canal,
    may your feelings come to ease.
Let me trample down like dirt those who rage against me!
Make submissive those furious against me
    and flatten them under my feet!
May my prayers and entreaties sit well with you,
May your magnificent forbearance be with me,   (100)
That those who see me in the street
    may magnify your name,
And that I too may proclaim your divinity and
    valor to the black-headed folk,
"Ishtar is pre-eminent, Ishtar is queen,
"The lady is pre-eminent, the lady is queen,
"Irnini, the valiant daughter of Sin, has no rival."   (105)

(The later version ends with a subscript calling it an "Incantation of Raising of the Hand" [in prayer, see General Introduction, F.1] and follows with four lines of instructions for a ritual, in the course of which the text is recited three times. The ritual and recitation are to deal with frustration or the like.)

Text: (a) Ehelolf, KUB 37 36, 37; (b) King, STC II, pl. LXXV-LXXXIV; duplicate cited JCS 21 (1967), 262.
Edition: (b) Ebeling, AGH, 130-136; (a) Güterbock-Reiner, JCS 21 (1967), 257-262, with parallel lines from (b) and a translation of the Hittite version.
Translation: von Soden, SAHG, 328-333 no. 61; Stephens, ANET³, 383-385; Labat, *Religions*, 253-257; Seux, *Hymnes*, 186-194.
Literature: Güterbock-Reiner, essential for comparing the two versions in Akkadian, and the basis for the interpretation presented here.
Notes to Text: (a 12) WGL. (b 34) WGL. (b 96) Seux, *Hymnes*, 193 note 65.

III.28 LITERARY PRAYER TO ISHTAR

This relates the speech of a sufferer, variously in the first or third person, who falls ill and is given up for lost because of the goddess' withdrawal of favor (compare also III.14). The only wickedness the speaker can think of is evil things he did and said during his physical and mental disintegration (compare IV.17), so he does not know what caused initial disgrace. The final hymn of praise, perhaps originally a separate composition, is addressed to a group of women, and stresses the merciful and protective nature of Ishtar, hoping thereby to bring these qualities to bear on the supplicant. This "great prayer," like the others in its style, appears to be a composite of various sources, but all the same the product of an erudite and ardent poet.

(The first sixty or more lines of the text are lost or badly damaged. From them one gleans that the text opened with a hymn of praise to Ishtar, mentioning her loud cry, her power, her shearing-off of mountains, her command of the four winds, her strong arms, and wide stance. Around line 47 the speaker refers to the circumstances that brought him low: he is surrounded, restrained, and various parts of his body are afflicted.)

[   ] the utterance of my mouth is stopped short,
[   ] my hearing is blocked,   (65)
[O Ishtar], bespeak, drive out the demon that binds me!
I have been remiss, I have sinned, I have made light (of my
    obligations), I have committed iniquity:
All of them are my sins and [my] iniquities!
I have done I know not what wrong,
    I have transgressed your orders,
[I] have been false to my vow to you,
    I have not observed your due.   (70)

I trample my misdeeds on the ground [   ]
[   ] ..., my iniquities are ...
Ishtar can rescue from danger,
When fear is revealed to her, she knows how to save.
Who among the gods can measure up to you?   (75)
None has ever been seen for answering prayers like you!

She braces the one who reveres her while he prays,
She [entrusts him?] to a protective spirit.
She is not slow to resuscitate [   ],
Anger is closely followed by reconciliation [   ].   (80)

Since you forgot your servant [   ],
He has no father [   ]
Confusion covers him [   ]
A fearless tormentor [   ]
A chill has seized him [   ]   (85)
Paralysis consigns him ... [   ]
His shanks are sluggish, [his knees] are crumpling,
His neck is bent [   ]
He has trouble keeping his balance [   ]
Like a tottering wall [   ]   (90)

You have been gracious to him, you will open [   ]
His life [   ]
His arms [   ]
He was moaning like a dove [   ]

(five lines lost or fragmentary)

May he not be crushed [   ]
May your breeze waft upon him [   ]   (100)

... his neck ...
He who defeated an opponent must have heeded his goddess,
His prayer was surely set before his god.

(eight lines fragmentary, then gap)

At your command [   ]
Your splendor which you [   ]
His throat quivers [   ]
His songs of joy are bitter [   ]
Awash in tears, he weeps [bitterly].   (145)
His mourners cal[led in] his family,*
For a bitter lamentation over him did [his] kin assemble.

By day he lacerates himself(?), at night he sobs,
Pity and pleading have withdrawn from him.
He is seared(?), cast aside, completely boxed in.   (150)

By an ill wind from(?) a god he [   ] out of his mind,
His feet are weak, [his] hands shake,
His chest is bruised, his tongue [   ].
He has grown short of breath, his arms fell limp,
His temperament is grim, his vigor gone,   (155)
He has suffered hearing loss(?), nor does he comprehend* [ ],
He has lost his mind, he forgets himself.
How has he neglected you that you ... his ...?
In mourning weeds and unkempt hair he ... [ ] your name,
Take his hand lest he be bruited as a curiosity(?) ...[1]   (160)

Fortify his path, fi[rm up] his foundations,
Strengthen the weak one,* let the [ ] be dissolved,
Rescue him from the maw of destruction lest he [ ].
The dream interpreters must not exhaust [   ].[2]
And the diviner must not [   ] the ... [   ]   (165)
So run to his aid [   ]
May he not linger so, [   ] his life!
May he go no [fur]ther without you,
He must get to the bottom of his trouble and [   ],
He ... [   ]   (170)

Companion and friend [   ] him alone,
He let himself become enraged [   ]
He let himself go berserk [   ]
"Of course my lips spoke blas[phemy],
"I uttered profanities, [I said] improper words.   (175)

---

1. Literally: "be asked about," that is, become a public spectacle where everyone asks, "What is the matter with him?"

2. That is, save him lest the experts he retains to find the reason for his troubles use up his resources without helping him. This refurbishes the topos of the bafflement of experts (compare Poem of the Righteous Sufferer [III.14] Tablet I line 52, Tablet II lines 7ff.; A Sufferer's Salvation [III.15] line 6'); differently Seux (*Hymnes*, 198 note 50).

"My flesh heaved, ... [   ]
"My eyes rolled up(?) like [   ]."
After he made [   ],
A comfortable bed [   ][1]

(*gap of about eighteen lines*)

[   ] let him turn around,
[   ] let me support,
[Stop the] pall [bearers] at your cry,[2]
Open wide [the sealed tomb].   (200)

[   ] make glow in the east
[   ] with my own ...,
[   ] walking around,
      he has cut short the bruit of curiosity,[3]
May the whole world [   ] ...
[   ] who calls on the mistress of the Anunna-gods.   (205)
[   ] relieve my suffering,
[   ] my [   ], that I may praise you,
[   ] like the father who begot me,
[Like the mother who bo]re me, take pity on me!
[   ] can relieve [   ]   (210)

The [   ] of the [daugh]ter of Sin is sweet to praise,
[   ] she releases the captive.
She reveals light to the [one in pri]son,
[To the   ] her mercy is close at hand,
[   ] swift her relenting.   (215)
Bow down[4] to her, [   ] of the gods,
Pray before her, [   ].
[From the rising of the] sun to the setting of the sun,

1. Perhaps a reference to his presumed final illness.
2. Literally: "basket [ ]." I understand the fragmentary reference to "basket" here to mean the people carrying his funerary goods to the tomb. His redemption comes at the very moment his funeral procession is moving through the streets.
3. See above, line 160.
4. Feminine plural, addressed to women adorants?

Continue to bless her [   ]
[Wherever   ] daises are established.   (220)

[Wherever   ] their "mountain" is invoked,
[   ] she alone is lofty,
[   ] she alone is mighty,
[   ] heroism,
[   ] leadership,   (225)
[   ] mercy and forgiveness.
Praise [Ishtar, who shows] kindness to their people,
Acquire a protective spirit [   ].
Receive herewith of me your offering [   ],
[   ] gifts, sacrifices.   (230)

[   ] extol and keep her in your thoughts,
Enlil [granted her power] to rescue and save,
Shalash[1] ordained her [power to   ] and forgive,
Her hands [are clean], her arms washed,
Support her [   ], provide for her,   (235)
Prayer and abjuration are yours, Ishtar!
[   ] your mercy!

Text: W. G. Lambert, AfO 19 (1959/60), pl. VIII-XI.
Edition: W. G. Lambert, AfO 19 (1959/60), 50-55.
Translation: Seux, *Hymnes*, 194-199.
Literature: von Soden, ZA 61 (1971), 48-49.
Notes to Text: (146) von Soden, ZA 61 (1971), 49. (156) *adima*, perhaps a learned pseudo-correction, intended for a stative of *idû*? (162) AHw, 1474a, but doubtful.

1. Wife of Adad and Dagan, for whom apparently Enlil is here substituted. Lines 211 to 237 may have been adapted from a hymn referring to Adad or Dagan, appended to the preceding psalm-like passage.

III.29 LITERARY PRAYER TO MARDUK

Marduk is both fierce and gentle. He is angry with a person, so let him now be
merciful to that person (compare III.14). Blandishments and excuses are
offered: a live servant is better than a dead one; a mortal cannot know right
from wrong as the gods understand them. The servant is truly repentant and
has been sorely tried. Now is an opportunity to proclaim the god's wondrous
power to the whole world, but only if the sufferer is spared to spread his story.
How else will the god's cult be maintained? At the end, the text returns to the
theme of anger and appeasement, with a final appeal for mercy. Language and
content set this text apart in Mesopotamian literature as the work of a master.
A fragment, said to be Old Babylonian in date,[1] suggests that this composition,
like III.26 and III.28, is a composite of various earlier texts.

O furious lord, let [your heart] be c[almed],	(1)
Be eased in your feelings for [ ],	
O furious Marduk, let [your heart] be calmed,	
Be eased in your feelings for [ ]!	
Your look is a serpent, the crushing power [of a flood],	(5)
The onslaught of a conflagration, where is your equ[al]?	
O Marduk, whose look is a serpent,	
the crushing power of a fl[ood],	
The onslaught of a conflagration, where is your equal?	
[ ] in your fury, you can h[elp],	
[Gentle your pity], like a father's your mercy,[2]	(10)
[O Marduk, in your fury, you] can help,	
[Gentle your pity], like a father's] your mercy.	
You know how to pardon the flagrant* crime,	
To waive the punishment in even grievous cases,	
O Marduk, you know how to pardon the flagrant crime,	(15)
To waive the punishment in even grievous cases.	
Your heart is merciful, your feelings [ ],	
[You can?] show [favor?] in guilt and wrong-doing,	
O Marduk, [your] heart is merciful, your feelings [ ],	

1. Examination of the original is not conclusive. The piece could be Middle Babylonian or
even, like the "Old Babylonian" Anzu, a late manuscript affecting Old Babylonian script.
2. Old Babylonian version: "like a merciful father."

[You can?] show [favor?] in guilt and wrong-doing!   (20)
O lord, you are [of] understanding,
Who holds deep counsel [   ], wise,
O Marduk, you are [of] understanding,
Who holds deep counsel [   ], wise!
O receiver of prayers, who accepts entreaties,   (25)
Guardian of life, solicitous god,
O Marduk, receiver of prayers, who accepts entreaties,
Guardian of life, solicitous god!
O hearer of blessings, who bestow[s li]fe,
To whom swift relenting is natural,   (30)
O Marduk, hearer of blessings, w[ho bestows life],
To whom swift relenting is natural,
What reason could any god besides you [   ],
[Rem]itting punishment, granting [favors   ]?
[O Marduk], what reason could any god besides you [   ],   (35)
[Rem]it punishment, grant [favors   ]?
Who is most fierce ... [   ]?
[Wh]o among the gods [can turn you back]?
O Marduk, who is most fierce [   ]?
Who among the gods can turn [you back]?   (40)
O Lord, you are ra[ging] in your fury,
Amidst the seas of the far-off [   ]
O Marduk, [you are raging in your fury],
Amidst [distant seas   ],
Every day the tide [   ]   (45)
The flood has raised [   ]
The (sufferer) bound in helplessness ... [   ],
He re[   ]ed to himself,
He arose [   ],
He leaned up [   ],   (50)
He cannot [stand   ].
They take hold of his feet [   ] ...
You are the lord, [   ] his life!
He has turned into clay, [   ] ...
You are Marduk, [   ] his life!   (55)
He has turned into clay, [   ] ...

O lord, look upon your exhausted servant,
Let your breeze waft, release him quickly,
Let your heavy punishment be eased,
Loosen his bonds, let him breathe right away!   (60)
[Break] his manacle, undo his bonds,
[In ev]il(?)* have regard for him, be solicitous for him,
Let him not be murdered [in] your [fury], spare his life!
O Marduk, [   ] have regard for him,
        be solicitous for him,
Let him not be murdered [in] your fu[ry], spare his life!   (65)
Do not destroy the servant who is your handiwork,
What is the profit in one who has turned [into] cl[ay]?
It is a liv[ing] servant who reveres his master,
What benefit is dead dust* to a god?
[He has from of ol]d* counsel and solicitude,   (70)
[He is always ...   ] to remit guilt
[   ]
In his fury [   ]
He did not know [   ]
The servant [   ] his lord.   (75)

(lines 76-103 lost or fragmentary)

Who is he that [   ], not s[inned]?
Who is he so watchful that has incurred no sin?   (105)
Which is he so circumspect that has committed
        no wrong-doing?*
People do not know their invisible [fault]s,
A god reveals what is fair and what is [fo]ul.
Sins are overcome by one who has a god,
He who has no god has much guilt.   (110)
When you, his god, are at his side,
His words were well chosen and his speech controlled.

(lines 113-124 lost or fragmentary)

Illness, head pain, [debil]ity(?), sleeplessness,   (125)
They have relentlessly imposed upon him
        wasting-away, exhaustion.

Nagging anxiety, nervousness, panic, terror,
Are let loose upon him and banish his zest for living.
He has reviewed his ills, he is weeping to you,
His feelings are afire, he burns for you, (130)
He is given over to tears, he rains them down like a mist,
He sobs and makes much weeping,
      [like] a woman who cannot give birth.
Like a hired wailer he makes bitter his cries,
He speaks of his sleeplessness in his lamentation,
"What has my lord ... and devised against his servant? (135)
"Let me bring his acknowledgment* that he did not know!
"Many are my guilty deeds, I have sinned in every way!
"My lord, I have indeed transgressed, let me escape from distress,
"Many are my guilty deeds, I have sinned in every way,
"O Marduk, I have transgressed, let me escape from distress!" (140)
He bears a curse, he has donned heavy punishment.
They took him, gloomy of face,
      remanding him to the place of judgment.
His arms are bound at the court[1] of your punishment,
While he tries to explain to you all he intended.
They are addressing you in prayers, (145)
Let the text of Ea[2] appease your heart,
Let his right wording hold you back on high,
Let sighs and pity speak to you for mercy.
Look upon the wretchedness dealt him!
Let your heart be calmed, have mercy on him, (150)
Take his hand, absolve his guilt,
Banish from him head pain and sleeplessness.
Your servant is cast into the maw of destruction,
Lift your punishment, save him from the morass.
[Break] his manacle, undo his hands, (155)
Make [his face] beam, entrust him to the god who created him.
Revive your servant [that he may pra]ise your valor,
Let him pro[claim] your greatness [to] the whole inhabited world.

---

1. Literally: "gate." Legal proceedings and trials were often held at the city gate.
2. A reference to Ea's role as author of incantations, and a statement that the present text was a product of sublime wisdom.

Accept his present, take his offering(?).
Let him walk before you on firm ground of well-being,   (160)
Let him come to shower upon your dais a plenteous yield.
Ensure his perpetual upkeep of your house,
Let him bathe your door fastenings in oil, as if with water,
Let him lavish finest oil on your thresholds.
Let him burn cedar resin for you,   (165)
Delightful fruits, abundant grain,

(gap)

May your [ben]evolent eyes rest up[on him],
May he himself [   ] in your heart for benevolence.
Lay no wrong-doing [to his] charge,
Do not make him bear his guilt,
        do not make him bear (his) sin,
Raise his head, ... [   ],   (175)
May his protective spirit be greater than be[fore].*
May his king[1] [   ] the words he speaks.
At your command may he [   ]
May he fulfill his vow [   ].
The road and path [   ],   (180)
May he who sees him in the street [praise] your divinity,
May they say one to the other,
        "Indeed, the Lord c[an revive the dea]d!"
May he who sees him in the street pr[aise] your divinity,
May they say one to the other,
        "Indeed, Marduk ca[n revi]ve the dead!"
And as for the servant whom [   ] you spared,   (185)
[May he procl]aim your greatness to all peoples.
May he praise the one who revealed to him light
        while he was dying [ ],
May he continue to bless you [   ].
As your servant [   ] at [night]time,
To all peoples [in the day he made to] be heard.[2]   (190)

---

1. Presumably the sufferer's personal god is here meant; for "king" in this sense, see above, II.1.
2. If this restoration is correct, one may compare Erra and Ishum (IV.16) Tablet V lines 43ff.

(fragmentary lines, gap)

Have m[ercy] on him, pity for your servant!   (206)

Text: W. G. Lambert, AfO 19 (1959/60), pl. XII - XVI; Pinches, CT 44 21; Matouš, LTBA I 68 obv 1-4 (ref. WGL).

Edition: W. G. Lambert, AfO 19 (1959/60), 55-60.

Translation: von Soden, SAHG, 270-272 no. 18 (lines 125ff.); Seux, *Hymnes*, 172-181; Hecker, TUAT II/5, 754-758.

Literature: Sommerfeld, AOAT 213 (1982), 129-134.

Notes to Text: (13) Seux, *Hymnes*, 174 note 17. (62) von Soden, ZA 67 (1974), 283. (69) Seux, *Hymnes*, 175 note 28. (70) Restoration from Old Babylonian version: [*i-ba-aš-ši iš-t*]*u ul-la*. (106) Unpublished duplicate quoted CAD N/1, 3b. (136) Hecker: "*auch wenn dessen Mund vorbrachte* ..." (159) Emendation AHw, 367a (IGI!.SÁ-*e*); otherwise *pedû* "release, exempt." (176) von Soden, ZA 67 (1974), 283.

III.30 GREAT HYMN TO MARDUK

Like the other great hymns (see General Introduction, F.1), this is a masterpiece of intricate thought and expression. Too much of the text is lost to see its overall structure, but the preserved portions deal with the mercy of Marduk and the wisdom of walking in his ways.

<blockquote>

O lord, sage of the Igigi-gods, I praise your name,   (1)

Sweet is the thought of you, impetuous, willful one(?),

O Marduk, among the Igigi-gods I praise your name,

Sweet is the thought of you, impetuous, willful one.

Who guides the rivers inside the highlands,   (5)

Who opens the well springs inside the mountains,

Who releases the bounteous flood to the entire inhabited world,

Who makes abundant* the ... of the broad earth with grain,

[Who makes the] dew [fall] from the bosom of heaven,

[   ] the breezes, the sprinklings over the lea land,[1]   (10)

[Who ...] bountiful yields to the grain fields,

[   ] abundance, plenty, yields, increase.

[Who allots] to the Igigi-gods great food offerings,

[   ] all daises,

[a]nointing of the door fastenings.[2]   (15)

[w]ine, a meal of food portions and free-will offerings,

[   ] the Anunna-gods, the whole creation of

    "The Lord of Heaven and Netherworld,"[3]

[   ] your benevolences reached,

[al]l of them were fed.

[   ] your benevolences reached,   (20)

(lines 21-27 fragmentary)

[   ] pasture [   ]

[   ] he provides grass

[   ] and princes, speak well of him!   (30)

[   ] the merciful, solicitous god.

</blockquote>

1. Compare Creation Epic (III.17) Tablet V lines 49-51, 54; Tablet VII lines 1-4, 57-69.
2. Compare Literary Prayer to Marduk (III.29) line 163; Prayer to Anu (III.34) line 14.
3. Ea (Lambert, AfO 19 [1959/60], 62 note 17).

There is [none] among all the Igigi-gods who can boast before you,
You have [no] rival above or below.
Whatever the gods of all the inhabited world may have done,
> they cannot be like you, Lord!
[   ] of the depths of knowledge, where is your equal?   (35)
Anu who dwells in heaven made you greatest,
Nunamnir,[1] father of the gods, pronounced your name.
Ea in the depths bestowed upon you wisdom,
Ninmenna,[2] the creatress, clo[thed?] you with awesomeness,
Your head is raised high in [your] splendid temple,   (40)
Damgalnunna[3] made your genius terrible,
Your dread, O lord, is fearful to the gods.
Like the surge of battle, you swell massively ... the sea,
You incinerate the enemy like a raging conflagration.
Your rage is a dragon, you tie up evil ones,   (45)
You catch up with troublemakers, instigators, and malcontents,
Passing (unscathed) through corruption,
> you bring swift misfortune upon the enemy.
You select the few that are good,
> you make good the many (that are not),*
You cause the just to prosper, you leave the wicked wanting.
May the establisher of gifts, the warden of life,   (50)
Nabu, beloved of Shazu,[4] hear what was in their
> hearts and [learn?] about their behavior.
The just man and obedient ones are unlimited waters [   ],
Rationed sips are the corrupt, contentious, disobedient, [   ].
[   ] those obedient to him ... [   ],
He who spreads deceit,
> instigates [..., Marduk] is furious(?) with him.*   (55)
[He who spreads de]ceit, who utters [   ],
Who gives intelligence to those who were not given [   ],
You make short their days and [   ],

---

1. A name for Enlil.
2. A name for the mother goddess.
3. Wife of Ea, mother of Marduk.
4. Literally: "He knows the heart," presumably Marduk. See Creation Epic (III.17) Tablet VII lines 35ff.

You turn [their   ] into ruin heaps.
[   ] whose intentions change,   (60)
[They   ] and commit a crime,
The humble, the reverent, the prayerful follows the god,
[   ], the arrogant, the irreverent,
They plot hostilities like [   ],
His god does not g[o at his side but] lets him be overcome
        by corruption.   (65)
Marduk, god of the peoples [ ], who absolves everything,
The god of redemption, [   ], solicitous prince,
When he has given judgment, the Lord [ ] and appeases,
Marduk appeases [   ] for benevolence.
He accepts prayers [   ] night,   (70)
He raises the head of him whom he [   ] in the fury of his heart.
Marduk, [   ] your servant, the sage[1]
        whom you [   ], have mercy on him!
Take away, O Lord, his guilt, absolve his misdeed.
His own mouth has confessed the sin he committed [   ],
Lift him from the mighty torrents [   ]   (75)
Marduk, you rage where [   ] was destroyed,
He has turned and flown into a fury at [   ]

(fragmentary, then large gap)

(Several fragments of text remain.)[2]

[... O Mar]duk, precious life of the people,   (1′)
[ ] their [   ], he foregoes their punishment.
[He   ] the reverent, he makes the pious prosper,
He is benevolent to the obedient, he makes the upright prosper.
One is ever mindful of you, they are glad now, when
        your name is pronounced,   (5′)
They are in awe of your words, like the roar of thunder.
From among those afire with purpose,
You save the ones who worship Marduk,

---

1. Text: "Adapa." For this personage, see III.20.
2. English translations of the other pieces are found in Lambert, AfO 19 (1959/60), 64f. (also CAD N/1, 132a, restoration of iii middle 7 from unpublished duplicate).

you open up to them unending yield and flow(?).[1]
To the traffic of the ferry landing,
    where the way is crowded,
You make a quick path for the king of the world,
    unequalled and irresistible.[2]   (10′)
You guard property, you cle[ar] profit.
You grant (receipt of) offerings forever,
    and are always, in all respects, at your task.
You set up the weak, you give the wretched room,
You bear up the powerless, and shepherd the meek.
O Marduk, you extend your benevolence over the fallen,   (15′)
The weakling takes his stand under your protection,
    and you pronounce recovery for him.

(breaks off)

Text: W. G. Lambert, AfO 19 (1959/60), pl. XVII-XXIII; additional joins to ms B include K 16922 and Sm 1732, not used here.
Edition: W. G. Lambert, AfO 19 (1959/60), 61-66.
Translation: von Soden, SAHG, 253-254 no. 7 (10′ff.); Seux, *Hymnes*, 70-75.
Notes to Text: (8) Seux, *Hymnes*, 71 note 7. (48) Reading *la me-na* as *la mīna* "innumerable." (55) WGL.

1. The sense may be that Marduk favors, of all firebrands, the ones eager in his service, and makes them prosper. "Flow," if correctly understood, may refer metonymically to prosperity as an abundance of water.

2. That is, in the hurly-burly of everyday life, Marduk speeds the king's progress. With a similar metaphor, Ishtar of Arbela assures Esarhaddon in an oracle, "I will bring you over the river in good order" (IV R² 61 iv 3-4).

III.31 Great Hymn to Nabu

This hymn is dedicated to Nabu, god of scribal lore. Its recondite language suggests a late date. Despite its fragmentary condition, it clearly belongs to the Babylonian tradition of great hymns (General Introduction, F.1). Like III.28 and III.29, it takes the form of a narrative about a penitent's wretched condition and expresses his hopes for absolution. It contains original ideas and involved imagery, much of which is still imperfectly understood.

```
[O lord        ], cresting like a wave [    ],
[              ], your absolution [                ],                     (10)
[O Nabu        ], cresting like a wave [    ],
[              ], your absolution [                ].
[O lord, who ... the anxio]us like a [    ],
[              ] he has turned [                ],
[O Nabu, who ... the anxio]us like a [    ],                             (15)
[              ] he has turned [                ].
[    ] your [an]ger, your raging* yoke,
[You ... ab]undance, you release the yield,
[O Nabu, ...] your anger, your raging yoke,
[You ... ab]undance, you release the yield.                             (20)
[O lord, ...] in your [    ], fire in your pitilessness,
[      ] of the gods, you inspect Anshar,
[O Nabu, ...] in your [    ], fire in your pitilessness,
[      ] of the gods, you inspect Anshar.
[O lord  ] is your [    ], your glower is a (dark) cloud,               (25)
[                    ] you support the just.
[O Nabu, ... is your ...], your glower is a (dark) cloud,
[                  you] support the [just].
[O lord ...] your [    ] is an earthquake,
[                    ] they hold,                                        (30)
[O Nabu, ... your ...] is an earthquake,
[                    ] they hold.
[O lord, ... of heaven],
[        ] ... family, ... profit,
[O Nabu          ] ... of heaven,                                       (35)
[              ] ... family, ... profit.
```

O excellent [lord], be calm at once!
May your [feat]ures(?) relax, have pity!
O excellent [Na]bu, be calm at once!
May your [features?] relax, have pity!   (40)
O erudite l[ord], sage in ...,
Wise one, master of the literate arts,
O erudite Nabu, sage in ...,
Wise one, master of the literate arts,
O furious lord, you are angry with your servant,   (45)
Want and misery have beset him,
O furious Nabu, you are angry with your servant,
Want and misery have beset him!
He is cast into the midst of the billow,
     the flood cl[oses] over him,
The shore is far from him, dry land remote from him.   (50)
He languished in a mesh of machination,
     impossible to cut through,
He sprawled in a morass, held fast by the mire.
Take his hand, let not your servant go under,
Lift his punishment, raise him from the morass,
O Nabu, take his hand, let not your servant go under,   (55)
Lift his punishment, raise him from the morass.
He bellows in ter[ror],
     like a bull being slaughtered with a butcher's knife,
He is cast in the maw of something mighty,
     overpowering ... [   ]

(gap)

"I am fallen, let me be borne up, let me [   ],
"In order to expel the 'vengeance'[1] (from me),
     let me make straight for [   ].
"Like a vagrant(?), let me go about ou[tside].
"Indeed(?), why should a one-handed man(?) stand [ahead of me]?
"[   ] brings suffering and misery (upon me).   (80)
"You are the lord, you called [my] n[ame in the womb?],

---

1. See Poem of the Righteous Sufferer (III.14), p. 321 note 3.

"At your command the midwife [   ].

"You are Nabu, you called [my name in the womb?],

"At your command, the midwife [   ].

"From my father's 'It's my child!'[1] [   ],   (85)

"The 'It's my child!' of his ancestors [   ]

"[   ] not [   ]."

He staggers(?) [   ]

"My father ... (his personal) god painfully [   ]

"He unceasingly heeded (his personal) goddess."   (90)

Omnipotent lord, (let) iniquity (be) era[sed],

O Swift-to-forgive, (let) foul crime (be) for[given],

Omni[potent Nabu, (let) ini]quity (be) era[sed],

O Swift-[to-forgive, (let) fo]ul [crime] (be) forgi[ven].

(two lines lost)

[   ] overlook [his] misdeed,

[   ] negligence, banish [his] s[in].

[Without] your consent, O lord, there can be no [forgiveness],

[Un]less by you, my iniquity and crime [will not be absolved],   (100)

[Without] your consent, O Nabu, there can be no [forgiveness],

[Un]less by you, my iniquity and crime [will not be absolved].

Your servant [has done wron]g,

    and you continue to turn away from him in anger,

In your [   ] you cast down [   ].

[   ] ..., the burrowing beetle, a hostile deity [   ]   (105)

(The next eight fragmentary lines continue with a description of various plagues undergone by the sufferer.)

The horror of headlice was grievous upon him,

The symptoms of ...-disease(?) he showed on [his] face(?).   (115)

"How long, a whole year, must I keep on waiting?

"Let me praise the lord, your fury is anger,

"[   ] your awesomeness to heaven [for]ever,

"[Let me praise Nabu], your fury is anger,

1. Text: "by father's 'Indeed'(?). I take this to be the initial acknowledgment of paternity after birth of the child.

"[   ] your awesomeness to heaven forever.   (120)
"My [family]* is (well) supplied with beer,
    is (well) supplied with flour,
"The land set aside[1] for my ancestor's [   ]
    is (worth) a talent of silver.
[   ] associates, constantly, may the night be at an end(?).
[   ] let them dispatch that I may be set right for all time.

    (lines 125-172 lost or too fragmentary for translation)

Loose his fetters, break [his] chains!
A wall is created against the severity of the wintry blast,
For the whole land a breeze makes the summer heat
    easier to bear.[2]   (175)
The morn of my help, the first fruits of the tree,
    ... bitter ...
What has (seemed) always unpalatable he will sweeten like honey.
The (early) dates on the tree are bitter as stinkwort,
But later the good ones are sweet and the sprout [   ].[3]   (180)
The grain in its budding was affected by smut [   ],
(But) when it matured it [gave full] yield.
The putrid flux of the body's channels, something
    abhorrent to the gods,[4] is universal(?) among(?) people.
Where it was dark it is bright, the raging one (is) for[giving].
The obedient, dutiful son makes a special bles[sing]
    for his father,   (185)
The disobedient, undutiful son curses [him] who be[got him].
You discipline your servant,
    (now) give him a vent to breathe through,
Incline your face to him, turn your head towards him,

---

1. This and the preceding line may refer to his lavish maintenance of his ancestor cult.

2. While these lines refer to the relief brought upon the sufferer by Nabu's forgiveness, it is not clear precisely how they are to be understood. Is Nabu the wall and the breeze?

3. This and the following couplet may refer to a period of misery followed by a period of good, "darkest before dawn."

4. I take this to mean that men are by nature impure and disgusting to the gods, so, like the dutiful and ungrateful sons of line 185, men and gods are by nature poles apart. The "putrid flux" normally refers to urinary disease (CAD M/2, 46) or gonorrhea (Adamson, JRAS 1979, 5), but here may refer to semen that begins human life.

O Nabu, you discipline your servant,
 (now) give him a vent to breathe through,
Incline your face to him, turn your head towards him!   (190)
Produce a substitute[1] for him, let him [find] self-preservation.
At your command [ ] good [ ]

(gap)

[let] him build his storehouse,
[   ] let him build his sanctuary.
[   ] let his body be released,
[   ] let his[2] vision be clear.
[May your radiant features] turn towards him,   (205)
[Your servant, ... comp]assion, have pity on him,
[O Nabu], may your radiant features turn towards him,
Your servant, ... compassion, have pity on him!
May the [ ] fields be restored,
May the [ ] revenues be his forever.   (210)
May his sanctuary be in order in village and marshland.
May his mood brighten [in the] four world [regions].
[Ta]ke his hand that he may ever glorify your divinity,
Let him proclaim your greatness [to all] the world,
[O Nabu, t]ake his hand, let him ever glorify your divinity,   (215)
Let him proclaim your greatness [to all] the world!
[Accep]t his abasement, immobility, and entreaty,
[ ] his petition, may his prayer come true.
May all the [Igi]gi-gods take his part,
May the [hai]ry hero-man[3] ... speak in his favor.   (220)
[O lord, among] the gods your greatness is surpassing,
[The people] have sung your praises for all time,
[O Nabu, among the gods] your greatness is surpassing,
[The people] have sung your [pra]ises for all time!

(six or seven lines missing till end)

---

1. That is, someone to die in his stead.
2. Text: "their," possibly, but not likely, referring to eyes.
3. For these beneficent monsters, see p. 173 note 1. These are not to be confused with the primeval gods Lahmu and Lahamu (see p. 354 note 3).

Text: Brünnow, ZA 4 (1889), 252ff. (= K 2361+3193+Sm 389). Additional pieces, with collations of the earlier copies, published in transliteration by von Soden, ZA 61 (1971), 50ff.

Edition: von Soden, ZA 61 (1971), 44-71.

Translation: Seux, *Hymnes*, 181-185; earlier treatment by von Soden, SAHG, 263-264 no. 13.

Notes to Text: (17) So text; perhaps there is an implied comparison with a weapon. (121) [*kim*]*tija.*

III.32 THE SHAMASH HYMN

This hymn to the sun god, Shamash, was frequently copied and studied by Mesopotamian scholars of the Late period.[1] The text begins with Shamash as the all-seeing sun (1-20), whose energies and responsibilities lead him over the entire world every day (21-52). His importance in divination is alluded to (53f.), as well as his role in oaths, treaties, and contracts (55f.). His ability to illumine the darkest places leads to a celebration of his role in investigation, trial, and verdict (56-64). Mention of his concern for travelers and the homeless (65-74) is followed by a fragmentary passage dealing with his interceding mercy (75-82?) and his inexorable retribution against the wicked (83?-94). An interesting passage (95-121), perhaps another independent composition inserted here, delves into his role as supervisor of honest business transactions.[2] Shamash can see through the cleverest fast-talk and the most stringent false denial (122-128). He is the principal divine communicant with the perplexed, the lost, meek, venturesome, and the most wretched human beings beyond the pales of civilization (129-148). This leads to a reflection upon his relationship to the human race as a whole; he grants knowledge, and receives joyous cultic observances in return, including beer at wharfside in honor of his interest in commerce and shipping (149-162). In a climactic paean, the hymnist marvels at the sun's universal dominion, extending to the unseen corners and depths of the cosmos (163-179). He considers the alternately harsh and tender qualities of the god (180-185?). The text is fragmentary at the end, but may conclude with reference to a ceremony and a plea for the god's goodwill.

The language of the hymn suggests that it, like the other great hymns (General Introduction, F.1), is not of a piece, but is a second-millennium compilation using some older materials and reworking imagery known elsewhere.

> Illuminator of all, the whole of heaven,   (1)
> Who makes light the d[arkness for mankind] above and below,
> Shamash, illuminator of all, the whole of heaven,
> Who makes light the dark[ness for mankind a]bove and below,[3]

---

1. W. G. Lambert, BWL, 121ff.

2. Remarks on this topic are offered by J. Nakata, "Mesopotamian Merchants and Their Ethos," JANES 3 (1970/71), 90-100.

3. Either "in every direction," or a reference to Shamash's position in both heaven and netherworld.

Your radiance [spre]ads out like a net [over the world],   (5)
You brighten the g[loo]m of the distant mountains.
Gods and netherworld gods rejoiced when you appeared,
All the Igigi-gods rejoice in you.
Your beams are ever mastering secrets,
At the brightness of your light,
       humankind's footprints become vis[ible].   (10)
Your dazzle is always seeking out [   ],
The four world regions [you set alight] like fire.
You open wide the gate of all [sanctuaries],
You [   ] the food offerings of the Igigi-gods.
O Shamash, mankind kneels to your rising,   (15)
All countries [   ].
Illuminator of darkness, opener of heaven's bosom,
Hastener of the morning breeze* (for?) the grain field,
       life of the land,[1]
Your splendor envelops the distant mountains,
Your glare has filled all the lands.   (20)
Leaning over the mountains, you inspect the earth,
You balance the disk of the world in the midst of heaven
       (for) the circle of the lands.
You make the people of all lands your charge,
All those king Ea, the counsellor,
       has created are entrusted to you.
You shepherd all living creatures together,   (25)
You are their herdsman, above and below.
You cross regularly through the heavens,
Every day you traverse the vast earth.
High seas, mountains, earth, and sky,
You traverse them regularly, every day, like a ...[2]   (30)
In the lower regions you take charge of the netherworld gods,
      the demons, the (netherworld) Anunna-gods,
In the upper regions you administer all the inhabited world.

---

1. Or, "heats," in which case the meaning would be that the rising sun heats the breezes of morn from their night coolness.

2. Word broken, perhaps "cultivated field" or the like, in which case the sun is like a conscientious farmer going over his domain.

Shepherd of the lower regions, herdsman of the upper regions,
You, Shamash, are regulator of the light for all.
You cross time and again the vast expanse of the seas,   (35)
[Whose] depths not even the Igigi-gods know.
[O Sham]ash, your radiance has gone down to the deep,
[The hairy hero-m]an of the ocean can see your light.
[O Shamash], you tighten like a noose, you shroud like a mist,
Your [bro]ad protection is cast over the lands.   (40)
Though you darken each day, your face is not eclipsed,
For by night you traverse [the below?].[1]
To far-off regions unknown and for uncoun[ted] leagues
You have persevered, O Shamash,
        what you went by day you returned by night.
Among all the Igigi-gods there is none who does such
        wearisome toil but you,   (45)
Nor among the sum total of the gods one
        who does so much as you!
At your rising the gods of the land assembled,
Your fierce glare covered the land.
Of all the lands of different tongues,
[You] know their intentions, you see their footprints.   (50)
All humankind kneels before you,
[O Sha]mash, everyone* longs for your light,
[From] the diviner's bowl to the knots of cedar,[2]
[You are] the most reflective of dream interpreters,
        explicators of night visions.*
[The parties to] contracts[3] kneel before you,   (55)
[Be]fore you both wicked and just kneel down.
[No one] goes down to the depths without you.[4]
You clear up the case of the wicked and criminal,

1. The meaning may be that even though the sun sets, his brightness remains undimmed as he passes the other side of heaven, and he is not to be considered in eclipse.
2. For cedars in the diviner's ritual, see above, II.40a lines 7-8 (tied in the hair and piled up), and II.40b line 5. Perhaps totality is implied, "from alpha to omega."
3. Sworn documents, such as treaties and contracts, were Shamash's area of concern (see above, III.1).
4. Reiner, *Poetry*, 72 suggests that this refers to a water ordeal; compare III.14 Tablet IV; IV.13.

```
[                                    ]
```
He pours out sleep [   ]   (60)
You send back (to court?) the rogue surrounded
    by [false witnesses],
You rescue from the brink of hell
    the [innocent] one tied up in a lawsuit,[1]
What you pronounced in just verdict, O Shamash, [   ],
Your utterances are manifest, they cannot be changed,
    [you show] no favoritism.*
You give support to the traveler whose j[ourney] is trying,   (65)
To the seafarer in dread of the waves you lend [aid],
You are wont to g[uide] the roamer(?) on unexplored routes,
You always guide [on the ro]ad any who turn towards [Shamash].
You rescued from the flashflood
    the [mer]chant bearing his purse,[2]
You bring up* the one gone down to the deep,
    you set wings upon him.   (70)
You reveal havens in sea and [wastelan]ds,
You show the exile roads he did not know.*
[You set free] the one in hid[den dungeon],
You save the displaced cast in prison.*
[You reconcile promptly] the god [who is angry] with someone,* (75)
Upon seeing ... [   ]
You stand by(?) the si[ck man   ]
You investigate the cause [   ]
You bear [   ]
From the Land of No Return you [   ]   (80)
The angry(?) goddesses |]
You are exalted [   ]
O Shamash, with [your] battle net [you   ]
From your meshes no [can escape   ].
He who, in taking an oath [   ],   (85)
For the one who does not fear [   ],

1. Lines 61-62 may refer to the comfortable(?), scot-free evildoer being packed off for legal action, while the just man is rescued from the machinations of the law. For different views, compare Lambert, BWL, 129 and Seux, *Hymnes*, 56.

2. The bag used by commercial agents to carry their means, and, by extension, "capital."

Your wi[de] net is spread   [   ].
The man who co[vets] his neighbor's wife,
He will make to [   ] before his appointed day.
A snare is set for him, the wicked man will [   ],   (90)
Your weapon makes straight for him,
          there [will be no]ne to save him.
[His] own father will not be present at his trial,
Nor will his own brothers reply to the judge's queries.
He is caught unawares in a metal trap!
You blunt the horns of a scheming villain,   (95)
The perpetrator of a cunning deal is undermined.*
You show the roguish judge the (inside of) a jail,
He who takes the fee but does not carry through,
          you make him bear the punishment.
The one who receives no fee but takes up the case of the weak,
Is pleasing to Shamash, he will make long his life.   (100)
The careful judge who gives just verdicts,
Controls the government, lives like a prince.
What return is there for the investor in dishonest dealings?
His profits are illusory, and he loses his capital.
He who invests in long-range enterprises(?),
          who returns (even?) one shekel to the ... [   ],   (105)
Is pleasing to Shamash, he will make long his life.
He who [commits] fra[ud as he holds the ba]llances,
Who switches weights,[1] who lowers the [   ],
(His) profits are illusory, and he lo[ses the capital].
The one who is honest in holding the balance, [   ] plenty of [   ], (110)
Whatever (he weighs) will be given to him in plenty [   ].
He who commits fra[ud] as he holds the dry measure,
Who pays loans by the smaller standard,
          demands repayment by the extra standard,
Before his time, the people's curse will take effect on him,
Before his due, he will be called to account,*
          he will bear the consequence(?).   (115)

---

1. That is, buys with a heavy standard and pays back with a light one, taking advantage of varying local standards of weight.

No heir will (there be) to take over his property,
Nor will (there be) kin to succeed to his estate.
The honest merchant who pays loans by the [ex]tra(?)
      standard, thereby to make extra virtue,
Is pleasing to Shamash, he will grant him extra life,
He will make (his) family numerous, he will acquire wealth,   (120)
[His] seed will be perpetual as the waters of a perpetual spring.
For the man who does virtuous deeds, who knows not fraud,
The man who always says what he really means,*
      there will be [ ],
The seed of evildoers wi[ll not be perpetual].
The nay-sayers' speeches are before you,   (125)
You quickly analyze what they say.
You hear and examine them,
      you see through the trumped-up lawsuit.
Each and every one is entrusted to your hands,
You make their omens the right ones for them,
      you resolve what perplexes.
You heed, O Shamash, prayer, supplication, and blessing,   (130)
Obeisance, kneeling, whispered prayer, and prostration.
The feeble one calls you as much as his speech allows him,[1]
The meek, the weak, the oppressed, the submissive,
Daily, ever, and always come before you.
He whose family is far off, whose city is distant,   (135)
The shepherd [in] the afflictions of the wilderness,
The herdsman in trouble, the keeper of sheep among
      the enemy, come before you.
O Shamash, there comes before you the caravan, passing in fear,
The travelling merchant, the agent carrying capital.
O Shamash, there comes before you the fisherman with his net, (140)
The hunter, the archer, the driver of the game,
The fowler among his snares comes before you,
The skulking thief comes before Shamash,
The bandit on the wilderness paths comes before you,
The wandering dead, the vagrant spirit come before you,   (145)

---

1. Literally: "according to the hollow of his mouth."

O Shamash, you have listened to them all.
You did not hold back(?) those who came before you,
      you heeded them,*
For my sake, O Shamash, do not despise them!
You grant wisdom, O Shamash, to humankind,
You grant those seeking you your raging, fierce light.   (150)
[You make] their omens [the rig]ht ones for them,
      you preside over sacrifices.
You probe their future in every way.
You grant wisdom to the limits of the inhabited world.
The heavens are too puny to be the glass of your gazing,
The world is too puny to be (your) seer's bowl.   (155)
On the twentieth of the month you rejoice with mirth and joy,[1]
You dine, you drink fine brew,
      the tavernkeep's beer at wharfside.[2]
They pour barkeep's beer for you, you accept it.
You are the one who saved them, surrounded by mighty waves,
You accept from them in return their fine, clear libations.   (160)
You drink their sweet beer and brew,
You are the one who makes them achieve the goals they strive for.
You release the ranks[3] of those who kneel to you,
You accept prayers from those who are wont to pray to you.
They revere you, they extol your name,   (165)
They(?) praise your greatness(?) forever.
Imposters, those whose tongues urge sedition,[4]
Who, like clouds, have neither face nor ap[pro]ach(?),
Those that go all over the wide earth,
Those that tread the lofty[5] mountains,   (170)
The hairy hero-men [of the oce]an, filled with fearsomeness,
The yield of the ocean, which goes all over the deep,
The catch of the rivers, (are?) what pass, O Shamash, before you.

---

1. In Mesopotamian menology, the twentieth of the month was Shamash's day.
2. Refers to Shamash's protection of travelers and commercial venturers (see lines 66ff.).
3. Refurbishment (or conflation? so CAD K, 120a) of "release sins" and "break ranks." If intentional, this could mean that the submissive are spared the discipline reserved for the others.
4. Variant: "fra[ud]."
5. Variant: "pure."

Which are the mountains that are not arrayed in your beams?
Which are the corners of the earth that are not warmed
    by the brightness of your rising?   (175)
Brightener of gloom, illuminator of shadow,
Penetrator of darkness, illuminator of the wide world,
Who makes daylight shine,
    who sends down the heatglare of midday to the earth,
Who makes the wild world glow like flame,
Who can shorten the days and lengthen the nights,   (180)
[Who can cau]se cold, frost, ice, (and) snow,
[Who shuts ... the ga]te,* the bolt of heaven,
    opens wide the doors of the inhabited world,
[Who is master of] strike-point and pin, latch,
    and handlebar,[1]
[Who ...] is relentless, (but) bestows life,
[Who ...] the captive in a fight to the death.   (185)
[rea]son, counsel, deliberation, advice,
[   ] ... of morning(?) to the wi[despread] people
[   ] throne, rule, [   ]
[   ] strength, [   ]

               (gap of three lines)

[   ] shining, your splendid abode,
[   ] a banquet for(?) the four world regions.
[gover]nor, high priest, and prince,   (195)
[   ] may they bring you their tribute.
[   ] in a libation the yield of the lands,
[   ] may your throne dais be renewed,
[   ] whose utterance cannot be changed,
[May Aya, your sp]ouse, say to you in the bed chamber,
    "Be appeased!"]   (200)

---

1. A contrast is implied between the parts that lock the door and those that open it, suggesting a chiasm with the preceding line.

Text: W. G. Lambert, BWL, plates 33-36, 73 (see list on p. 125; additional fragments cited CAD A/1, 53b, A/2, 153a, N/1, 218a).

Edition: Lambert, BWL, 121-138, 318-323, 346.

Translation: von Soden, SAHG, 240-247 no. 4; Stephens, ANET³, 387-389; Labat, *Religions*, 267-274; Seux, *Hymnes*, 51-63; Reiner, *Poetry*, 68-84.

Literature: G. R. Castellino, "The Šamaš Hymn: A Note on its Structure," AOAT 25 (1976), 71-74.

*Notes to Text: (22) Seux, *Hymnes*, 53; Lambert, BWL, 318f. (42) Reading with CAD A/1, 107b ˹ta˺-ta-šu-uš ... pa-nu-ka; for tu-šaḫ-bat see von Soden, ZA 67 (1977), 281. (52) Or, mitḫurtu could be parallel to šunna lišānu of 49, rather than "totality" or the like. See Lambert, BWL, 128; Seux, *Hymnes*, 55 with note 30. (54) mu-ši-mi and restoration uncertain; WGL suggests šummû. (64) ul t[u-ub-bal], von Soden, ZA 67 (1977), 281. (70) Restored from Rm IV 177, unpublished duplicate quoted CAD A/1, 53b. (72) von Soden, ZA 67 (1977), 281. (74) Restored from BM 35077, unpublished duplicate quoted CAD A/2, 153a. (75) Seux, *Hymnes*, 56 note 47. (96) For opinions on this line, see Seux, *Hymnes*, 57 note 54; AHw, 1221b. (115) Literally: "asked about," see Lambert, BWL, 321; reading here iššal; see also Seux, *Hymnes*, 58 notes 61, 62; Moran, *Studies Tadmor*, 329f. (123) Seux, *Hymnes*, 59 note 64. (147) For a suggestion to this line, see CAD K, 97a (ta-šal ta-ti). (182) [KÁ].GAL, see von Soden, ZA 67 (1977), 281. (200) Restoration suggested by Lambert, BWL, 138.

E. DEVOTIONAL AND RITUAL POETRY

III.33 TO ADAD

Adad was the god of thunderstorms. The three texts translated below have been chosen to illustrate different aspects of the god's nature as seen in devotional literature.

(a) AGAINST THUNDER

This prayer is addressed to the thunderstorm in the hope of averting portended evil. It ascribes to Adad certain feats of Ninurta, such as slaying of the Anzu-bird (III.22). A fragmentary Middle Babylonian manuscript from Hattusha in Anatolia, with variants and lines not attested in the later manuscripts, attests to the antiquity of this prayer. Two copies are known edited for Sargon II of Assyria.

O most great and perfect one, heir of divine Duran[ki].[1]* (1)
Storm unabating, who keeps up str[ife and combat],
O Adad, great and perfect one, [heir of divine Duranki],
Storm unabating, who keeps up str[ife and] combat,
Founder of the clouds, master of the deluge, (5)
Who strikes with his[2] lightning bolts,
    [who blitzes] Anzu with his lightning bolts!
O overwhelming, perfect one, furious and fierce,
Unrelenting and a wh[irlwind],
O Adad, overwhelming, perfect one, furious and fierce,
Unrelenting and a whir[lwind], (10)
Who overturns raging (enemies), lord of strength,
Fetter that restrains the haughty,
[Fur]ious, stately, awe-inspiring sovereign of the heavens,
Heir of Esharra, who is perfect one among his brothers, hero,
The one who makes lightning flash,
    who carries [torches?] and flame, (15)
Who destroys mountains, peaks, and boulders!

1. "Divine Duranki" is a way of referring to Enlil, commonly used in the Anzu poem (III.22).
2. Variant omits.

[Who for]ms* clouds in the midst of heaven,
[Who brings dow]n* the scorching heat,
     who rains down abundance!
[O Adad, who fo]rms clouds in the midst of heaven,
[Who brings down the scorching he]at,
     who rains down abundance,   (20)
The one at whose clamor[1] people are struck
     dumb with terror,
The meadows [quiver], the steppe heaves!
O Adad, at whose clamor people are struck
     dumb with terror,
The meadows [quake], the steppe heaves,
May you, who hears the secrets of Anu,
     perfect one, mighty one among [his brethren?],   (25)
Most awe-inspiring of the great gods, lord of combat,
Accept my prayer, hear my entreaty!
May (each) day bring me well-being, month joy,
     and year its prosperity.
[   ] ... my fault,
Take away my sin, accept my entreaty!   (30)
I have sought after you,
     I have turned to your divine power,[2]
Grant to me that my words be heard!
Let me proclaim your greatness, let me sound your praises!

Text: Ebeling-Köcher-Rost, LKA 53; King, BMS 20, 8-20 (+) BMS 49, obv 21 (= 1), rev 22-33 (= 11ff.); "Konstantinopel 517" = Ebeling, AGH, 96-98 (transliteration only); Weidner, KUB 4 26a (variants in general not noted here).
Edition: Ebeling, AGH, 96-99.
Translation: Seux, Hymnes, 305-307.
Literature: Mayer, UFBG, Adad 1a.
Notes to Text: (1) Mayer, UFBG, 378. (17) Seux, Hymnes, 306 note 13. (18) Seux, Hymnes, 306 note 14.

1. Later versions add "of his mouth."
2. Variants add here a prayer in the name of Sargon II, king of Assyria, to avert the evil portended by an eclipse, the standard phraseology of which is as follows: "on account of the evil portended by the eclipse of — on the month — on the day —, on account of the evil portended by signs and evil, unfavorable omens, either in my palace or in my country."

(b) AGAINST LIGHTNING

This is a prayer against the effects of lightning. The first part of the text is lost or damaged, but the surviving fragments complement well the preceding.

(gap)

O lord of [lightning, whose she]en illumines [the gloom],
Might[y   ] whose [command] cannot be altered,
Irriga[tor of heaven and earth],
    who rains down [abundance], (5)

(fragmentary lines)

Who [destroys the wic]ked, storm unrelenting,
I cal[l upon you, lord], in the midst of [holy] heaven, (12)
I, [your servant], come before you,
    I seek you out and [kneel be]fore you,

(fragmentary lines)

[O Adad, fire] has come down and [fallen] upon my city, (16)
[At] your [command fire] has come down [from] heaven.
(If) the brickwork of the temple [or the palace],
    or the foundation of the city wall have collapsed,
[Or, ... during] a rainstorm or hail, lightning and fire
[Have consumed my] city god o[r any ot]her [god?], (20)
O Adad, great lord, I [call upon] you, I invoke you,
[Stand?] by me, I invoke you!
[I come before you this d]ay,
    receive my lamentations, accept my ple[as]!
Let the [evil] portended by your utterance not come near me,
    [approach me, draw] nigh me, nor reach me,
Let me proclaim your greatness,
    let me so[und your praises] to the numerous peoples! (25)

Text: King, BMS 21, 1-23 + K 6612 (plate 76).
Edition: Ebeling, AGH, 98-101.
Translation: Seux, Hymnes, 307-309.
Literature: Mayer, UFBG, Adad 4.

(c) IN GRATITUDE FOR RAIN

This is a grateful paean to the beneficent rain storm.

O Adad, [thun]derer, splendid, mighty god,   (1)
[ter]ror, doughty warrior,
[Who forms?] clouds, who curtains daylight,
 ... everything,
Who wields lightning, master of the deluge,   (5)
Who administers heaven, mountains, seas,
Your [na]mes are [good],* your invocation is heard abroad.
At [your] clamor the mountains rejoice,
The meadows are joyous, the fields are happy,
[The people] are exuberant,
          they sound praises of your valor!   (10)
You relieve dr[yn]ess by night and day,
You make abundant greenery, you reconcile the angry.
Maintain your kindnesses [to] me, your servant,
Ordain mercy for me, let me sound your praises,
Let me extol your good [names] to the numerous peoples!   (15)

Text: King, BMS 21, 76-90.
Edition: Ebeling, AGH, 104-105.
Translation: Seux, *Hymnes*, 311-312.
Literature: Mayer, UFBG, Adad 2.
Notes to Text: (7) Seux, *Hymnes*, 312 note 6.

III.34 TO ANU

Anu, god of the sky, was head of the pantheon, and to human beings a remote, inaccessible figure. This bilingual prayer to Anu was used in royal lustration rituals (see III.50h) and is one of the rare devotional compositions addressed to him.

O most great lord, whose lu[strations are pure in heaven],*   (1)
O Anu, greatest lord, [whose] purifications [are pure in heaven],
God¹ of heaven, lord [of heaven],*
Anu, god of heaven, [lord of heaven],
Who releases the day, [crowned] lord, lord of signs,   (5)
Anu, who releases the day, c[rowned] lord, lord of signs,
Dispeller of evil, wicked, and terrifying dreams,
     evil signs and portents,
May my wickedness, [sin, and grave mis]deed
Be absolved with your [life-giving] incantation,
And all that I have committed or neglected
     against my (personal) god
     [and my (personal) goddess] be absolved.²   (10)
May the angry hearts of my (personal) god and
     [my (personal) goddess] be re[conciled to me],
May your furious heart b[e calmed],
And [your] feelings be eased, have mercy!
Let me endow [your] temple richly,
     and anoint your door bolt [with oil],
Let me sou[nd] my lord's praises,   (15)
Let me ever exalt the greatness of your great divinity!

Text: King, BMS 6, 1-16; Campbell Thompson, CT 51 211; Ebeling-Köcher-Rost, LKA 50.
Edition: Ebeling, AGH, 34-36.
Translation: Seux, Hymnes, 270-271.
Literature: Mayer, UFBG, Anu 1.
Notes to Text: (1) Seux, Hymnes, 270 note 3, though CT 51 211 omits *ina*. (3) Seux, Hymnes, 270 note 6.

1. Variant: "Lord."
2. Variant: "O averter of wickedness, sin, and grave misdeed, may the afflictions which have be[set me] and which continue to harass and hamper me ..."

III.35 TO DUMUZI

Tammuz/Dumuzi is celebrated in various Sumerian religious poems as the shepherd boy who wooed and married the youthful Inanna/Ishtar and subsequently met a violent death.[1] He was also known as a netherworld deity, and is here referred to as a son of Ea (Nudimmud, line 2). The following incantation prayer to Dumuzi exists in two versions, of which this is the earlier. It was at some time inserted in a medical ritual. This appeals to Dumuzi in his aspects as shepherd and lover of Ishtar.

> O lord Dumuzi, awe-inspiring shepherd of Anu, (1)
> Lover of Ishtar the queen, eldest son of Nudimmud,
> O mighty one, leader without rival,
> Who eats pure loaves baked in embers,
> Who is clad in a cloak and carries a staff, (5)
> Who drinks water from a ... waterskin,
> Creator of everything, lord of the [sheep]fold,
> You are the lofty prince, the noble one!
> Drive away from me the "evil gazer," the worker of evil,
> [Who] has fixated upon me
>   and is trying to cut short my life. (10)
> Herewith I bring you my life!
> I hand him over to an evil spirit,[2] a merciless demon,
> Let him be cut off from me, grant me life!
> Tear out the "evil gazer" who is present in my body,
> Let me sound your praises
>   until the end point of these (my) days. (15)

Text: Köcher, BAM 339, 33'-42'.
Edition: Farber, *Ištar und Dumuzi*, 190-192, lines 33-42.
Translation: Farber, *Ištar und Dumuzi*, 191-193; Seux, *Hymnes*, 440-441.
Literature: Mayer, UFBG, Dumuzi 1b.

---

1. T. Jacobsen, "Towards the Image of Tammuz," *History of Religions* 1 (1961), 189-213 = HSS 21 (1970), 73-101.
2. Later version substitutes "Humba," a name of uncertain significance; compare III.16d (16). This problem is discussed by Farber, *Ištar und Dumuzi*, 148 and 173.

III.36 TO EA

As god of wisdom, knowledge, and skill, Ea was a particular favorite among diviners and exorcists; indeed, magic was one of his special concerns. For the nature of this divinity, see J. Bottéro, "L'Intelligence et la fonction technique du pouvoir: Enki/Ea," in *Mésopotamie* (1987), 280-302; S. N. Kramer and J. Maier, *Myths of Enki, The Crafty God* (Oxford, 1989). A more technical study will be found in H. D. Galter, *Der Gott Ea/Enki in der akkadischen Überlieferung* (dissertation, Graz, 1981).

(a) FOR SUCCESS IN DIVINATION

Excerpted from an exorcistic work, this bilingual prayer expresses the exorcist's hope for success and professional high repute.

O Ea, king of the depths, finder of [good counsel],★ (1)
I am the exorcist your servant.
Come to my right hand, hasten to my left,
Set your sacral spell for mine,
Set your sacral utterance for mine, (5)
Make my sacral word effective,
Make what I say successful.
Command that my procedures be pure,
Let me succeed wherever I shall go.
Let the person I treat become well. (10)
Let favorable comments precede me,
Let favorable gestures follow me.
Be my protective genius,
Be my good fortune!
May Marduk, the god who brings (me) success, (15)
[Bring]★ success wherever my going.
Let the patient's (personal) god speak of your greatness,
Let this man sound your praises,
I too, the exorcist, let me sound your praises!

Text: Campbell Thompson, CT 16 7, 8, 260-297.
Edition: Campbell Thompson, *Devils* I, 26-29.
Translation: Seux, *Hymnes*, 239-240.
★Notes to Text: (1) Seux, *Hymnes*, 239 note 2. (16) Seux, *Hymnes*, 240 note 11.

(b) PROTECTOR OF THE KING

This prayer is extracted from a ritual for royal lustration, for which see III.50h.

O wise king, perceptive creator,   (1)
Lofty prince, ornament of the E-absu,[1]
Enlilbanda,[2] artful, venerated one,
Hero of Eridu, sage of the Igigi,
Lord of the E-[engur]ra,[3] protection of the E-unir,[4]   (5)
Bringer of the high waters (that cause) abundance,
        who makes the rivers joyful,
In oceans and in reed thickets you make plenteous prosperity,
In the meadows you create the livelihood of the peoples.
Anu and Enlil rejoice because of you,
The Anunna-gods bless you in their holy places,   (10)
The peoples of the land extol your weighty command,
You give counsel to the great gods.
O Ea, the moribund need not die, thanks to your life-giving spell.
Raise up my head, call (my) name!
At your command, may my words be heard,   (15)
At your utterance, may I achieve good fortune.
Grant me life, let me live a long time.
May what I say be pleasing to god and goddess,[5]
May god and king do what I order.
May mouth and tongue say good words for me,
May [   ] not [   ],   (20)
May nothing evil, nothing bad reach me,
Nor any actions of sorcerer or sorceress.
O Ea, thanks to your life-giving spell,
        may everything evil, everything bad retreat,
May the spell of Eridu undo the preparations
        of sorcerer and sorceress,

1. Name for temple in Eridu, city of Ea.
2. "Little Enlil," an epithet of Ea.
3. Name for temple in Eridu.
4. Name for temple in Eridu.
5. Variant: "king."

May Marduk, prince of the gods,
    undo their evil preparations.[1]   (25)
May my limbs be pure, my members healthy for me.
May the heavens rejoice because of you,
May the depths rejoice because of you,
May the great gods nobly(?) acclaim you,[2]
May the Igigi-gods speak favorably of you!   (30)

Text: Ebeling, KAR 59, obv 29-36, rev 1-22; King, BMS 10, 1-5 (same text, but addressed to Marduk); Loretz-Mayer, AOAT 34 33, 34; Finkelstein, STT 67; von Weiher, SBTU II 55, compare III 78.
Edition: Mayer, UFBG, 442-449.
Translation: von Soden, SAHG, 295-296 no. 40; Seux, *Hymnes*, 275-277.
Literature: Mayer, UFBG, Ea 1a.

1. Variant: "magic knots."
2. Variant: "[sa]tisfy [your he]art" and "may the gods of the universe bless you."

III.37 TO EA, SHAMASH, MARDUK

Ea, god of wisdom, Shamash, god of justice, and Marduk, son of Ea, were a group frequently invoked in magical prayers and rituals. Marduk is sometimes referred to with a by-name, Asalluhi, as in (b). Their functions in such contexts are not normally differentiated, save that, in a general way, Ea provides the spell, Marduk the effective execution of it, and Shamash the powers of purification. In this respect the last line of (b) is unusual.

(a) AGAINST CONGENITAL GUILT

O Ea, Shamash, and Marduk, what is my guilt?   (1)
An abomination has confronted me,
    evil has me in its power.
My father begot me, my mother bore me,
They laid their plans and like a snake I [   ],[1]
From the dark within I came forth and saw you, O Shamash!   (5)
An ill wind has brought down my branches,*
A mighty tempest has bent low my crown.
My pinions were shorn like a bird's,
I moulted my plumage, I could not fly.
Paralysis has seized my arms,   (10)
Debility has befallen my knees.
I moan like a dove night and day.
I am feverish and weep bitterly,
Tears are coursing from my eyes.
O Shamash, abatement is within your reach: (15)
Dispel, drive off the guilt of my mother and father.[2]
Go away, curse (upon me)!

---

1. This line may express parents' hopes and ambitions for their child. As Lambert points out, p. 294, the "snake" is an image for the child wriggling through the birth canal from the womb (the "dark within" of line 5; compare IV.48c). The sense of the whole passage seems to be that the first thing this sufferer did was to behold the sun, so his life began auspiciously. Furthermore, the sun should know all about him, since he was born as he is now. This speaker is evidently wrestling with the problem of personal guilt.

2. The text seems to impute the sufferer's trouble to his parents (compare III.45c line 5), who made him the mere human that he is; for a different interpretation, that the speaker has wronged his parents and is therefore being punished, see Seux, *Hymnes*, 171 note 22.

Drive it away, O Ea, king of the depths,
    [and A]salluhi, lord of exorcism!
May my guilt be 3600 leagues far distant,
May the river accept (it) from me
    and take (it) down within.   (20)
O Ea, Shamash, and Marduk, come to my help!
Let me be clean in your presence,
    let me be pure before you.

Text: Myhrman, PBS 1/1 14, 1-23; W. G. Lambert, JNES 33 (1974), 308 (Rm 414, 21-22).
Edition: W. G. Lambert, JNES 33 (1974), 274-275, lines 1-22.
Translation: von Soden, SAHG, 338-339 no. 65; Seux, *Hymnes*, 199-201.
*Notes to Text: (6) Seux, *Hymnes*, 200 note 7.

(b) AGAINST ANY EVIL

This prayer could be used against the consequence of any unfavorable omen.

O Ea, Shamash, and Asalluhi, great gods,   (1)
You are the ones who judge cases for the land.
Ordainers of destinies, the ones who draw up designs,
Apportioners of lots for heaven and earth,
In your power is decreeing of destinies
   and drawing-up of designs,   (5)
The destiny of life is yours to ordain,
The design of life is yours to draw up,
The ruling for life is yours to render.
Your spell is life, your utterance well-being,
   your speech is life.
You are the ones to pass judgment on the land,   (10)
Who tread the vast netherworld, who tread
   the distant heavens, as far as the heavens extend.
O opponents of evil, upholders of good,
Who obliterate evil signs and portents,
   terrifying, evil, foul dreams,
Who cut the wicked skein,
   who make defensive magic effective,
Wherever there are signs and portents,
   as many as there are,   (15)
I, so-and-so, son of so-and-so,
Whose (personal) god is so-and-so,
Whose (personal) goddess is so-and-so,
Against whom evil signs keep occurring,
I am afraid, frightened, and terrified!   (20)
Let me escape the evil (portended by)
   an eclipse of the moon,
The evil (portended by) an eclipse of the sun,
The evil (portended by) the stars (and) the stars of Ea,
   Anu, and Enlil,
The evil (portended by) the planets
   which approach the path of the stars,

(gap and fragmentary lines)

The signs and evil portents,	(1′)
[Lest I perish, be injured], or be turned ov[er to] a demon,	
[Let a good] wind [blow] and this evil not,	
[Let] the [south] wind [blow] but this evil not,	
[Let] the [no]rth wind [blow] but this evil not,	(5′)
[Let] the east wind [blow] but this evil not,	
Let the west wind blow but this evil not!	
At your sublime command, which cannot be altered,	
And your firm assent, which cannot be changed,	
Let me live in well-being!	(10′)
O Ea, Shamash, and Asalluhi, let me sound	
at this very time praises of your great divinity,	
O Shamash, make great the exorcism which Marduk,	
sage of the gods, performs.[1]	

Text: Ebeling-Köcher-Rost, LKA 109; Langdon, OECT 6 pl. XXII K 2784 + King, BMS 62; Caplice, OrNS 40 (1971), pl. IX, 54C, pl. X, 51D; Laessøe, *Bit Rimki*, pl. III no. X Sm 290 (slightly variant).
Edition: Caplice, OrNS 40 (1971), 157-158, no. 54, lines 1-20.
Translation: von Soden, SAHG, 339-340 no. 66; Seux, *Hymnes*, 349-351.
Literature: Mayer, UFBG, Ea, Šamaš, Marduk/Asalluhi 1a.

1. Variant omits this line.

(c) AGAINST SNAKEBITE

This is a general prayer which has been made specific in the case of the surviving manuscript to deal with snakebite. The manuscript was discovered at Hama in Syria and dates to the ninth century B.C. Its general entreaty is very similar to the preceding.

O Ea, Shamash, and Asalluhi, great gods,   (1)
[Who judge] cases for heaven and earth,
        ordainers [of destinies],
[Who ren]der rulings, who expand holy places,
[Who fou]nd sanctuaries and guarantee [their]* portions,
[Who dra]w up designs and apportion lots,   (5)
[Who ca]re for sanctuaries,
Who make lustrations purifying,
        [who] understand purification,
In your power is to ordain destinies, to draw up designs!
The destiny of life is yours to ordain,
The design of life is yours to draw up,   (10)
The ruling for life is yours to render.
You sur[vey] completely sanctuary of god and goddess,
You, O great gods, administer rulings for heaven
        and earth, depths and seas.
Your command is life, your utterance well-being,
        your speech is life.
You tread the remotenesses of heaven,   (15)
You drive away evil and establish good,
You dispel evil signs and portents; foul, terrifying dreams,
You cut the wicked skein!
I, w[hose speech is pur]e, who k[now] the pure rites
        of <the great gods>(?),
I have cast [pure] water and purified the [gro]und for you.   (20)
I have set up pure [chai]rs for you to sit on.
I have bestowed upon you a (bright) red garment [   ],
I have set up for you the (cultic) apparatus.
I have libated for you a pure libation,
I have set up for you a bowl of light beer,

I have libated wine and fine beer for you.
Because the power to execute the authority of the g[reat gods]
    and to perform lustrations rests with you,   (25)
Stand by me at this time,
[Or]dain majestically a fate for this unconscious man
    who [ ] before you,
That his [mo]uth may eat, that his ears may hear.
Let this [man] be pu[re] as [heaven],
    [clean] as the netherworld,
Let him shine like the innermost sky!   (30)
Let all evil speech stand aside.
I, so-and-so, son of [so-and-so], your servant,
    am afraid, frightened, and terrified,
    on account of the evil of a snake.

(breaks off)

Text: Laessøe, *Iraq* 18 (1956), pl. XIV (after p. 60).
Edition: Laessøe, *Iraq* 18 (1956), 60-67.
Translation: Seux, *Hymnes,* 352-354.
Literature: Mayer, UFBG, Ea, Šamaš, Marduk/Asalluhi 1b.
*Notes to Text: (4) Seux, *Hymnes,* 353 note 17.

(d) AGAINST A GHOST

This prayer uses a figurine of the ghost afflicting the patient as part of its magical procedure. The figurine is equipped for a journey and dispatched to the netherworld. With the departure of the figurine, the ghost was expected to quit the patient.

> [O administrator of all the] numerous [peoples],
>> light of the earth, Shamash the judge,   (1)
> O mighty [lord Ea], Eridu's [tru]st,
> O sage of the universe, raging Marduk, [lo]rd of E'engurra,[1]
> O Ea, Shamash, and Marduk, run to my aid,
> Let me advance with your assent!   (5)
> O Shamash,[2] a terrifying ghost has attached itself
>> to my back for many days, and does not release its hold,
> It has harassed me all day, terrified me all night,
> Always at hand to hound me, making my hair stand on end,
> Pressing my forehead, making me dizzy,
> Parching my mouth, paralyzing my flesh,
>> drying out my whole body.[3]   (10)
> Be it a ghost of my kith or kin,
> Be it a ghost of someone killed in battle,
> Be it a wandering ghost, this one, this is its figurine!
> O Shamash, I have worked on it before you:
> I have portrayed on it clothes to wear, sandals for its feet,[4]   (15)
> A belt for its waist, a waterskin for it to drink from, and flour,
> I have given it provision for a journey.
> Let it go to the setting sun,
> Let it be entrusted to Pituh,[5]
>> great gatekeeper of the netherworld,
> May Pituh, great gatekeeper of the netherworld,
>> keep it under close guard,[6]   (20)

1. Temple of Ea at Eridu.
2. Variant: "O figurine."
3. Variant omits.
4. Variant: "great Shamash."
5. Literally: "Open!" See Deller, *Nabu* 1991/18.
6. Variant omits this line.

May he hold fast the bolt (against) their keys(?).

O Shamash, at your sublime command,
　　which cannot be changed,[1]

At the command of the sage of the gods, Marduk,

Drive it from my body, cut it off [from] my [bo]dy,
　　remove it from my body!

Be it conjured by your life! Be it conjured
　　by the life of Ea and [As]alluhi! (25)

Be it conjured [by the life of the gre]at
　　[gods of heaven and netherworld]![2]

May it not approach me, may it not draw near me!

[May it not reach me], may it not catch up with me!

May it cross river, go beyond mountain,

[May it be 3600 l]eagues distant from my person! (30)

May it mount to the skies like smoke,

[Like an] uprooted [tamar]isk,
　　may it not return where it was![3]

May (this) tamarisk purify [me],

[May] (this) [... plant re]lease me!*

May the netherworld receive (it) of me, (35)

May it give me its awe-inspiring sheen,
　　may it remove my sickness!

[O Ea] and Marduk, run to my aid!

Remove the [sic]kness of my body,
　　that the one who sees me may sound your praises,

Eradicate the disease of my body!

I turn to you, grant me life! (40)

Text: King, BMS 53; Ebeling, KAR 267, rev 1-24.
Edition: Ebeling, TuL, 140-142.
Translation: von Soden, SAHG, 340-342 no. 67; Seux, *Hymnes*, 416-418.
Notes to Text: (34) von Soden, ZA 43 (1936), 269; AHw, 198a.

---

1. Variant adds here a prayer to avert the evil portended by an eclipse; see p. 546 note 2.
2. Variant omits.
3. This formula is encountered elsewhere; compare III.50a lines 7ff., III.50 i lines 101ff., III.500 lines 35ff., IV.46b line 14.

III.38 TO ENLIL

As chief god of the Sumerian pantheon, Enlil continued in Assyro-Babylonian tradition as one of the great gods. His domain was the earth, though he is often portrayed in Akkadian literature as inimical to mankind, angry, harsh, and malevolent.

(a) SPOKEN BY A PERSON IN AUTHORITY

[He who has ga]thered to himself all,
  king of heaven and netherworld, swift god,*   (1)
Wise one who knows the people's portents,
Who surveys (all) qua[rters],
Noble sovereign, whose [command] cannot be changed,
Whose utterance cannot be altered, [   ] ...   (5)
The command of whose lips no god can set aside,
Greatest lord, mountain of the Igigi-gods,
Sovereign of the Anunna-gods, solicitous noble one,
Enlil, greatest lord, mountain of the Igigi-gods,
Sovereign of the Anunna-gods, solicitous noble one,   (10)
Ever-renewing one, whose command cannot be altered,
The command of whose lips no god can set aside,
Lord of lords, king of kings,[1]
  father who begot the great gods,
Lord of destinies and designs, last resort for judgment,
You are the leader of heaven and netherworld,
  lord of the lands!   (15)
At your command humankind is born,
You nominate king and governor.
Of all the stars of heaven,
... it is your name I have invoked,
I have been attentive to you.   (20)
Ordain a favorable [destiny] for me,
[Grant me]* your great prosperity.
[Set upon me] your great vitality.

1. Variant: "king of the world."

[May god?],* king, lord, prince es[teem me],
[Ma]y the one who sees me extol [your] greatness.   (25)
May the people's mouths speak praise of me.
Set [as]sent, obedience, and peace upon my lips.
[By] your eternal assent, which cannot be changed,
Let my (personal) god stand at my right,
Let my (personal) goddess stand at my left,   (30)
Let the god who keeps (me) in well-being
     always be at my side,
Let courtier and official speak a favorable word for me.
Look upon me, lord, accept my supplication!
Reconcile with me the hearts of my angry, furious,
     wrathful (personal) god and my (personal) goddess
     which are angry, furious, and wrathful with me,
As well as the heart of your great divinity!   (35)
Each day, as long as I live,
Let me proclaim your greatness, let me sou[nd] your praises!

Text: Ebeling, KAR 68; KAR 25, iii 21-33; see also III.38b.
Edition: Ebeling, AGH, 20-23.
Translation: Seux, *Hymnes,* 271-273.
Literature: Mayer, UFBG, Enlil 1b.
Notes to Text: (1) Mayer, OrNS 46 (1977), 388. (22) CAD Ḫ, 168b. (24) Seux, *Hymnes,* 273 note 19.

(b) PROTECTOR OF THE KING

This prayer, to be spoken during a royal lustration ritual (see III.50h), is partly
a duplicate of the preceding, but then turns specifically to the needs of one in
authority.

> O greatest lord, mountain of the Igi[gi]-gods,   (1)
> Sovereign of the Anunna-gods, solicitous prince,
> O [En]lil, greatest lord, mountain of the Igigi-gods,
> [So]vereign of the Anunna-gods, solicitous prince,
> Ever-renewing one, whose command cannot be altered,   (5)
> The command of whose lips no god can set aside,
> Lord of lords, king of kings, father who begot the great gods,
> Lord of destinies and designs, leader of heaven and netherworld,
> Lord of the lands,
> Last resort for judgment, whose command cannot be altered,   (10)
> Who ordains destinies for all the gods,
> At your command humankind is born,[1]
> You nominate king and governor.
> Because creation of god and man is in your power,
> And because you can make the weak equal to the strong,   (15)
> From among all the stars of heaven,
> My lord, I put my trust in you, extol you,
> And I have been attentive to you.
> Ordain for me a destiny of (long) life,
> Command a good name for me.   (20)
> Dissolve evil and establish justice,
> Take away [po]verty and give me prosperity,[2]
> Set upon me your great vitality.
> May [god] and king esteem me,
> May noble and prince do what I command,[3]   (25)
> May the one who sees me act in awe of me,
> May my word be heeded in the assembly,
> May the protective spirit of speaking, hearing, and

1. Variant adds a prayer to avert the evil portended by an eclipse; see p. 546 note 2.
2. Variant for 21/22: "take away evil and give favor."
3. Variant: "what befits me."

acceptance go with me every day!
May my (personal) god exalt you,
  may my (personal) goddess seek you!* (30)
And as for me, your servant, may I live in well-being,[1]
Let me proclaim your greatness, let me sound your praises!

Text: Myhrman, PBS 1/1 17; King, BMS 19; compare Ebeling, KAR 25, iii 27-33, KAR 68, obv. 10-19 (above, III.38a).
Edition: Ebeling, AGH, 20-22.
Translation: von Soden, SAHG, 296-297 no. 41; Seux, *Hymnes*, 274-275.
Literature: Mayer, UFBG, Enlil 1a.
*Notes to Text: (30) Mayer, OrNS 46 (1977), 389.

1. Variant omits these two lines and ends here with an incomplete one: "At your sublime command, which cannot be altered, And your eternal assent, which cannot be changed ..."

(c) AGAINST ENLIL'S ANGER

This bilingual Sumero-Akkadian psalm is an example of a type intended to appease angry gods, a well-known genre in Sumerian called "heart-appeasing laments."[1] It invokes Enlil by various epithets, seeking to bring about his reconciliation with his people (the "black-headed folk," or Mesopotamians) and to restore order in the land. The preserved portion opens with an address to the god, hoping to stir his attention. The consequences of his withdrawal of favor are mentioned. There follows a lament over the destruction of the land; then the psalm ends with a plea for reconciliation. Compare III.49c.

How long, O lord, how long? Help me!   (1)
How long, ...? Help me!
How long, [O lord of the world]? Help me!
How long, [O lord of the sure command]? Help me!
How long, [O Mullil,[2] father of the land]? Help me!   (5)
How long, O shep[herd] of the black-headed folk? Help me!
How long, [O keeper of your own counsel]? Help me!
How long, [O wild bull who lets his herd stray]? Help me!
How long, [O sleeper of feigned sleep]? Help me!
How long, O lord of Nippur? Help me!   (10)
How long, O lord, how long will a mighty foe have had
         full control of your land?
[How long, O lord, will an enemy] destroy your land?
[   ] has scattered the people of your land to a distant [la]nd,
[   ] has left the cult centers moaning,
[   ] has scattered [   ]   (15)

                              (gap)

[May Asalluhi-Marduk, lord of Babylon],[3] (join) my prayer,
[May his wife, Panunan]ki-Sarpanitu, (join) my supplication.
[May your trusty messenger?, Muz]ebbasa'a-Nabu,
         (join) my prayer,

1. E. Dalglish, *Psalm Fifty-one* (Leiden, 1962), 21–35; Maul, HBKl.
2. Sumerian dialectal form for Enlil.
3. The hyphenated names that follow are Sumerian names or epithets of gods followed by Akkadian names or epithets of the same gods.

[May the daughter-in-law?], eldest child of Urash,
    (join) my supplication.
May the righteous princess, Gashankateshsiga-Tashmetu,
    join my prayer,   (5')
May the great princess, the lady Nanay,
    (join) my supplication.
May your father Enki, who begot you,
    (your mother) Ninki, (join) my prayer,
May your beloved wife, the great mistress Ninlil,
    (join) my supplication.
May your trusty messenger, the commander Nusku
    (join) my prayer:
May they say to you, "[Look steadfastly upon him]!"   (10')
May they say to you, "[Incline your head towards him]!"
May they say to you, "[Let your heart be calmed]!"
May they say to you, "[Let your feelings be soothed]!"
[As if my real mother, let your heart be reconciled],
[As if my real mother, my real father,
    let your heart be reconciled]!   (15')

Text: Maul, HBKl, pl. 6-7.
Edition: Maul, HBKl, 90-96 no. 3.
Translation: Seux, *Hymnes*, 147-149.

III.39 TO FAMILY GHOSTS

While Mesopotamians believed in the finality of death and a dreary eternity in a dusty, cheerless netherworld (see III.18 lines 7-11, III.19b iii 2' - 5'), they accepted as well the possibilities of traffic with spirits of the dead. Survivors of the deceased were responsible for providing food and water for the spirit in the netherworld. Spirits of the dead not properly interred or cared for might exercise a baneful influence. There is evidence at various periods for a household ancestral cult as well.[1] This is alluded to in the Great Hymn to Nabu (III.31), lines 121ff. For spells against ghosts, see also IV.39b, c.

O ghosts of my family, progenitors of the grave(?),* (1)
My father, my grandfather, my mother, my grandmother,
 my brother, my sister,
My family, kith, and kin,
 as many as are asleep in the netherworld,
I have made my funerary offering,
I have libated water to you, I have cherished you, (5)
I have glorified you, I have ho[no]red you.
Stand this day before Shamash and Gilgamesh,[2]
Judge my case, render my verdict!
Hand over to Namtar, messenger of the netherworld,
The evil(s) present in my body, flesh, and sinews! (10)
May Ningizzida, prefect of the vast netherworld,
 guard them well,
May Pituh, great gatekeeper of the netherworld,
 [cover?] their faces.
Seize (them)[3] and send (them) down
 to the Land of No Return!
May I, your servant, live in well-being,
Let me be purified* [in] your name from witchcraft, (15)

1. See J. Bottéro, "La Mythologie de la mort," CRRAI 26 (1979), 25-52 = *Mésopotamie*, 323-346; "Les Morts et l'au-delà dans les rituels en akkadien contre l'action des 'revenants'," ZA 73 (1983), 153-203; M. Bayliss, "The Cult of Dead Kin in Assyria and Babylonia," *Iraq* 35 (1973), 115-125.
2. Here a netherworld deity.
3. Text: "it," though preceding line has objects of verb in plural.

Let me libate cool water in your drinking pipe,[1]
Revive me, let me sound your praises!

Text: Ebeling, KAR 227, rev iii 8-24; Ebeling-Köcher-Rost, LKA 89, rev right, 3-7.
Edition: Ebeling, TuL, 131-132.
Translation: Seux, *Hymnes*, 431-432.
Literature: Mayer, UFBG, *eṭemmū kimtija* 1.
Notes to Text: (1) Reading von Soden, ZA 43 (1944), 266; translation uncertain. Seux suggests "builders of tombs(?)"; variant has "Anunna-gods." (15) Seux, *Hymnes*, 432 note 9, following Mullo Weir, reads "let me invoke your name," but this does not accord well with LKU 89, rev 16, where [*i*]*na* MU-*ku-nu* supports Ebeling's reading.

1. Conduit for water to the netherworld where the dead could receive fresh water, if offered to them by the living.

III.40 TO GIRRA

Girra, the fire god, was frequently invoked in rituals against black magic. In magic rituals fire was used to consume a figurine or other representation of the witch believed to be afflicting the patient. The selections translated below illustrate different appeals to the fire god's power. Many such prayers are found in two large magical works entitled "Burning" (*Maqlû*) and "Incineration" (*Šurpu*) respectively (see IV.44 and Introduction to Chapter IV, p. 695 notes 4 and 5). For a general study, see J. Bottéro, "Le feu dans les textes mésopotamiens," in *Le feu dans le Proche-Orient Antique, Actes du Colloque de Strasbourg (9 et 10 juin 1972),* (Leiden, 1973), especially 24-26.

(a) ILLUMINATOR

O blazing Girra, firstborn of Anu, (1)
You are the one to render judgment
 (on what is) spoken and secret,
You illumine darkness,
You set straight confusion and perturbation.
You make decisions for the great gods, (5)
Without you, no god reaches a verdict,
You are the giver of instruction and direction.
You straightaway restrain the evil-doer,
You straightaway overcome the wicked enemy.
I, so-and-so, son of his (personal) god,
 whose (personal) god is so-and-so,
 whose (personal) goddess is so-and-so, (10)
Have been afflicted by sorcery, I stand before you,
Being cursed before god and king, I ... before you,
Being [ob]noxious to whoever s[ees me],
 I kneel at your feet.
O Girra, most great one, pure god,
Now, before your great divinity, (15)
I have made for your power two bronze figurines
 of my sorcerer and of my sorceress,
I have made crossed marks(?) upon them, before you,
 I have given them over to you.

Let them be the ones to die, let me live,
Let them be the ones to be taken astray,
>   let me go straight,
Let them be the ones to come to an end,
>   let me be productive,   (20)
Let them be the ones to be weak, let me be strong![1]
O stately Girra, eminent one of the gods,
Overcome them,
>   you who overcome the evil and the enemy,
>   that I be not oppressed.
Let me, your servant, live in well-being
>   and stand before you.
You are my god, you are my lord,   (25)
You are my judge, you are my help,
You are my champion!

Text: Tallqvist, *Maqlû* II 69-90; Ebeling, KAR 235, obv 8-20; Gurney, STT 140, obv + Finkelstein, STT 79, 76-84, 81, obv 96-102.
Edition: Meier, *Maqlû,* 15-16, lines 76-102.
Translation: von Soden, SAHG, 347-348 no. 73; Seux, *Hymnes,* 384-385.
Literature: Meier, AfO 21 (1966), 73; Mayer, UFBG, Gira 2.

1. Possibly (Seux, *Hymnes,* 385 note 12) a reference to progeny.

(b) MELTER

O stately Girra, firstborn of Anu,   (1)
Pure offspring of sublime Shalash,[1]
Stately, ever-renewing,
       eternal requirement(?)[2] of the gods,
Giver of food portions to the Igigi-gods,
Who imparts brilliance to the Anunna, the great gods,   (5)
Raging Girra, who burns up canebrakes,[3]
Brave Girra, who destroys trees and rocks,
Who burns up evil ones, the tribe of sorcerer and sorceress,
Who destroys malefactors,
       the tribe of sorcerer and sorceress,
Stand by me this day in my case,   (10)
Overcome the seditious, corrupter(?), the evil one!
Just as these figurines dissolve, melt, drip away,
Let my sorcerer and sorceress dissolve, melt, drip away.

Text: Tallqvist, *Maqlû* II 124-135; Ebeling, KAR 235, rev 6-12.
Edition: Meier, *Maqlû*, 18, lines 135-147.
Translation: von Soden, SAHG, 349 no. 75; Seux, *Hymnes,* 387.
Literature: Mayer, UFBG, Gira 5.
Notes to Text: (6) Meier, AfO 21 (1966), 73; Seux, *Hymnes,* 387 note 4.

1. Normally the wife of Adad or Dagan, but here assigned to Anu; compare above, p. 519 note 1.
2. Uncertain. See p. 407 note 2.
3. Variant: "enemies."

(c) JUDGE

O Girra, mighty one, terrifying storm,   (1)
You govern gods and sovereigns,
You judge the case of the oppressed man and woman.
Stand by me in my case, and, like the warrior Shamash,
Judge my case, render my verdict!   (5)
Burn up my sorcerer and my sorceress,
Consume my enemies,
     devour those who are wicked to me,
Let your furious storm overcome them!

Text: Tallqvist, *Maqlû* II 114-121; Ebeling, KAR 235, rev 1-4.
Edition: Meier, *Maqlû*, 17-18, lines 126-133.
Translation: von Soden, SAHG, 348 no. 74; Seux, *Hymnes,* 386-387.
Literature: Mayer, UFBG, Gira 4.

(d) REFINER

O Girra, sage, exalted in the land,   (1)

Valorous one, son of Apsu, exalted in the land,

O Girra, with your pure flame*

You provide light to the House of Shadows,

You ordain the destiny* of whatever is called by name.   (5)

You are the one who mixes copper and tin,

You are the one who refines gold and silver.

You are the companion of the fermentation goddess,

You are the one who, at night, turns back the evildoer.

May the limbs of (this) man,

    son of his (personal) god, be purified!   (10)

May he be pure as the heavens,

May he be pure as the netherworld!

May he shine like innermost heaven,

[May] the evil [tongue stand] aside.*

Text: Pinches, IV R² 14 no. 2 = Haupt, ASKT 9, rev 6-29 (bilingual, translation follows Akkadian); Gurney, OECT 11 40.
Edition: Reiner, *Šurpu*, 53, lines 6-29.
Translation: Seux, *Hymnes*, 251-252.
Notes to Text: (3) Sumerian adds "clear." (5) Sumerian: "you put a branding mark on."
(14) Sumerian only.

III.41 TO GODS OF THE NIGHT

(a) AGAINST PESTILENCE

This prayer was used in a ritual against pestilence.

> The steppe is deathly still, doors are barred,
> > [gates are sh]ut,* (1)
> Bolts are set, the go[ds of the night][1] are hushed,
> (But) the gr[eat?]* gates of heaven are open.
> O great gods of the night, whose p[ath?] is discernible,
> Come in, O gods of the night, gre[at] stars, (5)
> Yoke-star, Sipazianna,[2] Shulpa'e,[3] [   ],
> Chariot,[4] Jupiter, Kidney, Mouse,[5] Field,[6]
> Come in, gods of the night, goddesses [of the night ...],
> Of south and north, of east and west.
> Come, Ninsianna,[7] great lady, and the many ... stars, (10)
> That he who is mindful of you may attain his desire,
> That so-and-so, who is mindful of you,
> > may attain [his desire].*
> From of old there has been acceptance [   ],
> Vitality, obedience, and revival <are yours (to grant)>,*
> Yours is to dissolve bondage, anger, fury, and scheming. (15)
> Accept the speech of him* who has invoked you,
> > dignify [his] speech,
> Accept the speech of [so-and-so],
> > who has invoked you, dignify his speech!

> *(obscure lines, then gap)*

1. So the parallel from Hattusha, though this is hard to reconcile with line 4.
2. Orion?
3. Procyon?
4. Great Bear.
5. Centaurus?
6. Pegasus?
7. Venus.

Text: K 3507 = Langdon, OECT 6 pl. xii = Sidersky, JRAS 1929, 786 (collated).
Edition: Ebeling, TuL, 163-164.
Translation: Seux, *Hymnes*, 243-245.
Literature: Meier, ZA 45 (1939), 197 (parallel from Hattusha in Anatolia); Oppenheim, AnBi 12 (1959), 291; Mayer, UFBG, *ilū mušīti* 2c.
Notes to Text: (1) Seux, *Hymnes*, 243 note 3. (3) Seux, *Hymnes*, 244 note 6. (12) Langdon's copy conflates the first half of tablet line 18 with the second half of tablet line 19; see Sidersky's copy. (14) *ittikunu* was apparently omitted by the scribe. (16) Seux, *Hymnes*, 245 note 26. First preserved sign is šá, not a.

(b) AGAINST CULTIC IMPURITY

This prayer was used in a ritual designed to protect a person from the evil incurred from an improperly performed cultic rite. For other prayers of this type, see von Soden, SAHG, 343 no. 69; Seux, *Hymnes*, 248-250 (a) = Caplice, OrNS 39 (1970), 128-129.

> Stand by me, O gods of the night,   (1)
> Heed what I say, O gods, lords of silence!
> O Anu, Enlil, Ea, great gods,
> O Ninshiku, exceedingly wise!
> I call upon you, Ishtar, mistress of silence,   (5)
> I call upon you, Night, bride of Anu, laden with splendor!
> O Yoke-star, stand at my right,
>   O Yoke-star, stand at my left!
> God sends you as a messenger to man and man to god,
> It is I who sends you to the god who eats my bread,
>   who drinks my water, the one who receives my offering.

Text: Ebeling, KAR 38, rev 18-27; Caplice, OrNS 39 (1970), pl. II K 8863.
Edition: Caplice, OrNS 39 (1970), 127, 130, no. 38, lines 18-27.
Translation: Seux, *Hymnes*, 250 (b).
Literature: Mayer, UFBG, *ilū mušīti* 3b.

(c) AGAINST WITCHCRAFT

I call upon you, O gods of the night, (1)
Along with you I call upon night, the veiled bride,
I call upon the evening, midnight, and dawn watch.
Because a sorceress has bewitched me,
(And) a deceitful woman has denounced me, (5)
They have driven away from me my (personal) god and
     my (personal) goddess,
I have become obnoxious to whoever sees me,
I am burdened with sleeplessness, day and night.
They keep filling my mouth with skeins(?),[1]
They have deprived my mouth of food, (10)
They have diminished my drinking water.
My joyful song is a dirge, my happiness sorrow.
Stand by me, O great gods, hear my complaint,
Judge my case, learn of my proceeding!
I have made a figurine of my sorcerer and of my sorceress, (15)
Of him and her who contrive against me,
I have set (them) before you, I plead my case.
Because she has done evil and has attempted villainy,
May she be the one to die, let me live!
May her sorcery, spells, and black magic be dissolved, (20)
May the full-crowned tamarisk absolve, purify me,
May the palm that withstands all winds absolve me,
May the ...-plant, full of pulp(?),[2] cleanse me,
May the pine cone, full of seeds, absolve me.
Before you I have become pure as the grass, (25)
I have become clean and pure as soap plant.
Her spell, that of the wicked sorceress,

---

1. Variant: "silence" (Meier, *Maqlû*, 66). According to CAD Q, 304b, "silence" is an erroneous variant; according to AHw, 925b, 927b, "skeins" is erroneous. Tying thread on the mouth as a metaphor for blocking speech and effectiveness is known in other magical contexts, though not filling the mouth with thread. Line 12 is in favor of "thread." For a magical procedure that involves stopping up a mouth with wool, see Falkenstein, ZA 45 (1939), 26.

2. Literally: "Earth." The symbolism of the trees may include tallness, strength, inner resources, and promise of productivity for the future, all attributes that might desert a man under an evil spell.

Her speech is turned back to her mouth,
    she is tongue-tied.
May the gods of the night strike her
    on account of her sorcery,
May the three watches of the night
    dissolve her wicked spells!   (30)
May her mouth be tallow, her tongue be salt,
May she who said the evil word against me melt like tallow,
May she who worked sorcery be dissolved like salt,
May her magic knots be untied,
    her contrivances be destroyed,
May all her words fill the wilderness,   (35)
At the command spoken by the gods of the night!

Text: Tallqvist, *Maqlû* I 1-36; Finkelstein, STT 78, 1-36.
Edition: Meier, *Maqlû*, 7-8, lines 1-36.
Translation: Seux, *Hymnes*, 375-377; Farber, TUAT II/2, 262-263.
Literature: Meier, AfO 21 (1966), 70-71; Mayer, UFBG, *ilū mušiti* 1; Abusch, *Witchcraft,* 85-147.

III.42 TO GULA

Gula was goddess of healing and the physician's arts. For additional hymns to Gula, see C. J. Mullo-Weir, "Four Hymns to Gula," JRAS 1929, 1-18, and above, III.25.

(a) HEALER

This song invokes her by various names and extols her life-giving powers.

> [Let me sing of y]our [pr]aises,
>> let me extol your [sovereign]ty,   (1)
> Let me exalt your [divin]ity, let me glori[fy your val]or,
> [O Gula], let me sing of your praises,
>> let me extol your sovereignty,
> Let me exalt your [divin]ity, let me glorify [your] valor.
> Let me proclaim [your] name to the black-headed folk,[1]
>> however many they be,   (5)
> You keep healthy (people's) bod[ies] in all world regions
>> you have allowed to fete you.
> O Gula, great physician, there is no equal to you,
>> great is [your] responsibility!
> Let me glorify your sovereignty,
>> let me exalt your na[me] in all holy places,
> You dwell in Ekur, in Esharra go [your pa]ths.[2]
> [   ] your [   ] among the gods you are warrior,
>> who among the gods can [   ] your sovereignty?   (10)
> You are the one [   ] who, with the great gods,
>> ordains destinies.
> You stand out [   ] ..., O lady,
>> the mention of your name is un[ ],
> Who [   ] dogs,[3] who gives health to god and man,
>> they call on you as "mistress of health."

1. The Mesopotamians.
2. This may refer to a temple in Assur.
3. The dog was associated with the goddess of healing.

You give [   ] to the great lords,
  they call on you in all of Baltil,[1]
You govern human beings [on] earth,
  you exalt [your] na[me] to the great gods.   (15)
You judge cases and ordain destinies
  [in response to?] prayers,
You hold [sov]ereignty of heaven,
  you give instructions to the Igigi-gods.
Which destiny among the gods' [   ] have you not ordained?
You prolong the days of the [ki]ng(?) [   ],
  you let him see light,
[   ], as he grows old, his eyes will see much,   (20)

(three lines fragmentary)

He who was plunged [into dis]as[ter],
  you saved him from distress,
You gave subsis[tence to the poor].   (25)
O merciful [   ], may your heart be cal[med],
O [   ] ..., may your feelings be ap[peased]!
May the mori[bund] revive [at] your sublime [command],
At your firm as[sent], the moaning
  world regions shout for joy,
They summon you as "queen of (all) world regions" [   ], (30)
Your names are important [   ], O spouse of Uta'ulu,[2]
[Me]me,[3] who establishes festivals for the lords
  who lo[ve you].
[   ] of the Anunna-gods, [your] responsibilities* are lofty.
[Allu]ring [goddess], who grants heirs(?),*
  who makes abundant [   ],
Beloved [   ], crea[tr]ess,
  mistress of the lords of [heaven],   (35)
[   ], pre-eminent spouse whose sovereignty has no rival,

---

1. Assur; see p. 227 note 4.
2. Name for Ninurta.
3. Like Ba'u in line 40, here another name for Gula. Lines 32ff. may explain Meme hermeneutically or may extol this aspect of the goddess. The fragment K 232, not included here, lists numerous other names of Gula; see Mullo-Weir, JRAS 1929, 9ff. and compare above, III.25.

You are greatest [among ...] the gods,
    who is as capable as [you]?
You pull up the bo[dy] of the [fallen   ],
[You make splen]did the [ ] of heaven and netherworld,
    O mer[ciful la]dy,
O [Ba]u, let praise of you [ ] on people's lips,   (40)
Let them [gl]orify [your] sovereignty [in] all lands,
[In all world reg]ions* you are the greatest, [ ]
[Grant?] health, strength, [ ], a fortunate course,
[ ] of body [   ]
[ ], let me glorify your greatness!   (45)

Text: Ebeling-Köcher-Rost, LKA 17.
Edition: Ebeling, OrNS 23 (1954), 346-349.
Translation: Seux, *Hymnes*, 103-106.
Notes to Text: (33) Compare K 232, line 17 = Mullo-Weir, JRAS 1929, 11. (34) Seux, *Hymnes*, 106 notes 33, 34. (42) Seux, *Hymnes*, 106 note 40.

(b) INTERCESSOR

O Gula, most great lady, merciful mother,
    who dwells in the great heavens,   (1)
I call upon you, my lady, stand by me and hear me!
I seek you out, I turn to you, I grasp your hem[1]
    as if it were that of my (personal) god
    and my (personal) goddess.
Because judging the case, rendering the verdict,
Because reviving and granting well-being
    are yours (to grant),   (5)
Because you know how to save, spare, and rescue,
O Gula, most great lady, merciful mother,
I turn to you, from among all the stars of heaven,
O my lady, I turn to you, I am heedful of you.
Accept of me my flour offering, receive my plea,   (10)
Let me send you to my angry (personal) god,
    my angry (personal) goddess,
To the god of my city who is in a rage and furious with me.
On account of omens and dreams
    which are continually besetting me,
I am afraid and always anxious.
O Gula, most great lady, with the utterance of your sublime
    command, which is greatest in Enlil's Ekur,   (15)
And with your firm assent, which cannot be changed,
May my angry (personal) god return to me,
    may my angry (personal) goddess relent to me,
May the god of my city who is in a rage and furious with me,
Who is angry, calm down; he who was vexed,
    may he be soothed!
O Gula, most great lady, who intercedes for the weak,
Intercede for me with Marduk, king of the gods,[2]
    the merciful lord; say a favorable word.

---

1. Gesture of petition; see further Finet, *Annales du Centre d'Études des Religions* 3 (1969), 101ff. and III.43b line 25.
   2. Variant omits.

May your broad protection
    and imp[osing] forgiveness be wi[th] me,
[Grant me] favor and life,
Let me proclaim your greatness,
    [let me] sound your praises!

Text: King, BMS 6, 71-94, BMS 37, 7'-13'; Loretz-Mayer, AOAT 34 18; Ebeling, KAR 341; Finkelstein, STT 59, rev 1-23. King, BMS 7, 9'-33'; Loretz-Mayer, AOAT 34 19; Scheil, SFS 6(?) are texts of the same hymn addressed to Belet-ili. Variant manuscripts insert additional prayers not included here.
Edition: Mayer, UFBG, 450-454.
Translation: Mullo-Weir, JRAS 1929, 1-4; von Soden, SAHG, 327-328 no. 60; Seux, *Hymnes*, 337-339.
Literature: Mayer, UFBG, Gula 1a.

III.43 TO ISHTAR

Ishtar, one of the most complex figures in Mesopotamian religion, is early attested as a goddess of warfare and as the morning and evening star (see II.1, III.26, III.43b). Partly through syncretism with the Sumerian goddess Inanna, she became as well a goddess of fertility, reproduction, and love (see III.43d). She is often portrayed as harsh, capricious, and vindictive (III.28); fearless and joyful in the battle fray (II.4, 6); urgent, ardent, and alluring as a lover (II.1, IV.51). She was also associated with prostitution, sexual impersonation, self-mutilation, and homosexuality (p. 407 note 3, p. 797 note 3, IV.51). Penitential and devotional literature tends to stress her valor and queenly tenderness. For further discussion and documentation of Ishtar, see Wilcke, "Inanna/Ištar," RLA 5, 74-87 and R. Harris, "Inanna-Ishtar as Paradox and a Coincidence of Opposites," *History of Religions* 30 (1991), 261-278.

(a) AGAINST SORCERY

O pure Ishtar, lofty one of the Igigi-gods,	(1)
Who makes battle, who brings about combat,	
Most stately and perfect of goddesses,	
At your command, O Ishtar, humankind is governed.	
The sick man who sees your face revives,	(5)
His bondage is released, he gets up instantly.	
At your command, O Ishtar, the blind man sees the light,	
The unhealthy one who sees your face becomes healthy.	
I, who am very sick, I kneel, I stand before you,	
I turn to you to judge my case, O torch of the gods,	(10)
I have seen your face, may my bonds be released.	
Do not delay,* I am confused and anxious.	
I live[1] like one bastinadoed.	
I did what you said to do, O Ishtar!	
A sorcerer or a sorceress,	(15)
Whom you know, but I do not know,	
With magic rites of malice and assassination,	
Which they have worked in your presence,	

---

1. Literally: "My life has become like one ..."; variant "my family."

Have laid figurines of me in a grave,

Have come to assassinate me! (20)

They have worked in secret against me,

    I work against them openly!

By your sublime command, which cannot be altered,

    And your firm "yes," which cannot be changed,

May whatever I say come true.

Let life come forth to me from your pure utterance,

(May) you (be the one to say) "What a pity about him!"

    O you who are the (supreme) goddess among the gods. (25)

Text: Ebeling, KAR 92, rev 9-33; Ebeling-Köcher-Rost, LKA 144, obv 3-17; Farber, *Ištar und Dumuzi* pl. 20 BM 54650, obv ii 1-25; pl. 22 Rm 247, rev.

Edition: Farber, *Ištar und Dumuzi*, 238-240, lines 3′-29′.

Translation: von Soden, SAHG, 337-338 no. 64; Seux, *Hymnes*, 457-458.

Literature: Mayer, UFBG, Ištar 24.

Notes to Text: (12) Seux, *Hymnes*, 458 note 6.

(b) THE GREATNESS OF ISHTAR

This devotional composition contains unusual and obscure expressions, such as suggest an effort at originality. It stresses the astral character of the goddess and her control of destinies.

> O warrior Ishtar, most cherished of goddesses, (1)
> Torch of heaven and earth,
> > splendor of the four world regions,
> Innini, first-born of Sin, offspring of Ningal,
> Twin sister of the bearded, magnificent warrior, Shamash,
> O Ishtar, you are (supreme like) Anu, you rule the heavens, (5)
> [With] Enlil the counsellor you order the inhabited world.
> O Mother-Matrix,[1] bringer into being of rites and lustrations,
> At(?) the revelation of Ea,
> > you hold the bonds in the depths,[2]
> Wheresoever floor plans are laid, brickwork built,*
> Like the sun, you take charge of whoever
> > has the power of speech. (10)
> Who is your equal even among the Igigi-gods,
> Who is your rival even among the Anunna-gods?
> You are the one who, in the womb* of humankind,
> > establishes poverty and wealth,
> You reverse destiny so the unlucky may have good fortune.
> I sought among gods, prayers were given to you,
> > I turned to goddesses, for you was entreaty. (15)
> Before you is a protective spirit, behind you is a guardian spirit,
> At your right is justice, at your left good fortune.
> Obedience, acceptance, and peace are established in your presence,
> Round about you are set life and well-being.
> How sweet to pray to you,
> > how near at hand your listening, (20)
> Your look is hearing, your speech light!
> Have mercy upon me, O Ishtar, order my prosperity,

1. Akkadian *mummu*; see above, p. 354 note 1.
2. Line not clear; precise sense of "bonds" uncertain.

Look upon me steadfastly, accept my entreaty!
I have followed your guidance, let there be wealth (for me),
I have seized your litter,[1]
    let there be satisfaction (for me).   (25)
I have borne your yoke, grant release!
I have waited upon you, let peace come directly,
I have gazed upon your radiance,
    let there be hearing and acceptance,
I have sought out your brilliance, may my face beam,
I have turned to your dominion,
    may there be life and well-being (for me).   (30)
May I acquire the protective spirit which is before you,
May I acquire the guardian spirit which goes behind you,
May I add (to mine) the wealth at your right,
May I attain the good fortune at your left.
Order that my speech be heeded,   (35)
That the word I shall say be agreed to, as I say it.
Guide me each day in good health and happiness,
Prolong my days, grant life.
Let me live in well-being, let me glorify [your] divinity,
Let me I attain whatever I desire.   (40)
May heaven rejoice because of you,
    the depths rejoice because of you,
May the gods of the universe bless you,
May the great gods please you.

Text: King, BMS 5, 11-19 + K 7243+; BMS 8, 1-19 [(+) BMS 48]; BMS 1, 29-35; Ebeling, KAR 250 obv; Loretz-Mayer, AOAT 34 14; Mayer, OrNS 59 (1990), 488 BM 57532.
Edition: Geers-von Soden, ZA 42 (1934), 220-225; Ebeling, AGH, 60-63; Sperling, WO 12 (1981), 8-20.
Translation: von Soden, SAHG, 333-336 no. 62; Seux, *Hymnes,* 321-323.
Literature: Mayer, UFBG, Ištar 1.
★*Notes to Text:* (9) Mayer, OrNS 46 (1977), 389. (13) Veenhof, RA 79 (1985), 94-95, confirmed by BM 57532.

1. The image is of the goddess being carried through the streets in a sedan chair. The petitioner has rushed forward to grasp a part of it in entreaty. Perhaps this is a refurbishment of the expression "grasp the hem," more common in devotional literature (see III.42b line 3); IV.2b iv line 18).

(c) AGAINST IMPOTENCE

Like the preceding, this prayer dwells on the astral character of Ishtar and asks
her help in a magical procedure.

> O luminary of heaven, capable Ishtar, (1)
> Mistress of the gods, whose "yes" (means) "yes,"
> Noble one among the gods, whose command is supreme,
> Mistress of heaven and netherworld, ruler of all settlements, (5)
> Ishtar, (at?) your invocation(?) all lords are kneeling,
> I, so-and-so, son of so-and-so, kneel before you.
> I, against whom sorcery has been done,
>   figurines of whom have been laid in the ground,
> May my body be pure as lapis,
> May [my] features be bright as alabaster, (10)
> Like pure silver, red gold, may I never tarnish,
> May (these seven) plants[1] drive away the magic against me!

Text: Ebeling, KAR 236, obv 25 - rev 4; KAR 243, rev! 1-4; Ebeling-Köcher-Rost, LKA 99b,
d I 10-19; Gurney, STT 280, iii 7-17; Biggs, *ŠÀ.ZI.GA*, pl. 3 K 11076.
Edition: Biggs, *ŠÀ.ZI.GA*, 28.
Translation: Seux, *Hymnes*, 400-401.
Literature: Mayer, UFBG, Ištar 27.

---

1. Seven plants are listed here, the modern names of which are unknown.

(d) A GIFT TO ISHTAR

You are Ishtar, whose lover is Dumuzi,
The valorous daughter of Sin, who traverses pasturelands,
You are she who loves rustic shelters,[1] who loves all mankind.
I have given your great gift:
A lapis vulva, a star of gold, as befits your divinity.[2]
Intercede for me with Dumuzi your lover,
May Dumuzi your lover take away my tribulation.

Text: Farber, *Ištar und Dumuzi* pl. 10 K 2001+ (114-120); pl. 16, BM 76976, rev i 3-9; Ebeling, KAR 57 rev i 1-16 + Ebeling-Köcher-Rost, LKA 70.
Edition: Farber, *Ištar und Dumuzi*, 146-149, lines 114-120.
Translation: Seux, *Hymnes*, 440.
Literature: Mayer, UFBG, Ištar 19.

1. Protection for shepherds, for whom Dumuzi was patron deity.
2. Compare above, Hymn to Papulegarra (II.3), p. 73 note 2.

(e) ISHTAR WILL NOT TIRE

A damaged manuscript from Nippur preserves part of a Mature or Late period hymn to Ishtar that a subscript ascribes to the time of Hammurabi (Classical period, see II.6). Each line is followed by a refrain: "The city's built on pleasure!" Refrains are unusual in Akkadian poetry, and may be a sign of Sumerian influence; compare III.2 and III.38c. For the explicit language of love, compare II.10, 11, 33; IV.22, 45, 51, 54.

(seven lines fragmentary)

One comes up to her ...,	*(refrain)*	
"Come here, give me what I want ..."	*(refrain)*	
Then another comes up to her,	*(refrain)*	(10)
"Come here, let me touch your vulva."	*(refrain)*	
"Since I'm ready to give you all what you want,	*(refrain)*	
"Get all the young men of your city together,	*(refrain)*	
"Let's go to the shade of a wall!"	*(refrain)*	
Seven for her midriff, seven for her loins,	*(refrain)*	(15)
Sixty then sixty satisfy themselves in turn		
upon her nakedness.	*(refrain)*	
Young men have tired, Ishtar will not tire.	*(refrain)*	
"Get on with it, fellows, for my lovely vulva!"	*(refrain)*	
As the girl demanded,	*(refrain)*	
The young men heeded, gave her what she asked for.	*(refrain)*	(20)

(Hymn of praise to Ishtar)

Text: von Soden, OrNS 60 (1991), pl. CVI (photo HS 1879).
Edition: von Soden, OrNS 60 (1991), 339-342.

III.44 TO MARDUK

Marduk, god of Babylon, emerged as pre-eminent in the Babylonian pantheon during the second half of the second millennium B.C. (see p. 290 note 3). Although his original role as a vegetation deity and warden of spring waters is alluded to in devotional literature, he is often appealed to as father, warrior, and ruler. Some hymns to Marduk, such as b, e, and f below, may allude to the Creation Epic (III.17) or use the same phraseology. For further discussion and documentation of Marduk, see Sommerfeld, "Marduk," RLA 7, 360-374.

(a) AGAINST MARDUK'S ANGER

This unilingual prayer, related to the bilingual psalms (see III.34) and "heart-appeasing" laments (see III.38c), is one of the finest of its type. An agnostic theme, taken up at length in the Poem of the Righteous Sufferer (III.14) and penitential psalms (see III.54), is balanced with expressions of goodwill (lines 12f.) and resignation (lines 14f.). The unanswered cries of the penitent provide a dramatic opening address, at once a reminder of the penitent's past observance and a description of his physical and emotional distress. His becoming an old man through Marduk's punishment (line 6) suggests that youth is a metaphor for his happy condition prior to Marduk's punishment, rather than his actual youth. This figure is carried through by the conclusion, whereby the supplicant becomes, if forgiven, a child of his god again (compare III.45b). Although there is scarcely a line in this poem that does not have parallels elsewhere, the harmony and effectiveness of the whole are striking and set this composition apart as a masterpiece.

> O warrior Marduk, whose anger is the deluge, (1)
> Whose relenting is that of a merciful father,
> I am left anxious by speech unheeded,
> My hopes are deceived by outcry unanswered,
> Such as has sapped my courage, (5)
> And hunched me over like an aged man.
> O great lord Marduk, merciful lord!
> Men, by whatever name,
> What can they understand of their own sin?*
> Who has not been negligent, which one has committed no sin? (10)

Who can understand a god's behavior?
I would fain be obedient and incur no sin,
Yes, I would frequent the haunts of health!
Men are commanded by the gods to act under curse,
Divine affliction is for mankind to bear.   (15)
I am surely responsible for some neglect of you,
I have surely trespassed the limits set by the god.
Forget what I did in my youth, whatever it was,
Let your heart not well up against me!
Absolve my guilt, remit my punishment,
Clear me of confusion, free me of uncertainty,   (20)
Let no guilt of my father, my grandfather, my mother,
      my grandmother, my brother, my sister,
      my family, kith, or kin
Approach my own self, but let it be gone!
If my god has commanded (it) for me,
      purify me as with medicaments.*   (25)
Commend me into the hands of my (personal) god
      and my (personal) goddess for well-being and life,
Let me stand before you always in prayer, supplication,
      and entreaty,
Let the fruitful peoples of a well-ordered land praise you.
Absolve my guilt, remit my guilt!
O warrior Marduk, absolve my guilt, remit my guilt!   (30)
O great lady Erua–Sarpanitu, absolve my guilt,
O Nabu of the good name, absolve my guilt,
O great lady, Tashmetu, absolve my guilt,
O warrior Nergal, absolve my guilt,
O gods who dwell <in> Anu's <heaven>,*
      absolve my guilt!   (35)
The monstrous guilt that I have built up from my youth,
Scatter it hence,[1] absolve it sevenfold.
Like my real father and my real mother,
Let your heart be reconciled to me.
O warrior Marduk, let me sound your praises!   (40)

---

1. Variant: "and disperse it."

Text: King, BMS 11; Ebeling-Köcher-Rost, LKA 61; Loretz-Mayer, AOAT 34, 35-39; additional manuscripts cited by Borger, HKL 2, 124.

Edition: Ebeling, AGH, 72-75.

Translation: von Soden, SAHG, 298-300 no. 43; Seux, *Hymnes*, 169-172.

Literature: von Soden, *Iraq* 31 (1969), 83; Mayer, UFBG, Marduk 4.

*Notes to Text: (9) Mayer, OrNS 46 (1977), 387. (25) Mayer, OrNS 46 (1977), 388. (35) WGL.

(b) AGAINST ILLNESS

This exorcistic prayer is one of the longest and most elaborate of its type. Its apparent allusions to the Creation Epic (III.17) suggest a first millennium date for its composition. See General Introduction, D.3.

> O Marduk, lord of the world, ra[ging], terrifying,   (1)
> Stately, ever-renewing, perfe[ct, ca]pable,
> Lofty, magnificent, whose [com]mand cannot be altered,
> Capable one, profound of understanding,
>   [no]ble one(?), sa[ge ...]!
> O Marduk,[1] eminent, surpassing,
>   whose [pos]ition is on hi[gh],   (5)
> Mighty, powerful, eminent van[guard],
> "Deluge weapon,"[2] [hopeless] to combat,
>   [whose onslaught] is furious!
> O Dumuduku,[3] most perfect [of ..., or]dainer of [des]tinies,
> Son of Lugal-du[ku[4]   ] of the great gods!
> O planet Marduk, lord [   ] prosperity![5]   (10)
> O Marduk, lord of abundance and prosper[ity,
>   w]ho rains down luxuriance,[6]
> Lord of underground springs, mountains, and seas,
>   who overlooks the mountains,
> Who opens wells and waterholes,
>   who guides watercourses,[7]
> Overseer of grain god and sheep god, creator of ear and fiber,
>   who makes abundant green plants,[8]

---

1. Variant adds: "lord."

2. Compare Creation Epic (III.17) Tablet IV line 49, 75; Tablet VI line 125. As Lambert has indicated to me, "deluge" (*amaru*) plus "weapon" (TUKUL) is a play on Marduk, etymologized as (A)mar(u)tuku(l).

3. Compare Creation Epic (III.17) Tablet VII line 65. Marduk is here etymologized as "son of the holy hill" (that is, of Ea).

4. According to Seux, *Hymnes*, 444 note 7, an allusion to Creation Epic (III.17) Tablet VII line 126.

5. Compare Creation Epic (III.17) Tablet VII line 65.

6. Compare Creation Epic (III.17) Tablet VII line 69.

7. Compare Creation Epic (III.17) Tablet VII line 60.

8. Compare Creation Epic (III.17) Tablet VII lines 2, 69, 79.

You create food for god and goddess,
  you are creator of the cropland for them.   (15)
O dragon of the Anunna-gods, monitor of the Igigi-gods,
Wise son of Enanki,[1] creator of all humankind,
You are the lord, you are like "father" and "mother"
  in people's speech,
You are the one who, like the sun,
  illumines their darkness.
Each day you give justice to the oppressed and abused,   (20)
You administer the destitute, the widow,
  the wretched and anxious.
[You] are what they listen for,
  [the shepherd who leads them],
[At] your weighty [command],*
  the numerous lands and peoples prosper.
You are merciful, lord,
  you rescue the weak* from danger and hardship,
[You look upon the] exhausted and des[perate],
  the one whom his god punished,*   (25)
You are comrade of [   ] ..., you release the captive,
[You t]ake the hand and raise the injured from his bed,
You make the [cap]tive in darkness and prison,
  the [hos]tage, see light.
[I] your [servant], so-and-so, son of so-and-so,
  whose (personal) god is so-and-so,
  whose (personal) god[dess] is so-and-so,
Bathed, clean of hands,
  [I have set up] for you pure utensils,[2]   (30)
I have spread out a [clean] red cloth beneath your feet,*
Hearken to my prayer, ac[cept] my [en]treaty.
You know the illness from which I suffer, I do not.
It flattens me like a net, shr[ouds me like a me]sh.
Torment, head pain, and fatigue, inflammation,
  an[xiety? and ... have ...] my limbs,   (35)

---

1. "Lord of Heaven and Netherworld" = Enki/Ea.
2. Variant adds: "I have made you a pure (offering)."

Foul disease, oath and curse, make my flesh cr[ee]p.
They have made my frame feverish,
     I am clothed in them as if with a garment.
Symbols(?) and images of me are interred.[1]
They have collected dust from under my feet,
     they have taken my measure,
     they have taken away my vitality.
I am infected and beset by people's wicked machinations,   (40)
The fury of my (personal) god and goddess[2]
     and mankind are against me.
My dreams are terrifying, awful, evil,
My signs and omens are confused
     and have no clear interpretation.
O my lord, stand by me this day, hear what I say,
     judge my case, render my verdict!
Banish the disease which is set upon me,
     drive the head pain from my person!
May my (personal) god and goddess and mankind
     be reconciled with me.[3]   (45)
At your command may no evil approach me
     from machinations of sorcerer or sorceress,
May no spell, enchantment, sorcery,
     nor wicked machination of mankind approach me,
May no evil portent from dreams, signs,
     or portents celestial or terrestrial approach me,
May no evil portents for city or land affect me personally,
May I be safe in your presence from evil thought
     and speech of mankind,   (50)
May the amulet set around my neck
     keep all evil away from me,

---

1. This refers to a magical procedure whereby an image of the person to be bewitched is ritually interred, presumably to bring about the death of the person represented. "Symbols" (is/lqu) may refer to objects intended to represent the person who is the target of the spell (Nougayrol apud Seux, Hymnes, 446 note 38).
2. Variant omits.
3. Variant adds: "May they have pity on me."

May it drive away curse against me
>or utterance portending evil,[1]

May my light shine like alabaster, may I have no gloom,[2]

May my life be as precious as lapis in your sight,
>let there be mercy for me.

May my (personal) god and goddess be reconciled with me,
>as with gold, (55)

May people speak well of me,

May I keep away my troubles
>as if with (imperishable?) wood,[3]

May no wicked, foul curse against me
>come near or approach me,

May my descent and progeny prosper in my sight,[4]

May the (medicinal) plants and salves you cherish
>drive out my faults, (60)

May they let no divine fury or anger come nigh me,

May they release (me from) affliction(?), crime, or sin,

May prayer and invocation of the great gods
>release an oath or curse (against me),

May I progress proudly at your command,
>order that I live (long)!

May I be pure as heaven from enchantment against me, (65)

May I be clean as the netherworld from foul sorcery.

May I gleam like innermost heaven,
>may the wicked devices against me be dispelled,

May the tamarisk purify me, may the ...-plant release me,
>may the palm bough dispel my sin,

May the water stoup of Asalluhi bestow favor upon me,

May the censer and torch of Girra and Kusu[5] cleanse me. (70)

At the command of Ea, king of the depths,
>father of the gods, Ninshiku,

---

1. That is, directed malice and random malice.
2. Variant: "curse or gloom."
3. Text: "sissoo wood," an exotic wood used for fine woodwork.
4. That is, may he attain old age and see his descendants happy.
5. A minor deity often mentioned in connection with purification rituals (Seux, *Hymnes*, 448 note 62; Bauer, *Altorientalische Notizen* 19 [1982], 4-7).

May your heart be calmed at my prayer![1]
O Asalluhi, exorcist of the great gods,
    sage of the Igigi-gods,
I shall heed Ea's command,
    and queen Damkina will guide me to the right.*
May I, your servant, so-and-so, son of so-and-so,
    live in well-being,   (75)
May I exalt your divinity and sound [your] praises,
May my (personal) god exalt [your] valor,
May my (personal) goddess speak of your greatness.
(May I too, the exorcist, your servant, sound your praises!)[2]

Text: King, BMS 12, 17-94; Loretz-Mayer, AOAT 34 40-46; Mayer, OrNS 59 (1990), 487 K 20155.
Edition: Ebeling, AGH, 76-83; von Soden, Iraq 31 (1969), 84-89 (partial).
Translation: von Soden, SAHG, 302-306 no. 46; Seux, Hymnes, 443-449.
Literature: Mayer, UFBG, Marduk 5; Abusch, Witchcraft, 45-75.
*Notes to Text: (23ff.) Restored from unpublished duplicate (courtesy WGL). (31) Mayer, OrNS 46 (1977), 391. (74) Seux, Hymnes, 449 note 66.

1. Variant: "may my prayer be the right one that your heart ..."
2. Lines 1-78 are to be spoken by the sufferer; the exorcist adds his lines at the end as the attending professional.

(c) PROTECTOR OF THE KING

This prayer was used in royal lustration rituals.

O mighty, resplendent, noble one of Eridu, (1)
Lofty prince, first-born of Nudimmud,
Raging Marduk, who rejoices E-engurra,[1]
Lord of Esagila, Babylon's trust,
Who loves Ezida,[2] who safeguards the living, (5)
Foremost one of Emahtila,[3] renewer of life,
Protection of the land,
     bestower of benevolence upon the numerous peoples,
(Protective) dragon of all daises,
Sweet is your name on the lips of people everywhere!
O Marduk, great lord, merciful god,[4] (10)
Let me live in well-being at your steadfast[5] command,
     that I may glorify your divinity.
Let me attain whatever I desire!
Set truth on my lips,
Set good words in my heart,
May courtier and functionary speak well of me. (15)
May my (personal) god stand at my right,
May my (personal) goddess stand at my left,
May my guardian deity always be at my side.
Grant me hearing and acceptance of what I say,
May the word I say be accepted even as I say it. (20)
O Marduk, great lord, grant me life
     and command that I may live it,
Let me proceed, radiant, before you, to my heart's desire,
May Enlil be happy because of you,
     may Ea rejoice because of you,

---

1. Temple of Ea (= Nudimmud) at Eridu, city of Ea.
2. Temple of Nabu at Borsippa, city of Nabu.
3. Part of Ezida.
4. Variant omits.
5. Variant: "sublime," "eminent."

> May the gods of the universe bless you,
> May the great gods please you.[1]

Text: Ebeling, KAR 59, obv 1-25; KAR 25, i 29-38; KAR 23, i 1-17; Finkelstein, STT 55, 1-24; King, BMS 9, obv; BMS 54; Lutz, PBS 1/2 108; Loretz-Mayer, AOAT 34 26-30; von Weiher, SBTU III 78, rev.
Edition: Meier, AfO 14 (1941/4), 140-143; Ebeling, AGH, 64-67.
Translation: von Soden, SAHG, 297-298 no. 42; Seux, *Hymnes*, 290-292.
Literature: Mayer, UFBG, Marduk 2.

---

1. Variants add a prayer, in one instance for Shamash-shum-ukin, king of Assyria, against the evil portended by an eclipse (see p. 546 note 2); other variants have rearrangements of the text not noted here.

(d) REVIVER OF THE SICK

O Marduk, great lord, merciful god,   (1)
Who grasps the hand of the fallen,
[Who releases] the bound, revives the moribund,
[For wro]ng-doing known or not known,
[Which] I committed [through carelessness],
    negligence, or malfeasance,[1]   (5)
[Which] against your great divinity,
    [as against] one's own father,
I committed [through carelessness], negligence,
    or malfeasance,
[I bring] my life before your great divinity.
May the [soo]thing [water] be accepted by you,
May your [angry] heart be calmed.   (10)
May your [swee]t forgiveness,
Your great [absol]ution,
[Your] migh[ty] indulgence [be mine],
Let me sound the praises of your great divinity!

Text: Ebeling, KAR 23, i 19-31; KAR 25, ii 1.
Edition: Ebeling, AGH, 12-13.
Translation: von Soden, SAHG, 300-301 no. 44; Seux, *Hymnes*, 292-293.
Literature: Mayer, UFBG, Marduk 18.

---

1. Variant adds: "[I] feared and was frightened."

(e) LORD OF THE UNIVERSE

This hymn may allude to the Creation Epic (III.17, see III.44b).

> O most great one, prince of the gods, mighty Marduk,   (1)
> Counsellor, beloved of Ea, whose utterance cannot be changed,
> To whose stately utterance the great Igigi-gods pay heed,
> Before whom the Anunna-gods are ever kneeling,
> Lord of living creatures, merciful one, who increases grain,   (5)
> Giver(?) of food offerings to the gods,
>   maintainer of holy places,[1]*
> Who governs underground springs and watercourses,
>   who opens wells,[2]
> Lord of the gods, king of heaven and netherworld,
>   who heaps up prosperity,
> God without whom no people's destiny is ordained in the depths,
> You look upon all the inhabited world,
>   you quickly wipe out the hostile,   (10)
> You strike blind(?) the narrow and shifty-eyed,*
> You destroy quickly the talk of gossipers,*
> You harshly force the stiffest neck to bow.*
> What god in heaven or netherworld can come forth against you?
> You are higher than all the gods!   (15)
> Your counsel is supreme among the gods,
> You are superior to Ea, the father who begot you,

(fragmentary lines, then breaks off)

Text: K 3505b = Hehn, BA 5, 385; Scheil, SFS 7.
Edition: Ebeling, AGH, 92-95.
Translation: von Soden, SAHG, 310-312 no. 48; Seux, *Hymnes*, 289-290.
Literature: Mayer, UFBG, Marduk 1.
Notes to Text: (6) Seux, *Hymnes*, 289 note 3; CAD K, 512b. (11) CAD M/2, 245a, with collation. (12) CAD L, 211b, with collation. (31) CAD K, 147a, with collation.

1. Compare Creation Epic (III.17) Tablet VI line 109.
2. Compare Creation Epic (III.17) Tablet VII line 60.

(f) PRINCE OF THE GODS

This fragmentary hymn, like the preceding, may allude to the Creation Epic
(III.17, see III.44b).

> [Valorous] prince, son of Ea, l[ofty] hero, (1)
> [Forem]ost one of a[ll] heaven and netherworld,
> > ordainer of destinies,
> [Lord] Mard[uk?], ... w[ho is surpassing] of form,[1]
> [   ] form of Tutu,[2]
> [Sarpanitu], great queen, bride of Shazu,[3] (5)
> Lo[rd En]lil,[4] prince surpassing of perception.[5]
> Battle formation and warfare are in the hand
> > of the sage of the gods, Marduk,
> He at whose warfare the heavens quake,
> At whose cry the depths are roiled,
> At whose blade edge the gods retreat. (10)
> There was none came forth against his furious onslaught.[6]
> Awe-inspiring lord,
> > none like whom has arisen among the gods,[7]
> Stately is his progress through the shining firmament,
> Heavy his responsibilities in Ekur,[8]
> > the cherished dwelling.
> In the ill wind[9] his weapons are flashing,
> Tortuous mountains are destroyed by his flame,[10] (15)
> The surging(?) ocean[11] tosses up its waves.

1. Restoration doubtful; compare Creation Epic (III.17) Tablet I line 93.
2. One of the fifty names of Marduk; see Creation Epic (III.17) Tablet VII lines 9, 15, 19, 25, 33.
3. One of the fifty names of Marduk; see Creation Epic (III.17) Tablet VII lines 35, 41, 43, 47, 51, 55.
4. That is, Marduk as supreme god; compare Creation Epic (III.17) Tablet VII line 49.
5. Compare Creation Epic (III.17) Tablet I lines 95-98.
6. Lines 8-11 may refer to Marduk's vanquishing Tiamat and her forces.
7. Perhaps a reference to Creation Epic (III.17) Tablet I line 91.
8. Enlil's temple in Nippur; compare line 6.
9. One of Marduk's weapons; see Creation Epic (III.17) Tablet IV lines 45, 96, 98.
10. Creation Epic (III.17) Tablet IV line 40.
11. Reference to Tiamat?

His name is "Heir to Esharra,"[1]
　　he is called "Warrior of the Gods."
He is lord of all the gods of the inhabited world,
　　from the farthest depth.
They clustered against heaven before his furious bow,[2]　　　　(20)
Those who slumbered in the high sanctuary
　　cowered and shook.
[　　　　] all the Anunna-gods,
[　　　　　] the Igigi-gods.

(breaks off)

Text: King, STC I 205.
Edition: Ebeling, AGH, 94-95.
Translation: Seux, *Hymnes*, 76-78.
Literature: Mayer, UFBG, Marduk x = p. 399 *"unsicher."*

1. Compare Creation Epic (III.17) Tablet IV line 145. This name was also given to Ninurta; see further p. 377 note 3 and p. 630 note 1.
2. Compare Creation Epic (III.17) Tablet IV line 35, Tablet VI lines 82-91.

(g) SYNCRETIC HYMN TO MARDUK

This text suggests henotheistic tendencies in that it represents the other gods as aspects of Marduk. A parallel is provided by the text known as the "Marduk Theology," for translations and discussion of which see T. J. Meek, *Hebrew Origins* (New York, 1960), 197-198; W. G. Lambert, *Unity and Diversity*, 197-198.

(gap)

Sin is your divinity, Anu your sovereignty,
Dagan is your lordship, Enlil your kingship,
Adad is your might, wise Ea your perception,   (5)
Nabu, holder of the tablet stylus, is your skill.
Your leadership (in battle) is Ninurta, your might Nergal,
Your counsel is Nus[ku], your superb [minister],
Your judgeship is radiant Shamash,
        who arouses [no] dispute,
Your eminent name is Marduk, sage of the gods.   (10)
Your hurtling arrow is a piti[less li]on.
O eminent lord, who tramples down all foes,
        who wards off attack,
Your escort is the Pleiades,
        O judge just and true of gods and goddesses.
Your greatness is the Igigi-gods,
        your primacy(?) is the warrior Irnini,
Your[1] basin is the depths,
        your incense stand is Anu's heaven,   (15)
Your ... is the vast netherworld, ...
The one who in the temple has ... offerings,
The widow with roasted grain,
        the rich man with sheep call upon you.
Come hither to the food and drink
        from those who revere you,   (20)
By your unalterable utterance absolve their misdeeds,
Let me proclaim your greatness, let me sound your praises!

---

1. Text uses the plural pronoun, perhaps referring to Marduk as the sum total of all the gods, whereas previously only individual aspects were referred to.

Text: Ebeling, KAR 25, ii 3-24.
Edition: Ebeling, AGH, 14-15.
Translation: von Soden, SAHG, 301-302 no. 45; Labat, *Religions*, 73-74; Seux, *Hymnes*, 129-131.
Literature: von Weiher, AOAT 11 (1971), 66-67.

(h) FOREMOST OF THE GODS

O Marduk, great lord,
    foremost one of heaven and netherworld,   (1)
Sage of the universe, who knows everything,
Merciful god, who accepts prayers,
Who receives entreaties,
Who watches over the life of mankind,
Who grasps heaven and netherworld,
Wise king who loves to revive,   (5)
Lord of fresh water depths and the seas,
    who [puts a stop to?] combat,
Bringer of abundance,
    who makes abundant grain for the numerous peoples!
O Marduk, great lord, lofty one of the gods, without rival,
Proud(?) god, glorious with the tiara of supreme divinity,
You are the light of the corners (of the universe),
    the shepherd of mankind!   (10)
Without you, heaven and netherworld create no [   ],
Without you, Sin, luminary of heaven,
    ... no sign to the people,
Without you, Shamash judges no case,
Without you, no verdict is rendered for the land,
Without you, no god whatsoever keeps in good order the
    sanctuary of god or goddess,   (15)
Without you, the wise gods hold no festivals,
Without you, Shamash the judge does not set in the sheep
    the right coil (of the intestines),
    the correct (state of) the lungs,[1]
Without you, the diviner does not do
    his manipulations correctly,
Without you, the exorcist does not
    bring his hand to the sick man,
Without you, the conjurer, ecstatic, snake charmer
    do not pass through the st[reet],   (20)

1. References to divination; see General Introduction, E.9 and Chapter IV, Introduction.

Without you, they escape neither strait nor hardship,
Without you, the destitute and widow are not cared for,
The destitute and widow call upon you, "O Lord!"
You give a husband to those who have no ...,
It is you, O [lor]d, who has [ ] pi[ty] on them.   (25)
The strong, the common man, the rich man call upon you,
Each day ...,
All lands call upon Marduk!

(Prayer concludes with a long list of ills and ends with a plea for purification plus the usual offer to sing the god's praises together with those of his spouse, Sarpanitum.)

Text: Ebeling, KAR 26, obv 11–rev 6; here in excerpt only.
Edition: Ebeling, ZDMG 69 (1915), 96–101.
Translation: von Soden, SAHG, 306–310 no. 47; Seux, *Hymnes*, 449–453.
Literature: Abusch, *Witchcraft*, 45–75.

III.45 TO NABU

Nabu, son of Marduk and Sarpanitum, was in later Assyro-Babylonian tradition god of the scribal arts. His principal cult center was at Borsippa, near Babylon, and was called the Ezida (see IV.13).

For other prayers to Nabu, see W. G. Lambert, RA 53 (1959), 134-138; "Nabu Hymns on Cylinders," in B. Hruška and G. Komoróczy, eds., *Festschrift Lubor Matouš* (Budapest, 1978), 2: 75-111; Seux, *Hymnes*, 299-300. For a general study of this deity, see F. Pomponio, *Nabu, Il culto e la figura di un dio del pantheon babilonese ed assiro, Studi Semitici* 51 (Rome, 1978).

(a) FOR PROTECTION FROM BLACK MAGIC

O foremost prince, firstborn of Tutu,[1] (1)
Proven leader, offspring of Panunanki,[2]
Nabu, who bears the gods' tablet of destinies,[3]
   monitor of Esagila,
Lord of Ezida, protection of Borsippa,
Beloved of Nudimmud,[4] bestower of life, (5)
Foremost one of Shuanna,[5] guardian of life,
Protection of the inhabited world, rescuer of mankind,
   lord of sanctuaries,
Invocation of you is an especially sweet protection
   on the lips of the people!
O son of the great prince Marduk, at your steadfast word,
At your eminent word,
   at the command of your great divinity, (10)
I, so-and-so, son of so-and-so, your sick, very sick servant,
Who have been seized and hounded by the power of a ghost,
   black magic, and something accursed,
Let me live in well-being, may I attain whatever I plan,
Put truth on my lips,

---

1. Name for Marduk, see Creation Epic (III.17) Tablet VII lines 9, 15, 19, 25, 33.
2. Sarpanitum, wife of Marduk.
3. For tablet of destinies, see p. 360 note 1.
4. Ea; variant has Panunanki.
5. Babylon.

Set a good word in my heart!   (15)
May courtier and functionary speak well of me,
May my (personal) god stand at my right,
May my (personal) goddess stand at my left,
May a good guardian deity and a good protective spirit
        be [clo]se by me,
Grant me hearing and acceptance [of what I say],   (20)
May my speech be of good purport.
O son of great prince [Marduk], gr[ant me li]fe!*
Let me proceed in all confidence before you,
May Shazu[1] be h[appy because of you,
        may Nudimmud] rejoice because of you,
May the gods of heaven and netherworld bless you,   (25)
May heaven [and netherworld ...] exalt you,
[May the] great [gods please you],
May Tashm[etum, your beloved spouse,
        confirm my life] in E[zida].

Text: King, BMS 22, obv 1-29; Loretz-Mayer, AOAT 34 54-58; Ebeling-Köcher-Rost, LKA 56.
Edition: Mayer, UFBG, 473-475.
Translation: von Soden, SAHG, 312-313 no. 49; Seux, *Hymnes*, 297-299.
Literature: Mayer, UFBG, Nabu 3.
*Notes to Text: (22) Seux, *Hymnes*, 298 note 18; Mayer, UFBG, 474.

1. Name for Marduk, see Creation Epic (III.17) Tablet VII line 35.

(b) AN OLD MAN'S PRAYER

This prayer appeals to Nabu as intercessor with his father, asking his help in averting divine displeasure. The speaker notes, perhaps with nostalgia, that Nabu counts off the years (lines 3, 17). Perhaps, as with III.44a, the speaker's old age is a metaphor for his being bowed down by suffering, but a more literal reading has been preferred in this instance.

O [Nab]u, eldest (son), rightful heir, (1)
[Holder] of the tablet stylus, of profound intelligence,
[Who ... the days], who examines the years,
[Who safeguards] life, who requites good,
[Foremost one] of the gods, of eminent name! (5)
The father who begot him does not change his command,
Tutu does not change the utterance of Nabu his son,
His word is supreme among the gods his peers.
You turn the face of a god towards the victim of his anger,
You reconcile with him the goddess* who is hostile, (10)
You absolve the wrong-doing of the [   ].
[I], so-and-so, son of so-and-so,
        the servant who reveres you,
In my youth I prayed ...*
Now that I am old,
        my hands make petition to all the gods,
I am breathless [from] prostration! (15)
[Before] mankind I am like a whirlwind![1]
My days have elapsed, my years have come to an end.
I have seen no favor, I have had no mercy.
O rightful [heir], mighty Nabu,
[I] pray(?) to you, show me[2] the light,
Let me proclaim your [grea]tness,
        let me sound your praises!

1. I take the line as hyperbole, referring, perhaps humorously, to the speaker's continuous prostrations, rather than as a metaphor for his poor physical condition. For different views, see Seux, *Hymnes*, 302 note 15; Mayer, UFBG, 471.
2. Variant: "Let me see."

Text: Finkelstein, STT 55, 28-48; Ebeling, KAR 25, i 1-19; Loretz-Mayer, AOAT 34 73.
Edition: Mayer, UFBG, 469-472.
Translation: Seux, *Hymnes,* 301-302.
Literature: Mayer, UFBG, Nabu 1.
Notes to Text: (10) Text: "destiny," see Mayer, UFBG, 472. (13) Differently CAD M/2, 37a, but there seems to be no basis for the reading proposed there; see Mayer, UFBG, 472.

(c) DISCOURAGEMENT

This sad prayer reflects on the joy of premature happiness and the bitterness of premature sorrow. All has gone by too quickly, and the supplicant begs that his life be made worth living.

(gap)

O Nabu, lest I sin, O son of the Lord, [lest] I offend,
[On account of the heed]less deeds of my ancestors and
    kinfolk, who heedlessly neglected
    [the rites of Tashmetu],★   (5)
I have longed [for] Ezida, the high ground,
    the house in which we put our trust,
I have longed for Ezida, the threshold of delight, ...
[Even as] an infant(?), I have longed for the collegium,
    to take my place in (its) house of learning,
My strength was the precious offerings
    of the temple of Nabu,★
I was ever mindful of its beauties,
    it was the fire of Ezida that stoked my heart.   (10)
I gained wealth,
    I attained what I wanted ahead of my time.
(Now) old age has me bedridden prematurely,
I am wasted by suffering,
    as if I were not fearing your divinity.
I weep, for I have not seen the beauty of my life.
I have become the smallest of the small,
    I am become the lowest of the low,   (15)
My (begging) hands are outstretched
    (even) to the poverty-stricken who frequent my door,
I have entreated slaves and slavegirls,
    whom I used to buy in commerce,[1]
When I moved against an enemy,
    a sorceress splashed water on my back.★

---

1. Literally: "by the scales."

I am cut off from my community,
    enemies of (my) family glower at me,
Anguish, sickness are upon me,
    I am stricken with weakness   (20)
I keep crying out to estranged gods,
    raising my hands (in prayer) in heed of my goddess.
I have gone everywhere for a mother,
    she has shrunk from me and is clawing at me.*
Death has tantalized me like a precious stone.
I constantly go up to the roof to jump off,
    but my life is too precious, it turns me back.
I try to encourage myself,
    what is there for me to encourage?   (25)
I try to keep control of my thoughts,
    but what is there for me to control?
O Nabu, where is your forgiveness,
    O son of the [Lo]rd, where are your oracles?
Where is your favorable breeze
    which wafts over your weakling (subjects)?
O lord, how long will there be darkness
    in my time of trouble?*
The sun lights up for the land, (but) for me [   ].   (30)
Prosperity rains down on the people,
    (but) for me rains down [ ] and gall.
My life is spent, O account-keeper of the u[niverse],
    where shall I go?
I have reached death's door, O Nabu,
    why have you forsaken me?
Do not forsake me, my lord,
    for the [com]pany of my numerous ill-wishers,
To the hands ... of my sorceress do not forsake me,
    O god called by the good name!   (35)
I am a weakling who fears you,
    do not shame me in public!
I am a guardian of truth,
    do not destroy the truth [I have] guarded!

May the lonely one not die,
>who has called up to you, O lord!
O Nabu, take the hand of the fallen one
>who attends your divinity,
Spare the life of the weakling,
>whom ill-wishers hemmed in, (40)
Whom baleful witches have splashed with conjured water.
Let the dead man revive [by your] breeze,
Let his squandered life become gain!

Text: Finkelstein, STT 65.
Edition: Livingstone, *Court Poetry*, 30-32.
Literature: W. G. Lambert, RA 53 (1959), 129-131; Deller, OrNS 34 (1965), 458-461.
Notes to Text: (5, 9, 18, 22) von Soden, WdO 22 (1991), 191. (29) Reading *ma-ru-<uš>-ti-ya*.

(d) COMPOUND ACROSTIC PRAYER TO NABU

This fragmentary prayer, in four- or five-line strophes, forms an acrostic at the beginning and end of each line, though its meaning is not clear. The tight restriction of form and meter make for artificiality of expression.

i

I understand the deed [   ]
I hamstring(?) myself,
      I make my heart cry out in mourning,
My inmost self wails a dirge like [   ]   (5)

ii

No [head] can be raised (proudly) among the gods
            without your approval.
You strengthen the weak and lowly,
One who is girt about with sickness and disease
            waits on you,
May your favorable breeze blow upon me
            and grant me release!

iii

I call upon you, O Nabu, be gracious to me, O brave one.   (10)
I abased myself among the multitude,
      I always held my peace.*
I became like one possessed, I ... I know not what.
I kept calling out to the gods, but all was silence!

iv

The lowly who trusts in you will have his fill of abundance,
You strengthen the foundations of the righteous
            and make firm his support,   (15)
You grant me good fortune, you banish sin,
You can turn a rock wall into clay.

(rest fragmentary)

Text: K 8204 (collated) = Strong, PSBA 17 (1895), 137-138.
Edition: Strong, PSBA 17 (1895), 139-140.
Literature: Ebeling, "Alliteration," RLA 1, 71.
Notes to Text: (11) CAD Q, 75b.

(e) THE NAMES OF NABU

Like the prayer to Nabu by Nabu-ushebshi (f), this hymn assigns to Nabu many of the attributes ascribed in other compositions to Marduk. The text uses phraseology known from the Creation Epic (III.17) and may date to the seventh century B.C. See General Introduction, D.3.

[Let me ever sp]eak of your grandeur, O Nabu,
    glorious king,   (1)
[Let me] exalt your greatness,
    O dragon of the gods, stately leader,
[L]et me proclaim your lordship, O sage of the depths,
    firstborn of the gods,[1] bearer of king[ship],
Hear ever of the valor of the leader of the gods, Marduk.[2]
Let me praise the names of the king(?),
    [heir?] of Esagila, torch of the gods,   (5)
Which other [c]reator of the whole inhabited world,
    of all regions, should I be speaking of?
Your command is the strongest(?)* in the universe
    and sublime, (for) you are Nabu!
O Dimmerankia,[3] "divine lord, king of heaven
    and netherworld" they cal[led]* your name.
Your first name is Shazu,[4]
    "who knows the hearts of the gods,"
    "who shall not examine [his] enemy,"[5]
Your second name is Urrunzu,[6] whose name [ ],   (10)

1. Or, perhaps, "the god" (= Marduk).

2. Nabu may be referred to here as "Marduk of the gods."

3. Compare Marduk's name, Lugaldimmerankia, of Creation Epic (III.17) Tablet VI line 139. Perhaps one should restore "lord" (EN) at the beginning of the name so as to account for the "lord" of the explanation.

4. One of the names of Marduk in the Creation Epic (III.17) Tablet VII lines 35, 41, 43, 47, 51, 55.

5. A misquotation of the Creation Epic (III.17) Tablet VII line 35. This should read "who examines the inside." Here the line may mean something like "no enemies appear before him" (because he is so mighty).

6. Approximately, "the one of the moon," an attribute peculiar to Nabu (Ebeling, WdO 1, 477; Seux, Hymnes, 135 note 16).

Your third name is Asari,[1]
    "clasher at arms(?), who provides incense offerings,"[2]
Your fourth name is "Bearer of the Tablet of Divine Destinies[3]
    (of) all the su[preme] Igigi-gods."
Your fifth name is "Hana,"[4] <who grasps> the circumference
    of heaven and netherworld, who establishes [   ]
Your sixth name is "Incorruptible Judge, Who Enforces [Justice],"[5]
Your seventh name is "The Seven,"[6] valiant hero,
    who scans [the mountains],
Your eighth [name] is "Sirsirra,"[7] offspring of Qingu,[8]
    who [   ].
O lord, you grew high from the depths
    and are warrior [in the land], (for) you are Nabu!

Text: Ebeling-Köcher-Rost, LKA 16.
Edition: Ebeling, WdO 1, 476-479.
Translation: Seux, *Hymnes*, 134-136.
Literature: Pomponio, *Nabu* (see III.45a), 170-173.
Notes to Text: (7) Seux, *Hymnes*, 135 note 11. (8) Seux, *Hymnes*, 135 note 13.

1. Name of Marduk, Creation Epic (III.17) Tablet VII line 1.
2. Creation Epic (III.17) Tablet VII line 39 (for a different interpretation, see Seux, *Hymnes*, 135 note 25).
3. For the tablet of destinies, see p. 360 note 1.
4. According to Seux, *Hymnes*, 136 note 22, to be understood as Hayya (written Ḫa-NI), spouse of the grain goddess. The grain goddess was also a patron deity of scribal lore. One may also see here an allusion to Marduk's sojourn in Hana, for which see III.13.
5. See Creation Epic (III.17) Tablet VII line 39 (noted by Seux, *Hymnes*, 136 note 25).
6. For the Seven, see Erra and Ishum (IV.16), Tablet I.
7. See Creation Epic (III.17) Tablet VII lines 70-77, a mythological episode there assigned to Marduk.
8. Since Qingu was an enemy of Marduk and was executed in the Creation Epic, Marduk took over his name and it is here given to Nabu. See Lambert, *Atrahasis*, 153; Livingstone, *Explanatory Works*, 234; Pomponio, *Nabu*, 173f.

(f) ACROSTIC PRAYERS OF NABU-USHEBSHI

These prayers to Marduk and Nabu form compound acrostics at the beginning and end of each line. The beginning signs of both prayers spell "Nabu-ushebshi the exorcist." In prayer (i) the end signs of the lines spell "the servant who proclaims your lordship"; in prayer (ii) "the supplicant servant who reveres you." Nabu-ushebshi was presumably the author of both prayers. He may have lived about the middle of eighth century B.C. The author displays both cleverness and a penchant for rare vocables.

(i) To Marduk

Sun to his forefathers, exalted leader Asari,[1]   (1)
Skilled, acute grantor of longevity of days,
Yours is to keep alive and in well-being!
Mortals magnify your worthy name,
Afflicted and lowly are attentive to you.   (5)
[You hear] their prayers, you grant offspring.
The peoples of the land m[aintain]* daily their song of praise,
Living creatures ex[tol] your sweet appellation.
May there be protection for Nabu-ushebshi,
    the [sup]plicant [s]erv[ant],
May he have the destiny of mankind, progeny and descent,   (10)
May his descendants last for all time before you!

(Eleven lines not set in paragraphs,* the beginning and end of each line
may be read in two directions.)[2]

(ii) To Nabu

O lofty hero, Asari's son,   (1)
Who called (into being) all that is, [who h]ears prayers,
Radiant of feature, coun[s]ellor of h[is] forefathers,
Dragon without equal, heir to Nudimmud,[3]
Archetype of the Igigi-gods, lord of w[isdom],
    who [gathers to himself] all learning,   (5)

---

1. Name for Marduk; see Creation Epic (III.17) Tablet VII line 1.
2. Scribal indication, meaning that the text is an acrostic.
3. Ea, god of wisdom, grandfather of Nabu.

The lore(?)[1] of heaven and netherworld is forever [in your hand].
O merciful* Nabu, you can ordain a favorable destiny,
Quicken [Nabu-ush]ebshi, your thrall,
[May he reach] a fullness of life-span, a ripe old age,
[May all that is] sound the praises of your valor! (10)

Text: W. G. Lambert, JAOS 88 (1968), 131.
Edition: W. G. Lambert, JAOS 88 (1968), 130-132.
Translation: Seux, *Hymnes*, 264-266.
Literature: R. F. G. Sweet, "A Pair of Double Crostics in Akkadian," OrNS 38 (1969), 459-460.
Notes to Text: (i 7) Seux, *Hymnes*, 265 note 7. (i 12) AHw, 1514b. Not clear, but perhaps refers to indentations or paragraphing used to mark off sections. (ii 7) Sweet, OrNS 38 (1969), 460 note 3.

1. The word used here (*šipkat*) is not clear, but may mean something like "things piled up."

III.46 To Nergal

Nergal, a major netherworld deity with his sanctuary at Cutha, in northern Babylonia, is portrayed as a pitiless, destructive warrior. This hymn may refer to the Creation Epic (III.17); see General Introduction, D.3. Nergal is often associated with battle, plague, and violence. For further information, see E. von Weiher, *Der babylonische Gott Nergal*, AOAT 11 (1971).

(a) NERGAL THE WARRIOR

> O warrior, splendid one,
> > offspring of Nun[amnir],[1]   (1)
> Let me sound your [praises?],*
> > O lordly one, arrayed in awesomeness.
> O bearer of pointed horns,[2] clad with frightening sheen,
> > first-born son of Kutumshar,[3]
> Monitor of the lower world, overseer of the Six Hundred,[4]
> > let me always praise your greatness!
> You are supreme in strength, overwhelming all disobedient,
> > forcing the ...* to submit.   (5)
> O tireless mighty one,
> > who gladdens Enlil's heart,
> Mighty of arms, broad of chest,
> > perfect one without rival among all the gods,
> Who grasps the pitiless deluge-weapon,
> > who massacres(?)* the enemy,
> Lion clad in splendor,
> > at the flaring-up of whose fierce brilliance
> The gods of the inhabited world took to secret places,
> > evil-doer and wicked have found their way into crevices.   (10)
> [   ] has adorned you [   ] ... with awesomeness,

---

1. Name for Enlil.

2. Nergal is sometimes referred to as a bull; in general, horns were a Mesopotamian symbol of divinity.

3. Name for Ninlil, Enlil's wife.

4. Gods of the netherworld; compare Creation Epic (III.17) Tablet VI line 44 and General Introduction, D.3.

Nudimmud[1] has bestowed [upon you] irresistible weaponry,
[   ] has [   ] your [   ] among the gods your brethren.

(breaks off)

Text: K 9880, Rm 290 (collated) = Böllenrücher, *Nergal* No. 8 (p. 50), transliteration only.
Edition: Böllenrücher, *Nergal,* 50-52.
Translation: Seux, *Hymnes,* 84-85.
★Notes to Text: (2) Z[À.MÍ.MEŠ-k]a? (5) K 9880 has MUŠ.ŠID, not clear. Rm 290 inserts *pa-ni-šú* after *ma-gi-ri.* (8) *etem/nu,* meaning unknown.

1. Another name for Ea, god of wisdom.

(b) THE TERRORS OF NERGAL

This hymnic fragment is known from a manuscript of the Achaemenid period. The scribe was fond of visual effects in that the first writing of certain key words is logographic and the second syllabic.[1] Note also that the third line of the first four distiches has the god's name in initial rhythmic position. The disjointed expression and unusual style suggest a late date for the composition of this text, perhaps by someone familiar with, but not well-versed in, traditional Akkadian hymnic style. Compare IV.11.

Warrior among his brothers, princely god,*   (1)
Lord surpassing all the Igigi-gods,
Nergal, princely god,
Lord surpassing all the Igigi-gods,
He has fastened on a vestment of divine splendor
    and awesomeness,   (5)
The god who is furious in joy(?) (and) fe[arsomeness],[2]
Nergal has fastened on a vestment of divine splendor
    and awesomeness,
The god who is furious in joy(?) (and) fea[rsomeness]!
His cheekbones gleam like the glint* of a gem,
His cheeks flash like a lightning bolt,   (10)
Nergal's cheekbones gleam like the glint of a gem,
His cheeks flash like a lightning bolt!
His weapon is mighty, his onslaught irresistible,
Like a tempest (and) overwhelming flood, he has no equal,
Nergal's weapon is mighty, his onslaught irresistible,   (15)
Like a tempest (and) overwhelming flood, he has no equal!
Impetuous warrior, lord, proven one of the gods,[3] untrammeled,
Valorous heir of Belet-ili, who brings satisfaction to Enlil,

---

1. Nougayrol (RA 41 [1947], 38) suggests that the text was written respectively for an expert, then for apprentices, but this is not convincing. Perhaps the second writing is simply an explanation of the first (though often elementary), in the spirit of other texts that explain names and attributes (see, for example, III.17, 26, 45e).

2. This may mean that Nergal is terrible even in a good frame of mind or that he is happiest when in a fury.

3. Or: "proven god."

Valorous courier, fleet of foot,★

Inspector of everything, beautiful heir,★ untrammeled,   (20)

Ninlil gave him a full quiver,

She has placed a splendid bow in his hands.

(manuscript ends)

Text: Nougayrol, RA 41 (1947), 40.

Edition: Ebeling, AGH, 118.

Translation: Seux, *Hymnes,* 88-90.

★*Notes to Text*: (1) For a different reading, see Seux, *Hymnes*, 88 with note 3: "Héros de ses frères les dieux, (leur) souverain." (9) <*ni*>-*ip-ḫu* with Seux, *Hymnes,* 89 note 7. (19) *birbirki,* called for by the meter, may be a reduplicated form for emphatic effect, not a dittography. (20) *bānu aplu šammar*, perhaps a refurbishment of *bāni apli* "creator of an heir."

(c) SUBLIME NERGAL

This hymn is known from a small fragment said to have come from Uruk. The allusion to the Creation Epic (III.17) in line 7 suggests a late date of composition; the manuscript itself dates to late in the first millennium.

> [O Nergal], warrior of the gods,
>> who possesses the lofty strength of Anu,   (1)
> [Lion] with gaping maw,* marauding lion monster,
>> who takes his place nobly in the height of heaven,
> [Who hol]ds lordship, whose features ever glow in heaven,
> [Who bears] bow, shaft, and quiver,
>> who grasps glaive, fearing no battle,
> [Van]guard whose strength is sublime,
>> mounted on a steed, deluge irresistible,   (5)
> Stately [offspring] of Anu, fair in horns,
>> worthy of a lordly vestment,
> [Adorned] in splendid array, masterful, deeply courageous,
> Impossible to perceive, difficult to understand.[1]
> [O Nergal, warrior]* of the gods, long of arms,
>> whose divine splendor is sublime in heaven,
> [Star] ever shining, sublime of features,
> [Who] holds [lord]ship [   ],
>> who wields a knife, who knows fighting,   (10)
> [Vict]orious [   ], who flashes wickedly in strife,
> [Who   ] weapon and staff, whose sleep is a feint,
> [Who] has no rival [in me]lee or battle.
> [   ] of Uruk, who slaughters evil demons,
> [   ] who annihilates the foe, who uproots the enemy,   (15)
> [who le]vels the hostile land,
> [who holds the hand] of the fallen

(breaks off)

---

1. The same expression occurs in Creation Epic (III.17) Tablet I line 94. Seux (*Hymnes*, 87 note 10) suggests that this is a direct allusion to the passage; see General Introduction, D.3.

Text: Böhl, BiOr 6 (1949), pl. vi, vii.

Edition: Böhl, BiOr 6 (1949), 165-170, updated in *Opera Minora* (Groningen, 1953), 207-216, 496-497.

Translation: Seux, *Hymnes*, 85-88.

Notes to Text: (1) [Pirig]-kaduha, see Seux, *Hymnes*, 86 note 3. (9) Seux, *Hymnes*, 87 note 11.

III.47 TO NINURTA

Ninurta was a warrior and vegetation deity. He appears as the hero of the Anzu-poem (above, III.22).

(a) PRESCRIPTIVE HYMN TO NINURTA

This fragment, known from a Middle Assyrian bilingual tablet, is the remains of a text similar to the Shamash hymn (III.32) in content. The second part describes a ceremony of the citizens of Nippur and of the Mesopotamians in general ("black-headed folk").

(gap)

Grievous is the guilt of him who has intercourse with
    (another) man's wife.   (4)
He who says frivolous words, the backbiter,
Who points the finger of malice towards his equal,   (10)
Who impugns the unspeakable to (his) brother,
Who oppresses the poor,
Who gives the weak over to the strong,
Who [   ] a fellow citizen with calumny,   (16)
Pilferer(?) who [   ] from his neighbor's field,

(gap)

(Songs) are sung to you with tympani, drum, and [... har]p.   (3)
Fatted cattle, [fatted sheep] are slaughtered for you
    as the king's offering,
Young men of strength compete with each other
    in wrestling and athletic games [in your honor].
The citizens of Nippur, clan by clan,
    [keep the occasion] in abundance,   (9)
The black-headed folk sing your songs of praise.
When [you] set your face towards that place,
When [you] enter the sanctuary gate as a shower of rain,   (15)
When y[ou] pass through the square of the sanctuary gate
    as it is full of rejoicing,

When you enter Eshumesha,[1] the house
　　which stretches to heaven and netherworld,
When [you] behold your beloved [　　　　] (21)

　　　　　(breaks off)

Text: W. G. Lambert, BWL pl. 32 (VAT 10610) = Ebeling, KAR 119.
Edition: W. G. Lambert, BWL, 118-120.

---

1. Temple of Ninurta at Nippur.

(b) PROTECTOR OF THE KING

This text was incorporated in the royal lustration ritual "House of the Ritual Bath," for which see III.50h.

> O mighty heir, firstborn son of Enlil,   (1)
> Most great one, perfect one, offspring of Esharra,[1]
> Who is clad in terror, arouses chilling fear,
> Uta-'ulu,[2] whose battle is irresistible,
> Whose (celestial) station is outstanding among the great gods,   (5)
> Your head is raised high in the Ekur, splendid house,
> Enlil your father has given you
> (His) power of command over all the gods,
>   you hold it in your hand.[3]
> You judge the case(s) of mankind,
> You do justice to the wronged, the powerless,
>   the destitute girl,   (10)
> You grasp the weak by the hand, you exalt[4] the helpless,
> You bring back the person
>   who is being sent down to the netherworld,
> You absolve the guilt of the guilty.
> You promptly reconcile the man whose (personal) god
>   or goddess[5] is angry with him.
> O Ninurta, foremost of the gods, you are the warrior.   (15)
> I, so-and-so, son of so-and-so,
>   whose (personal) god is so-and-so,
> I have prepared an offering for you, given you flour,
> I have given you sweet-smelling incense,[6]
> I have libated to you sweet beer (made from) grain.
> May the gods of Enlil[7] stand with you,   (20)

1. Name of the temple of Enlil in Nippur; hence Ninurta is son of Enlil.
2. Name for Ninurta, personification of a storm.
3. Or, perhaps, "(which) is held in your hand."
4. Variant: "make esteemed."
5. Variant omits.
6. Variant omits this line.
7. Group of astral deities in the celestial path of Enlil.

May the gods of Ekur stand with you.[1]
Look steadfastly upon me and hear what I say,
Accept my entreaty, receive (my) prayer!
May what I say content you,
Be reconciled with me,* who reveres you. (25)
I have seen your face, may I prosper.
You are regardful, regard me steadfastly.
Absolve my guilt, dissolve my wrong-doing,
Dismiss my crime, undo my sin.
May my (personal) god and my (personal) goddess
      esteem me and speak favorably (of me), (30)
Let me proclaim your greatness, let me sound your praises!

Text: King, BMS 2, 11-41; BMS 3, 10-16; Loretz-Mayer, AOAT 34 3-7; Mayer, OrNS 59 (1990), 486 K 16934; Ebeling-Köcher-Rost, LKA 41.
Edition: Ebeling, AGH, 24-27.
Translation: von Soden, SAHG, 314-316 no. 51; Seux, *Hymnes,* 314-316.
Literature: Mayer, UFBG, Ninurta 1.
Notes to Text: (25) Seux, *Hymnes,* 315 note 12.

---

1. Variant adds here prayer against the evil portended by an eclipse; see p. 546 note 2.

(c) SYNCRETIC HYMN TO NINURTA

This henotheistic hymn syncretizes various gods, male and female, with organs of Ninurta; compare III.44g.

(gap)

[   ] of the great gods has exalted [you],
O Ninurta, warrior, you [   ]
You [   ], who gather to yourself their powers,   (5)
You take their responsibilities, you [   ].
Kingship of lords is [entrusted]* to your hands.
O lord, your anger is a [   ] deluge,
O warrior of the gods, you are lofty [   ].
O lord, your face is Shamash, your locks [Nisaba],   (10)
Your eyes, O lord, are Enlil and [Ninlil],
Your eyeballs are Gula and Belet-il[i],
Your eyelids, O lord, are the twins Sin [and Shamash],
Your eyebrows are the corona of the sun which [   ],
Your mouth's shape, O lord, is the evening star,   (15)
Anu and Antu are your lips, your speech [is Nusku?],
Your discoursing tongue(?) is Pabilsag, who [   ] on high,
The roof of your mouth, O lord, is the circumference
        of heaven and earth, abode of [   ],
Your teeth are the Seven, who slay evil-doers,
Your cheeks, O lord, are the rising of bri[lliant] stars,   (20)
Your ears are Ea and Damkina, sages of wisdom [   ],
Your head is Adad, who [makes] heaven and earth
        [resound] like a smithy,
Your brow is Shala, beloved [sp]ouse
        who contents [Adad's heart],
Your neck is Marduk, judge of heaven [and netherworld],
        the deluge [ ],
Your throat is Sarpanitum, creat[ress of peo]ple,*
        who [   ],   (25)
Your chest is Shullat, who examines [   ],

Your upper back[1] is Hanish, who establishes p[lenty,
    who r]ains down* abundance,
Your right side[2] is Uta-ulu, who [   ],
Your left side[3] is Ninpanigingarra [   ],
Your fingers are [   ],   (30)
Your [   ] are Dagan [   ],
Your navel, O lord, is [   ],
Your [   ] is Zababa [   ]

        (fragmentary lines, then breaks off)

Text: Ebeling, KAR 102+328; Gurney, STT 118 rev.
Edition: Ebeling, *Quellen* 1, 47-49.
Translation: von Soden, SAHG, 258-259 no. 101; Labat, *Religions,* 93; Seux, *Hymnes,* 131-133.
Literature: H. Lewy, ArOr 18 (1950), 355-356 (dates to Middle Assyrian period or earlier); T. J. Meek, *Hebrew Origins* (New York, 1960), 198.
Notes to Text: (7) Seux, *Hymnes,* 131 note 5. (25) Seux, *Hymnes,* 133 note 25. (27) Seux, *Hymnes,* 133 note 27.

1. Variant adds "O lord."
2. Variant adds "O lord."
3. Variant adds "O lord."

(d) NINURTA AS SIRIUS

In this prayer a diviner calls upon the Sirius star for aid in the divination he is to perform.

O greatest Ninurta, warrior god,
    vanguard of the Anunna-gods,
    commander of the Igigi-gods,   (1)
Judge of the universe, who oversees (its) equilibrium,
    who makes bright darkness and illumines gloom,
Who renders verdicts for teeming mankind!
O my splendid lord, who satisfies the needs of the land,
    at whose [   ] fell head pain takes to corners(?),
The critically ill recovers,   (5)
Merciful one, who spares life, reviver of the d[ea]d,
Who grasps truth and justice and destroys [   ],
[Un]swerving arrow[1] that [kills] all enemies,
Great storm, who grasps the leadrope
    [of heaven and netherworld],
Judge of verdicts, diviner of oracle[s   ],   (10)
Conflagration that incinerates and burns up the wick[ed   ],
Whose celestial name is "Straight Dart,"
    whose [   ] is the greatest among the Igigi-gods,
Among all the gods your divinity is singular.
When the stars come out, your features shine [like] the sun,
You survey the entire inhabited world,
    [ ] of your light [ ],   (15)
To set [right] the distressed and sleepless(?)
    of humankind [   ],
You are the [   ] of the one who has no one to trust in,
You rescue the kidnapped and abandoned [   ],
You summon him back to life from hell [   ].
On the one who, in the thick of battle,
    seems destined to die and calls your name,   (20)

---

1. "Arrow" is a name for Sirius, Sumerian kak-si-sá "Straight Dart."

On him you have mercy, O lord,
　　you rescue him from disaster.
And as for me, the reverent diviner, your servant,
I was anxious by day, I was essaying a bad case,
The verdict is extremely trying and difficult to discover,
I am far from getting to the bottom of it.　　　　　　　　(25)
In the daylight(?) I came(?),* in the night I await you.
I take my place before you to discover the outcome,
　　to make the right verdict.
I have my hands raised (in prayer); stand by me and [in] the
　　pure heavens hear what I say.
Absolve (any) guilt, efface (any) mistake,
　　may my handiwork be blessed by you.[1]
May my presents soothe your heart,
　　do not disdain to stand by me!　　　　　　　　　　　(30)
[Ren]der a verdict, accept my entreaty, and hear my prayer.
In all I have planned give a verdict.
Let me say what is needful for your firm assent.
As for me, may I live a long life in your service.
O greatest Ninurta, O pure [god], attend this sacrifice.　　(35)
In what I say and pray, in whatsoever I do,
In the inquiry I ask your blessing on, let there be truth!
(Prayer to Sirius when it is in position at sunrise)

Text: K 128 = Burrows, JRAS 1924 *Centenary Supplement*, plates II–III.
Edition: Burrows, JRAS 1924 *Centenary Supplement*, 33–36.
Translation: von Soden, SAHG, 275–277 no. 22; Seux, *Hymnes*, 480–482.
Notes to Text: (26) Differently CAD A/1, 423b "O Shamash!" This would equate Ninurta with
Shamash. For the reading *ikušamma*, see Deller-Mayer, OrNS 58 (1989), 275. Note, however, in
favor of *ašašu* that the diviner has had a worrisome day (*urri dalḫakma*) and awaits the intervention
of Sirius with hopeful trepidation.

1. A request to overlook faults of procedure and to consider only the offerings and the divinatory medium.

III.48 TO NUSKU

Nusku, courier of the gods, is invoked in prayers as a protective, beneficent deity.

(a) GUARDIAN OF THE NIGHT

O Nusku, king of the nighttime, illuminator of shadows,   (1)
You stand forth in the night, you examine the people.
Without you, no meal is prepared in Ekur.[1]
The protector-demon, the watcher-demon,
    the lion-headed demon, the oppressor-demon,
    the *gallu*-demon, the lurker-demon, the wicked deity,
The phantom, the male ghost, the female ghost
    which lean in hidden corners,   (5)
By means of your divine light, drive out the malignant demon,
    expel the phantom, overcome the wicked one,
The lion-demon who goes about at night,
    the touch of whom is death.
I look upon you, I turn towards your divinity,
Set above me a watcher of well-being and life,
Station at my head a protective guardian,
    a god who safeguards,
Let them be looking out for me all night until daybreak.
O Nusku, perfect one, lord of wisdom,
Let me proclaim your greatness before Shamash every day!

Text: Ebeling, KAR 58, obv 39-50; Figulla-Walker, CT 51 149, rev 1'-3'; von Weiher, SBTU
II 7; three unpublished fragments cited by Mayer, UFBG, 485-486.
Edition: Mayer, UFBG, 485-486.
Translation: von Soden, SAHG, 351-352 no. 78; Seux, *Hymnes*, 254-255.
Literature: Mayer, UFBG, Nusku 4.

1. Variant adds here a line: "Without you, no judgment or verdict is [rendered in ...]."

(b) COURIER OF DREAMS

O Nusku, sublime vizier, who wal[ks abroad at night],   (1)
[Light?] of the gods of the (four) world regions,
     lord of sublime powers, sa[ge],
Whose battle cry mankind hears from afar,
I, so-and-so, son of so-and-so, entreat you,
     inform me [ab]out my case!
[With res]pect to [my] case, provide [merc]y(?) (for me),   (5)
Do not go [to] another case.
May the evening watch, the midnight watch,
     the morning watch
Bring me a [dre]am, that I may sing your praises.
O [An]zagar, Anzagar,[1] who transports mankind,[2]
Messenger of prince Marduk,   (10)
O Nightfall, awesomeness of the nighttime,
O three watches of the night, who are wakeful,
     watchful, alert, and non-sleeping,
Since you are wakeful, watchful,
     alert, and non-sleeping,
You will grant a verdict to wakeful and sleeping,   (15)
You will fulfill your responsibility,
     you will look out all night until the morning watch.
May one (of you) bring me <a dream(?)>,*
Let me sound your praises!

Text: Ebeling, KAR 58, rev 1-17.
Edition: Ebeling, AGH, 40-41.
Translation: von Soden, SAHG, 350-351 no. 77; Seux, *Hymnes*, 320-321.
Literature: Mayer, UFBG, Nusku 5.
*Notes to Text: (17) Seux, *Hymnes*, 321 note 16. The passage as it stands is not clear.

1. Dream god.
2. That is, transports men in their sleep?

(c) FORFENDER OF NIGHTMARES

O Nusku, you are companion to the sun,   (1)
You are the judge, judge (my) case!
This dream which was brought to me in the evening,
    midnight, or morning watch,
Which you understand but I do not,
If it is propitious,
    may the good (it portends) not pass me by,   (5)
If it is evil, may the evil (it portends) not overtake me,
It is not for me!
Just as this pulled-up reed cannot return to its place,
And (as) this hem cut from my garment,
Being cut from it, cannot return to my garment,   (10)
So may the evil (portended by) this dream,
Which was brought to me in the evening, midnight,
    or morning watch,
Not overtake me, it is not for me!

Text: Oppenheim, *Dreams*, 361, K 8583; 362, 75-7-8,77.
Edition: Oppenheim, *Dreams,* 340, 343; 298.
Translation: Seux, *Hymnes,* 373.
Literature: Mayer, UFBG, Nusku 12.

(d) PROTECTOR AGAINST SORCERY

O Nusku, most great one, offspring of Anu, (1)
Likeness of (your) father, firstborn of Enlil,
Raised in the depths, creation of Enanki,[1]
I have raised a torch, I have made you glow.
A sorcerer has bewitched me, bewitched me
    with the sorcery he worked against me, (5)
A sorceress has bewitched me, bewitched me
    with the sorcery she has worked against me,
A male witch has bewitched me, bewitched me
    with the witchcraft he has worked against me,
A female witch has bewitched me, bewitched me
    with the witchcraft she has worked against me,
A worker of spells has bewitched me, bewitched me
    with the spells she has worked against me!
Those who have made figurines that are figurines of me,
    who have made a likeness of my features, (10)
Who have taken of my spittle,
    who have plucked out (a lock) of my hair,
Who have cut off a piece of my clothing,
    have collected dust where my feet have passed,
May Girra, the warrior, dissipate their spells!

Text: Tallqvist, *Maqlû* I 122–134; Finkelstein, STT 78, 122–134.
Edition: Meier, *Maqlû,* 11–12 lines 122–134; see also AfO 21 (1960), 72.
Literature: Mayer, UFBG, Nusku 10.

---

1. "Lord of heaven and netherworld," a name for Ea. Variant reads Ninmen[na].

III.49 TO A PERSONAL GOD

Belief in personal gods, supposed to act as protectors and intercessors for the individual, is widely expressed in Assyro-Babylonian literature. Pleas to them express a range of feelings such as guilt, frustration, sorrow, even anger and reproof. The selections translated below sample the variety of this class of prayers, a treatment of which will be found in W. G. Lambert's study, DINGIR.ŠÀ.DIB₂.BA Incantations," JNES 33 (1974), 267-322. For a study of the personal god, mostly based on evidence from the Classical period, see R. Albertz, *Persönliche Frommigkeit und offizielle Religion: religionsinterner Plurismus in Israel und Babylon* (Stuttgart, 1978), and above, General Introduction (E.8).

(a) GOD OF MY FAMILY

O my god, my lord, who created my name,[1]
Guardian of my life, producer of my progeny,
O angry god, may your heart be calmed,
O angry goddess, be reconciled with me.

Who knows where you dwell, O my god?   (5)
Never have I seen your pure standing place (or sleeping) chamber.[2]
I am constantly in great distress: O my god, where are you?
You who have been angry with me, turn towards me,
Turn your face to the pure godly meal of fat and oil,
That your lips receive goodness. Command that I thrive,   (10)
Command (long) life with your pure utterance.
Bring me away from evil that, through you, I be saved.
Ordain for me a destiny of (long) life,
Prolong my days, grant me (long) life!

Text: Myhrman, PBS 1/1 14, 41-54; W. G. Lambert, JNES 33 (1974), 307, 309; Ebeling-Köcher-Rost, LKA 26, 27 (collated Lambert, 317).
Edition: W. G. Lambert, JNES 33 (1974), 276-277, lines 40-53.
Translation: von Soden, SAHG, 353 no. 79; Seux, *Hymnes*, 204-205.

1. Variant places lines 1-4 at end, thus beginning with line 5.
2. Variant adds: "sublime."

(b) FURIOUS GOD

My god, I did not know (how) [har]sh
    [your] punishment would be! (1)
I have sworn lightly a solemn oath by your name,
I have disregarded your rites, I went too far,
I have skirted(?) your duty in difficulty,
I have trespassed far beyond your limits. (5)
I certainly did not know, much [   ].
My crimes being (so) numerous, I do not know all I did.
O my god, clear, forego, dispel your ire,
Disregard my iniquities, accept my entreaties,
Transmute my sins into good deeds. (10)
Your hand is harsh, I have seen your punishment.
Let him who does not revere his god and goddess
    learn from my example.
O my god, be reconciled, O my goddess, relent!
Turn hither your faces to the entreaty of my prayer.
May your angry hearts be calmed,[1] (15)
May your feelings be soothed, permit me reconciliation,
Let me ever sing your praises, not to be forgotten,
    to the numerous peoples.

Text: Myhrman, PBS 1/1 14, 24-40; W. G. Lambert, JNES 33 (1974), 306, 308, 318.
Edition: W. G. Lambert, JNES 33 (1974), 274-277, lines 23-39.
Translation: von Soden, SAHG, 352 no. 79; Seux, *Hymnes*, 203-204.

1. Variant adds: "May the hostile goddess be reconciled with me."

(c) THE PITEOUS SUFFERER

This bilingual lament portrays the suffering of a man who believes himself forsaken by his god. Compare Dialogue Between a Man and His God (II.5).

(gap)

[In agony of] heart, in terrible weeping,   (1')
He abides in grief.
With bitter plaint, agony of heart,
Terrible weeping, terrible grief,
He moans like a dove, in crushing distress, night and day.   (5')
He lows[1] like a cow to his merciful god,
He keeps setting forth his bitter grief,
He abases himself before his god in supplication.
He weeps and knows no restraint in sobbing:
"Shall I speak of what I did?
    What I did is unspeakable!   (10')
"Shall I repeat[2] what I said?
    What I said should not be repeated!
"O my god, shall I speak of what I did?
    What I did is unspeakable!
"O my lord, shall I speak to someone (of it)?
    It is unspeakable!
"Shall I repeat what I said?
    What I said should not be repeated!
"I am deaf, I am blindfolded, I cannot see.   (15')
"You have gone beyond what you intended,[3]
"Let your sweet breeze wa[ft upon me].
"I am caught up like reeds in the wind.
"My god, [absolve] my sin,
"My god, look steadfastly upon me from your abode,[4]   (20')
"Take pity on me, may your angry heart be calmed,

1. Variant: "cries out."
2. Variant: "speak of."
3. Literally: "commanded." I take this to mean that the punishment has exceeded the limits imagined by the sufferer to have been imposed upon it by the god.
4. Variant: "wherever," omits last two lines.

"[May your heart, like a real mother's, like a real father's],
    be [restored],
[Like a real mother's, like a real father's, may it be restored]."

Text: Maul, HBKl, pl. 31-35 (with numerous variants not noted here).
Edition: Maul, HBKl, 216-228 no. 40-42.
Translation: Seux, *Hymnes*, 143-145.

(d) WHO HAS NOT SINNED?

Be it [offen]se, crime, iniquity, sin,   (1)
[I] have offended against my god,
    I have sinned against my goddess.
I have (indeed) perpetrated [all] my crimes,
    all my sins, all my iniquities.
[I] gave my word, then changed (it),
    I was trusted but did not deliver.
I did [un]seemly deeds, I said something harmful.   (5)
I repeated [what should not be spoken of],
    harmful (speech) was on my lips.
[I was ig]norant, I went too far!
Absolve, my god ... [   ]
Let my [iniquities] be dissolved,
    [transmute] my sins into good deeds.
You decide [   ]   (10)
Save safe and sound the one who sinned [   ]!
Who is there who is guilty of no sin against his god?
Which is he who kept a commandment forever?
All human beings there are have sin.
I, your servant, have committed every sin,   (15)
I stood before you, (but) I ... falsehood,
I uttered lies, I indulged crimes,
I spoke harmful words, you know what they are.
I committed an abomination against the god who created me,
I acted sacrilegiously, I kept on doing evil.   (20)
I envied your vast possessions,
I yearned for your precious silver,
I lifted my own hand to touch what should not be touched.
I entered the temple without being pure,
I committed one terrible outrage after another against you,   (25)
I went beyond your limits of what was offensive to you,
I cursed your divinity in the rage of my heart.
I have persisted in every sort of crime,
I kept on going as I liked and incurred iniquity.
It is enough, O my god, let your heart be calmed!

May the goddess who grew angry be pacified completely. (30)
Dissolve the ire you harbored in your heart,
May your inmost self, which I swore by,
    be reconciled with me.
Though my crimes be numerous, clear my debt,
Though my iniquities be seven(-fold),
    let your heart be calmed.
Though my [si]ns be numerous,
    show great mercy and cleanse [me]. (35)
[O my god], I am exhausted, grasp my hand,
[from the gr]ound and hold up [my] head,
[ ] save my life!

(thirteen lines fragmentary)

Let the day be joyful [for] the shepherd of the people,
[Let me si]ng of you, let me p[r]aise your divinity,
Let me sound your praises [to] the numerous [peoples]!

Text: Ebeling, KAR 39, "rev?" 18-27; KAR 45 "rev" + KAR 39, "obv"; W. G. Lambert, JNES 33 (1974), 314-315, with collations, p. 322.
Edition: W. G. Lambert, JNES 33 (1974), 280-285, lines 121-175.
Translation: von Soden, SAHG, 272-273 no. 19 (partial); Seux, *Hymnes*, 206-208.

III.50 TO SHAMASH

Shamash, the sun, was the god of justice and fair dealing. He was often invoked in prayers against evil magic and in the prayers of diviners, as investigation and perception of the truth were his special responsibility. Compare also III.32.

The cosmology of the hymns to the sun can seem contradictory and confusing to the modern reader, especially in connection with the word pair *šamê u erṣetum* (usually translated "heaven and earth," see General Introduction, C.8). The second word in the pair can mean "earth" or "netherworld," and it is often difficult to decide which is meant. For example, in III.50a, the opening lines refer to "heaven and —, above and be[low, lord of the dead, gui]de of the living" (assuming the restoration is correct, see Caplice, OrNS 39 [1970], 140). The contrasts above/below and dead/living, presumably inverted for poetic reasons, imply that "below" and *erṣetum* refer to the netherworld. However, the relationship could be understood as symmetrical and tripartite (heaven : earth // netherworld : earth), in which case *erṣetum* should refer to the earth. In III.50h the sun "administers dead and living ..., scrutinizes all there is," implying, like the preceding, that the sun had access to the netherworld, even if the dead themselves were bereft of light (see III.18, line 7ff.). The next line calls the sun "light of heaven and —, splendor of the world." This could be tripartite, and so be read as heaven : netherworld : world, or it could be bipartite, with the last word parallel to the middle one, heaven : earth // world. A further example, in III.50n, calls the sun "king of heaven and —," with parallel "Anu and Enlil convene no assembly in heaven, Nor would they take counsel concerning the land." This implies bipartite division, heaven : earth / / gods : land. The solution to this difficult conceptual problem may be that in poetry a contrast can be drawn between heaven and that which is below it, earth and netherworld being considered as a unit in opposition to heaven. Further development within an individual poem can separate earth from netherworld, or define that larger unit more closely, as in III.50h, where the sun is judge of heaven and —, then "light of the gods, light of living things." For these reasons, the pair *šamê u erṣetum* might best be translated with an awkward paraphrase such as "heaven and world-below," but out of deference to tradition and the need for intelligibility, "heaven and earth" has been retained, except where it seemed clear that the netherworld was meant.

(a) AGAINST IMPENDING EVIL

O Shamash, king of heaven and earth, judge above
    and be[low, lord of the dead, gui]de of the living,   (1)
You are preserver of life, the great leader of humankind,
You are [averter of sp]ells, signs, and portents,
    whatever they may be,
You are the one to cut off evil, celestial or terrestrial.
Because of the evil of sorcer[y, witchcraft, magic], and
    machinations which have seized me
    and are not dissolved,
Because of the evil of unfavorable signs and portents
    which are present in my house,
    which have stymied me,[1]
Each day I am afraid, anxious, terrified.   (5)
Now, may the evil of this sorcery which has been put upon me,
    the evil of the signs and portents
    which are present in my house,
    not approach me or my house,
    nor bes[et me, n]or affect me.
May that evil cross river, may it go beyond mountain,
May that sorcery be 3600 leagues distant from my person.
May it mount to the skies like smoke, like an uprooted tamarisk,
    may it not return where it was.
May the river receive the[se evils] from me,
    may the river redeem me.   (10)
Let me live in well-being and proclaim your greatness,
Let me sound your [pra]ises to the numerous peoples!

Text: Caplice, OrNS 39 (1970), pl. vi K 2773 +; OrNS 36 (1967), pl. lix K 8932; Ebeling-Köcher-Rost, LKA 111, obv 7-rev 3; Gadd, UET 6/2 405.
Edition: Caplice, OrNS 39 (1970), 134-135, 137-138 no. 40, lines 8-17.
Translation: Seux, *Hymnes*, 356-357.
Literature: Mayer, UFBG, Šamaš 24.

1. Variant same to here, then goes on with another prayer against the evil portended by a stray cat (compare III.50d).

(b) AGAINST A KNOWN SORCERER

O Shamash, judge of heaven and earth,
    judge of upper and lower regions,
Who administers the black-headed folk,[1]
    who releases the prisoner,
    who revives the moribund,
O Shamash, these images[2] are of my enemy,
    of my persecutor, of my opponent,
Who [has worked?] against me witchcraft, subversion,
    foul disease, assassination, injustice, suppression,
    every sort of evil and machination.
O Shamash, in the presence of your great divinity,
    may their own persons retain the assassination
    they are attempting!

Text: Caplice, OrNS 39 (1970), pl. vi K 2773+.
Edition: Caplice, OrNS 39 (1970), 136, 139 no. 40 lines 35-40.
Literature: Mayer, UFBG, Šamaš 8.

1. The Mesopotamians.
2. Refers to a set of six figurines, male and female, inscribed with names and subsequently buried in a magic ritual (compare III.50f).

(c) AGAINST SNAKES

O Shamash, king of heaven and earth,   (1)
Lord of truth and justice,
Lord of the Anunna-gods, lord of the Igigi-gods,
Whose assent no god can change,
Whose command cannot be transgressed,   (5)
O Shamash, in your hands is revival of the dead,
    loosing of the bound.
O Shamash, I, your servant, so-and-so, son of so-and-so,
Whose (personal) god is Marduk,
    whose (personal) goddess is Sarpanitum,
I come before you,*
    I have seized the hem of your garment.[1]
On account of the evil omen of a snake
    which I saw come right into my house for (its) prey,   (10)
I am afraid, anxious, frightened.
Deliver me from this evil!
Let me proclaim your greatness, let me sing your praises,
Let those who see me sound of you praises forever!

Text: Schollmeyer, *Šamaš* p. 139, VAT 5.
Edition: Schollmeyer, *Šamaš*, 64-66, no. 9.
Translation: von Soden, SAHG, 320-321 no. 55; Seux, *Hymnes*, 364-365.
Literature: Mayer, UFBG, Šamaš 25.
Notes to Text: (9) Copy not clear, but this is what is expected; see also Seux, *Hymnes*, 365 note 4.

1. Gesture of entreaty.

(d) AGAINST DOGS

O Shamash, king of heaven and earth,
    judge of above and below,   (1)
Light of the gods, guide of mankind,*
Who judges the cases of the great gods,
I turn to you, I seek you out.
Command among the gods life (for me),   (5)
May the gods who are with you speak favorably of me.
On account of this dog that has urinated on me,
I am afraid, anxious, frightened.
Deliver me from the evil of this dog,
Let me sound your praises!   (10)

Text: Ebeling, KAR 64, obv 24-33; KAR 221, 8-12; Gurney, STT 64, 11-17; Caplice, OrNS 36 (1967), pl. 1 DT 169.
Edition: Caplice, OrNS 36 (1967), 2-3, 5-6 no. 12 lines 24-33.
Translation: Caplice, SANE 1/1, 21; Seux, *Hymnes*, 363-364.
Literature: Mayer, UFBG, Šamaš 9.
Notes to Text: (2) Variant (perhaps): "the living," see Seux, *Hymnes*, 364 note 3.

(e) AGAINST GHOSTS

O Shamash, noblest of the Anunna-gods,
    most lordly among the Igigi-gods, sublime leader, guide,   (1)
Judge of heaven and earth, not changing in his command,
O Shamash, who controls darkness,
    who provides light for the people,
O Shamash, when you set, the peoples' light is darkened,
O Shamash, when you rise, the four quarters brighten.   (5)
The destitute, widow, waif, female companion,
At your rising, all humanity is warmed.
Beasts, living creatures, animals of the steppe,
Bring(?) you(?) their life(?), their wealth(?).*
You judge the case of the oppressed man and woman,
    you administer their verdicts.   (10)
I, so-and-so, son of so-and-so, exhausted, kneeling,
Who am bound by the anger of a god or goddess,
A ghost, a lurking demon, a spirit, a "wind" spirit,
    goose pimples, dizziness, paralysis(?), vertigo,
Joint pain, irrational behavior, have exacted a toll
    of me and each day have left me (more) stunned.
O Shamash, you are the judge, I bring you my life,   (15)
I kneel for a verdict on the disease that has its hold upon me.
Judge my case, give a verdict for me,
Do not go [ ] to another case.
After you have administered case and verdict,
And my constraint is loosed and flown away from my [body],*   (20)
I will always trust in you.
May the gods bless(?) you,*
May the heavens rejoice on account of you,
May the earth rejoice on account of you.

Text: Köcher, BAM 4 323, obv 19-35; Gray, SRT, pl. XII K 2132.
Edition: Ebeling, *Quellen* I, 43-45.
Translation: von Soden, SAHG, 323-324 no. 57; Seux, *Hymnes*, 426-427.
Literature: Mayer, UFBG, Šamaš 73.
Notes to Text: (9) CAD M/2, 41a; AHw, 629a, 698a. (20) Seux, *Hymnes*, 427 notes 24, 25.
(22) Seux, *Hymnes*, 427 note 26.

(f) AGAINST A CURSE

O Shamash, king of heaven and earth,
    who administers above and below,   (1)
O Shamash, it is in your power to revive the moribund,
    to release the bound.
Incorruptible judge, administrator of the peoples,
Sublime offspring of the lord Brightly Rising God,[1]
Mighty son, splendid one, light of the world,   (5)
You are Shamash, creator of all there is of heaven and earth.
O Shamash, because of a curse which, many days ago,
Has attached itself to my back and cannot be removed,
Expense, loss, and poor health have beset me,
It has reduced my household, livestock, everything.   (10)
It fills me with a relentless distress of disease,
Anxiety and weight loss have beset me,[2]
And so I am afflicted with insomnia day and night,
With digestive troubles and poor health
    I am bringing myself to an end.
I go on, downcast in misery,   (15)
I enfeeble myself with hardship and misery.
When I was young I was an ignoramus,
    I did not understand the crime I committed!
Even as a youngster I had sinned,
I transgressed the boundaries of my (personal) god.
O lord, stand by me, hear my prayer!   (20)
O Shamash, stand by me, hear me!
Because of a curse of disease that besets me and hounds me,
Or a curse of my father or an accursed thing of my mother,
Or a curse of seven generations of my father's house,
Or a curse of my family or relatives,   (25)
Or a curse of my kith or kin,
Or a curse of a dead or living person,
Or a curse of descendants new born or yet to be,

---

1. Namrasit, a name of Sin, the moon god.
2. Variant omits.

Or a curse thing I swore or did not swear,
Or that I swore by father or mother, (30)
Or that I swore by brother or sister,
Or that I swore by friend or comrade,
Or that I swore by watercourse or well,
Or that I swore by weapon or spindle,
Or that I swore falsely by the life of my (personal) god, (35)
Or that I sw[ore] by human, beast,
    or anything whatsoever of wilderness or city,
O Shamash, great lord, command that the curse
    of disease which has a hold on me [be dissolved],
[May] Ea [dissolve] the substitution[1] for me
    which has been made,
May Marduk dis[perse] the stand-ins for me
    which have been produced.

(Text continues with list of demons and describes fashioning of a magic figurine.)

Text: Gray, SRT, pl. IV, S 787+833+303+949 (= Craig, ABRT 2, 3-5); K 8457+8926+2387+6300 (all collated), see Gray, SRT, pl. XX.
Edition: Schollmeyer, *Šamaš*, 96-99 no. 18.
Translation: von Soden, SAHG, 321-323 no. 56; Seux, *Hymnes*, 403-405.
Literature: Mayer, UFBG, Šamaš 78.

1. That is, figurines or other representations of a person fashioned to work black magic against him (compare III.50b).

(g) GOLDEN TIARA OF THE HEAVENS

O great lord who occupies an awe-inspiring
     dais in the pure heavens,   (1)
Golden tiara of the heavens, fittest for kingship,
O Shamash, shepherd of the people, noble god,
Who scrutinizes the land, leader of the people,
Who guides the escapee to the right path,   (5)
O Shamash, judge of heaven and earth,
Who directs the Igi[gi]-gods,
Who grants incense offerings to the great gods,
I, Assurbanipal, son of his (personal) god,
Call upon you in the pure heavens,   (10)
[And] I seek (you) out in your radiant dwelling.
I invoke your name at the great gods' table,
I libate [   ] before you.
Learn(?) my [   ] and direct me.
[Whatever I have done], from my youth [until] my adulthood,   (15)
May it not affect me!
May it be 3600 leagues [dis]tant from my person!
[I], Assurbanipal, your servant,
[Who ever seeks out] the ways of your great divinity,
Cleanse me bright [as] your daylight!   (20)
[Let] me li[ve] in well-being,
Let me proclaim your greatness [with my] mouth,
Let me sound [your pr]aises!

Text: Ebeling, KAR 55.
Edition: Ebeling, AGH, 52-53.
Translation: von Soden, SAHG, 317-318 no. 53; Seux, *Hymnes*, 286-287.
Literature: Mayer, UFBG, Šamaš 2.

(h) PROTECTOR OF THE KING (1)

This prayer was used in the ritual series "House of the Ritual Bath." This was a royal lustration procedure that took place in various bathing chambers of a bath house, during which an officiant pronounced some prayers and the king others. While many of the officiant's were in Sumerian, the king was expected to speak only Akkadian prayers. Each stage was accompanied by elaborate rituals. The basic procedure involved washing off evil from the king and transferring it magically to those believed to be the source of it. In this instance a figurine is splashed with the dirty wash water. One cycle of this series was devoted to Shamash, from which this and the following prayers have been excerpted. For more information on the ritual bath, see Laessøe, *Bît Rimki*, 9-19, 99-102, W. G. Lambert, BiOr 14 (1977), 227, and p. 695 note 3.

(said by the king)

O Shamash, king of heaven and earth, lord of truth and justice, (1)
You are purifier of god and man.
O Shamash, I take my place before you
 in the reed booth of the house of the ritual b[ath],[1]
O Shamash, I do not know who has a hold over me,*
 assuming a woman, here is a figurine (to represent) her.
O Shamash! Since it is made of pure barley,[2]
 which creates mankind, (5)
The figurine is like a (human) shape,
 the head is like a (human) head,
The shape of the body is like the shape of a (human) body.
O Shamash! This is the figurine of the witch
 (who is doing the) sorcery, who has harassed me,
 who is making the attempt against me,
Who has said to a sorceress, "Bewitch!"
 who has said to a harasser "Harass!"
 who has incited another, (10)
Who has made me eat (bewitched) bread,
 who has made me drink (bewitched) beer,

1. Variant: "so-and-so, son of so-and-so, be[fore you]."
2. The figurine is made of a grain paste.

Who has made me wash in (bewitched) water,
> who has made me anoint with (bewitched) oil,

Who has made me eat (bewitched) food:

Because of whatever she made me eat,
> because of whatever she made me drink,

Because of whatever she made me wash with,
> because of whatever she made me anoint with,
> or dispatched against me,   (15)

Because she pronounced my name with evil intent,
> interred symbols of me,

Made figurines of me and took my measurements,

Collected dust grains from my footprints, took up my spittle,

Plucked out a lock of hair, cut off a piece of my clothing,
> snooped for something bad about me,

Because she has made accusations against me,
> hampered me, seized me, polluted me,   (20)

Has made me full of stiffness and debility,

Has seized my heart, has turned the heart <of my god> against me,*

Has twisted my muscles, weakened my strength,

Has overthrown my arms, hobbled my feet,

Has set upon me discord, ill temper,
> misery, anxiety, panic,   (25)

Terror, cursing, fear, worry, loss of sleep, speechlessness, depression,

Misery,[1] dissatisfaction, illness,

Has cast "dog tongue"[2] between us,

O Shamash, this is she, here is her figurine!

Even though she is not here, her figurine is here!   (30)

I wash the water off upon her,
> whatever is known to me of her or not known,

I pollute her with it, let her receive it from me.

She has worked against me furtively,
> but I wash myself off on her openly* before you.

Through the greatness of Ea and the procedures of Asalluhi, (35)

Through the command of Marduk and Sarpanitum,

---

1. Variant omits.
2. Meaning unknown, perhaps expression for "bad blood."

Through the command of Nabu and Tashmetum,[1]
I wash myself off upon her, I bathe myself off upon her.
Just as the water is cleared from my body
    and goes upon her and her form,
So do I cast off upon her wrong and bondage!
May all evil in my person, flesh, and sinews   (40)
Be cleared like the water from my body
    and go against her and against her form!
O Shamash, her own wicked intents and actions
    turn against her and her form.
On account of the evil of signs and [bad, unfavorable] portents
    which are [present] in my palace [and in my land],[2]
O Shamash, may my sorceress fall and may I rise,
May she be hamstrung but I proceed,   (45)
May she be polluted but I become pure,
May she die but I live!
O Shamash, let me proceed straight on my way,
    according to your judgment.
O Shamash, since I did not work against her
    — it was she who worked against me —
O Shamash, since I did not harass her
    — it was she who harassed me —   (50)
I have washed myself off upon her,
    I have bathed myself in water upon her,
I have polluted her, may she receive it from me!
Just as the water is cleared from my body and goes to this (figurine),
May all evil in my person, my flesh, my sinews
Be cleared from my body and leave my body.   (55)

Text: Laessøe, *Bît Rimki*, pl. 1 no. 1-3; pl. II, no. 4; Lutz, PBS 1/2, 129; Finkelstein, STT 76, 77.
Edition: Laessøe, *Bît Rimki*, 37-47.
Translation: Seux, *Hymnes*, 388-392.
Literature: Mayer, UFBG, Šamaš 41.
Notes to Text: (4) W. G. Lambert, BiOr 14 (1977), 229; Borger, AfO 18 (1957), 139.
(22) Reiner, JNES 17 (1958), 207. (34) Variant obscure.

1. Variant omits.
2. Variant omits.

(i) PROTECTOR OF THE KING (2)

Bilingual incantation prayer from a royal lustration ritual, see III.50h.

(To be spoken by the exorcist)

O Shamash, when you come forth from the great mountain,   (1)
When you come forth from the great mountain,
    the mountain of the deep,
When you come forth from the holy hill
    where destinies are ordained,
When you [come forth] from the back of heaven
    to the junction point of heaven and earth,
The great gods attend upon you for judgment,   (5)
The Anunna-gods attend upon you to render verdicts.
Mankind, including (all) peoples, await your command,
Livestock, wildlife, all four-footed creatures,
Fix their eyes upon your great light.
O Shamash, you are greatest of sages
    and your own (best) counsellor,   (10)
O Shamash, you are greatest of leaders,
    judge of heaven and earth.
Whatever is (secret) in the heart is spoken out [before you?],
All people's passing thoughts speak (as if aloud) to you.[1]
You strike down instantly the party in the wrong,   (15)
You single out truth and justice.
The oppressed and maltreated,
The one trapped inadvertently in an oath,
The one who encountered the unforeseen,
The one in the grip of contagion,
The one held hostage by a fiend,   (20)
The one beset by a malignant phantom,
The one smothered in his bed by a malignant apparition,
The one flung down by a malignant shade,
The one slain by a huge spectre,

---

1. *ziqīqu*, a disembodied spirit that can express a person's motivation or will, here apparently referring to unspoken thoughts.

The one whose limbs a malignant god twisted,   (25)
The one whose hair a malignant lurking demon stood on end,
The one taken by a Lamashtu,
The one flung down by a paralyzing demon,
The one made feverish by a snatching demon,
The one wedded by a female ghost,   (30)
The young man frustrated by a female ghost,
The one thwarted by a bad sign,
The one bound by a curse,
The one despised by a mouth of malice,
The one cursed by a tongue of malice,   (35)
The one glowered at balefully by an eye of malice,
The one bound by witchcraft,
The target of machination,
Shamash, you have the power to revive (all of) them.
You resolve conflicting testimony as if it were one.   (40)
I (the exorcist) am the messenger of Ea,
He sent me to revive th(is) troubled man,
I repeat to [you] Ea's commission,
"Ren[der] a verdict for the king, son of his god,
"Ban[ish] the foul sickness from his body,   (45)
"[Pour out] pure water, clean water, clear water upon him.
"When [he bathes] the image of his substitute in the bath water,
"When the water [flows] from its body,
"May the malignant phantom, malignant apparition,
        malignant shade, malignant spectre, malignant god,
        malignant lurking demon,
"Lamashtu, paralyzing demon, snatching demon,   (50)
"Male ghost, female ghost,
"Contagion, fiend, foul sickness,[1]
"(All) flow like water from the body of the king,
        son of his (personal) god, and [quit?] his person!"
O Shamash, whose mightily (given) command
        cannot be ch[anged],

---

1. Variant adds: "bad signs, curse, mouth of malice, tongue of malice, lips of malice, enchant-ment, witchcraft, magic, machination" (Borger, JCS 21 [1967], 6 "Einschub C").

This day let his wrong be dissolved.   (55)
May the tongue of malice be deflected,
May the king's god proclaim your greatness!
May the king [sound] your praises,
And I too, the exorcist, your servant, will render you homage.

(to be spoken by the king)

O Shamash, judge of heaven and earth,
    lord of above and below,
Light of the gods, guide of living things,[1]
Who sets free the captive, who revives the moribund,
Who averts the evil of [   ],
Who dispels darkness and brings illumination,   (90)
I, so-and-so, son of so-and-so, your servant, turn to you,
    seek you.
Stand in judgment upon my case this day,
Illumine my darkness, clear up my confusion,
    set right my uncertainties!
Save me from bad signs and portents, from magic circles,   (95)
    or any human agency which may block my progress,
Release my bond, give me life, for I am afraid, anxious,
    terrified of the evil (consequences of) bad signs
    and portents which are present in my house.
Avert from me the evil (consequences) of the signs
    and portents, lest I die or come to harm.   (100)
May this evil not approach me, may it not draw near me,
[May it not reach me, may it not catch up with me],[2]
[May it cr]oss river, may it go beyond mountain,
[May it be 3600 leagues distant from my person],
May it mount to the skies [like smoke],
[Like an uprooted tamarisk], may it not return where it was!
[Let me proclaim your greatness], let me sound your praises!   (105)

1. Variant: "mankind" (Borger, JCS 21 [1967], 9).
2. Variant may have ended here; for the presumed restorations of the longer version, I follow
Seux (*Hymnes*, 358 note 6), differently Borger (JCS 21 [1967], 10); see III.37d lines 27ff.

Text: Ebeling-Köcher-Rost, LKA 75; Gray, SRT, pl. XII Sm 166+; XIII (K 4922) + Borger, JCS 21 (1967), 16 (K 4977+), K 4830+; XV (K 4654+), K 3462, K 5069+; XVI (K 5069+), K 3138+; XVII (K 4986+) + Borger, JCS 21 (1967), K 4998, K 4610+, K 5135+; Haupt, ASKT 7; Pinches, V R 50-51 + Borger, JCS 21 (1967), 16 (K 5196); see further Borger, ZA 61 (1971), 84-88.

Edition: Borger, JCS 21 (1967), 2-7, 9-10 (lines 1-59, 86-101).

Translation: Seux, *Hymnes*, 357-358 (= 86-101).

Literature: Mayer, UFBG, Šamaš 42 (= portion to be spoken by king).

(j) PROTECTOR OF THE KING (3)

From a royal lustration ritual (see III.50h), this prayer stresses the centrality of
the sun for the gods and creatures of the universe, especially the Mesopotamians
("black-headed folk").

(bilingual, to be spoken by the exorcist)

O great lord, when you come forth from the pure heavens,   (1)
O warrior Shamash, young hero,
    when you come forth from the pure heavens,
When you raise the latch pin
    from the lock of the pure heavens,
When you free the bolt of the pure heavens,
When you open the great door of the pure heavens,   (5)
When you cross the sublime boo[ths] of the pure heavens,
Anu and Enlil greet you with joy,
[Ea] and Belet-ili stand happily in attendance upon you,
[Asalluhi] stands in attendance upon you each day
    to calm your feelings,
The great [gods of the] sanctuaries of all lands
    pay close heed to you,   (10)
[The Anunna-gods?] of the high daises of heaven and earth
    stand in attendance upon you.
[You ordain their destinies], you render verdicts for them,
[You look upon the beasts of the] steppe
    [who live on grain and water].
You make the [black-he]aded folk have [truth and justice],
You set right [the oppressed and maltreated],   (15)
You look on [the numerous gods and men].
[O Shamash, sublime judge,   ] night and day,
You [absolve] sin, you remove wr[ong-doing].
Freeing the captive and reviving the sick are in your power.
A man's (personal) god stands in attendance upon you
    for his devotee's sake.   (20)
The lord sent me, the great lord (Ea) sent me,
Stand by, learn what he said, render his verdict!

As for you, when you come,
    you set right the black-headed folk.
Establish for him (the king) protective splendor,
    let his illness be set right. (25)
Th(is) man, son of his (personal) god, has sinned
    and has been punished,
His members are painfully diseased, he lies painfully in disease.
O Shamash, heed my prayer!
Eat his food (offering), accept his sacrifice,
    set his (personal) god at his side.
At your order, may his offense be dissolved,
    his wrong-doing removed, (30)
May he be released from his bondage,
    may he revive from his illness,
Let this king live!
As long as he lives, let him proclaim your greatness,
Let the king sound your praises!
And I, the exorcist, your servant, let me sound your praises! (35)

Text: Pinches, IV R² 17, obv 1-rev 6; Gray, SRT, pl. XIII Bu 91-5-9, 180; BM 99077+99257 (Sumerian only) (all collated).
Edition: Langdon, OECT 6, 45-48.
Translation: Seux, *Hymnes*, 226-229.

(k) PROTECTOR OF THE KING (4)

From a royal lustration ritual, see III.50h.

(to be spoken by the king)

I call upon you, Shamash, in the pure heavens,   (1)
Take your seat in the shade of cedar,
Let your feet be set on a platform* of juniper.
The lands rejoice over you, the humming (world) exults over you,
All peoples behold your brilliant light!   (5)
Your net embraces all lands,
O Shamash, you are the one who understands their arrangements.
O destroyer of the wicked,
        implementer of preventive rituals
(Against) bad signs and portents, terrifying nightmares,
O cutter of the magic knot that can destroy people and land,   (10)
I have drawn before you the worker
        of witchcraft, magic, and sorcery,
I have made figurines of them in pure flour.
Those who worked magic against me, plotted treachery,
Their hearts are perverted and full of malice.
Stand by me, Shamash, light of the great gods,   (15)
Let me be the one to prevail
        over the one working magic against me,
Let my (personal) god, who created me, sta[nd] by my side.
My mouth is washed, my hands are set right,
Set me right, lord, light of the universe, Shamash the judge!
May day, month, year, [seventh], fifteenth, [twentieth],
        and thirtieth day undo their plots.   (20)
[May   ] dissolve the sorcery.*
[Accept my entreaty], dissolve my bondage,
[Let me, your servant], sound [your praises]!

Text: Pinches, IV R² 17, rev 8-30.
Edition: Langdon, OECT 6, 48-49.
Translation: von Soden, SAHG, 324-325 no. 58; Seux, *Hymnes*, 392-394.
Literature: Mayer, UFBG, Šamaš 43.
Notes to Text: (3) Seux, *Hymnes*, 393 note 3. (20f.) Mayer, OrNS 46 (1977), 390.

(l) PROTECTOR OF THE KING (5)

This prayer is attested with the royal "washing-of-the-mouth" ritual (p. 695 note 2), a purification procedure somewhat similar to the "ritual bath" (see III.50h), used as well as for apotropaic and medical purposes.

O most great, perfect, son of the Brightly Rising God,[1]   (1)
Perpetually renewing light, beacon of the people,
    discloser of light,[2]
O Shamash, who administers dead and living,
    who scrutinizes all there is,
O Shamash, light of heaven[3] and earth,
    splendor of the world,
O lord of Sippar, protection of the Ebabbar,[4]   (5)
Twin of Marduk, Babylon's trust,
The peoples heed your light,[5]
The Igigi-gods await your command,[6]
The numerous black-headed folk[7] praise your valor.
You provide a comrade for the lonely man,   (10)
You give an heir to the impotent,
You open wide the fast doorbolts of heaven,
You provide light for the one who cannot see.
You can read the cased tablet that has not been opened,
You inscribe omens in sheep, you provide a verdict.[8]   (15)
O judge of the gods, lord of the Igigi-gods,
O Shamash, you are master of the land's destiny,[9]
Ordain my destiny, make my course a propitious one!
May my signs be favorable,
May my dreams be propitious,

1. Namrasit, a name of Sin, the moon god.
2. That is, to those bereft of light, such as the sick.
3. Variant: "of the gods."
4. Temple of Shamash at Sippar.
5. Variant omits.
6. Variant: "heed."
7. Variant: "god and king, the black-headed folk" (Mesopotamians).
8. Variant omits.
9. Variants list specific prognostications here (e.g., rodents) or rearrange lines.

Make the dream I had[1] a propitious one for me,   (20)

Let me proceed in favor and acquire a comrade.[2]

May there be good fortune in my days,

Grant me a good repute!

May my speech be acceptable in public,[3]

May I pass my days in pleasure and joy,   (25)

May truth stand at my right,

May justice stand at my left,

May a safeguarding god go ever at my side,

May a watcher of well-being never cease to be behind me.

May Bunene, the courier,

    speak to you a favorable word (of me),   (30)

May Aya, your beloved wife, say, "Peace upon you!"[4]

O Shamash, you are foremost of the gods, have pity![5]

May the heavens rejoice because of you,

    may the earth rejoice because of you,

May the gods of the universe bless you,

May the great gods content your heart.[6]

Text: King, BMS 6, 97-130; Loretz-Mayer, AOAT 34 23; Myhrman, PBS 1/1 12; Langdon, OECT 6 pl. XXX, K 2854+K 17249 (not used); Gurney, STT 60, 61, 122; von Weiher, SBTU II 18; abbreviated version King, BMS 10, 7-25.
Edition: Mayer, UFBG, 503-510.
Translation: von Soden, SAHG, 318-320 no. 54; Seux, *Hymnes*, 283-286.
Literature: Mayer, UFBG, Šamaš 1.

1. Variant: "will have."

2. Variant: "comrades" = protective spirit(s)?

3. Literally: "in the street"; variant adds, "May god and king es[te]em me, May nobleman and prince do what I say."

4. Variant omits.

5. Variant adds: "May a god content your heart ..."

6. Variant replaces this and preceding with "May Anu, Enlil, and Ea grant [   ]."

(m) ABSOLVER

O Shamash, you are supreme judge of the great gods,   (1)
Whether, as I walked through a street,
        an accursed man touched me,
Or, when I crossed a square, I stepped in a puddle of wash water,
Or, I walked over nail pairings, shavings from an armpit,
A worn-out shoe, a broken belt, a leather sack
        (holding things) for black magic, a leper's scales,   (5)
(Any)thing unlucky for mankind,
Let it be released for me, let it be dissolved for me!
O Shamash, if in your view I have been neglectful this day,
If I sinned or erred or committed a crime,
Let it be released for me, let it be dissolved for me!   (10)
Through all my misdeeds, all my sins, all my crimes,
May the one who does not revere his (personal) god
        or his (personal) goddess learn from my example,
One who was neglectful of his (personal) god or of his (personal)
        goddess, who sinned, erred, committed a crime.
I gave my word then changed (it),
        I was trusted but did not deliver,
I did unseemly deeds, harmful speech was in my mouth,   (15)
I repeated what should not have been told.
I am an ox who does not recognize his forage,
I am the water of a watercourse that knows not where it runs.
The misdeeds and crimes of mankind outnumber
        the hairs of their heads!
My misdeeds, sins, and crimes, that are heaped up like chaff,
        I have trampled them,   (20)
Let them be released for me, let them be dissolved for me!

(fragmentary lines)

Text: K 3059+ = Reiner, JNES 15 (1956), 142-143 (transliteration only); Ebeling, KAR 295
"1. Seite"; Finkelstein, STT 75, 26'-41'.
Edition: Reiner, JNES 15 (1956), 142-143, lines 40'-58'.
Translation: Seux, *Hymnes*, 409-410.
Literature: Compare also IV.46b, extracted from the same group.

(n) THE SUPREMACY OF SHAMASH

This text glorifies Shamash as the central creative power of the universe. Sin the moon god, great as he may be, must take a secondary position.

i (= a 'rev', b 'rev' 1-17)

Without Shamash, king of heaven and earth,
 jud[ge] of the upper and lower regions,   (1)
Who renders verdicts, the young king Shamash,
Anu and Enlil would convoke no assembly in heaven,
Nor would they take counsel concerning the land.
They would produce no harvest in summer,
 nor in [win]ter dew, fog, and ice.   (5)
Pasturage, waterholes, grass, ear, or green plants,
[Vege]tation, subsistence for the beasts of the lands,
Without Shamash none would be granted!

Sin, chief god of heaven, great son of Enlil,
Sin, principal(?) light of heaven and earth,   (10)
Who goes out before[1] the gods his brethren,
 prince whose command is [un]alterable,
The radiant god, splendid, noble [ ],
[Who determines] how many days (make) a month, a year,

(gap)

(fragmentary lines)

The gods convene when Sin appears,
Kings, bringing their pure offerings, prostrate themselves,
Whether to settle lands or to abandon them,
Whether to make them hostile to one another
 or war on one another:
They heed[2] Sin, the very luminary.   (10')
Without Sin and Shamash,

---

1. Reference to precedence of Sin, perhaps referring to the appearance of the moon at night before the stars.
2. Both an allusion to the crescent moon and to Sin's divinity.

No other god in heaven will give an affirmative reply.[1]
Without Shamash, Sin does not ...[2] in heaven,
Scepter, crown, throne, staff(?), where would they be?
They are not granted to king or his land without Shamash!   (15′)

Without Shamash, king of heaven and earth,

(large gap = col ii, iii)

iv (= a 'obv', b 'obv')

(Without Shamash ...)
Shakkan, the son(?) whom you love,   (1′)
The pure herdsman, the leader for Anu,
Who carries the staff of office before his body,
Lord of headpiece, garment, and cloak,
Who carries a sublime staff, who is clad in a robe,   (5′)
Who covers the nakedness*[3] of the world,
No garment of rank* nor royal attire,
No splendid crown, symbol of lordship,
Brings he, whatsoever, to king or to his land,
Without Shamash, none is granted.   (10′)

Without Shamash, king of heaven and earth,
Latarak,[4] king of the steppe,
Who is supreme among the beasts,
Who overcomes cattle, sheep, wild beasts, and men,
Could not bring on his punishment,   (15′)
Nor without Shamash [ ] would ...*
The wild creatures fall into no pit ...

(a breaks off, b ends excerpt)

1. Reference to divination.
2. Verb broken, but the passage is evidently intended to subordinate the moon to the sun.
3. That is, wool and leather provide clothing for the human race.
4. Disease demon.

Text: (a) Ebeling, KAR 19 (archaizing script); (b) Ehelolf, KBo 1 12 (excerpt tablet).

Edition: Ebeling, OrNS 23 (1954), 209-216.

Translation: Seux, *Hymnes,* 66-70, whose ordering of the text I follow.

Notes to Text: (i 10) Beginning of line problematic. von Soden, AHw, 989b derives *rīšu* from *ri'āšum*; though *rēšu* "head" (for *rēštu*?) might be preferable on the basis of the parallelism. (iv 6′) CAD B, 352a reads *būl ṣēri* "who clothes the beasts of the steppe." (iv 7′) Seux, *Hymnes,* 69 note 34. (iv 16′) b adds "Shakkan" here, perhaps a misunderstanding of ANŠE?

(o) HEALER

The following address to Shamash is part of an elaborate ritual against a variety of afflictions, including impotence, death of a spouse, and black magic of all types. It describes the sun's importance to the gods and the human race, especially the Mesopotamians ("black-headed folk").

[O Sham]ash, pure lord, who administers heaven and earth,
    O Shamash the judge,   (1)
[O Shamash, l]ight of above and below,
    who brings about renewal,
[ ] Shamash, pure lord, who administers heaven and earth,
    divine jud[ge],
[O Shamash], light of above and below,
    who brings about renewal,
O magnificent [or]b, who knows all and whose [ ] is final,   (5)
[O Shamash, c]reator of all there is, who makes all omens
    appropriate and understandable,
[Who defines] time spans, who illumines all world regions
    and mountains,
[O Shamash], yours is power to revive the dead,
    to release the captive,
[O Shamash], the human race cannot continue without you,
[Nor without you] can the decisions of heaven
    and netherworld be made.   (10)
[Without you] the gods of the universe smell no incense,
[Without you] the (netherworld) Anunna-gods accept
    no funerary offering,
[Without you] no case is judged in the land, no decision is
    made in the land.
[Without you] the dream interpreter
    performs no rite for the king,
[Without you the exorcist] cannot he[lp] the sick man,   (15)
[Without you Anu gives] no scepter, diadem,
    or st[aff?]* to the king.
[Beloved of En]lil, leader of huma[nkind],*
[Faithful shepherd] of the black-hea[ded] folk,

(one line lost)

[O Shamash, w]ithout you the [sick man cannot surviv]e,   (20)
[O Shamash, y]ou are the shepherd of all [numerous] mankind!
[I, so-and-so, son] of so-and-so, call upon you,
    exhausted, des[perate, sleepless].
[... affliction] has beset me, I knee[l before you].
[Lo]ss, des[truction], and ev[il against my spouse],
[And] my wives, my sons and daughters [have fastened]
    upon me and relentlessly cru[sh me].   (25)
[O Shamash],★ yours is power to save, spare, and res[cue],
As you are generous, [spa]re life!
As you are wont to look with [radiant] features,
    let [the lord of lords]★ so look upon me!
O lord, let me see [your light], let me warm myself
    in the [warmth] of your [rays].★
Let me praise your divinity [to] gods and goddesses,   (30)
L[et me proclaim] your [val]or [to all] the human race.
[Let me si]ng [your glorification, let me] sound your praises,
[And let] the ... [your servant], exalt your valor!★
[O Shamash, as you are foremost of the gods], have pity!
[Make my evil go] beyond mountain and cross river,★
    drive it 3600 leagues distant from my person.   (35)
[May it mount to the skies] like sm[oke],
    like an uprooted tamarisk, may it not return where it was.
May the tamarisk cleanse me,
    [may the tragacanth?] release me,
May the <earth>★ give me its splendor,
    may it take away [my aff]liction.
May the south wind blow towards me,
    but the evil [   ] not blow,
May the north wind blow towards me,
    but the evil [   ] not blow,   (40)
May the east wind blow towards me,
    but the evil [   ] not blow,
May the west wind blow towards me,
    but the evil [   ] not blow!
According to your august command which cannot be ch[anged],

And your eternal assent which cannot be altered,
May I, so-and-so, son of so-and-so, live in well-being,
Let me praise your greatness, [let me sound] your [praises]!

Text: Campbell Thompson, AMT 71-72/1, obv 27 - rev 24.
Edition: Ebeling, ZA 51 (1955), 170-179, obv lines 27-44, rev lines 1-24; most of the restorations used here are from him.
Notes to Text: (16) Seux, *Hymnes*, 455 note 11. (17) Ebeling, ZA 51 (1955), 172, 177. (26) Seux, *Hymnes*, 456. (28) Text: EN.E[N.MEŠ]: "the lords(?)." (29, 33) Mayer, OrNS 46 (1977), 392. (34) Text uncertain here, though the expressions are well known; see III.37d. (38) Seux, *Hymnes*, 457 note 32.

(p) AGAINST THE CONSEQUENCES OF A NIGHTMARE

You have burst into light, Shamash,   (1)
    from the Mountain of Cedars,
The gods rejoice on account of you,
    mankind is glad on account of you.
The diviner brings you cedar, the widow a flour offering,
The poor woman oil, the rich man a lamb from his wealth.
I bring you a lump of earth, product of the depths.   (5)
You, lump, product of the depths,
Part of me is pinched off in you,
Part of you is pinched off in me.
My clay is mixed with your clay,
Your clay is mixed with my clay.
Just as you, lump, dissolve and disappear
    when I throw you into water to dissipate you,   (10)
So may the evil [portended by the dream] I had last night,
Which I had of a god, which I had of a king,
    which I had of a noble, which I had of a prince,
    which I had of a dead man, which I had of a living man,
Which I went around ... right ... left,
May it, like you, fall into water to dissipate,
Dissolve, and disappear!
Sheep of the storm, slaughtered with a knife of the wind,   (15)
The dead eat it and drink it, it is nothing but wind!
Just as the instep of the foot does not come near the heel,
May the evil (portended) by the dream I had during the night
    not approach me nor come near me!

Text: Oppenheim, *Dreams*, pl. II, K 3333; Gray, SRT, pl. III K 3286 obv; Ebeling, KAR 252, rev ii 20-36.
Edition: None.
Translation: Oppenheim, *Dreams*, 301; Seux, *Hymnes*, 369-371.

(q) HOMECOMING

This little bilingual prayer, designated to be used at sunset, portrays the sun coming home to his abode, Ebabbar, at the end of the day. His gates hail him, his advisor escorts him inside, his wife meets him happily, and he has his evening meal.

> O Shamash, when you enter innermost heaven,   (1)
> May the pure bolt of heaven greet you,
> May the door of heaven salute you.
> May Justice, your beloved vizier, bring you straight in.[1]
> Show your splendor to the Ebabbar, your lordly dwelling.   (5)
> May Aya, your beloved wife, meet you happily,
> May she make you relax,
> May your godly meal be set before you.
> O youthful warrior Shamash, let them ever praise you.[2]
> O lord of Ebabbar, go straight on your path,   (10)
> Make straight your way, go the true course to your dwelling.
> O Shamash, you are judge of the land, administrator of its verdicts.

Text: Bertin, RA 1 (1886), 157-161; Abel-Winckler, *Keilschrifttexte zum Gebrauch bei Vorlesungen* (Berlin, 1890), 59-60.
Edition: Langdon, OECT 6, 11-12, 101.
Translation: Falkenstein, SAHG, 221 no. 42; Seux, *Hymnes*, 215-216.
Literature: Heimpel, JCS 38 (1986), 129-130.

1. Wordplay in the original, justice and straightness having the same root.
2. Sumerian adds: "with one voice."

III.51 TO SHAMASH AND ADAD

The following group of diviner's prayers are addressed to the principal deities of divination. They form part of a procedure in which ritual acts and prayers are interspersed. They are translated here as prose, though they are arranged in poetic form in the original manuscripts.

(a) THE CLEANSING WATER

O Shamash, lord of judgment, O Adad, lord of divination, cleanse yourselves! O Shamash, lord of judgment, O Adad, lord of divination, [here are brought you] pure water of the Amanus, sprigs from the mounts of apples(?) and cedar, fruit of cedar, cypress, alum, juniper, reed, and incense from the abode of [Irnina?]. The "pure mountains," the "children of Anu,"[1] are set up for you and fully purified, their [   ] are provided. Stand by me, O Shamash and Adad! In whatever I ask your blessing on, in what I [say] or pray, in whatsoever I do, in the inquiry I ask your blessing on, let there be truth!

Text: Zimmern, BBR, pl. LXII no. 75, 5-10.
Edition: Zimmern, BBR, 190-191.
Translation: Seux, *Hymnes*, 471-472.

1. Types of offerings.

(b) LIGHTING THE INCENSE

O Shamash, lord of judgment, O Adad, lord of divination, I burn for you pure cedar incense, branches, sprigs, sweet sap, bunches of pure cedar, beloved of the great gods. I burn thick cedar as befits your great divinity. May the cedar linger, may it invite the great gods to render a verdict for me. Take your places and render a verdict! O Shamash and Adad, stand by me! In what I say or pray, in whatsoever I do, in the inquiry I ask your blessing on, let there be truth!

Text: Zimmern, BBR, pl. LXIII no. 75, 56–61; pl. LXIV no. 78, 56–61.
Edition: Zimmern, BBR, 192–193.
Translation: von Soden, SAHG, 278 no. 23a; Labat, *Religions*, 278; Seux, *Hymnes*, 472–473.

(c) PLACING THE FLOUR OFFERING

[O Shamash, lord of judgment], O Adad, lord of divination, accept (this)![1] O Shamash and Adad, who dwell in the pure heavens, O Shamash and Adad, may your great divinity accept (this)! O Shamash and [Ad]ad, accept this, accept the meal of all the great gods! O Anu, Enlil, Ea, Sin, Shamash, Belet-seri, Ninurta, accept this! In what I say and pray, in whatsoever I do, in the inquiry I ask your blessing on, let there be truth!

Text: Zimmern, BBR, pl. LXIV no. 78, rev 69–74.
Edition: Zimmern, BBR, 194–195.
Translation: von Soden, SAHG, 279 no. 23c; Seux, *Hymnes*, 470–471.

1. Refers to flour the diviner is placing on the incense stand.

(d) THE SACRIFICIAL GAZELLE

This prayer is notable for its lyrical portrayal of the growth of a young gazelle in the wilderness. It forms part of a group of diviner's prayers arranged for the offering of specific animals.

> O Shamash, lord of judgment, O Adad, lord of divination, I bring and ask your blessing upon a pure fawn, offspring of a gazelle, whose eyes are bright-hued, whose features are radiant(?), a pure, tawny sacrificial animal, offspring of a gazelle, whose mother bore him in the steppe, and the steppe set its kind protection over him. The steppe raised him like a father, and the pasture like a mother. When the warrior Adad saw him, he would rain abundance(?)* upon him in the earth's close: grass grew up, he would rejoice in (its) fullness, the ... of the livestock would sprout luxuriantly. He would eat grass in the steppe; never would he want for water to drink at pure pools. He would feed on the ...-plants and then return (to his haunts). He who never knew a herdsman [   ] in the steppe, from whom the lamb was kept away, I ask your blessing (upon him as my offering). O Shamash and Adad, stand by me! In what I say and pray, [in whatsoever I d]o, in the inquiry I ask your blessing on, let there b[e] truth!

Text: Craig, ABRT 1 60-62, obv 12-22 (see 2, x).
Edition: Zimmern, BBR, 214-217 (with collations).
Translation: von Soden, SAHG, 278 no. 23b; Labat, *Religions*, 277-278; Seux, *Hymnes*, 473-474.

(e) THE SACRIFICIAL LAMB

[O Shamash, lord of judgment, O Ada]d, lord of divination, I bring and ask your blessing upon (this) yearling [lamb] which no ram has mounted, into which [no] beast's seed has fallen. It ate grass on the plains, it always drank water from pure pools, the male lamb was kept away from it. I ask your blessing upon (this) lamb, I set in this lamb's mouth pure cedar in bunches, sprigs, and sweet sap. O Shamash and Adad, stand by me in this lamb (offering). In what I say and pray, in whatsoever I do, in the inquiry I ask your blessing on, let there be truth!

Text: Craig, ABRT 1 61-62, obv 10-17.
Edition: Zimmern, BKBR, 216-217.
Translation: Labat, *Religions*, 277; Seux, *Hymnes*, 474-475.

III.52 TO SIN

(a) FOR HELP IN HARUSPICY

This prayer to the moon god is one of many for the use of diviners preparing at night to examine the livers and entrails of animals to be slaughtered for divinatory purposes. It glorifies the beauty and majesty of the moon, seeking his help in the rite to follow.

O Sin, shining, radiant god, luminary of [heaven],
    eldest son of Enlil, [foremost one] of Ekur,   (1)
You reign as king of the uni[verse],
    you s[et] your throne [in] the [shining] heavens,
You set out a superb linen, you [don] the resplendent tiara
    of lordship whose waxing never fails!
O noble Sin, whose light goes be[fore] the people,
    resplendent prince
Whose command is never cha[nged],
    whose intents no god can know!   (5)
O Sin, at your appearance the gods convene,
    all sovereigns do obeisance,
O luminary Sin, [   ],
    you come out amidst shining carnelian and lapis.
At sight of Sin, the stars are jubilant, the night rejoices.
Sin takes his place in the center of the shi[ning] heaven,
    Sin, the cherished eldest son, belo[ved] offspring.
Solicitous prince, eldest son of Enlil, foremost [ ],   (10)
Luminary of the skies, lord of all lands
    whose [head?] is h[igh?] in Ekur,
Whose word is assented to in Eridu [   ],
You founded Ur on a [ ] dais
    [and raised its] head(?) [on high],*
O Sin, luminary of heaven, protection
    of [the inhabited world?], shining god [   ],
Foremost one, Sin, you [open] the gates of heaven
    when you appear.   (15)

At your appearance, the peoples rejoice,
    all the black-headed folk[1] [are joyful],*
The peoples pray to you, all humankind convenes before you.
Sheep, goats, and cattle, creatures of the steppe
    all convene before [you].
Sin has come forth, lord of crescent and halo,
    who administers pasture and drink[ing place],*
Stand by me, Sin, in the midst* of shining heaven,
    may the [great] gods stand by.   (20)
May the divine judges stand by with you,
    the ... [ ] stand by,
May Alammush your vizier inform you,
    bring the case before you,
May he set the diviner's qu[ery] before you.
    O Sin, shining god, [stand by me] in this offering!
In what I say or pray, in whatsoever I do, in the inquiry
    I ask your blessing on, let there be truth!

Text: K 3794 + Ki 1904-10-9,157 = Perry, *Sin*, pl. I K 3794 (17ff. =1-13 of this translation) + Langdon, RA 12 (1915), 190 (= 13-24 of this translation); K 2792+7973+9242+10011+13785 = Perry, *Sin*, pl. II (ii 13ff. = 1-16 of this translation), all mss. collated.
Edition: Perry, *Sin*, 23-24 + Langdon, RA 12 (1915), 191-192.
Translation: Seux, *Hymnes*, 478-480.
Notes to Text: (13) *pa-rak-*[*kí*]. The AR.KI copied by Langdon at the top of his plate are not clear on the tablet; perhaps ʼ*ri-ší*ʼ. (16) Seux, *Hymnes*, 479 note 20. (19) Seux, *Hymnes*, 479 note 23. (20) Seux, *Hymnes*, 479 note 24.

1. The Mesopotamians.

(b) ILLUMINATOR OF DARKNESS

O Sin, luminous and splendid one, foremost of the gods,   (1)
O perpetually renewing Sin, illuminator of darkness,
Provider of illumination to the teeming peoples,
Your brilliance is released to the black-headed folk.[1]
Your rising illumines the p[ure?] heavens,   (5)
Your torch[2] is magnificent, your ra[diance?] is like fire.
The vast earth is filled with your luminosity,
The people proud(ly) vie to see you.
O Anu of the heavens, whose counsel no one can learn,
Your rising is superb, [your] offspring is like the sun.   (10)
The great gods kneel before you,
    the verdict(s) of the world are placed before you.[3]
The great gods inquire of you and you give advice,[4]
They sit in assembly, they debate at your feet.   (15)
O Sin, splendid one of the Ekur, they inquire of you
    and you give (reply) to the gods' inquiry.
Your day of disappearance is your day of splendor,
    a secret of the great gods.
The thirtieth day is your festival,
    day of your divinity's splendor.
O Brightly Rising God,[5] strength without rival,
    one can learn,[6]
I make for you a pure night offering,
    I libate for you the finest sweet beer.[7]   (20)
I take my place on my knees, as I seek you(r attention),
Grant me a favorable and just repute.
My (personal) god and <my> (personal) goddess,
    who have been angry with me for many days,

1. The Mesopotamians.
2. Variant: "rising."
3. Variant inserts prayer to avert the evil portended by an eclipse; see p. 546 note 2.
4. Variant adds seven different lines, mostly fragmentary.
5. Namrasit, a name for Sin.
6. Variant adds here a royal name, with "your servant."
7. Variant adds: "With the holy ... I invoke your name and call upon you, my lord, in the pure heavens."

May they be reconciled with me in truth and justice.

May my path be propitious, my way straight. (25)

I have commissioned Anzagar, god of dreams,

Let him absolve my wrong in a dream.

Let me hear my punishment, that I may be cleansed,*

Let me sound your praises forever!

Text: King, BMS 1, 1-27; Loretz-Mayer, AOAT 34 1; Finkelstein, STT 56, 19-37; Ebeling-Köcher-Rost, LKA 39; Langdon, PSBA 40 (1918), pl. VII; Scheil, SFS 18; additional mss. cited by Mayer, UFBG, 490. Minor variants and rearrangements of the text in the mss. are not noted here.
Edition: Mayer, UFBG, 490-494.
Translation: Stephens, ANET[3], 386; von Soden, SAHG, 316-317 no. 52; Labat, *Religions*, 284-285; Seux, *Hymnes*, 278-280.
Notes to Text: (28) von Soden, SAHG, 317 against CAD A/2, 297a.

III.53 TO SIN AND SHAMASH

A royal prayer to be said upon commencing an enterprise.

> O Sin and Shamash, gods both,   (1)
> Sin of the night, Shamash of all the day,
> You <pronounce> the verdicts of heaven and earth.
> You look each day upon the dimensions of day, month, and year.
> O Sin and Shamash, it is you ordain the destiny of the lands,   (5)
> You are the remote gods
> Who daily control(?)* the speech of the people.
> Without you, no regular offering is set out among the Igigi-gods,
> You light all the Anunna-gods like the day.*
> You prepare(?) their food portions, you take care of their chapels. (10)
> The lands rejoice at your appearance,
> They watch for you carefully,[1] [n]ight [and day].
> It is you who stands by to dissolve the unfavorable signs
>   of heaven and earth.
> I, your servant, who watch for you,
> Who daily gaze upon your faces,   (15)
> Who am attentive to your appearance,
> Make my unfavorable signs pass away from me,
> Set for my person propitious and favorable omens,
> Order for me that my reign be long-lasting
>   and watch over (it) together!
> Grant me your radiant beacons,   (20)
> Let me constantly bless you, night and day,
> And let me proclaim your greatness to the heights!

Text: Lutz, PBS 1/2 106, rev 3-25.
Edition: Ebeling, ArOr 17 (1949), 179-181.
Translation: von Soden, SAHG, 342-343 no. 68; Seux, *Hymnes*, 490-491.
Literature: Mayer, UFBG, Sin und Šamaš 1.
Notes to Text: (7) Seux, *Hymnes*, 459 note 5; CAD Ḫ, 119b; AHw, 343a. (12) von Soden, SAHG, 490.

1. Perhaps a reference to lunar observation, for example, time of appearance and disappearance.

III.54 TO ANY GOD

According to its subscription, this bilingual address, consisting of a prayer, confession, lament, and concluding supplication, could be used for any deity.

May (my) lord's angry heart be reconciled,   (1)
May the god I do not know be reconciled,
May the goddess I do not know be reconciled,
May the god, whoever he is, be reconciled,
May the goddess, whoever she is, be reconciled,   (5)
May my (personal) god's heart be reconciled,
May my (personal) goddess's heart be reconciled,
May (my) god and (my) goddess be reconciled (with me)!
May the god who [has turned away]* from me
    [in anger be re]conciled,
May the goddess [who has turned away from me
    in anger be reconciled],   (10)
[I do not know] what wrong [I have done],
[   ] the wrong [   ].
[My god did not call my name]* with favor,
[My goddess did not call my name] with favor,
[My god did not] pronounce my name [with favor],   (15)
[My goddess did not pronounce my name with favor].
I could not eat for myself the bread I found,[1]
I could not drink for myself the water I found.
I have perpetrated un[wittingly] an abomination to my god,
I have unwittingly violated a taboo of my goddess.   (20)
O (my) lord, many are my wrongs, great my sins,
O my god, many are my wrongs, great my sins,
O my goddess, many are my wrongs, great my sins,
O god, whoever you are, many are my wrongs,
    great my sins,
O goddess, whoever you are, many are my wrongs,
    great my sins!   (25)
I do not know what wrong I have done,

---

1. That is, he offered it all to his gods in vain (Maul, HBKl, 245).

I do not know what sin I have committed,
I do not know what abomination I have perpetrated,
I do not know what taboo I have violated!
A lord has glowered at me in the anger of his heart,   (30)
A god has made me face the fury of his heart,*
A goddess has become enraged at me
      and turned me into a sick man,
A god, whoever he is, has excoriated me,
A goddess, whoever she is, has laid misery upon me!
I keep on searching, but nobody will help me,   (35)
When I wept, they would not draw near,
When I would make a complaint, no one would listen,
I am miserable, blindfolded, I cannot see!
Turn towards me, merciful god, as I implore you.[1]
I do homage to you, my goddess,
      as I keep groveling before you,   (40)
O god, whoever you are, [turn towards me,
      I implore you],
O goddess, [whoever you are, turn towards me,
      I implore you],
O lord, tur[n towards me,
      I implore you],
O goddess, lo[ok upon me,
      I implore you],
O god, [whoever you are, turn towards me,
      I implore you],   (45)
O goddess, whoever [you are, turn towards me,
      I implore you]!
How long, O my god,
      [until your furious heart is calmed]?
How long, O my goddess,
      [until your estranged heart is reconciled]?
How long, O god whosoever you are,
      until y[our angry heart is calmed]?

1. Here and in the next three lines Akkadian has "I keep turning toward my merciful god."

How long, O goddess, whosoever you are,
  until your estranged heart is reconciled?   (50)
Men are slow-witted and know nothing,
No matter how many names they go by,
  what do they know?
They do not know at all if they are doing good or evil!
O (my) lord, do not cast off your servant,
He is mired in a morass, help him!   (55)
Turn the sin which I perpetrated into virtue,[1]
Let the wind bear away the wrong I committed!
Many are my crimes, strip them off like a garment,
O my god, though my wrongs be seven times seven,
  absolve my wrongs,
O my goddess, though my wrongs be seven times seven,
  absolve my wrongs,   (60)
O god, whosoever you are, though my wrongs be
  seven times seven, absolve my wrongs,
O goddess, whosoever you are, though my wrongs be
  seven times seven, absolve my wrongs,
Absolve my wrongs, let me sound your praises!
As if you were my real mother, let your heart be reconciled,
As if you were my real mother, my real father,
  let your heart be reconciled!

Text: Pinches, IV R² 10 (see also Maul, HBKl, pl. 38).
Edition: Maul, HBKl, 236-246.
Translation: Stephens, ANET³, 391-392; Falkenstein, SAHG, 225-228 no. 45; Seux, *Hymnes,* 139-143.
Literature: Y. Rosengarten, *Trois aspects de la pensée religieuse sumérienne* (Paris, 1971), 133-163.
Notes to Text: (9) Seux, *Hymnes,* 140 note 8. (13) Falkenstein, SAHG, 226. (31) Differently Seux, *Hymnes,* 141 note 20.

1. Sumerian in this and the following lines has preterites, "he turned ..."

III.55 PRAYER FOR LAYING THE FOUNDATION OF A TEMPLE

O Enmesharra,[1] lord of the netherworld,
    prince of the infernal regions,   (1)
Lord of (this)* place and of the land of no return,
    mountain of the Anunna-gods,
Who pronounces the verdicts of the netherworld,
    great bond of Andurunna,[2]
O great lord, without whom Ningirsu regulates
    no dikes or canals, nor forms furrows,
Champion who mastered the netherworld by his strength,   (5)
Who made heavy its fetter,
    grasping the circuit of the netherworld,
Grantor of scepter and staff(?) to Anu and Enlil,
May, at your command, the foundation of this place
    endure before you,
May this brickwork be as lasting as your lordly abode
    in the netherworld!
May Anu, Enlil, and Ea take up lasting residence there.   (10)
And I too, so-and-so, the prince, your servant,
May I always be called by a good name
    in your divine presence.
May th(is) abode of the great gods be eternal(?),
May all my land dwell in peaceful abode.

Text: Craig, ABRT 2 13, 1–16 (+, see Borger, ZA 61 [1971], 72ff.).
Edition: Borger, ZA 61 (1971), 72–80, lines 42–57.
Translation: von Soden, SAHG, 345–346 no. 71; Seux, *Hymnes*, 492–493.
*Notes to Text: (2) So Seux, *Hymnes*, 492 note 6 (compare line 8); otherwise, perhaps a euphemism for the netherworld.

1. Netherworld deity, ancestor of Anu and Enlil.
2. A cosmic locality, here evidently meaning where heaven and netherworld are linked. Compare Andurna, p. 355 note 1.

III.56 LITIGANT'S PRAYER

This little bilingual prayer, written in Akkadian on one side of the tablet and in Sumerian on the other, forms part of a family archive of legal and business documents from Kassite Babylonia (ca. 1500-1200 B.C.). It may reflect the anxieties of a person embroiled in a lawsuit or other difficulties. Some idea of the troubles this family faced may be gleaned from Text 96 in the archive, a list of transactions including several outrages or abuses. First a plow was taken away on the day cultivation was supposed to begin, second some equipment, including a wagon, was stolen or misappropriated, and third, the remaining wagons were purloined and someone was incapacitated from work or detained at threshing time. While there is no reason to assume that the texts are related to each other, these are the sorts of problems that the supplicant had on his mind.

> Shamash, my ... has sealed it,
> Nabu, master of my truthfulness, has sealed it,
> May my harasser disappear!
> May my ill-wisher be plucked out!
> I put my trust in my god,
> Let Nabu judge(?) my case(?),
> Let me see a favorable (outcome) through the command of Nabu!

Text: F. Peiser, *Urkunden aus der Zeit der dritten babylonischen Dynastie* ... (Berlin, 1905), 92.
Edition: Peiser, *Urkunden*, 4.

CHAPTER IV

THE LATE PERIOD
(1000 – 100 B.C.)

The Late period of Assyro-Babylonian literature is characterized both by preservation and standardization of Mesopotamian written tradition and by production of vital new works. It is often difficult to decide whether a text was composed in the Late or Mature periods.[1] Scholars agree that many important and original works, such as Erra and Ishum, were composed during the Late period, even if they disagree over what other works to date to this period.

As part of the standardization of Assyro-Babylonian written tradition in the Late period, related texts were compiled into "series." Within a series, the title of which was normally the first half-line of text (incipit), the tablets were numbered in sequence. Numbered tablets therefore correspond to chapters of modern works.[2] Colophons at the ends of tablets in a series provided information such as the number of tablets in the series; the name, title, parentage, and family name of the copiest; the date the manuscript was copied; a statement about the collation of the text (for example, copied from an older manuscript, compiled from manuscripts from different cities); an injunction to safeguard the manuscript.[3]

The largest and most important group of these tablet series consists of scholarly works, which are essential components of the Mesopotamian literary heritage. A brief survey of these series follows.

Lexical texts are lists of names, words, and phrases from Sumerian, Akkadian, and other ancient Mesopotamian languages. These are attested in standardized forms as early as the mid-third millennium B.C. Many appear to be pedagogically oriented. One important group of lexical texts is arranged graphically,

---

1. W. von Soden, "Das Problem der zeitlichen Einordnung akkadischer Literaturwerke," MDOG 85 (1953), 14-26; E. Reiner, "First-Millennium Babylonian Literature," CAH³ 3/2, 293-321.

2. W. W. Hallo, "New Viewpoints on Cuneiform Literature," IEJ 12 (1962), 23f.

3. H. Hunger, *Babylonische und assyrische Kolophone*, AOAT 2 (1968); E. Leichty, "The Colophon," *Studies Oppenheim*, 147-154.

that is, by cuneiform signs, simple and compound. Another group is arranged semantically; for example, words for animals, stones, wooden objects, fish, pottery, and other things. Lists can include divine and personal names, stars, planets, and temples, as well as Sumerian legal formulae that could have been encountered in contracts and legal documents as late as the mid–second millennium B.C. Lists of foreign, rare, and dialectal Akkadian words occur, as well as lists that assign numbers to cuneiform signs as if for cryptographic purposes.[1]

Texts on divination make up the bulk of Assyro-Babylonian scholarly writings. Divination, in its many forms, was both the most highly esteemed intellectual endeavor in Mesopotamian civilization and the one for which Babylonia was famed in the Mediterranean world. Divination was related to Mesopotamian historical tradition because it sometimes preserved prognoses of certain significant events of the past, such as the death of kings under unusual circumstances. Divination was concerned not so much with the cause of an event, that being a matter of divine will, as it was with what an event might presage. The scientific labor of divination required collection of portents and consequences in encyclopedic form. This allowed a diviner to identify portents from the past similar to those before him, and to know consequences of those portents in the past. Knowledge of portents could lead to control of events, because a diviner could then take corrective or preventive measures to save a person from harm or ensure him good fortune. Some of the omens collected in the series were actual occurrences; others were evidently reasoned analogically or hermeneutically according to principles not always apparent to a modern reader.[2]

Collection of omens into series resulted in several large compilations including different types of information. Certain collections had individual significance, whereas others contained omens affecting the community at large.[3] Taking of omens for events of public significance (for example, construction of a monumental building, beginning a military campaign, installing a high official in office) is attested by the third millennium B.C. and continued until the end of cuneiform tradition.[4]

1. A. Cavigneaux, "Lexikalische Listen," RLA 6, 609-641.

2. J. Bottéro, "Symptomes, signes, écritures," in J. P. Vernant, ed., *Divination et Rationalité* (Paris, 1974), 70-193; *La Divination en Mésopotamie Ancienne* (Paris, 1966).

3. A. Sachs, "Babylonian Horoscopes," JCS 6 (1952), 49-75; F. Rochberg-Halton, "Babylonian Horoscopes and their Sources," OrNS 58 (1989), 102-123.

4. See, for example, III.7b.

Some omens were deductive: based on observation and assessment of events. These might include the behavior of animals,[1] sounds overheard in the street,[2] dreams,[3] or monstrous births.[4] Other omens were deliberately induced by following certain procedures and then studying and recording the consequences. These procedures included sacrificing a sheep and studying its entrails, liver, and gall bladder under controlled conditions,[5] pouring oil on water and studying its appearance,[6] or burning incense and watching the smoke rise.[7]

Medical series form an important sub-group of omens.[8] Some deal with physical symptoms, others with events observed by the exorcist or physician on his way to the patient's bedside.[9] Others are physiognomatic omens that assess various human physical and behavioral characteristics as favorable or unfavorable.[10]

Extensive astrological omen collections, made in the Late period, tend to presage events affecting the king, the government, or the community.[11] So great was the esteem astrology enjoyed in the Late period that the astrological series "When Anu and Enlil" (seven thousand or more astrological omens) was

1. Bottéro, *Symptomes* (p. 692 note 2), 105-106.

2. A. L. Oppenheim, "Sumerian: inim.gar, Akkadian: *egirrû* = Greek kledon," AfO 17 (1954/6), 49-55; Bottéro, *Symptomes* (p. 692 note 2), 98-99.

3. A. L. Oppenheim, *The Interpretation of Dreams in the Ancient Near East, with a Translation of the Assyrian Dream-Book, Transactions of the American Philosophical Society* NS 46/3 (1956), 179-373. A brief account is found in G. von Grunebaum *et al.*, eds., *The Dream and Human Societies* (Berkeley, 1966), 341-350.

4. E. Leichty, *The Omen Series šumma izbu*, TCS 4 (1970).

5. Bottéro, *Symptomes* (p. 692 note 2), 179ff.

6. G. Pettinato, *Die Ölwahrsagung bei den Babyloniern, Studi Semitici* 21-22 (Rome, 1966).

7. G. Pettinato, "Libanomanzia presso i Babilonesi," RSO 41 (1966), 303-327; R. D. Biggs, "À propos des textes de libanomancie," RA 63 (1969), 73-74; E. Leichty, "Smoke Omens," *Studies Finkelstein*, 143-144; I. Finkel, "A New Piece of Libanomancy," AfO 29/30 (1983/4), 50-55.

8. R. D. Biggs, "Medicine in Ancient Mesopotamia," *History of Science* 8 (1961), 94-105; "Medizin," RLA 7, 623-629. See also General Introduction, p. 35 note 1.

9. R. Labat, *Traité akkadien de diagnostics et prognostics médicaux* (Leiden, 1951); R. Labat, "Une nouvelle tablette de prognostics médicaux," *Syria* 33 (1956), 119-130; J. V. Kinnier Wilson, "Two Medical Texts from Nimrud," *Iraq* 18 (1956), 130-146; "The Nimrud Catalogue of Medical and Physiognomatic Omina," *Iraq* 24 (1962), 52-62; P. Herrero, *Thérapeutique mésopotamienne*, ed. M. Sigrist (Paris, 1984).

10. F. R. Kraus, *Die Physiognomischen Omina der Babylonier*, MVAeG 40/2 (1935); *Texte zur babylonischen Physiognomatik*, AfO Beiheft 3 (Berlin, 1939); "Weitere Texte zur babylonischen Physiognomatik," OrNS 16 (1947), 172-205; "Ein Sittenkanon in Omenform," ZA 43 (1936), 77-113; E. Reiner, "A Manner of Speaking," *Studies Kraus*, 282-289.

11. Sachs, JCS 4 (1952), 51-52; A. Ungnad, "Besprechungskunst und Astrologie in Babylonien," AfO (1941/4), 251-284.

said to have been written by the antediluvian sage Adapa.[1]

The most extensive omen series is the terrestrial group entitled "If a City is Situated on a Height." This series of over one hundred tablets deals with settlements and houses, atmospheric phenomena, birds, animals, reptiles, insects, plants, trees, and other aspects of the every day Mesopotamian environment.[2] Even when large series were standardized, empirical collection of ominous data continued throughout the Late period.[3]

Divination and ritual were closely connected. Divination implies the ability to read and predict divine will, ritual, to avert presaged evil or to bring about desired consequences. Ritual texts contain prescribed utterances, such as incantations or prayers, together with complicated magical procedures often described in detail. Such texts are known in great numbers from the Late period.[4] Rituals and their accompanying prayers and incantations were largely concerned with matters of health and well-being, including physical illness that could be treated pharmacologically or by exorcism, as well as mental illness: depression, feelings of inadequacy, persecution, neurosis, psychosis, abnormal behavior.[5] Sympathetic magic played an important part in medical rituals, which often prescribed symbolic washing off of the evil or interment, submersion, or burning of the sorcerer in the form of figurines created for the purpose.[6] Apotropaic rituals could ward off potential evils, while healing rituals dealt with evil already encountered.[7] Charms sought to bring about a personal consequence such as sexual contact, love, marriage, or successful childbirth.[8] Texts focusing on magic figurines, or on monsters and demons and their

---

1. E. Weidner, "Die Astronomische Serie Enûma Anu Enlil," AfO 14 (1941/44), 172-195, 308-318; AfO 17 (1954/56), 70-89; AfO 22 (1968/69), 65-75; F. Rochberg-Halton, *Aspects of Babylonian Celestial Divination: The Lunar Eclipse Tablets of Enūma Anu Enlil*, AfO Beiheft 22 (1988).

2. F. Nötscher, *Haus und Stadtomina der Serie šumma âlu ina mêlê šakin*, Or 31 (1928); *Die Omen-Serie šumma âlu ina mêlê šakin*, Or 39-42, 51-54; Zur Omen-Serie "šumma âlu," Or NS 3 (1934), 177-195; S. Moren, *The Omen Series Šumma Alu: A Preliminary Investigation* (University of Pennsylvania Dissertation, 1978).

3. D. J. Wiseman, "Assyrian Writing Boards," *Iraq* 17 (1955), 3-13.

4. H. Zimmern, BKBR.

5. J. V. Kinnier Wilson, "An Introduction to Babylonian Psychiatry," AS 16 (1968), 289-298; Edith K. Ritter and J.V. Kinnier Wilson, "Prescription for an Anxiety State: A Study of BAM 234," AnSt 30 (1980), 23-30.; J. V. Kinnier Wilson, "Mental Diseases of Ancient Mesopotamia," in D. Brothwell et al., eds., *Diseases in Antiquity* (Springfield, IL, 1967), 723-733.

6. See for example III.50h, lines 31ff., III.40b, lines 12ff.

7. See note 4.

8. IV.46, 48, 49.

appearances, underlie the imagery of IV.5.[1] Rituals having to do with statues and images are referred to as "Cleansing the Mouth" (of evil).[2]

The ritual series "House of the Ritual Bath" incorporated Sumerian and Akkadian prayers, the purpose of which was to cleanse the speaker, presumed to be the king, from contamination brought upon him by sorcery or other causes.[3] These prayers, sometimes called incantation prayers, often resort to legal phraseology, as if the god is judging the speaker's case or petition against an adversary in court (for example, II.35 and III.40c).

The exorcistic series called Maqlû "Burning" is primarily concerned with warding off the effects of black magic, especially through the burning or melting of figurines.[4] Shurpu "Incineration" is primarily concerned with evil from within the individual or of unknown origin, where fire purifies the affected person.[5] Various other series against sorcery, spells, and curses exist, some with long lists of possible evils in fixed sequences.[6]

---

1. F. Wiggermann, *Babylonian Prophylactic Figures: The Ritual Texts* (Amsterdam, 1986); E. Reiner, "Magic Figurines, Amulets, and Talismans," in A. Farkas et al., eds., *Monsters and Demons in the Ancient and Medieval Worlds: Papers Presented in Honor of Edith Porada* (Mainz, 1987), 27-36.

2. G. Meier, "Die Ritualtafel der Serie 'Mundwaschung'," AfO 12 (1937/9), 40-45; "Beschwörung mittels eines Mehlkreises," AfO 11 (1936/7), 365-367; S. Smith, "The Babylonian Ritual for the Consecration and Induction of a Divine Statue," JRAS 1925, 37-60.

3. J. Laessøe, *Studies on the Assyrian Ritual Series bīt rimki* (Copenhagen, 1955); A. Ungnad, "Bemerkungen zum bît-rimki-Ritual," OrNS 12 (1943), 196-198; C. J. Mullo-Weir, "The Prayer Cycle in the Assyrian Ritual bît rimki, Tablet IV," AfO 18 (1957/8), 371-372; C. Frank, "bit mesiri," ZA 36 (1925), 215-217; G. Meier, "Die zweite Tafel der Serie bīt mēseri," AfO 14 (1941/4), 139-152; R. Borger, "Die Beschwörungsserie Bīt Mēseri und die Himmelfahrt Henochs," JNES 33 (1974), 183-196. For extracts from these series, see III.50h-k.

4. G. Meier, *Die Assyrische Beschwörungsserie Maqlû*, AfO Beiheft 2 (1937); "Studien zur Beschwörungssammlung Maqlû," AfO 21 (1966), 70-81; T. Abusch, "Mesopotamian Anti-Witchcraft Literature: Texts and Studies," JNES 33 (1974), 251-262; T. Abusch, *Babylonian Witchcraft Literature, Case Studies* (Atlanta, 1987); "Maqlû," RLA 7, 346-351. For extracts from this series, see III.40c, 41c, 48d, IV.44.

5. E. Reiner, *Šurpu, A Collection of Sumerian and Akkadian Incantations*, AfO Beiheft 11 (1958); W. G. Lambert, "Two Notes on Šurpu," AfO 19 (1959/60), 122. For extracts from this series, see III.40d, IV.41.

6. F. Köcher, "Die Ritualtafel der magisch-medizinischen Tafelserie 'Einreibung'," AfO 21 (1966), 13-20; E. Reiner, "'Lipšur-Litanies'," JNES 15 (1956), 126-149; E. Knudsen, "An Incantation Tablet from Nimrud," Iraq 21 (1959), 54-61; O. R. Gurney, "An Incantation of the Maqlû Type," AfO 11 (1936/7), 367-368; R. Caplice, *The Akkadian Namburbi-Texts: An Introduction*, SANE 1/1 (1974); E. Weidner, "Beschwörung gegen Böses aller Art," AfO 16 (1952/3), 56. For a study of the witch or sorcerer, see T. Abusch, "The Demonic Image of the Witch in Standard Babylonian Literature: The Reworking of Popular Conceptions by Learned Exorcists," in J. Neusner, *et al.*, eds., *Religion, Science, and Magic In Concert and In Conflict* (Oxford, 1989), 27-58.

Incantations or magic spells were sometimes grouped into series according to the classes of demons against which they were directed. Among these is Lamashtu, the female demon attacking children and women in childbirth, incantations against whom date from the Archaic (I.6), Classical (II.26) and Late (IV.37) periods and later.[1] There are also incantations in series, mostly in Sumerian, against sickness demons of various kinds. The longest of these series is called "Malignant Phantoms," portions of which are known from the Classical period, and whose Sumerian forerunners date even earlier.[2]

Menologies and hemerologies deal specify propitious times for activities such as the construction of buildings.[3] They also arrange cultic activities in accordance with the calendar year.[4]

The social and historical background for late Assyro-Babylonian literary activity may be seen in the succession of empires — Assyrian, Babylonian, Achaemenid, Hellenistic, Arsacid — spanning the first millennium B.C.[5] Whereas Assyria reached its apogee in the eighth century and was destroyed towards the end of the seventh, Babylonia remained strong for most of the millennium and flourished under Persian and Seleucid rule.[6] The grand side of empire is reflected in texts like IV.1, 48, 50, 51, with fulsome praises of the king

1. D. Myhrman, "Die Labartu-Texte, babylonische Beschwörungsformeln gegen die Dämonin Labartu," ZA 16 (1902), 141-183; W. Farber, "Lamaštu," RLA 6, 439-446.

2. R. Campbell Thompson, *The Devils and Evil Spirits of Babylonia* (London, 1903); M. J. Geller, *Forerunners to UDUG-HUL, Sumerian Exorcistic Incantations*, FAOS 12 (1985). For extracts from this series, see III.36a, IV.32.

3. R. Labat, *Un calendrier babylonien des travaux, des signes et des mois (series iqur ipuš)* Bibliothèque de l'École Pratique des Hautes Études 321 (Paris, 1965); R. Labat, "Un almanach babylonien (V R 48-49)," RA 38 (1941), 13-40; "Nouveaux Textes hémérologiques d'Assur," MIO 5 (1957), 307-315; "Un calendrier cassite," *Sumer* 8 (1952), 17-36; L. Matouš, "L'Almanach de Bakr-Awa," *Sumer* 17 (1961), 17-66; R. Labat, *Hémérologies et ménologies d'Assur*, (Paris, 1939); P. Hulin, "A Hemerological Text from Nimrud," *Iraq* 21 (1959), 42-53; R. Labat, "Tablette de Tešrit et autres prescriptions," *Iraq* 23 (1961), 88-94. For a survey of the genre of hemerologies and almanacs, see R. Labat, "Hemerologien," RLA 4, 317-323.

4. See in general S. Langdon, *Babylonian Menologies and the Semitic Calendars* (London, 1935), as well as the works cited in note 3.

5. For surveys of Mesopotamian history in the first millennium B.C., see P. Garelli, V. Nikiprowetzky, *Le Proche-orient asiatique: Les Empires Mésopotamiens, Israël, Nouvelle Clio 2 bis* (Paris, 1974); J. Brinkman, *Prelude to Empire, Babylonian Society and Politics, 747-626 B.C.* (Philadelphia, 1984); CAH³ 3/2 (with extensive bibliographies).

6. For considerations of scholarly conditions in the first millennium B.C., see Parpola, LAS 2 (1971), 6-47; A. L. Oppenheim, "The Position of the Intellectual in Mesopotamian Society," *Daedalus* Spring 1975, 37-46; "Divination and Celestial Observation in the Late Assyrian Empire," *Centaurus* 14 (1969), 97-135; M. A. Dandamayev, *Vavilonskij Pisci* (Moscow, 1983), with extensive bibliography;

and his prowess. The dark side is seen in Erra and Ishum (IV.16), in which the indiscriminate cruelty and wanton destruction of the age are lamented, and the question is raised of how, in a world supposedly controlled by gods, violence and destruction, even of sanctuaries, could take place. The old theme of divine justice and its relationship to human affairs is debated in IV.17 (compare III. 14 and II.7).[1] The rights, duties, responsibilities, pretensions, and limitations of kings are dealt with prescriptively in IV.12 and elsewhere by implication (Gilgamesh), even satirically (IV.22).

Literary developments specific to the Late period include tendencies towards henotheism (III.44g, 47c), and perhaps an increase in religious skepticism (Gilgamesh Epic). Such traditional Mesopotamian literary concerns as divine hegemony (IV.23) and death (IV.5) continue to be explored in the Late period. Certain gods, especially Nabu, achieve greater prominence in the Late period than they had in the Mature period (see III.45). Marduk seems to age from a youthful warrior in the Creation Epic (III.17) to a remote, sage-like figure in Erra and Ishum (IV.16). Ishtar tends to shed her militarism, as seen in II.8, to reveal her qualities as princess, lover, even prostitute (IV.22, 23; Gilgamesh Epic). Texts such as IV.22 and IV.16 provide glimpses into aspects of her persona that may have seemed horrifying and perverted to some Babylonians (compare also IV.2d, line 10f.).

The personalities of Late period rulers can be reflected in the literature of their times: the vainglory of Sargon II,[2] the anxieties and superstitions of Esarhaddon,[3] the scholarly interests of Assurbanipal,[4] the idiosyncratic theology of Nabonidus.[5]

J- Pečirková, "Divination and Politics in the Late Assyrian Empire," ArOr 53 (1985), 155-168. For Babylonia under Persian rule see Oppenheim, *Cambridge History of Iran* 2, 529-587. For the Hellenistic period, see J. Oelsner, *Materialien zur babylonischen Gesellschaft und Kultur in Hellenistischer Zeit* (Budapest, 1986); A. Kuhrt and S. Sherwin-White, eds., *Hellenism in the East, The Interaction of Greek and non-Greek Civilizations from Syria to Central Asia after Alexander* (Berkeley, 1987).

1. W. von Soden, "Das Fragen nach der Gerechtigkeit Gottes im Alten Orient," MDOG 96 (1965), 41-59; J. Bottéro, "Le Problème du Mal en Mésopotamie ancienne. Prologue à une etude du 'Juste souffrant,'" *Recherches et documents du Centre Thomas More* no. 15 (1977), 1-43.

2. See IV.2a and Grayson, CAH³ 3/2, 86-102.

3. See W. von Soden, *Herrscher im alten Orient* (Berlin, 1956), 118-126; Parpola, LAS 2 (1971), 46-47; Grayson, CAH³ 3/2, 122-141.

4. See IV.3 and von Soden, *Herrscher* (note 3), 127-138; Grayson, CAH³ 3/2, 142-161.

5. Nabonidus is one of the most controversial figures of Mesopotamian antiquity; see IV.10 and the bibliography in P.-A. Beaulieu, *The Reign of Nabonidus King of Babylon 556-539 B.C.*, YNER 10 (1989).

Sometimes traces of resistance to foreign rule can be found. Perhaps anti-Persian sentiment lies behind redaction of the "Kedor-Laomer" Texts (III.11). A group of late apocalypses or prophecies may well express Babylonian cultural resistance to the Achaemenids and Seleucids.[1]

Towards the end of the Late period, when Mesopotamia was under Greek rule, Akkadian was dying out as a spoken language. Some of the latest hymns show an awkwardness of expression that suggests that the authors were not native speakers of Akkadian (III.46b, IV.11). Acrostics and word games lend a precious, Alexandrian flavor to certain works of the Late period (III.45c, e; IV.2c, 4d, 8k, 17). The substrate influence of Sumerian, so prominent in works of the Classical period, was replaced by that of Aramaic.[2] Sumerian ossified into an academic and cultic argot known only to the most scholarly.[3]

Knowledge and wisdom, as seen in the literature of the Mature period, continue to be important in literature of the Late period, with increasing emphasis on learning and scholarship. Slavish imitation of ancient styles or selected classics was not the norm; Akkadian literature was spared the sterility brought about by imitation and anthologizing. Above all, what is most impressive about Akkadian literature of the Late period is that it remained vital and productive even in the face of two thousand years of literary tradition.

---

1. The theme of resistance is taken up in A. Finet, ed., *La Voix de l'opposition en mésopotamie* (Brussels, 1973); A. K. Grayson, BHLT, 24ff.

2. J. C. Greenfield, "Babylonian-Aramaic Relationship," CRRAI 25 (1978), 471-482. For a survey of the role of Arameans in Assyria, see N. Postgate, "Ancient Assyria — A Multi-Racial State," *Aram* 1 (1989), 1-10. See also p. 3 note 2.

3. G. Goosens, "Au déclin de la civilisation babylonienne: Uruk sous les Séleucides," *Bulletin de la Classe des Lettres et des Sciences morales et politiques*, series 5, vol. 27 (1941), 223-244; M. E. Cohen, *The Canonical Lamentations of Ancient Mesopotamia* (Potomac, MD, 1988), 1:24-27. For a detailed survey of cuneiform documents from Mesopotamia of the Hellenistic period, see Oelsner, *Materialien* (p. 696 note 6), 137-246. See also p. 3 note 3.

A. ASSYRIAN POETRY AND PROSE

IV.1 SHALMANESER III

Shalmaneser III (858-824 B.C.) was an Assyrian warrior king who made extensive conquests in Syria, Palestine, Anatolia, and the mountain lands of present-day Kurdistan. He was also drawn into Babylonian affairs and fought the Chaldaeans threatening Babylonian cities. For a historical survey of his reign, see Grayson, CAH³, 3/1, 259-269.

(a) SHALMANESER IN ARARAT

This text is a poetic account of a campaign by an Assyrian king, Shalmaneser III, probably against Urartu, the region centering around Lake Van in eastern Anatolia. W. G. Lambert has suggested that it was produced by a specific Assyrian poetic school; see above, III.4. The historicity and geographical setting of the text are uncertain in many points; much of the narrative in the unique manuscript is fragmentary, poorly written, or obscure. Even the sequence of speeches in the text is difficult to discern. I propose the following interpretation:

1-9: Opening invocation, in which Shalmaneser's conquests in north Syria are referred to.
10-24: Shalmaneser orders his general, Assur-bel-ka'in, to secure his new domains while the king marches against Urartu. The king exhorts his officers.
25-30: The god Assur encourages Shalmaneser.
31-60: Shalmaneser narrates his own campaign in the style of Assyrian royal inscriptions.
61-64: The text concludes with a narrative of a festival for Ishtar of Arbela and a triumphant return to Assur.

[O Shalmaneser], lord of the world, shepherd of all rulers, (1)
[   ] the lofty one, the lady of Nineveh,
[   ] justice,
[admin]isters everything,
[un]sparing, (5)
The Lord and Anu have [en]trusted you(?) ... [dis]tant [   ]!

[Having   ] ... the stubborn Bit-Adinian[1] slave,
Having t[orched] Til-barsip,[2] the mighty stonghold,
Having laid waste the dwellings of the Hittite kings,[3]
He spoke <to> Assur-bel-ka'in the general ... as follows,   (10)

"Let the fortresses be entrusted to you,
        let your security be strong,
"Let your preparedness be high, take their tribute.
"I have forced the rulers of the Hittites to submit,
"I will go see how to approach the Urartians,
"...   (15)
"Assurnasirpal[4] ... Nairi[5] [   ] is aroused."

He inspects his officers that they keep discipline high,
"My fierce warriors! ...
"I will go [   ] you(pl.) to ... the campaign of Assur.[6]
"Let the iron swords be sharpened(?) ...   (20)
"The sharp darts [which pierce?] the heart [   ],
"[   ] coats of iron mail for the horses.
"Do not [   ] your powerful force,
"[   ] the warfare of the Urartian slave(s)![7]
"Assur gave me confidence and s[howed me   ]."   (25)

The people of Assyria heard(?)* ... [   ]
Good fortune ... to the lord,

"Go, O lord of kings, ... [   ],
"May Nergal go before you, Girra [behind you],
"[   ] at your command, we will be full [   ]."   (30)

---

1. An Aramean state in North Syria and south-central Asia Minor in the ninth century B.C.

2. Modern Tell Ahmar, a city in North Syria, where the remains of a palace of this period have been excavated, capital of Bit-Adini.

3. The so-called "Neo-Hittite states," various small kingdoms in North Syria in the first part of the first millennium B.C.; see Hawkins, CAH³ 3/1, 372-441.

4. See III.4.

5. Corresponds roughly to Kurdistan, see M. Salvini, Nairi ed Uruadri (Rome, 1967).

6. Lambert suggests emending to "Assurnasirpal," but this is not adopted here.

7. This seems to be a poetic word for troops, and need not be derogatory; compare III.1 v 32'.

They set out on the march ... [   ]
[   ] of his battle like ... [   ]:

"[   ] picks of iron, arrows of [   ]
"Difficult [   ] mountains, [ ] ravines,
"[   ] ... we ... [   ]   (35)
"[The city Ubum]u together with the land of Shubri
      [I] like [ ],
"[ ] crossing the vast [ ] towards [ ],
"[I] rapidly [...the whole?] of the land of the Urartians,
"I conquered [st]rong [cities] and la[id waste] fortifications,
"I reminded(?) them of [fi]erce Assurnasirpal.   (40)
"On the first of September, [I] drew near [his] royal capital,
"The king(s) ...
"Terror of the lord of the world regions fell upon them.
"They forsook their cities,
      they went into [mountains] and forests,
"The enemy(?) went into forbidding mountains
      to save their lives,   (45)
"Hard upon their heels,
      I drove them <into> arduous mountain terrain.
"I felled 18,000 of the enemy with my battle weapons,
"I cast their corpses(?) in the open country like ...,
"I seized as booty innumerable mules, horses, and donkeys.
"I pillaged his palace for nine days,   (50)
"I burned down his numerous residences.
"I paraded the women(?) of his land[1] before my troops,
"..., his royal capital, I burned with fire.
"I set up images of my power by mountains and seas.
"I trampled down all the Nairi-lands, ...   (55)
"I received horses as tribute
      from the cities Tikki and Hubushkia,
"I received the rest(?) of the tribute from(?) the city Turushpa.
"I ... [ ] to Assur, my god.
"I entered the temple of [   ] with a blithe heart,

---

1. Or, possibly, "booty" (grammatically difficult).

"I [   ] the festival of the lady of Arbela."   (60)

The king, ... a lion, [   ] in Assur with joy,
He showed [his weapons?],
    with all his territories he [entered] before Ishtar.
He hailed ...
He donated ... [   ] for joy.
"[   ] suitable for you."   (65)

Text: Gurney, STT 43.
Edition: W. G. Lambert, AnSt 11 (1961), 143-158; Livingstone, *Court Poetry*, 44-47.
Literature: Schramm, EAK 2, 82 (from which several restorations are taken); Kinnier Wilson, *Iraq* 26 (1964), 107f. For historical background on this campaign, in addition to Lambert's study, see B. B. Piotrovsky, *Il Regno di Van: Urartu*, trans. M. Salvini (Rome, 1966), 71-82. For a review of the chronological and geographical problems raised by this text, see J. Reade, "Shalmaneser or Ashurnasirpal in Ararat," SAAB 3 (1989), 93-97.
Notes to Text: (26) AHw, 1212a.

(b) TO NINLIL

This text is an address by Shalmaneser III(?)[1] to the goddess Ninlil(?)[2] commemorating his repairs to her cultic harp and asking for her blessing.

(large gap)

The priest who [   ],
Pious prince, favorite of Ishtar, ...
Reliable general of the gods, beloved of Ishtar,   (5′)
Who leads you in procession,*
    who proclaims your divinity,
(When) you beheld him, O my lady,
    you desired that he be lord.
May they(?) hail his kingship above all other kings.
The diademed kings, whom you commit to his power,
    are assembled, kneeling, and doing homage to him.   (10′)
The faithful shepherd, the provider for san[ctuaries],
Son of Assurnasirpal, priest of ... A[ssur],
Descendant of Tukulti-[Ninurta, ...   ]
Who guarantees your offerings,
    who maintains [your] food offerings,
The faithful shepherd who watches over(?) ... [   ]   (15′)
The most great one, first in rank,
    who performs [your] rites:
The great harp which played(?) your songs of praise(?)
    having deteriorated,
He made [the ... of that] harp,
The harp ... [   ]
He made once again splendid and greater
    than it was [before].   (20′)
He placed on your head a brilliant gem,
    shining like a star.
He who kneels and glorifies you,
    proclaiming your dominion,

1. Borger, HKL 1, 99; Schramm, EAK 2, 95.
2. M.-J. Seux, *Épithètes royales akkadiennes et sumériennes* (Paris, 1967), 165 note 57.

O Ninlil, of your own free will bestow
    (long) life upon him!
As for the harp and drum beloved to [your] divinity,
Which are agreeable to you
        and which your loftiest feelings delight in,   (25′)
He restored(?) the ... and ornamented its inside,
He decorated it(?) with a gazelle and onager(?),
    creatures of the high mountain.
They put earrings of finest gold on her ears,
[   ] joy ...

(four more fragmentary lines, then breaks off)

Text: Ebeling, KAR 98.
Edition: None.
Literature: See Schramm, EAK 2, 95.
★Notes to Text: (3) Reading *qa-at!-ka*.

IV.2 SARGON II

Sargon II (721-705 B.C.) came to the throne under mysterious circumstances. He may not have been of royal lineage nor in direct line for succession. He proved to be a valorous warrior and undertook an extensive series of campaigns, on one of which he died in battle. Sargon's throne name, "The-King-is-Legitimate," was of course programmatically reminiscent of Sargon of Akkad (see Chapter I, Introduction). For a historical survey of his reign, see Grayson, CAH³ 3/2, 86-102.

Sargon II constructed a new capital city for himself at Dur-Sharrukin, modern Khorsabad, not far from Nineveh. This city was destined to be occupied for less than fifty years and lies today as an impressive memorial to the will of a single man. Its grandiose plan included numerous temples and a royal palace. The prayers translated here (IV.2a) were composed for the new temples at Dur-Sharrukin. Each appeals to a specific aspect of the deity's powers: rainfall (Adad), protection (Assur, Nabu), wisdom and spring water (Ea), progeny (Ningal), strength and prowess (Ninurta), and truth (Sin).

(a 1) TO ADAD

This prayer was inscribed on the threshold of the entrance to the Adad-temple at Dur-Sharrukin.

> O Adad, irrigator of heaven and earth, who brightens daises, for Sargon, king of the world, king of Assyria, governor of Babylon, king of the land of Sumer and Akkad, builder of your cella, bring the rains from heaven and the floods from underground in good season. Garner grain and oil in his leas, make his subjects lie down in safe pastures amidst plenty and abundance. Make firm the foundations of his throne, let his reign endure.

Text: Jacobsen *apud* G. Loud *et al.*, *Khorsabad* I, OIP 38 (1936), 130 no. 4.
Edition: Jacobsen, *Khorsabad* I, 130-131; Meissner, ZDMG 98 (1944), 32-33.
Translation: von Soden, SAHG, 280 no. 24d; Seux, *Hymnes*, 529.

(a 2) TO ASSUR

This prayer concluded an inscription on the pavement of a palace gate at Dur-Sharrukin.

> May Assur, father of the gods, look steadfastly with the radiance of his holy features upon this palace. May its renewal always be ordered, until distant days. Let it be established from his holy utterance that the protective spirit and the safeguarding god be on the watch day and night within it and never leave its sides.
>
> At his command may the sovereign who built it live to a ripe old age. From his holy lips may (these words) fall, "May he who made it grow old, far into the future." May he who dwells therein rejoice within, in good health, happiness, and blithe spirits. May he enjoy well-being in full measure.

Text: H. Winckler, *Die Keilschrifttexte Sargons II*. (Leipzig, 1889), pl. 39-40, 131-150.
Edition: Borger, BAL II, 58 131-150.
Translation: von Soden, SAHG, 281-282 no. 24g.

(a 3) TO EA

This prayer was inscribed on the entrance to the Ea-temple at Dur-Sharrukin. It addresses Ea using his by-name Ninshiku, which may mean "leader" or the like.

> O Ninshiku, lord of wisdom, creator of all and everything, for Sargon, king of the universe, king of Assyria, governor of Babylon, king of the lands of Sumer and Akkad, builder of your cella, make your underground depth open up, send him its spring waters, provide his leas with plentiful, abundant water. Ordain for his destiny great wisdom and profound understanding, make his project(s) succeed, may he enjoy well-being in full measure.

Text: Jacobsen *apud* G. Loud, *et al.*, *Khorsabad* I, OIP 38 (1936), 132 no. 6; H. Winckler, *Die Keilschrifttexte Sargons II*. (Leipzig, 1889), pl. 49, no. 3B.
Edition: Jacobsen, *Khorsabad* I, 132-133; Meissner, ZDMG 98 (1944), 35.
Translation: von Soden, SAHG, 279 no. 24a; Seux, *Hymnes*, 527-528.

(a 4) TO NABU

This prayer was inscribed on the threshold and around the steps in the sanctuary area of the Nabu-temple at Dur-Sharrukin.

O Nabu, universal scribe, who checks on all, look steadfastly, in the fidelity of your heart, upon Sargon, king of the universe, king of Assyria, governor of Babylon, king of the lands of Sumer and Akkad, builder of your cella, and direct your just countenance upon him. Grant him days of good health till furthest time, ordain for his destiny years of happiness. Make his reign last as long as heaven and earth, let him continue to exercise shepherdship of all lands. May his support endure as (this) structure and its platform.

Text: Jacobsen *apud* G. Loud *et al.*, *Khorsabad* II, OIP 40 (1938), 103-104 no. 1.
Edition: Jacobsen, *Khorsabad* II, 103-104; Meissner, ZDMG 98 (1944), 36.
Translation: von Soden, SAHG 281, no. 24f; Seux, *Hymnes*, 529-530.

(a 5) TO NINGAL

This prayer was inscribed on the threshold of the entrance to the Ningal-temple at Dur-Sharrukin.

O preeminent lady, exalted Ningal, [inter]cede for Sargon, king of the universe, king of Assyria, governor of Babylon, king of the land of Sumer and Akkad, builder of your cella, with Sin, your beloved spouse, speak a word favorable of him that his reign be [sta]ble. Let him ordain his destiny to live a life long of days. May his offspring hold dominion over all inhabited regions till the end of time.

Text: Jacobsen *apud* G. Loud *et al.*, *Khorsabad* I, OIP 38 (1936), 133 no. 7.
Edition: Jacobsen, *Khorsabad* I, 133; Meissner, ZDMG 98 (1944), 33.
Translation: von Soden, SAHG, 280 no. 24c; Seux, *Hymnes*, 528.

(a 6) TO NINURTA

This prayer was inscribed on the threshold of the entrance to the Ninurta-temple at Dur-Sharrukin.

> O Ninurta, athlete of surpassing strength, bestow old age upon Sargon, king of the universe, king of Assyria, governor of Babylon, king of the land of Sumer and Akkad, builder of your cella. May he enjoy well-being in full measure. Make firm his reign in Esagila and Esharra. Guide straight his steeds, safeguard his teams, grant him [un]rivalled strength and manly might, make his weapon at the ready that he kill his foes.

Text: Jacobsen *apud* G. Loud *et al.*, *Khorsabad* I, OIP 38 (1936), 131 no. 5; H. Winckler, *Die Keilschrifttexte Sargons II.* (Leipzig, 1889), pl. 49 no. 3A.
Edition: Jacobsen, *Khorsabad* I, 131-132; Meissner, ZDMG 98 (1944), 34.
Translation: von Soden, SAHG, 281 no. 24e; Seux, *Hymnes*, 529.

(a 7) TO SIN

This prayer was inscribed on the threshold of the entrance to the Sin-temple at Dur-Sharrukin.

> O Sin, pure god who renders verdicts and discloses decisions,[1] look steadfastly in the fidelity of your heart upon Sargon, king of the universe, king of Assyria, governor of Babylon, king of Sumer and Akkad, builder of your cella, and direct your just countenance upon him. Grant him days of good health till furthest time, ordain for his destiny years of happiness, make his reign last as long as heaven and earth, make firm his throne over the four world regions.

Text: Jacobsen *apud* G. Loud *et al.*, *Khorsabad* I, OIP 38 (1936), 130 no. 3.
Edition: Jacobsen, *Khorsabad* I, 130; Meissner, ZDMG 98 (1944), 34-35.
Translation: von Soden, SAHG, 280 no. 24b; Seux, *Hymnes*, 528.

1. Reference to divination.

(b) TO NANAY

This fragmentary hymn includes a description of musicians and performers in col i, a blessing on Sargon II, and a prayer against crop pests. The fighting alluded to in the first preserved lines may be war games that formed part of a ceremony in honor of this goddess.

i

(gap)

The naked sword [   ],
The pointed axe, symbols of [her?] divinity,
Battle is drawn up to her right and left.
First-ranked of the gods, whose amusement is combat,   (5)
Vanguard to those with seven companions.
Skilled singers kneel before her,
Performers on the lyre, the small harp, and clappers,
Flute, shawm, and pipes,
Impersonators (who carry) spindle, lash(?), whip,   (10)
Relax her mood with "sweet reeds."[1]

(fragmentary lines, then gap)

ii

Daughter-in-law of Esagila,[2] princess [   ],
Spouse of Muati, beloved of the Lord [his] father,
Whom Belet-ili cherishes among all goddesses,
Be up and on the way,[3] most valiant of goddesses!   (5)
O capable lady, who acquits well a warrior's duty,
[   ] the hearts of those who spare no combatant,
[   ] till the end of time

(fragmentary lines, then large gap)

---

1. Possibly a reference to incense (so CAD K, 558a), but more likely a reference to music.
2. That is, bride to Nabu = Muati, Marduk's son.
3. To battle?

iv

(fragmentary lines)

The knowledgeable physician
    whom she does not [guide],
His hand is fal[tering] before his clients.[1]
Without her, who can do it right?
Hasten forth, learn her (song of) praise!   (10)
Cherish the merciful one, each month forever,
She who enriches the impoverished, prospers the poor.
Hear, O regions of the world, the praise of queen Nanay,
Glorify the beautiful one, extol her of voice resounding,
Exalt the splendid one, hail the mighty one,   (15)
Make continuous prayer and entreaty to her.

Calm yourself, O daughter of Sin, take up your abode.
Bless Sargon who grasps your hem in entreaty,[2]
The shepherd of Assur, who walks behind you,
Ordain for his destiny a life long of days,   (20)
Make firm his throne, make his reign endure,
Safeguard the steeds hitched to [his] yoke,
Keep affliction and loss afar off from him:
The fell locust plague which destroys the grain,
The vile cicada-pest which denudes the orchards,   (25)
That cut off the food offerings of god and goddess.
Enlil is heeding you, Tutu[3] awaits you,
At your command may they vanish into thin air!
[May] the protection and good fortune
    standing before you [   ],
[   ] steppe, mountains, and [   ]   (30)

(breaks off)

1. This line is apparently the end of a list of professionals whose duties are the goddess's special concern (for the reading, Livingstone, *Court Poetry*, 14).
2. See III.42b line 3, III.43b line 25.
3. Marduk, see Creation Epic (III.17) Tablet VII lines 9, 15, 19, 25, 33.

Text: K 3600 + DT 75 = Craig, ABRT 1, 54-55 = Macmillan, BA 5 (1905), 626-629 (collated).
The parallel K 9898 and duplicate K 13773 have not been used here.
Edition: Livingstone, *Court Poetry*, 13-16.
Translation: Seux, *Hymnes*, 107-109.
Literature: Lambert, AnSt 11 (1961), 143-144.

IV.3 ESARHADDON AND ISHTAR OF ARBELA

Esarhaddon (680-669 B.C.) ruled the Assyrian empire in one of its most powerful and prosperous periods. This king is sometimes reputed to have been
unusually superstitious and much under the influence of exorcists and diviners.
These devised elaborate rituals for him to avoid evils, real or imagined. For a
historical survey of his reign, see Grayson, CAH³ 3/2, 122-141.

Tablets from Nineveh preserve prayers of Esarhaddon and his son,
Assurbanipal, together with divine responses, or oracles. About fifty such
oracles are known; for English translations of others, see Biggs, ANET³, 449-
451.

> I am Ishtar of [Arbela]. O Esarhaddon, king of the land of
> As[syria], I give long days and eternal years to Esarhaddon, my king
> in the City,[1] in Nine[veh], Calah, and Arbela. I am your great
> midwife, I your good wetnurse. I have made firm your throne for
> long days and eternal years under the great heavens. I watch over
> you in a golden abode in the midst of heaven.
>
> Fear not, O king! I have taken you in trust,* I did not disappoint
> you. I made [your] trust, I did not let [you] come to shame. I
> brought you over the river in good order(?).* O Esarhaddon,
> legitimate heir of Ninlil, ..., I will finish off your enemies with my
> own hands. Esarhaddon, king of the land of Assyria, is a cupful of
> lye, an axe weighing (only) two shekels.[2]
>
> In the City I give you long days and eternal years, O Esarhaddon,
> in Arbela, I am your good shield.

Text: Pinches, IV R² 61, iii 15-iv 59.
Edition: Weippert, ZATW 84 (1972), 84-85.
Literature: M. Weippert, "Assyrische Prophetien," in F. M. Fales, ed., *Assyrian Royal Inscriptions:
New Horizons in Literary, Ideological, and Historical Analysis*, OAC 17 (1981), 71-115.
*Notes to Text: (11) Weippert, "Prophetien," 85 note 2. (14) Weippert, "Prophetien," 85 note 28.

---

1. Assur.
2. This may mean that Esarhaddon is ineffective as a warrior without Ishtar's assistance.

IV.4 ASSURBANIPAL

The last great Assyrian king, Assurbanipal succeeded to the throne of the empire in 669 B.C. The events surrounding his accession are referred to in IV.4c below. Among his many military achievements was the conquest of Elam, the traditional enemy of Babylonia (see above, III.11 and III.12). This event is referred to in a prayer to Marduk[1] and other literary texts too fragmentary for translation here.[2]

At Assurbanipal's order was assembled a library at Nineveh, the largest known collection of Akkadian literary and scholarly texts (see General Introduction, B.2 and IV.4g). In his inscriptions Assurbanipal boasts of his scholarly attainments (IV.4d, g), so it is tempting to see in the turgid and verbose style of the compositions in his name some imprint of the royal personality. For another hymn in the name of Assurbanipal, see III.50g. For a historical survey of his reign, see Grayson, CAH[3] 3/2, 142-161.

(a) CORONATION PRAYER

This prayer was evidently composed for the coronation[3] of Assurbanipal. It alludes to the Middle Assyrian prayer translated above, III.8.

> (1) May Shamash, king of heaven and earth, elevate you to shepherdship of the four [world regions]. May Assur, who bestows [the scepter], prolong your days and your years. Enlarge the land at your feet, may my god(?) ascend to yours![4] (5) Just as grain and silver, oil, cattle, and the salt of Bariku[5] are desirable, so too may the name of Assurbanipal, king of Assyria, be desirable to the gods. May they grant him speaking and hearing, truth and justice.
>
> May the [resident] of Assur obtain 30 kor[6] of grain for 1 shekel of silver, may the [resi]dent of Assur obtain 30 quarts of oil for 1 shekel of silver, (10) may the [resident] of Assur obtain 30 minas of

---

1. S. Strong, *Journal Asiatique* 9 série 1893, 361-380.

2. Livingstone, *Court Poetry*, 48-51.

3. Ebeling, AfO 13 (1939/41), 324.

4. Obscure. The speaker may be the personage presiding at the ceremony; he may be saying that Assur is to become the king's personal god (differently Livingstone, *Court Poetry*, 26 note 4).

5. A place, the salt from which was used at the gods' repast.

6. Roughly 170 bushels. This and the following schematic figures are supposed to convey great prosperity.

wool for 1 shekel of silver. May the [great] listen when the lesser speak, may the [lesser] listen when the great speak, may harmony and peace be established [in Assur].

(15) Assur is king, it is Assur who is king! Assurba[nipal is vicegerent* ...] for Assur, his handiwork. May the great gods ensure his reign, may they protect [the life? of Assurba]nipal, king of Assyria. May they give him a just scepter to enlarge [his] land and people. May his reign be ever renewed, may they establish his royal throne forever. May they bless him day, month, and year, may they [make] his reign [out]standing. (20) [During] his years, may the rain from heaven and the flood from the underground depths be unfai[ling].

Grant to Assurbanipal, king of Assyria, our lord, long [days], m[any] years, a strong [wea]pon, a long reign, [year]s of abundance, a good name, and reputation, contentment, happiness, good rep[ute] and first rank among kings.[1]

(26) Anu has given [his] crown, Enlil has given his throne, Ninurta has given his weapon, Nergal has given his splendor, (30) Nusku has sent (wise) counselors to stand in attendance upon him.

He who shall speak insolence or falsehood to the king, be he important, he will die violently; be he rich, he will become poor. He who shall harbor ev[il] against the king in his heart, Erra will call him to account in a plague. (35) He who thinks disrespectful thoughts of the king, a whirlwind will crush him, his property(?) will be empty air.

Assemble, all ye gods of heaven and netherworld, bless Assur-banipal, king, counselor, man![2] Deliver the weapon of com-bat and battle into his hand. (40) Give him the black-headed folk,[3] that he serve as their shepherd.

Text: Ebeling-Köcher-Rost, LKA 31.
Edition: Weidner, AfO 13 (1939/41), 210-213, 324-325; Livingstone, *Court Poetry*, 26-27.
Translation: Seux, *Hymnes*, 110-112.
Notes to Text: (15) Seux, *Hymnes*, 111 note 10. (34f.) Mayer, OrNS 56 (1987), 66 and Seux, *Hymnes*, 112 note 21; Livingstone: "his foundation is (but) wind, the hem of his garment is (but) litter."

1. A direction is inserted here for the officiant: "As soon as he has made the blessing, he turns around and makes a blessing towards the 'Censer Gate', that is, towards Shamash."

2. Perhaps a compound is intended, "counselor-man."

3. The Mesopotamians.

(b) TO ASSUR

This hymn glorifies Assur as Anshar, a primeval deity.[1] It concludes with a blessing upon the text and its royal speaker.

Most great one, noblest of the gods, omniscient,	(1)

Most great one, noblest of the gods, omniscient,   (1)
Eminent, supreme Enlil[2] of the gods, ordainer of destinies,
Assur, most great lord, noblest of the gods, omniscient,
Eminent, supreme Enlil of the gods, ordainer of destinies,
[Let me ex]alt* Assur, the powerful,
    noblest of the gods, lord of the world,   (5)
[Let me pro]claim his greatness,
    let me ever make splendid his praise,
Let me proclaim the renown of [As]sur,
    let me exalt his name,
[He who] dwells in E-hursaggalkalamma,[3]
    let me ever make splendid his praise.
Let me ever invoke [the powerful one],*
    let me praise his valor,
[Him who] dwells in Esharra,[4] Assur,
    who ordains destinies,   (10)
Let me disclose for all time, to [rev]eal to mankind,
[Let me bequeath] a reminder for later ones to hear,
[Let me exalt] the sovereignty of [Assur] forever.
[Cap]able one, profound of wisdom,
    sage of the gods, princely one,
[Father], creator of what is in the heavens and earth,
    who formed the mountains,   (15)
[Assur], creator of gods, begetter of goddess(es),
[Whose heart] is inscrutable, whose mind is ingenious,
Lofty [hero] whose name is feared,

1. Assur is here written Anshar. According to the Creation Epic (III.17) Tablet I line 14, Anshar was the father of Anu; here he is equated with Assur in order to give Assur a place among the primeval deities (ahead of Marduk). See also Livingstone, *Court Poetry*, xvii; Tadmor, JCS 12 (1958), 82.
2. That is, supreme god of the pantheon.
3. Part of the Assur temple in Assur.
4. The Assur temple in Assur.

His ow[n counselor], Assur,
    whose utterance is profound,
The basis [of his word], like a mountain,
    cannot be moved,   (20)
[His command], like the graven signs of the starry sky,[1]
    cannot miss its appointed time.
[He whose] word cannot be [alter]ed,*
    whose command is sure,
[Assur, the basis of his word], like a mountain,
    cannot be moved,
[His command], like the graven signs of the starry sky,
    cannot miss its appointed time.
Your wo[rd] is [   ], spoken from of old!   (25)
No god, O Anshar, can comprehend [   ] of your [great]ness,
The reason for your [   ] cannot be perceived!
[w]hose battle is irresistible,
[   ], which splits open mountains,
[None can withstand him,
    who] relies upon his own strength   (30)

(fragmentary lines, then gap)

[A]nu, Enlil, Ea, Belet-ili, and [Ninl]il,
Who acknowledged the sovereignty of Assur
    in the Assembly Place of the Gods,[2]
Have said, "May Assurbanipal, vicegerent for Assur,
    alone be the provider!"[3]
Among descendants, in far-off days,
For future reigns, years without number,   (10')
May th(is) praise of Assur be not forgotten,
    may it* keep one mindful of Esharra!
Let it be in (every) mouth,
    may it never cease to enlarge understanding,

---

1. The stars and planets, compared to writing, as if on the dome of the sky.
2. Ubshu-ukkenna, see Creation Epic (III.17) Tablet II line 160, Tablet III line 119. This passage refers to an Assyrian version of the Epic in which Assur was substituted for Marduk.
3. Provider for temples, that is, the king.

So that, as to me, Assur will deliver into your[1] hands
     sovereignty of land and people.
Splendid is the name of Assur, most great his divinity.
The praise of Assur, lord of lords, the valiant one,
     is (doubly) sweet.*

Text: K 3258 = Craig, ABRT 1 32-34 = Macmillan, BA 5 (1905), 652-653.
Edition: Livingstone, *Court Poetry*, 4-5.
Translation: von Soden, SAHG, 254-256 no. 8 (whence many of the restorations used here);
Seux, *Hymnes*, 90-93.
*Notes to Text: (5) Seux, *Hymnes*, 90 note 4. (11) Seux, *Hymnes*, 91 note 8. (22) Seux, *Hymnes*,
92 note 22. (11') Against Seux, *Hymnes*, 93 notes 38-40, and the literature cited there, I take this
to refer to the text of this hymn (*tanittu*); see General Introduction, D.1. (15') Text: TAB-*bat*,
an artificed writing for *ṭābat(?)*, perhaps in D-stem?

---

1. Future kings.

(c) TO ISHTAR OF NINEVEH AND ARBELA

At the beginning of his reign, Assurbanipal shared the empire with his brother, Shamash-shum-ukin, referred to diplomatically as the "twin." Assurbanipal, however, received larger territory. Since the inhabitants of the brother's domain were forced to swear allegiance to Assurbanipal, the division of power may have been more nominal than actual. The assertion of line 13 (see also IV.5) and the oblique allusion to the subsequent struggle with and disappearance of the brother (see line 39) refer to Assurbanipal's irregular succession, perhaps contrary to the will and preparations of his father, Esarhaddon.

Extol, glorify the divine lady of Nineveh,	(1)
Exalt, praise the divine lady of Arbela,	
Those who have no rival among the great gods.	
Their names are precious to goddesses,	
Their holy places, all their sanctuaries, are unequalled.	(5)
The speech on their lips is a fire breaking out,	
Their utterance is cherished forever.	
I (am) Assurbanipal, their hearts' desire,	
Great seed of Baltil,[1] [bo]rn at Nineveh,	
Formed in the [Emashmash][2] and the Egashankalamma,[3]	(10)
Whose kingship they [sum]moned(?)	
from the [crown prince's] palace.	
They have [ordered] with their holy command	
that my throne long endure.	
I knew neither human father nor mother,*	
I grew up on my goddesses' knees,	
The great gods have guided me like an infant.	
They have gone with me at my right and left,	(15)
They have set at my side spirits of protection and good fortune,	
They have confided my survival	
to the guardians of well-being and life.	
They made my physique splendid,	
they made mighty my strength,	

1. Assur; see III.1 note 17.
2. Temple of Ishtar of Nineveh. See also IV.4f.
3. Temple of Ishtar of Arbela (see Seux, *Hymnes*, 101 note 8).

They exalted my name over any other ruler's.

[All] e[nemies] heard, trembling with fear,*   (20)

Rebellious [lands] which did not submit to the kings my ancestors,

And which submitted neither [gifts] nor presents before them,

[I], Assurbanipal, handiwork of the great gods,

(gap)

[   ] their command,

[   ] their words.

Neither [... by] my [might] nor by the might of my bow,

(But) by the st[rength and by the] might of my goddesses,

Did I cause the lands [disob]edient to me

    to submit to the yoke of Assur.   (30)

[Numerous] gifts, unceasing, year by year they bring me,

They keep watch(?) each day at the great gate of Assur and Ninlil.[1]

They seek peace with me in supplication and plea,

With prayer and petition they do homage at my feet.

It was I, Assurbanipal, of the blood royal,   (35)

Victor over rebels, who appeases the hearts of the gods,

Whom the great gods have given courage,

    whose weaponry they blessed!

The Lady-of-Nineveh, the mother who bore me,

Has given (me) an unrivalled kingship.   (40)

The Lady-of-Arbela, who created me, has ordered a long life for me.

They have ordained it my destiny

    to exercise sovereignty over all the inhabited world,

They have made all its kings submit at my feet.

O Lady-of-Nineveh, mistress of poetry, bless your king forever!

Text: Langdon, OECT 6, pl. XI; photo AfO 25 (1974/7), 46.
Edition: von Soden, AfO 25 (1974/7), 45-49 (with numerous improved readings adopted here); compare Livingstone, *Court Poetry*, 10-13; von Soden, WdO 22 (1991), 190.
Translation: Seux, *Hymnes*, 100-102.
Notes to Text: (13, 20) Restoration von Soden, AfO 25 (1974/7), 46.

1. This may refer in a general way to vassalage, but Assurbanipal is known to have put a defeated king to watch at a city gate in company with a bear and a dog (M. Streck, *Assurbanipal* [Leipzig, 1916], 66 viii 11); differently von Soden, WdO 22 (1991), 190.

(d) ACROSTIC HYMN TO MARDUK

This hymn is divided into distiches and occasional tristiches, the first signs of which form an acrostic reading "I am Assurbanipal, who has called upon you. O Marduk, grant me life, let me sing your praises!" The lines of verse are exceptionally long so as to give the impression of prose, the style known as "*Kunstprosa.*" There are various allusions to the Creation Epic (III.17). While this piece is of little aesthetic interest, it is included here as an example of late Assyrian style at its most ponderous.

I praise your name, O Marduk, mighty one among the gods,
    irrigator[1] of heaven and earth [   ],   (1)
Who were fair created, are alone on high [   ].

You bear the responsibilities of Anu, Enlil, and Ea,
    lordship and kingship [   ],
You have gathered to yourself all wisdom,
    O perfect of strength [   ].

O cherished counsellor, sublime prince,
    omnipotent, most great [   ],   (5)
(Who) made splendid his lordship,
    (who) drew up for Anu's battle [   ].[2]

You are sublime in heaven, king in the netherworld,
    resourceful counsellor of the god[s   ],
Who establishes all habitations,
    who grasps the circumference of the starry sky
    and the [world   ].

You are the [gre]atest among the gods.
    Nudimmud[3] has formed your features fair [   ],

---

1. Creation Epic (III.17) Tablet VII line 62.
2. This refers to the battle against Tiamat. Anu went out to her first, but returned unsuccessful; Creation Epic (III.17) Tablet II lines 96ff.
   3. Ea.

The great gods let you grasp the tablet of destinies in
      your hand, (the power) to raise and lower [is yours].   (10)
[w]ho has made [the gods?] do homage at your feet,
      saying as they hailed (you), "He is [our king]!"[1]

[   ] of omens have exalted you, and Enl[il]
[gr]eatest of the gods, brilliant glow, lightning flash [ ],
[   ] who traverses innermost heaven [   ].

[   ] who struck the pate of Anzu,[2] overwhelmed [   ],   (15)
[who defeated] the lion man, bison man, scorpion man,[3]
K[ing   ] who divided them [   ].[4]

Heir of N[udimmud ...] your eyes [   ]
Bow, arr[ow,   sw]ord, [battle] gear,
You defeated vast Tiamat [   ] Qingu [her] sp[ouse].[5]   (20)

May Babylon rejoice over you, may Esagila be joyful [over you   ],
      who judge [in truth] and justice,
Who render decisions and op[en wells],[6]
You rain down copious rainfall, you [ ] mas[sive] floods [   ].

Great is the greatness of the Lord, irrigator of heaven,
      much mightier than [the gods, his fathers],[7]
He is surpassing in stature, lofty of form,
      splendid [   ] for his lordly garment.   (25)

He summoned the Igigi and Anunna-gods,
      they were kneeling before him,
      as the gods his forefathers sat in silent awe before [him   ],

---

1. Creation Epic Tablet IV line 28 (Seux, *Hymnes*, 116 note 11).
2. For the Anzu story, see III.25. Here the exploit of Ninurta is assigned to Marduk. For discussion of this motif, see W. G. Lambert, CRRAI 32 (1985), 55ff.
3. Monsters created by Tiamat in the Creation Epic Tablet I lines 142f. See p. 359 note 1.
4. Creation Epic (III.17) Tablet VI lines 39-40, 46, 145 (Seux, *Hymnes*, 120 note 45).
5. Creation Epic (III.17) Tablet I lines 95-104.
6. Creation Epic (III.17) Tablet VII line 60 (if restoration is correct).
7. Creation Epic (III.17) Tablet I line 19.

For taking counsel,
> to deliberate in lordly(?) deliberation are Marduk's,
They listen to Marduk alone.

Continuous are the offerings, the incense of the stand,
> the harp, the lyre, and the [   ],
They glorify the builder of Esagila,[1]
> Babylon rejoices and [   ] are joyful.

There bow before you the Igigi and Anunna-gods,
> gods and goddesses of holy places, s[anctuaries], and daises,   (30)
Governors and rulers pray [to you].

[Fir]stborn(?) of Nudimmud, first-ranked, valiant, mighty,
> tempest unrelenting, raging fire, [ ] flame,
Who engulfs enemies, who, in battle,
the clash of weapons, does not [fear   ].

Marduk is lofty of form, blazing sun, glowing torch,
> who, when he appears [   ],
(Who) purifies the impure and illumines [gloom   ],   (35)

May all gods and goddesses, Anu, [Enlil],
Constellations, depths, netherworld, Nudimmud,
> together with hairy hero men, ... [   ],
Cancer, the Battle Goddess, ...   [   ],
Behold the deeds of Marduk, lord of the gods,
> [may they] constantly [   ].

Give me for all time meal offerings, abundance of pure [   ],
(Which) the wrathful god established for living creatures,
> at [his] sublime command ... [   ].   (40)
Your [rad]iant name* is Sagmegar "noble,
> first-ranked god,[2] loftiest of the gods, [   ],

1. Marduk, see Creation Epic (III.17) Tablet VI line 62.
2. The planet Jupiter.

"Who, by his radiance, reveals a guidepost ... [   ]."
Splendid hero, En-gishgal-anna,[1] "g[reat] lord [who   ]
      the (celestial) positions of the Anunna-gods,"
Lustrations, rituals, offerings [   ]

Very great is your name, O furious Marduk [   ],   (45)
You are greatest among all the gods,
      among the gods your divinity is [   ].

O circumspect prince, ... [   ] in your net,
      [is] at [your] right,
At your left is Erragal, mightiest of the gods,
      before you are the va[liant] Seven, [   ]
To your right and left fire scorches, where you ra[ged].

Most honored one, splendid one, how magnificent is the god
      who [   ] his divinity to the [rev]erent one who kneels,   (50)
To all the gods who dwell on daises, he grants food offerings,
      and portions rejoice [   ].

Marduk grasps firmly in hand the lead-rope of the Igigi and
      Anunna-gods, the bond of he[aven and netherworld],
At rising and setting he set up constellations,[2]
      he gave them a path and a way to go [   ].

Your weighty invocation is "Judge of the Four World Regions,"
      willful Enlil of the great gods,
Who implements the decrees of the depths,
      who grants portions and offerings to the gods.[3]   (55)

Accept my entreaty, receive the prayers of supplicants,
      the petitions of the so[rrow-worn],
May one who pleases you always speak fair [to you].

1. "Lord-in the-Heavenly-Station," a name for the planet Jupiter.
2. Creation Epic (III.17) Tablet V line 2 (Seux, *Hymnes*, 120 note 45).
3. Creation Epic (III.17) Tablet VII line 85.

May Anu, Enlil, and Ea rejoice your mood
   and make you cheerful,
May Damkina, your great mother, [say to you in] Esagila,
   which you love, "Calm yourself!"

She is eminent, important, queenly, mighty,
   head of the family, spouse, goddess, mistress,
   splendid, great, lofty, fair, [ ],   (60)
O beloved of Tutu,[1] grant me (long) life, I will si[ng] your praises.

I will glorify your valor, O sublime princess, queen of Esagila,
   supreme goddess, queen of que[ens],
Lofty ruler of all [ ], merciful goddess who loves prayers!

I implore you, magnificent lord, may your furious heart be calm,
   may [your] mood, which had turned to fury,
   relent and be appeased.
Let me live in your (favorable) breezes,
   O lofty sage of the gods, Mar[duk]!   (65)

The humble, imploring scholar[2] extols the greatness of
Sarpanitu, great lady, spouse of Enbilulu,[3]
   daughter-in-law of Nud[immud],
He sings [her praises].

Text: Craig, ABRT 1, 29-31 + 2 x = Brünnow, ZA 4 (1889), 246-248 + ZA 5 (1890), 77-78;
1904-10-9,205 (unpub.); texts collated from photograph.
Edition: Livingstone, *Court Poetry*, 6-10.
Translation: von Soden, SAHG, 249-253 no. 6; Seux, *Hymnes*, 115-121; Hecker, TUAT II/5,
765-768.
Notes to Text: (27) Livingstone, *Court Poetry*, 8 note 27. (41) Seux, *Hymnes*, 119 note 36.

---

1. One of the names of Marduk in the Creation Epic (III.17) Tablet VII lines 9, 15, 19, 25, 33. The passage refers to Sarpanitu, Marduk's wife.

2. Assurbanipal, who was proud of his literacy; see H. W. F. Saggs, *The Might that Was Assyria* (London, 1984), 41; R. Labat, "Un prince éclairé: Ashurbanipal," *Comptes rendus de l'Académie des Inscriptions et Belles-Lettres* (1972), 670-676.

3. One of Marduk's names in the Creation Epic (III.17) Tablet VII line 57.

(e) TO SHAMASH

This hymn glorifies Shamash, apparently in connection with work done on his temple by Assurbanipal, and prays for the king's long life. Like the hymn to Assur (IV.4d), it alludes to Assurbanipal's accession and ends with an epilogue addressed to future kings and performers of the song.

[O lord, ra]diance of the great gods, light of the earth,
    illuminator of the world regions, (1)
[O Shamash], lofty judge, creator of the above and below,
You scan all lands in your light like a graven sign.
[w]ho never wearies of divination, you render daily
    verdicts for heaven and earth.
Your [rising] is a fire blazing,
    all the stars of heaven are covered. (5)
You alone are [mani]fest,
    no one among the gods can rival you.
You take counsel with Sin, your father,
    and issue instructions,
Nor do Anu and Enlil hold congress without you,
Ea, who judges cases in the depths, looks into your face.
All the gods are attentive to your brilliant rising, (10)
They [sm]ell incense, they receive pure food offerings.
Exorcists [kneel] before you to avert evil portents,
Diviners [pray?] to you to steady their hands,
    to interpret the omens (aright).
[ ], Assurbanipal, whose assumption of kingship
    you commanded by oracle,
[Who ...] the brilliant [ ] of your [divin]ity,
    who makes splendid the symbol of your divinity, (15)
[Who ...] your [greatne]ss,
    who proclaims your praises to the numerous peoples,
[Look steadfastly upon him], judge his [ca]se,
    render a favorable verdict for him,
[Grant him long life?], let him proceed in well-being
    in the dawn of your rising.

May he serve in justice as shepherd [for all time?]
    to the subjects you gave him.
[In the house] that he built,
    wherein he caused you to dwell in joy,   (20)
[May] his heart exult [ ], may his mood be joyful,
    may he enjoy life in full measure!
[The prince who?] performs this [song] of Shamash,
    who pronounces the name of Assurbanipal,
May he shepherd in prosperity and justice
    the subjects of Enlil [all] his days.
[The singer] who masters this text,
    who extols Shamash, judge of the gods,
May his god hold him in good esteem,
    may his performance be pleasing to people.   (25)
He who abandons this song to obscurity,
    who does not extol Shamash, light of the gods,
Or who makes substitution for the name of Assurbanipal,
    whose assumption of kingship Shamash
    commanded by oracle,
But names some other king,
May his string-playing be painful to people,
    May his joyful songs be the prick of a thorn!

Text: Ebeling, KAR 105, 361.
Edition: Ebeling, *Quellen* I, 25-27.
Translation: von Soden, SAHG, 247-249 no. 5; Stephens, ANET[3], 386-387; Seux, *Hymnes*, 63-66.

(f) ASSURBANIPAL AND NABU

For these oracles, compare IV.3.

[I sin]g your praise, O Nabu, among the great gods. [Among?] my [ill-wisher]s, may my life not be continually sought.[1] I keep turning to you, O most valorous of the gods his brethren, [in the temple of the lady of] Nineveh. [You are the tru]st of Assurbanipal henceforth, for all time. [Since childhood I] have cast myself at the feet of Nabu, [watch over me], O Nabu, among my ill-wishers!

Listen(?), O Assurbanipal, I am Nabu! Until the end of time, your feet shall not falter, your hands shall not tremble, nor shall these your lips weary of continual prayer to me, nor shall your tongue stumble at your lips, for I shall ever grant you fair speech. I shall raise your head and make you proud in Emashmash.[2]

(Nabu continues) That, your eloquent mouth, which always implores the lady of Uruk, and your own person, which I created, keep imploring me to remain(?) in Emashmash, your destiny, which I created, keeps imploring me as follows, "Bring good order(?) to Egashankalamma."[3] Your spirit keeps imploring me as follows, "Prolong the life of Assurbanipal."

Assurbanipal, on bended knee, keeps praying to Nabu his lord, "Listen(?), O Nabu, do not forsake me! My life is inscribed[4] before you, my spirit is entrusted to the lap of Ninlil. Listen(?), do not forsake me among my ill-wishers!"

1. Or, "May my ill-wishers not continually be seeking my life" (CAD K, 284a).
2. Temple of Ishtar at Nineveh.
3. Uncertain; the word translated here as "good order" may also mean a garment or headgear.
4. Reference to Tablet of Destinies, see p.360 note 1.

A dream-god answered him from the presence of Nabu his lord, "Fear not, Assurbanipal, I will give you long life, I will entrust fair breezes with your spirit. This, my eloquent mouth, will ever bless you among the great gods."

Assurbanipal, spreading his hands, kept praying to Nabu his lord, "May he who seized the feet of the Queen of Nineveh not be disgraced among the great gods! May he who grasps the hem of the Lady of Uruk not be disgraced among his ill-wishers. Do not forsake me, O Nabu, do not forsake my life among my adversaries!"

"You were young, O Assurbanipal, when I left you to the Queen of Nineveh, you were a baby, O Assurbanipal, when you sat on the knee of the Queen of Nineveh. Her four teats were set in your mouth, with two you were suckled and with two you drew milk for yourself. Your ill-wishers, O Assurbanipal, will fly off like insects from the water's surface, they will be squashed at your feet like bugs in springtime. You will stand, O Assurbanipal, opposite the great gods, that you may praise Nabu."

Text: Craig, ABRT 1 5.
Edition: Livingstone, *Court Poetry*, 33-35.
Translation: von Soden, SAHG, 292-294 no. 39.
Notes to Text: (5) Restoration Livingstone, 33.

(g) PIOUS SCHOLAR

Among the colophons scribes appended to the manuscripts they copied for Assurbanipal's library are prayers for the king and his muse.

> I, Assurbanipal, king of the universe, king of Assyria, on whom Nabu and Tashmetu have bestowed vast intelligence, who acquired penetrating acumen for the most recondite details of scholarly erudition, no predecessors of whom among kings having any comprehension of such matters, I wrote down on tablets Nabu's wisdom, the impressing of each and every cuneiform sign, and I checked and collated them. I placed them for the future in the library of the temple of my lord Nabu, the great lord, at Nineveh, for my life and for the well-being of my soul, to avoid disease, and to sustain the foundations of my royal throne. O Nabu, look joyfully and bless my kingship forever! Help me whenever I call upon you! As I traverse your house, keep constant watch over my footsteps. When this work is deposited in your house and placed in your presence, look upon it and remember me with favor!

Text: See Hunger, AOAT 2 (1968), 105-106 No. 338.
Edition: Hunger, AOAT 2 (1968), 105-106 No. 338.

IV.5 THE NETHERWORLD VISION
OF AN ASSYRIAN CROWN PRINCE

Much of this bizarre narrative remains obscure, owing to the bad condition of
the single manuscript that preserves it. The narrative was composed by a scribe
who professed to set down the exact words of an Assyrian prince who had a
vision of the netherworld.

The first fifteen lines of the text may deal with actions of the prince's father.
There is reference to administrative acts, then the king may give himself over
to gluttony and obsession with wealth. The mysterious scribe is introduced in
line 17 in connection with some event that seems to cause the king
considerable distress: he weeps, goes out alone in the streets, smashes things,
ignores food, characteristic actions of a man undergoing personal misfortune.[1]
He commits some final abomination which, one may surmise, was to name a
different heir to the throne.

In line 27 Kumaya, who may be a son of the king and the same person as the
"prince" referred to elsewhere in the narrative, incubates a dream, perhaps to
find out when he is going to die. This might again suggest some situation of
uncertainty with the succession. Ereshkigal, queen of the netherworld, appears
to him and promises to reveal to him what he wanted to know.

In line 37 Kumaya awakes and prays for the promised revelation. Kumaya's
second dream is narrated directly in the first person, as overheard and set down
by the scribe (line 73). Kumaya enters the netherworld, where he sees fifteen
demonic figures, each one more ghastly than the preceding. The last two are
so appalling that Kumaya cannot even name them. Next he sees a dark human
figure wearing a red cloak, and finally Nergal himself, who grabs him by the
hair to kill him.

The warrior god Ishum intercedes, asking that the man be spared to sing
Nergal's praises to the land. Nergal is pacified, and asks the prince a question,
perhaps why he prayed to Ereshkigal for the revelation. He then prophecies
difficulties, rebellion, and anxieties for the prince. Nergal apparently shows the
prince his own father, who, despite his innate excellence (67) has committed
some evil act before his death (in connection with the succession?) that will be
a cause of grief to the prince.

The prince awakens and declaims his misery in public, praising Nergal and

---

1. See, for example, III.1 Fragment C iii lines 7'ff.; III.14 Tablet II lines 88ff.

Ereshkigal who had vouchsafed him his revelation. The scribe remembers his words perfectly and out of loyalty reports them to the palace.

Following von Soden, it is tempting to associate this composition with Assurbanipal and his father, Esarhaddon. The delicacy of the matters referred to might explain the oblique diction. The scribe, who seems to have been in disgrace for some evil act of his own, calls to mind Urad-Gula, a scholar at the court of Esarhaddon, who lost his post after the accession of Assurbanipal. He is sometimes compared with Ahiqar, the unfairly disgraced vizier of Aramaic tradition. All of this is speculation, however.

The prince's brush with death raises him, like Gilgamesh, to the company of those who know the "alpha and omega" of human wisdom, matters before the flood and after death.

```
[                    ] responsibility for [    ]                           (1)
[                    ] of the house of examiners of
         ora[cles], he took coun[sel] with him [    ]
[        ] ... the wise administrators,
         who keep the [secre]ts of their lord,
[        ] the governors [and] great ones
         he commissioned together
         and reinforced the proper care of his possessions,
[        ] Dada, his cook, strong drink, whatever
         there was, wherever the sun illumined,                           (5)
[        ] he delivered over to him [his] subjects,
         but he, disregarding his inner promptings, forgot
             what he (should have) held in awe,
[        ] ... he held in contempt
         what he (should have) feared, and thought evil,
         though his heart urged him to do good.
[        ] he reckoned [its acc]ounts(?), day and night
         he would shower his treasuries with jewels fit for a king,
         as if with a bucket from a well,
[        ] income, wealth, ... beloved by(?) the human race,
         (was) like pitch or tar coming up from the depths ...
[Like] potter's clay, he covered it (with) plaster, great [   ]
         he crammed it from foundation to parapet with silver,          (10)
[        ] and the walls [   ], within Nineveh,
```

the royal city, the way of well-being and justice,
[   ] the good deeds(?) he had made it enjoy(?),
[   ] ... to enter Assur ..., made ready to speak
and [addressed him] as if he were a man,
[   ] in his heart, nor did ill-omened words [   ]
[   ] of the god, lest [   ].   (15)
[At] that time, [   ] darkness ...
[   ] ... he went to a certain scribe ... [   ]
[   ] he took up his official post and [   ] the treasury,
[never] resting, nor did he hold back weeping,
[   ] ...   (20)
[   ] alone [   ] he went along its streets,
   [   ] a joyful song in the nuptial chamber [   ],
[   ] he ... of massive,
ingenious workmanship with his sword ... [   ]
[   ] in the netherworld which does not [   ] ...
the royal repast, great banquets, all [   ] ...
[   ] his evil [   ] which were not rightfully his, [   ] ...
[   ] years of service and [   ] gold ... [   ] ...   (25)
[   ] an attack against [   ], they stood and ... [ ] ...
[   ] and the shepherd of ... people for good, eternally.
Then did Kumaya, son of [   ], enter the temple(?),
[   ] to go down to the netherworld ... [   ] ... he desired.
He set up an incense burner with juniper [ ] ... and prayed,
   ... and made the god angry(?)
   while he uttered blessings,
"O [   ], Allatu, Allatu, mistress of the netherworld,
   ... [   ] ...,   (30)
"... of the lost orphan, let her disclose her face and
   [   ] ....
"[On] lips that have spoken insolence, where there is no
   regret, as long as I live ...
"[   ] on the day of my death [   ] to the (netherworld)
   Anunna-gods let me ... [   ]
"[   ] mention of my name ... "
[E]reshkigal appeared in a dream in the middle
   of the night and said to him,

"I have re[gard for] your (very) first offering,
"I shall surely hear your [p]rayer, I shall surely
      reveal to you what you desire,   (35)
"[By com]mand of my great divine mouth,
      you may interpret dreams,
      (but) I (myself) will not answer you
      the meaning of the sign,*
      w[hy] did you [turn to me], and [   ] Shamash?"
Kumaya awoke and moaned like a dove, [saying],
      "My earth, my earth ..."
      He wept and [   ] the dream.
[Again] he prayed, entreating Ereshkigal, before Nergal,
      king of the netherworld, her spouse,
      were his tears flowing down,
"[   ] your substitute the teeming peoples [   ]
      whom they made to bow down,
"[   ] ... [   ] I destroyed,
      you opened to me a secret, ... [   ]."   (40)
[Ku]maya lay down and was seeing a vision of the night.
In his dream, ... [   ] "I saw his terrifying splendor, [ ]
"I saw [Na]mtar, courier of the netherworld,
      who issues decrees.
"A man stood before him,
      he was holding his hair in his left hand,
      he was [holding] a sword [in his right hand],
"[Na]mtartu, his female counterpart,
      had the head of a protective spirit,
      her hands and feet were human.
"Death had the head of a dragon,
      his hands were human, his feet [   ],
'Evil Spirit' had a human head and hands,
      it was wearing a crown, its feet were those of an eagle,
      with its left foot it trod upon a crocodile(?).
"Alluhappu had a lion's head, four human hands and feet.
"'Upholder-of-Evil' (had) the head of a bird,
      his wings were opened as he flew to and fro,
      (he had) human hands and feet.   (45)

"'Take-Away-Quickly', boatman of the netherworld,
  had the head of Anzu, four [ ] hands and feet.
"[ ] (had) an ox's head, four human hands and feet.
"'Malignant Phantom' (had) a lion's head,
  the hands and feet of Anzu.
"Shulak was a normal lion rea[ring] on his hind legs,
"[Ma]mitu had a goat's head, human hands and feet.
"Pituh, gatekeeper of the netherworld, (had) a lion's head
  human hands, bird's feet.
"'Whatever-is-Evil' (had) two heads,
  one a lion's head, the other [   ].
"[Muh]ra (had) three feet, the two front ones were bird's feet,
  the rear was that of an ox, it had terrifying splendor.
"Two gods whose names I do not know: one (had) the head,
  hands, feet of Anzu, in its left hand [   ],
"The other had a human head and was wearing a crown.
  In its right hand was a mace, in its left ...
"Fifteen gods in all were in attendance.
"When I saw them I prayed [to them].
"A certain man, his body was black as pitch,
  his face was like that of Anzu,
  he was dressed in a red cloak,
  in his left hand he carried a bow,
  in his right he was ho[lding] a sword,
  he was treading on a serpent(?),
  ... with his left f[oot],   (50)
"When I raised my eyes, there was valiant Nergal sitting
  on his royal throne wearing the royal crown,
  he held two terrible maces with both hands,
  each with two heads,
"[   ] were piled up ... lightning was flashing,
  the great (netherworld) Anunna-gods were knee[ling]
  to right and left [   ],
"The netherworld was full of terror,
  deep silence(?) reigned in the presence of the prince.
"He seized me by the forelock and dr[ew] me towards him.
"When [I] saw him my legs shook,

his wrathful splendor overwhelmed me,
    I kissed the feet of his [great] divinity, I knelt.
"When I stood up, he was looking at me,
    shaking his head.
"He gave me a fierce [c]ry and shrieked at me wrathfully,
    like a raging storm.
"He drew up his scepter, his divine symbol,
    ghastly as a serpent, to kill me!   (55)
"Ishum, his counselor, intercessor, savior of life,
    who loves truth and <justice>, said,

    'Do not kill th(is) young man,
        O m[ight]y king of the v[as]t netherworld!
    '... let the subjects of the land all
        and always hear your praises!'

"The heart of the formidable, mighty one,
    who captures the wicked,
    grew calm as pure well water,
... Nergal said(?) this,

    'Why did you ... my beloved spouse,
        queen of the netherworld?'
    '[By] her sublime command, which cannot be changed,
        may Bibbu, slaughterer of the netherworld,
        entrust you to Lugal-sula the gatekeeper,
        that he may take [you] out of the gate
        of Ishtar and Aya.
    'Do not forget me nor neglect me!
        I will not sentence you to death.
    'By the command of Shamash
        there shall gust upon you
        want, violence, and revolts, all at once,   (60)
    'You shall have no sleep because of their fierce clamor.
    'This [corpse] that is interred in the netherworld belongs
        to that magnificent shepherd who fulfilled the
        heart's desire of my father [Assur], king of the gods.
    '[Of the king] who made ...
        all the lands from sunrise to sunset,

he looked upon you as plunder, who ruled over all,
'(To) whom Assur,
> at the beginning of his high priestly office
> [ordai]ned(?) construction of the sacred new year's
> festival house on the steppe,
> surrounded by a lush garden,
> the likeness of Lebanon, ... forever,

'And whose person Iabru and Humba-Napruhu[1] watch over,
> whose seed they preserved in well-being, whose army
> and camp they kept safe, lest a [chario]teer(?)
> approach him(?) in battle,   (65)

'He is your l[oft]y father, who understood matters,
> he of profound wisdom and penetrating understanding,
> who had in v[iew?] the designs of (how) the earth
> is linked (to heaven),

'Whoever ignored common sense when he spoke,
> who did what is forbidden,
> committed an abomination,
> the terrifying splendor of his kingship
> will overwhelm you all, until you are empty air!

'This saying shall lie like a thorn in your hearts,
'Do you go forth to the upper world until once again
> I call you to mind!'

As he spoke I awoke."
Like a young man who has shed blood,
> who wanders alone in a swamp,
> whom a pursuer has overtaken,
> and his heart is pounding,

Or, like a lusty young boar, mounting his mate with innards
> aswell, who lets out wind at his mouth and behind,   (70)

He cried out a lament, saying "Woe is me!"
> He darted out into the street like an arrow and
> scooped up dirt from alley and square in his mouth,
> all the while setting up a frightful clamor,
> "Woe! Alas! Why have you ordained this for me?"

---

1. An Elamite deity, see Hinz, JNES 24 (1965), 353ff.

He was shouting in front of the subjects of Assur,
praising in his pain the valor of Nergal and Ereshkigal,
who had stood forth to aid the prince.
As for him, the scribe who formerly had accepted a present,
who assumed his father's post,
with the astuteness that Ea bestowed upon him,
he took th(ose) words of praise to heart,
saying to himself,
"Lest disloyalty bring me to harm,
I shall always do what [   ] commanded."
So he went and reported it to the palace, saying,
"This shall be my protection from evil."   (75)

Text: von Soden, ZA 43 (1936), pl. I - IV (photos only).
Edition: W. von Soden, "Die Unterweltsvision eines assyrischen Kronprinzen," ZA 43 (1936), 1-31 (most restorations and interpretations are taken from him); Livingstone, *Court Poetry*, 68-76 (with some improved readings and interpretations used here).
Translation: Speiser, ANET³, 109-110; Labat, *Religions*, 94-97.
Literature: Dalley, RA 74 (1980), 190 (to lines 44 and 48 rev.).
Notes to Text: (36) von Soden, *Nabu* 1987/11.

IV.6 IN PRAISE OF ARBELA

Arbela, modern Irbil, was an important city in Assyria noted for its sanctuary
of the goddess Ishtar.

Arbela, Arbela! (1)
Heaven without rival, Arbela!
City of joyful music, Arbela,
City of festivals, Arbela,
City of happy households, Arbela! (5)
O shrine of Arbela, sublime abode,
Spacious sanctuary, delightful dais,
The pride(?) of Arbela is [its] lofty holy place.
City of splendor, Arbela,
Abode of pleasure, Arbela, (10)
Arbela, home of reason and discretion.
Bond of the world, Arbela,
Sustainer of ancient rites, Arbela.
Arbela is established like heaven,
Her foundations are firm as the [netherworld]. (15)
Arbela's head is held high, rivalling [heaven].
Her image is Babylon, her double is [   ],
Sublime holy place, dais of destinies, gateway to heaven.

Tribute(?) from [all la]nds enters there,
Ishtar dwells within it, Nanay, daughter of Sin [   ], (20)
Irnina, foremost of the gods, firstborn goddess.

(rest too fragmentary for translation)

Text: Ebeling-Köcher-Rost, LKA 32.
Edition: Ebeling, *Jahrbuch fur Kleinasiatische Forschung* 2 (1952/3), 274-282; Livingstone, *Court Poetry*, 20-22.
Translation: Hecker, TUAT V/2, 768-770.

B. BABYLONIAN POETRY AND PROSE

IV.7 NABOPOLASSAR

The Neo-Babylonian kings were heirs to the great conquests of Assyria. Under their rule, Babylon was destined to become the greatest city of its time. Numerous prayers in the names of the Neo-Babylonian kings are preserved in building inscriptions. Their language bespeaks great piety and reverence, but they give little hint of the personalities of the kings they name. Furthermore, except for certain prayers of Nabonidus, they generally lack the personal and political allusions often to be found in Assyrian prayers of the Late period.

Nabopolassar (625-605 B.C.) was the founder of this dynasty. He allied with the Medes against Assyria, and, after the destruction of Assyria, set about to consolidate his substantial territorial gains. He bequeathed to his son, Nebuchadnezzar II, an empire stretching from southern Babylonia to the Mediterranean. For a historical survey of his reign, see D. J. Wiseman, CAH³ 3/2, 229f.

(a) TO MARDUK (1)

This prayer to Marduk concludes an inscription commemorating the reconstruction of the Etemenanki, temple of Marduk in Babylon.

O lord Marduk, look joyfully upon my good works and, according to your sublime command, which cannot be altered, may my handiwork endure forever. Even as the brickwork of Etemenanki shall stand firm for all time, so sustain my throne till distant days.

O Etemenanki, bless the king who renovated you. When, amidst jubilation, Marduk takes up his dwelling within you, do you, O house, speak favorably of me to Marduk, my lord.

Text: Hilprecht, BE 1 84, iii 38-59; Strassmaier, ZA 4 (1889), 134-136 lines 147-177.
Edition: Langdon, VAB 4, 64-65 no. 1, 31-61.
Translation: von Soden, SAHG, 283 no. 26; Seux, *Hymnes*, 505.
Literature: Berger, AOAT 4/1 (1973), Nabopolassar Zylinder III, 1.

(b) TO MARDUK (2)

This prayer concludes an inscription commemorating reconstruction of the city fortification wall called Nemetti-Enlil in Babylon.

O Marduk, Enlil of the gods, administrator of the four world regions, look joyfully upon my good works and, according to your sublime command, [grant] me [as my?] royal gift a just scepter, a firmly sustained throne, a reign till distant days, and that I proceed in the four world regions proudly, with head held high.

Text: Clay, BRM 4 51 = Stephens, YOS 9 84.
Edition: Clay, BRM 4, 48-50.
Translation: Seux, *Hymnes*, 505.
Literature: Berger, AOAT 4/1 (1973), Nabopolassar Zylinder II, 3.

IV.8 NEBUCHADNEZZAR II

The long reign of Nebuchadnezzar II (604-562 B.C.) saw expansion and consolidation of the empire founded by Nabopolassar. Babylon was extensively rebuilt, including new temples and a royal palace, the remains of which are still visible today. The prayers which follow all come from texts commemorating building projects of this energetic and successful king. For a historical survey of his reign, see D. J. Wiseman, CAH³ 3/2 230-240 and *Nebuchadrezzar and Babylon* (Oxford, 1985).

(a) TO MARDUK (1)

This prayer to Marduk, which exists in two variant versions, concludes an inscription commemorating construction of the royal palace in Babylon.

O lord Marduk, wisest of the gods, magnificent prince, it was you who created me and entrusted to me the kingship of all peoples. I love your lofty form as (my own) precious life.[1] None of your holy places in the whole inhabited world did I render more renowned than your holy place, Babylon. Even as I love your divine splendor and have ever sought after your dominion, so accept my entreaty, hear my prayer! Let me be a royal provider who pleases you, let me be your faithful shepherd who keeps your people safe,[2] let me be a skilled governor who provides for all your holy places.

At your command, O merciful Marduk, may the house I built long endure and may I enjoy its delights in full measure. May I reach old age and enjoy venerable years therein. May I receive therein the massive tribute of the kings of the four world regions and of all humankind. From horizon to zenith, wherever the sun comes forth, may I have no opponents nor encounter those to affright me. Within it may my descendants hold dominion over the black-headed folk[3] forever.

1. Omits.
2. Variant omits.
3. Mesopotamians.

Text: Norris, I R 58 ix 47 - x 19; Ungnad, VAS I 38, iii 34-54; Ball, PSBA 11 (1889), 159f. pl. VIII, iii 36-55; see also Stephens, YOS 9 143, 144.
Edition: Langdon, VAB 4, 120-121 no. 14, iii 36-55; 140-141 no. 15, ix 47 - x 19.
Literature: Berger, AOAT 4/1 (1973), Nebukadnezar Stein-Tafel X; Nebukadnezzar Zylinder III, 5.
Translation: von Soden, SAHG, 283 no. 27a; Seux, *Hymnes*, 506-507; Hecker, TUAT V/2, 782-783.

(b) TO MARDUK (2)

This prayer concludes an inscription commemorating the reconstruction of Etemenanki, temple of Marduk in Babylon.

O Marduk, fiercest of the gods, noble one, according to your command the holy place of the gods is built, its brickwork formed, the sanctuary restored, the temple completed. According to your sublime word, which has no alteration, may my offering be sound, may my handiwork be perfect, may whatsoever I attempt be lasting and long endure, may I enjoy its delights. Even as Etemenanki stands firm for all time, so sustain my throne forever.

O Etemenanki, bless me, Nebuchadnezzar, the king who renovated you. When [I shall have completed your work], according to the commands of Marduk, [do you, O house, speak favorably of me to Marduk, my lord].*

Text: Hilprecht, BE 1/1 3, iv 5-28.
Edition: Langdon, VAB 4, 148-149 no. 17, iv 5-28.
Translation: von Soden, SAHG, 284 no. 27b; Seux, *Hymnes*, 507.
Literature: Berger, AOAT 4/1 (1973), Nebukadnezar Zylinder IV,1.
Notes to Text: (28) von Soden, SAHG, 284; Seux, *Hymnes*, 507 note 2.

(c) TO MARDUK (3)

This prayer concludes an inscription commemorating construction of a fortification wall in Babylon.

> O Marduk, Enlil of the gods, my divine creator, may my works find your favor, may I live on forever. Grant me the gift of eternal life, venerable old age, a firm throne and an enduring reign. May you, Marduk, be my help and my trust. At your firm command, which cannot be altered, may my weapons be whetted and brandished, may they overwhelm the weapons of the enemy.

Text: Moldenke, JAOS 16 (1896), 76-77, lines 14-30; Ungnad, VAS 1 40, ii 13-32; Winckler, ZA 1 (1886), 341-342, lines 13-32.
Edition: Langdon, VAB 4, 82-83 no. 4, ii 13-32.
Translation: von Soden, SAHG, 284 no. 27c; Seux, *Hymnes*, 508.
Literature: Berger, AOAT 4/1 (1973), Nebukadnezar Zylinder II,8.

(d) TO MARDUK (4)

This prayer concludes an inscription commemorating construction of fortifications, including gates and a moat, at Babylon.

> O lord Marduk, look with favor upon my handiwork and grant me eternal life. Wherever are battle and warfare, may you, Marduk, be my help and my trust. May your raging weapons, which cannot be withstood, go beside me to slay my enemies.

Text: Winckler, ZA 2 (1887), 127, lines 17-29.
Edition: Langdon, VAB 4, 84-85 no. 5, ii 17-29.
Translation: von Soden, SAHG, 284 no. 27d; Seux, *Hymnes,* 508.
Literature: Berger, AOAT 4/1 (1973), Nebukadnezar Zylinder II,5.

(e) TO MARDUK (5)

This prayer concludes an inscription commemorating reconstruction of the old palace and construction of a new one at Babylon.

> What is there besides you, my lord? You have promoted the reputation and vouchsafed an honorable career to the king you love, whose name you pronounce, who is pleasing to you. I am the prince whom you preferred, your handiwork. It was you who created me and vouchsafed me kingship over all peoples. According to your favor, O lord, which you are always ready to bestow upon all of them, make your sublime lordship merciful upon me, instill in my heart reverence for your divinity, grant me what you please that you sustain my life.

Text: Norris, I R 53, i 55 - ii 1.
Edition: Langdon, VAB 4, 122-125 no. 15, i 55 - ii 1.
Translation: Seux, Hymnes, 508-509.
Literature: Berger, AOAT 4/1 (1973), Nebukadnezar Stein-Tafel X.

(f) TO NABU

This prayer concludes an inscription commemorating construction of a temple for Nabu at Borsippa.

> O Nabu, true heir, sublime courier, victorious one, beloved of Marduk, look joyfully upon my works for (my) favor. Grant me the gift of eternal life, venerable old age, a firm throne, an enduring reign, slaying of foes, conquest of the enemies' land. Proclaim from your steadfast tablet, which fixes the limits of heaven and netherworld, long days and a prolonged old age. Make my works acceptable to Marduk, king of heaven and netherworld, the father who begot you. Speak favorably of me, may this ever be on your lips, "Nebuchadnezzar is surely a provident king."

Text: Norris, I R 51 no. 1, ii 16-31.
Edition: Langdon, VAB 4, 98-101 no. 11, ii 16-31.
Translation: von Soden, SAHG, 286 no. 29; Seux, Hymnes, 511-512.
Literature: Berger, AOAT 4/1 (1973), Nebukadnezar Zyl. II,12.

(g) TO NABU AND MARDUK

This prayer, written out on a brick, concludes an inscription commemorating construction of a processional street in Babylon.

O Nabu and Marduk, as you go joyfully in procession through these streets, may words favorable of me be upon your lips. As I proceed before you within the(se streets), may I live a life enduring till distant days, in good health and [satisfac]tion forever.

Text: R. Koldewey, *Das Wiedererstandene Babylon*[4] (Leipzig, 1925), 54 figure 37.
Edition: Langdon, VAB 4, 196-197 no. 29, 5-7.
Translation: Seux, *Hymnes*, 513.
Literature: Berger, AOAT 4/1 (1973), Nebukadnezar Backstein BI,5.

(h) TO NINMAH

This prayer concludes an inscription commemorating reconstruction of the temple of the birth goddess in Babylon.

O Ninmah, merciful mother, look joyfully! May words in my favor be upon your lips. Multiply my descent, make numerous my posterity, administer in safety childbirth among my descendants.

Text: Ungnad, VAS 1 43, ii 5-19; Ball, PSBA 11 (1889), 249, ii 5-18; see also Bezold, ZA 1 (1886), 40-41, lines 23-30; Stephens, YOS 9 146.
Edition: Langdon, VAB 4, 84-85 no. 6, ii 5-19.
Translation: von Soden, SAHG, 287 no. 32; Seux, *Hymnes*, 514.
Literature: Berger, AOAT 4/1 (1973), Nebukadnezar Zylinder II,1; see also Backstein BI,12.

(i) TO SHAMASH (1)

This prayer concludes an inscription commemorating reconstruction of the temple of Shamash in Sippar.

O Shamash, great lord, as you enter joyfully Ebabbar, your radiant house, look steadfastly upon my precious handiwork, may words in my favor ever be upon your lips. At your steadfast command, may I enjoy venerable old age, the gift of life till distant days, and a firm throne. May my reign be long and prosperous forever. May a just scepter, good shepherdship, and a steadfast rod to safeguard the people be my royal portion forever.

O Shamash, be you the protection of my army amidst raging weaponry brandished for battle, answer me in oracle and divination. At your holy word, which cannot be transgressed, may my weapons be brandished and whetted, may they overwhelm the weapons of my foes.

Text: O'Connor, *Hebraica* 1 (1884/5), 207-208, lines 68-100.
Edition: Langdon, VAB 4, 102-103 no. 12, ii 41 - iii 30.
Translation: Seux, *Hymnes*, 509-510.
Literature: Berger, AOAT 4/1 (1973), Nebukadnezar Zylinder III,1.

(j) TO SHAMASH (2)

This prayer concludes an inscription commemorating construction of the Shamash temple at Larsa.

O Shamash, great lord, as you enter Ebabbar, your lofty abode, in joy and jubilation, look happily upon the works of my good hands. Let a life till distant days, a firm throne, and an enduring reign be upon your lips. May doorsill, doorbolt, locks, and door leaves of Ebabbar ceaselessly voice words in my favor before you.

Text: Norris, I R 51 no. 2, ii 12-26, see also Stephens, YOS 9 140.
Edition: Langdon, VAB 4, 96-97 no. 10, ii 12-26.
Translation: von Soden, SAHG, 285 no. 28b; Seux, *Hymnes*, 510.
Literature: Berger, AOAT 4/1 (1973), Nebukadnezar Zylinder II,4.

(k) ACROSTIC HYMN TO NABU

This acrostic hymn, the first sign of each stanza of which spells "God Nabu," glorifies him with many of the attributes normally ascribed to Marduk. It concludes with an account of the divine election of Nebuchadnezzar II to kingship.

> O [Nabu], counsellor of the gods of heaven [and netherworld],   (1)
> [of the god]s his forefathers, Enlil[1] of the gods, lord of the gods,
> [O   ] god, who loves truth and justice, who saves the [   ],
> Divine [Lugal]dimmerankia "king of the gods of all of heaven
>   and netherworld,"[2]
>   who ordains destinies for the [   ] gods,
> God whose divinity is greatest [above] in heaven,
>   whose [   ] is surpassing in the depths,   (5)
> God whose sublime [supervi]sion* has produced the grain
>   of the gods, god who [   ] food portions,
> [God] to whom the Anunna-gods do homage,
>   whose [kingship] they exalt,
> [God] whose word [the Igigi-gods he]ed,*
>   whose command they attend,
> [Divine] irrigator of heaven [and earth],
>   who provides prosperity [   ],   (10)
> [God whose lordship the gods?] of heaven and netherworld
>   have made supreme!*
>
> [   ], lord of lords, supervisor of the gods, offspring of [   ],
> [Shi]ning light of the Igigi and Anunna-gods, firstborn of [Marduk],
> [Beloved] of Ninshiku,[3] creative matrix of the [gods],
> [   ] who grasps the circumference of the p[ure] starry sky, (15)
> [   ] who renders judgments, who destroys all ev[il ones],
> [   ] ruler, foremost one, Enlil of the gods [   ],
> [Who grants scepter] and royal throne
>   to the king who reveres [him],

1. That is, supreme among the gods.
2. See Creation Epic (III.17) Tablet VI line 139, where this is a name for Marduk.
3. Name for Ea; see IV.2a(3).

[Who gives] truth and justice to those
who seek after [his sanctuaries],
[who] gives his ordinances in the pure heavens,   (20)
[who] has established obed[ience]
        throughout the wide world,

The pure [starry sky] which he made as a cover[1]
        [is entrusted]* to his hand,
An uncontested [deci]sion established the stations
        of the great gods within Ba[bylon],
His is to [ca]re for the sanctuaries and to restore the holy places,
He formed the shape of human [vi]sages, animate creatures,   (25)
He provided a shep[herd] for livestock and wildlife,
The lord of life, the god of [   ]
        grasps the living in his gentle hand.
Gods and m[en] are taught reverence for his sublime divinity,
All the gods of heaven and netherworld wait upon him,
        they stand and kn[eel] reverently [before him].
He has endowed the king's features with awesomeness
        beyond that of mortal men,   (30)
He has clad him in fearsomeness and [him]
        with divine splendor and radiance!

He has exalted his[2] lordship over all subject peoples,
He has subjected at his feet peoples and lands,
He has delivered the black-headed folk[3] into his hand,
        that he be their shepherd,
Finally, Marduk, who loves [his] kingship,   (35)
Resolved that Esagila and Ezida be provided for,
        and that Babylon, [his] beloved city, be restored:
He raised up for rulership Nebuchadnezzar,
        a prince who reveres him,
        who pleases him, [his] own handiwork,

1. See Creation Epic (III.17) Tablet IV line 38, where this is said of Marduk.
2. Nebuchadnezzar's.
3. The Mesopotamians.

[And], having regard for his righteous [d]eeds,
> he nominated [him] to exercise kingship over all peoples,

[He caused] him to grasp in his hand the just scepter that
enlarges the land,

[He placed] beside him mighty weaponry to vanquish his foes, (40)

[He bes]towed upon him a merciless mace
> that conquers enemies and opponents!

Text: Strong, PSBA 20 (1898), 155-157.
Edition: Strong, PSBA 20 (1898), 154-162.
Translation: Seux, *Hymnes*, 124-128.
*Notes to Text: (6) Seux, *Hymnes*, 125 note 12. (9) Seux, *Hymnes*, 126 note 15. (11) So CAD B,
203a *u-šá-t[i-ru]*, though the copy does not show enough room for this restoration. (22) Seux,
Hymnes, 127 note 37.

IV.9 NERIGLISSAR TO MARDUK

At the death of Nebuchadnezzar II began a period of political instability in Babylonia, wherein various kings reigned for short periods. Neriglissar (559-556 B.C.) was the most important of an undistinguished lot.

This prayer concludes an inscription commemorating reconstruction of the royal palace in Babylon.

> O Marduk, great lord, splendid Enlil of the gods, light of the gods his fathers, at your sublime command, which cannot be altered, may I enjoy the delights of the house I have built, may I grow old and attain a venerable old age within it. From horizon to zenith, wherever the sun comes forth, may I receive therein the massive tribute of the kings of the four world regions, of all peoples. May my offspring hold dominion therein over the black-headed folk[1] forever.

Text: Norris, I R 67, ii 31-42.
Edition: Langdon, VAB 4, 214-215 no. 1, 31-42.
Literature: Berger, AOAT 4/1 (1973), Ngl Zylinder II,3.
Translation: Seux, Hymnes, 575-576.

1. The Mesopotamians.

IV.10 NABONIDUS

Nabonidus (555-539 B.C.) came to the throne under obscure circumstances, ending a period of political instability. His reign was marked by religious controversy, for he promoted the cult of the moon god to an extent some Babylonians found offensive. Part of his reign he spent at Teima, in northern Arabia, for reasons that are as yet unexplained, but which may have to do with the growing power of the Medes across the northern flanks of Mesopotamia. After his return to Babylon his policies seem to have met increased resistance, though his theological innovations are not fully understood. The invading armies of Cyrus the Persian entered Babylon without hindrance, and this ended native rule in Babylonia. For a historical survey of his reign, see P. Beaulieu, *The Reign of Nabonidus, King of Babylon 556-539 B.C.*, YNER 10 (New Haven, 1989).

Some of the prayers translated below give elusive hints as to the personality and religious convictions of this complex and interesting man.

(a) TO ISHTAR OF AKKAD

This prayer concludes an inscription commemorating reconstruction of a temple of Ishtar in Babylon.

> Therefore, O Ishtar of Akkad, goddess of combat, look joyfully upon this house, your beloved dwelling, and command life (for me). Speak each day before Marduk, king of the gods, for the prolongation of my days and the increase of my years. Come to my side where there is battle and melee, may I kill my enemies and slay my foes.

Text: S. Smith, RA 22 (1925), 60 ii 16-31.
Edition: S. Smith, RA 22 (1925), 60-62 = Ehelolf, WVDOG 47 (1926), 136-137.
Translation: von Soden, SAHG, 290 no. 36; Seux, *Hymnes*, 523.
Literature: Berger, AOAT 4/1 (1973), Nabonid Zylinder II,3; Beaulieu, YNER 10 (1989), 39.

(b) TO MARDUK (1)

This prayer forms part of an inscription commemorating reconstruction of the Shamash temple in Larsa.

O lord, foremost of the gods, prince Marduk, without you no dwelling is founded nor is its design laid out. Were it not for you, who could do what? O lord, at your sublime command, let me do what is pleasing to you.

Text: Bezold, PSBA 11 (1889), pl. iv (after p. 96), 35-40.
Edition: Langdon, VAB 4, 238-239 no. 3, 35-40.
Translation: Seux, *Hymnes*, 516.
Literature: Berger, AOAT 4/1 (1973), Nabonid Zylinder III,1; Beaulieu, YNER 10 (1989), 27f.

(c) TO MARDUK (2)

This prayer forms part of an inscription commemorating reconstruction of the Ehulhul, temple of the moon god in Harran.

Let me be king after your own heart, I who, in my ignorance, had no thought of kingship, whom you, lord of lords, have given more responsibility than others you have named and who held dominion from of old. Prolong my days, let my years endure, that I may be the provider [for your sanctuary].

Text: Messerschmidt, MVAeG 1896/1, 79 vii 45-56.
Edition: Langdon, VAB 4, 280-281 no. 8, vii 45-56.
Translation: Seux, *Hymnes*, 516.
Literature: Berger, AOAT 4/1 (1973), Nabonid Stelen-Fragment XI; Beaulieu, YNER 10 (1989), 20f., 89.

(d) SHAMASH (1)

This prayer forms part of an inscription commemorating reconstruction of the Ebabbar, temple of Shamash in Sippar.

O Shamash, sublime lord, as you enter Ebabbar, seat of your repose, may the gates, entrances, chapels, and courtyards rejoice before you like flowers(?).[1] As you take up your residence in your lordly cella, your judiciary seat, may the gods of your city and of your household put your feelings in repose, may the great gods please you. May Aya the great bride, who dwells in the bedchamber, keep your features ever aglow and speak favorably of me every day.*

With your radiant features and joyful face look joyfully upon my precious handiwork, my good deeds, my inscription and my royal statue. May words in my favor be upon your lips, pronounce my name for all time. Let the house I built endure, may your dwelling be perpetual within it. May the god of the house, the design of the house, the crossbeams, lentil, doorframe, sill, bolt, threshold, anteroom, and door leaves guard my step and make straight your going, in your presence extol my deeds, and night and day may they invoke favor for me.

At your sublime command, which cannot be altered, at the word of your great divinity, which cannot be transgressed, may truth, justice, and the divine judge of the gods who sits before you, set for my feet a way of well-being and wealth, a path of truth and justice. May your sublime courier* who stands before you, Bunene, whose counsel is good, who rides (your) chariot, who sits on the driver's seat, whose onslaught cannot be withstood, who hitches up the valorous steeds whose legs tire not going or returning, who parades before you in street and way, make favorable report of me and advise you that my kingship be lengthy of days, may he come to your aid in your precious mission.* Send beside me the divine splendor of your lightning bolt, symbol of

---

1. Meaning uncertain, the simile may be that of a field full of spring flowers that seems to rejoice as the sunlight approaches. A similar expression occurs in IV.47b line 3.

dominion and the awesomeness of kingship, to plunder the land of my enemy. May I overwhelm my foe's land, may I kill my adversaries, may I partake of the booty of my enemy, may I garner to my land the possessions of all lands.

May I be a provident king who renews holy places, who completes sanctuaries for all time. At the invocation of my eminent name may all my enemies become timorous and weak, may they bow down before me. May they bear my yoke till distant days and bring their massive tribute before me in my city Babylon. May my dwelling be eternal within Babylon, may I enjoy the thoroughfare of its by-ways in full measure, may my service endure in Esagila and Ezida, which I love. Before lord Nabu and Nergal, my gods and the gods of the entire new year's festival house of the Enlil of the gods, Marduk,* may I always, for all time, proceed to offer flour sacrifices, to care for Edadihegal,[1] and to entreat the lord of lords.

Text: Pinches, V R 65, ii 15-52.
Edition: Langdon, VAB 4, 258-261 no. 6, 15-52.
Translation: von Soden, SAHG, 288-290 no. 35b; Seux, *Hymnes*, 519-521.
Literature: Berger, AOAT 4/1 (1973), Nabonidus Zylinder II,9; Beaulieu, YNER 10 (1989), 25.
Notes to Text: (20) Seux, *Hymnes*, 519 note 5. (32) Seux, *Hymnes*, 520 note 13. (38) Seux, *Hymnes*, 520 note 17. (50) Seux, *Hymnes*, 521 note 21.

1. Unclear, perhaps the name of a structure.

(e) TO SHAMASH (2)

This prayer forms part of an inscription commemorating reconstruction of the Ebabbar, temple of Shamash in Sippar.

O Shamash, great lord of heaven and earth, light of the gods his ancestors, offspring of Sin and Ningal, as you enter the Ebabbar, your beloved house, as you take your place upon your eternal dais, look joyfully upon my good works, mine, Nabonidus, king of Babylon, the prince who provides for you, who pleases you, builder of your sublime cella. Each day as you rise and set, make my signs favorable in sky and terrain. Receive my entreaties and accept my prayers. May I hold dominion forever with the legitimate scepter and staff which you let me hold in my hand.

Text: Pinches, V R 64, iii 11-21; Ungnad, VAS 1 53, iii 11-22.
Edition: Langdon, VAB 4, 226-227 no. 1, iii 11-21.
Translation: Seux, *Hymnes*, 518.
Literature: Berger, AOAT 4/1 (1973), Nabonid Zylinder III,2; Beaulieu, YNER 10 (1989), 34f.

(f) TO SIN (1)

This prayer concludes an inscription commemorating reconstruction of the Ekishnugal, temple of Sin the moon god at Ur. Here Nabonidus asserts that Esagila, temple of Marduk at Babylon, and Ezida, temple of Nabu at Borsippa, are also temples to the moon god, Sin. Thereby this prayer gives evidence for his personal convictions. The reference to possible wrong-doing of his son, Belshazzar, suggests resistance to his religious program, even within his own family. This inscription may date to near the end of Nabonidus' reign, after his return from Arabia.

O Sin, lord of the gods, king of the gods of heaven and netherworld, god of gods, who dwells in the great heavens, as you joyfully enter this temple, may there be upon your lips words favorable to Esagila, Ezida, and Ekishnugal, the temples of your great divinity. May its foundation last like heaven. Save me, Nabonidus, from wrong-doing against your great divinity, grant me the gift of a life long of days. Instill as well in the heart of Belshazzar, (my) first-born son, my offspring, reverence for your great divinity. May he commit no wrong-doing, may he enjoy the delights of living in full measure.

Text: Norris, I R 68, ii 3-31.
Edition: Langdon, VAB 4, 252-253 no. 5, ii 3-31.
Translation: Seux, *Hymnes*, 521.
Literature: Berger, AOAT 4/1 (1973), Nabonid Zylinder II,2; Beaulieu, YNER 10 (1989), 35ff.

(g) TO SIN (2)

This prayer, from stelae set up by Nabonidus at Harran, commemorates his reconstruction of the Ehulhul, temple of Sin there. The language of the prayer shows Nabonidus's policy of promoting Sin over the other Mesopotamian gods. This aroused resistance in Babylon and elsewhere. The prayer is characterized by use of conventional phraseology in unconventional ways and by rambling, profuse diction.

O Sin, lord of the gods, whose name on the first day of the month is "... of Anu,"[1] who can strike the heavens and shatter the earth, who appropriates the supremacy of Anu, who controls the supremacy of Enlil, who takes over the supremacy of Ea, who grasps all and every heavenly responsibility in his hands, supreme god[2] of the gods, king of kings, lord of lords, whose command they do not contest and whose word you speak not twice, with the awesomeness of whose great divinity heaven and earth are filled, as with whose features heaven and earth are overwhelmed,[3] without you, who can do anything?

The land you have resolved to make your dwelling, you will establish therein reverence for your great divinity for all time to come. The land you have resolved to shatter, you will remove reverence for you therefrom and you will overthrow it for all time to come.

(You are the one) whom all gods and goddesses dwelling in heaven watch for, whose utterance they carry out, (that being) the command of Nannaru,[4] the father who begot them, who controls the responsibilities of heaven and netherworld, without whose sublime command, which he speaks in heaven daily, no land can rest secure, nor will there be light in that land ... *(fragmentary lines, then gap)*

---

1. "Crescent," "Weapon," and "Prince" have variously been suggested, but the word remains obscure.

2. Text: Enlil, perhaps etymologizing as *il-ili* "god of gods."

3. The precise purport of "as" is not clear. It may be temporal, in the sense that as the moon's light overwhelms the earth, the awesome qualities of the moon fill the earth, or a simile may be implied, the earth being filled (from below) the way it is overwhelmed (from above).

4. Name for Sin.

Text: Gadd, AnSt 8 (1958), 60-62.
Edition: Röllig, ZA 56 (1964), 221-223.
Translation: Oppenheim, ANET³, 562-563.
Literature: Berger, AOAT 4/1 (1973), Nabonidus Stelen-Fragmente III.1; Moran, OrNS 28 (1959), 139; Beaulieu, YNER 10 (1989), 32ff., 60ff.

IV.11 ANTIOCHUS SOTER TO NABU

This stilted piece is primarily of interest because it is the latest datable Akkadian prayer. It concluded an inscription commemorating renovation of the Esagila and Ezida temples in the mid-third century B.C.

O Nabu, sublime son, wisest of the gods, stately one, worthy(?)* of praises, first-ranked son of Marduk, offspring of Arua,[1] queen who is fashioner of created things, look joyfully and, at your sublime command, (you) whose command cannot be changed, let overthrow of my enemy's land, attainment of my desire to stand in triumph over our foes, just kingship, prosperous reign, satisfaction, and venerable old age be the royal gift (to) Antiochus and Seleucus his son, forever.

O princely son Nabu, heir of Esagila, first-ranked son of Asaru,[2] offspring of Arua the queen, when amidst happiness and rejoicing you enter Ezida, the eternal house, the house of your divine supremacy, your pleasurable dwelling, by your eternal command, which cannot be set aside, may my days be long, may my years be many, may my throne be firmly founded, may my reign endure, through your sublime scepter, which fixes the limits of heaven and netherworld. May words favorable of me be always upon your pure lips. May I conquer the lands from the rising to the setting sun, may I behold their tribute and bring it for the perfection of Esagila and Ezida.

O Nabu, foremost son, when you enter Ezida, the eternal house, may there be on your lips a favorable word for Antiochus, king of the world, and favorable words for Seleucus the king, his son, and Stratonike his wife, the queen.

Text: Pinches, V R 66, i 16 - ii 29.
Edition: Weissbach, VAB 3, 132-135.
Translation: von Soden, SAHG, 291-292 no. 38; Oppenheim, ANET³, 317; Seux, *Hymnes*, 525-526.
Notes to Text: (1) Text: "established."

1. Name for Sarpanitum, wife of Marduk.
2. Marduk.

IV.12 ADVICE TO A PRINCE

This warning, composed in the casuistic style of omens, lists misdeeds of an unnamed king and their consequences. Most of the misdeeds center around royal abuse of the privileges of the cities Sippar, Nippur, and Babylon. The detailed charges suggest that the writer had a specific king in mind, perhaps Merodach-Baladan, an eighth-century ruler of Babylonia.[1] Since this text was copied for Assurbanipal's library, was quoted from memory(?) by a scholar in a letter,[2] and has turned up in a late manuscript from Nippur, it was evidently studied as a literary work, whatever its original political purpose may have been.

(1) If the king has no regard for due process, his people will be thrown into chaos, his land will be devastated. If he has no regard for the due process of his land, Ea, king of destinies, will alter his destiny and misfortune will hound him.[3]

If he has no regard for his nobles, his lifetime will be cut short. (5) If he has no regard for his advisor, his land will rebel against him. If he has regard for a scoundrel, the mentality of his country will alter. If he has regard for a clever trick,[4] the great gods will hound him for the sake of right counsel and the cause of justice.

If he denied due process to a citizen of Sippar, but granted it to an alien, Shamash, judge of heaven and earth, (10) will establish an alien due process in his land and neither princes nor judges will have regard for due process. If citizens of Nippur were brought to him for due process (and) he accepted the (customary) remuneration, (but) denied them due process, Enlil, lord of the world, will raise up against him a foreign enemy that will decimate his army,[5] his[6] commanders and administrators will prowl the streets like vagabonds.

---

1. For a study of his reign, see J. Brinkman, "Merodach-Baladan II," *Studies Oppenheim*, 6-53; *Prelude to Empire* (Philadelphia, 1984), 47ff.; R. van der Spek, JEOL 25 (1977/8), 56-66. The dating of the events referred to in the text to his reign was argued by Böhl, MAOG 11/3, 30ff. and afresh by Diakonoff, AS 16, 343ff., endorsed by Brinkman, *Studies Oppenheim*, 48. Labat, *Religions*, 316f., suggests that this text refers to actions of Sennacherib.

2. Reiner, *Studies Diakonoff*, 320ff.

3. Or: (Ea) "will hound him with misfortune," in contrast to line 8.

4. Literally: "a device of Ea."

5. Variant: "and will turn over his forces to the ruler of Elam"(?).

6. Or: "its" (the army).

(15) If he took money of citizens of Babylon and appropriated (it) for (his own) property, (or) heard a case involving Babylonians but dismissed (it) for a triviality, Marduk, lord of heaven and earth, will establish his enemies over him and grant his possessions and property to his foe.

If (he) imposed a fine or imprisonment (20) upon a citizen of Nippur, Sippar, or Babylon, the city where that fine was imposed will be razed to its foundations and a foreign foe will enter the place of imprisonment.

If he called up the whole of Sippar, Nippur, and Babylon to impose forced labor on the peoples aforesaid, requiring of them (25) service at the recruiter's cry, Marduk, sage of the gods, deliberative prince, will turn his land over to his foe so that the forces of his land will do forced labor for his foe. Anu, Enlil, and Ea, the great gods (30) who dwell in heaven and earth, have confirmed in their assembly the exemption of these (people from such obligations).

If he granted his steeds forage on the fodder of citizens of Sippar, Nippur, (or) Babylon, the steeds that consumed the fodder will be led off to an enemy's harness. (35) If the citizens aforesaid are conscripted into the king's forces in a time of national conscription, mighty Erra, [van]guard of his army, will shatter his front line and go at his [fo]e's side.

If he absconds with [their] oxen, alters [their] fields, (or) (40) grants (them) to an alien, Adad will come quickly. If he seizes [   ] their sheep, Adad, irrigator of heaven and earth, will decimate his pasturing livestock with hunger and offer them up(?)[1] to the sun.

(45) If an advisor or administrator on the king's service denounces them[2] (the citizens aforesaid) and extorts bribes from them, by the command of Ea, king of the depths, the advisor or administrator will die violently, the place they were will be obliterated to a wasteland, (50) the wind will carry away their remains, their achievements will be reckoned as a puff of air.

If he nullifies their contracts, alters their steles, sends them out on

---

1. Meaning of the verb not clear. I take it to refer to the corpses of the starved beasts lying under the hot sun.
2. Variant: "the case of a 'lord'"; I adhere to the reading of BWL.

service, or [forces] labor obligations upon them, Nabu, scribe of Esagila, who inspects the whole of heaven and earth, who directs everything, who appoints kingship, will nullify the bonds of his country and ordain misfortune (for it).

(55) If an officer or temple warden or royal administrator who holds wardenship of a temple in Sippar, Nippur, or Babylon, imposes forced labor upon them (the citizens aforesaid) for the temples of the great gods, the great gods will quit their sanctuaries in a fury, they will not enter their shrines.

Text: W. G. Lambert, BWL, plates 31, 32; Civil, *Studies Diakonoff*, 324-326 (variants not noted here).
Edition: W. G. Lambert, BWL, 110-115.
Translation: Labat, *Religions*, 316-319; von Soden, TUAT III/1, 170-173.
Literature: I. M. Diakonoff, "A Babylonian Political Pamphlet from about 700 B.C.," AS 16 (1965), 343-349; E. Reiner, "The Babylonian Fürstenspiegel in Practice," *Studies Diakonoff*, 320-323. For a critique of Diakonoff's interpretation of the text, see W. G. Lambert, JAOS 88 (1968), 124.

IV.13 THE KING OF JUSTICE

This text recounts certain signs and wonders of the reign of a Neo-Babylonian king that illustrate his concern for justice and the gods' favor for him. Of particular interest is the fullest description of a water ordeal to come down from antiquity. Important parts of the text are missing, notably the beginning and end, that latter of which contained, among other things, a description of the king's domain (unfortunately too fragmentary to translate). The preserved text contains various errors and what seem to be anacolutha, but, with all these problems, the composition is singularly appealing and a notable contrast to the formalities of the royal inscriptions of the period. Whereas the king was identified with Nebuchadnezzar II by Lambert, an attribution to Nabonidus is also possible.

i

(At the beginning remains of about twenty-seven lines of text are preserved. These suggest that the composition opened with a third person peroration with numerous dependent clauses ["He who ..."], with reference to the "Lord of Lords," climaxing in the mention of Babylon and the king's name [lines 10-11]. Thereupon the text may move into an account of his divinely directed birth and upbringing, and how he was chosen for dominion over the land.)

ii

... (2) nor would he make a decision concerning them (the cripple or widow). They would eat each other like dogs. The strong would oppress the weak, while they had insufficient means to go to court for redress. The rich would take the belongings of the lowly. Neither governor nor prince would appear before the judge on behalf of the cripple or widow, they would come before the judges but they would not proceed with their case; a judge would accept a bribe or present and would not consider it (the case).[1] They (the oppressors) would not receive an injunction (such as this):

---

1. Not clear. The line may mean that judges were bribed not to hear cases, not that the poor were unable to muster the fee to give to a judge to have a case heard.

(9) "The silver which you loaned at interest you have increased five-fold! You have forced households to be broken up, you have had fields and meadowland seized, families were living in front and back yards. You have taken in pledge servants, slaves, livestock, possessions, and property. Although you have silver and interest in full, these (mortgaged properties) remain to yourselves."[1]

(14) A man who had nothing came before him, but he, the judge who had made the decision, drawn up a tablet, and sealed it, threw the tablet away and would not give (it) to him.* Were the man to pursue him (the judge), he risked his life. Having no recourse, he would let out a cry and set up a sh[ou]t, invoking the lord of lords, "Award (me) my silver and interest, against (these) people!" [He (the judge) would not aw]ard it (to him), nor would he comfort them (widow and cripple), come to their help (the oppressed), nor consider (the case of the impoverished).

(22) For the sake of due process he (the king) did not neglect truth and justice, nor did he rest day or night! He was always drawing up, with reasoned deliberation, cases and decisions pleasing to the great lord Marduk (and) framed for the benefit of all the people and the stability of Babylonia. He drew up improved regulations for the city, he rebuilt the law court. He drew up regulations ... his kingship is forever. *(one line gone).*

iii

(2) The innocent man would take the ... [   ]. A man who returned to that law court (to reopen a case), such that, a tablet [having been written] and sealed, he was returning a second time for false and dishonest purposes, the king commanded the troops to cut off his head and paraded it through the land. The head ... cut off, he made a likeness of that man's head, and he had (the following) written upon that man's head and fastened forever after to the outer gate of that law court for all the people to see, "(This was) a man whose case was judged, whose tablet of verdict was written and sealed, but who afterwards changed and came back for

---

1. Translation doubtful. It seems that the rapacious creditor, though paid, has not let the debtor take his pledged property back.

judgment. His head was cut off on this wise." Base and wicked men would see it, abscond, and never be heard of again.

(14) He put a stop to bribes and presents among the people, he gave the people satisfaction, he caused the land to dwell in tranquility, allowing none to do them any alarm. He pleased his lords Sin, Shamash and Ishtar — they being Bel and Beltiya[1] — (and) Nabu who dwells in Esagila and Ezida, <and who loves his kingship>. They (the gods) were reconciled in his reign on account of the regular offerings.[2]

(21) A man charged a man with murder but did not prove it. They were brought before him (the king) and he ordered them (to be taken) above Sippar, to the bank of the Euphrates, before Ea, king of the depths, for trial. The troops of the guard, keeping both under close surveillance all night, lit a fire. At daybreak the prince, governor, and troops assembled as the king commanded, and took their places around them. Both went down (and) ... the river. Ea, king of the depths, in order to [ ] his royal beloved* (and) in order to see justice [done, did] what always had [   ] ... [The first] ... he had jump in, he (the river god) brought him safely t[o the bank]. The one who had charged him with murder* sank in the water. From morning until noon no one saw him nor was aught heard of [him].* As for the troops of the guard, who had stood around them at the riverbank from evening until daybre[ak], their hearts sank and they set out to search [ ], "What shall we report? How shall we answer the king?" When the king heard, he was furious at the troops. A courier was coming and going, "Did you not watch over the man? Has he gotten across the river and lain down in the open country?" Since none saw him at any time, they could not answer. Anxious boat(?) riders went along the river, bank to bank, checking the edge. When high noon came his corpse rose up from the river. He had been struck on the head, blood was running from the ears and nostrils. The top of his head was burned, as if with fire, his body was covered with sores. The people saw, and spoke (? of it) in reverence; all the world was borne down with awe. The enemy,

---

1. For the understanding of this line, see Lambert, *Iraq* 27 (1965), 10 note to iii 17: "the line states quite clearly that Šamaš and Ištar are identified with Marduk and Sarpanitum ..."
2. Text in disorder here; I have freely rearranged lines 18-20.

the wicked one, and the hostile betook themselves into hiding.

(iv 24) On another occasion, another man den[ounced]* another man. He swore an oath by Shamash (that he had not), and had no fear of the magic circle[1] [of Shamash], the great lord who is Marduk, residing in Esagila *(one line lost)*.

v

(1) [   ] he built anew. He hitched up strong horses to wagons. It being his desire,* the foremost of them were laden* with an offering to the gods, they lost no time hurrying along with (it).

(4) Before him (Marduk), every day, without ceasing, for food he gave him to eat abundant mighty oxen, fine fatted rams, [   ], geese, ducks, [wild fowl, pigeons], dormice, s[trings] of f[ish], cultivated [fr]uit in enormous [quantities], the [prid]e of orchards, [apples], figs, pomegranates, grapes, dates, imported dates, [dried figs?], [rai]sins, abundant vegetables, the [delight] of the garden, fine mixed beer, honey, ghee, refined oil, best quality milk, sweet emmer beer, fine wine. The finest of grain and vine of all mountains and lands, the best of what was his, the fair products of mountains and seas he offered in abundance before the great gods. What no one had ever done to such an extent, they received, in perpetuity, from his pure hands, and blessed his kingship. [In] conquering from Egypt to Hume, Piriddu, Lydia, [Mar]hashi, king of [remote] regions [   ] *(breaks off)*

Text: W. G. Lambert, CT 46 45.
Edition: W. G. Lambert, *Iraq* 27 (1965), 1-11.
Literature: J. Bottéro, "L'Ordalie en Mésopotamie ancienne," *Annali della Scuola Normale Superiore di Pisa, Classe di Lettere e Filosofia*, Serie III vol XI/4 (1981), 1005-1067 (cited below as "Bottéro, Ordalie"); von Soden, ZA 65 (1975), 283, where numerous new readings are proposed, many of which are adopted here. See also W. von Soden, "Kyros und Nabonid, Propaganda und Gegenpropaganda," *Archaeologische Mitteilungen aus Iran, Ergänzungsheft* 10 (1983), 61-68; Beaulieu, YNER 10 (1989), 4-5.
Notes to Text: (ii 16) von Soden, ZA 65 (1974), 283. (iv 2) See Bottéro, "Ordalie," 1049. (iv 6) von Soden, ZA 65 (1975), 283. (iv 9) Bottéro, "Ordalie," 1050 suggests: "calls upon his name were not heard." (iv 24) von Soden, ZA 65 (1975), 283. (v 2) *pa-nu-tú šá-a-šá za-a-na-tú*(?). *za-a-na-tú*(?) may be the same root *za'ānu* as in iv 22. (v 3) Reading *i-zab-bi-<la>-ma* or *i-zab-bi-la*!

1. In the Late period, oaths to Shamash could be sworn standing inside a magic circle; see p. 695 note 2.

IV.14 IN PRAISE OF EZIDA

Ezida was the temple of Nabu at Borsippa, an important city and center of learning to the south of Babylon. For Nabu, see III.45.

How like heaven is the city Borsippa!	(1)
Lofty Ezida is the likeness of Esharra.[1]	
The whole(?)* is delightful to (its) god,	
The gardens enhance the city's pride.	
Its summit reaches the clouds,	(5)
Its well-founded roots thrust to the netherworld.	
Its brickwork is of soapstone(?),*	
Its parapet is of finest, choicest gold,	
Its retaining wall is of alabaster,	(10)
The apparel of Ezida is blue (glazed) pegs.	
He who dwells therein is scribe to the gods,	
Nabu, son of Esagila,	
He bears the tablet of destinies for all the gods,[2]	
He gives the decision(s).	(15)
He holds the stylus of truth,	
He scrutinizes the black-headed folk[3] each day.	
Take up your abode in your dwelling, son of the lord,	
May your house, Ezida, be replete with splendor!	

Text: Köcher, ZA 53 (1959), 237.
Edition: Köcher, ZA 53 (1959), 236-240.
Notes to Text: (3) See von Soden *apud* Köcher, 239. (7) So Köcher, 240; see CAD L, 65b.

1. See p. 377 note 3. This may refer to the heavenly abode of all the gods.
2. For tablet of destinies, see p. 360 note 1.
3. The Mesopotamians.

IV.15 IN PRAISE OF BABYLON

(a) SUBLIME HOLY PLACE

This text was composed in fifteen(?) five-line strophes, each line of a strophe beginning with the same sign. While the date of the composition is uncertain, it is generally ascribed to some pro-Babylonian Assyrian monarch, for example, Assurbanipal (Strong, PSBA 17 [1895], 131) or, as preferred here, Sargon II (Seux, *Hymnes*, 124 note 34). This latter attribution is based on the possibility that Sargon II is named in the last line of the text. As suggested originally by Strong, the acrostic probably read "[I will extol] its (Babylon's) name in the four [world regions]."

(*gap*)

iv

May months and years bless sublime Esagila,   (5)
May its brickwork give blessing to noble Marduk.*
At the month of life, (at?) the New Year's festival,
     let a celebration be held,
Let the four world regions gaze fixedly upon his features,
May he bestow a satisfying life upon the shepherd[1]
     who provides for him.

v

He who devised the plans of the sanctuaries, restored the daises,   (10)
Who completed his great holy place Babylon,
     city of universal dominion,
Who restored all its mighty sanctuaries,
He confirmed its suspended regular offerings as they were before,
His [   ] responded with an omen of well-being and a verdict.

vi

[In] Babylon, the sublime holy place which [   ]   (15)
[   ] a brilliant garment

1. The king.

(gap)

xiii(?)

(fragmentary lines)

May the sublime princess Sarpanitum bless his kingship,
May she make numerous his descent and multiply his progeny.   (5)

xiv(?)

May he attain his ambitions with none to oppose him,
May daily talk of him be favorable and submissive,
May he proceed through Shuanna¹
    on a course of well-being and satisfaction,
May he go safely inside its temples and carry out its rites,
May he ever, in gladness, make rejoicing in sweet Babylon.   (10)

xv(?)

May its excellence be sung on the lyre and its hymn of praise ...
May he shower down finest oil in its famous holy places,
May he fill the coffers of its temples
    with precious goods beyond calculation,
May those deeds he performed be ... [   ],
May the name of Sar[gon   ].   (15)

Text: DT 83 = T. Pinches, *Texts in the Babylonian Wedge-writing* (London, 1882), 15 no. 4 (collated).
Edition: Strong, PSBA 17 (1895), 133-135.
Translation: Seux, *Hymnes*, 122-124.
Notes to Text: (6) Or, according to Poebel, AS 9 (1939), 23, "May they (the months and years) bless its brickwork for the sake of prince Marduk." While this rendering better fits the parallelism, it requires an emendation of the text.

1. Babylon.

(b) THE BABYLONIANS

This composition is known from a tablet containing excerpts of various texts, presumably the work of a student. There appear to be numerous mistakes. The text may not be complete.

> They set out (offering) shares of beverage,
>> How reverently they bless the g[od]!   (1)
> They are heedful of divine judgment, observant of truth,
>> They [   ] boundary, truth, and design.
> Strength of Ningirsu, wealth of the sweet harvest song,
>> Their ... cannot be compared with them.
> They have seemly ways(?), are well-advised and pleasing,
>> They brighten their mood and m[ake] merriment.
> Women who have gained understanding in their tasks,
>> High priestesses who are always faithful to their
>> (divine) husbands,   (5)
> Cloistered women who are skilled in keeping
>> the unborn child alive,
>> Holy Women who place [   ] in purifying water,
> Who observe interdicts and adhere to what is sacred,
>> They bless [   ] ...
> Reverent, circumspect, mindful of virtue,
>> The daughters of the gods always [   ] ...
> Well-tried in good works, they can (do) what is see[mly?],
>> The [   ] of all Babylon ...
> These are the ones whom Marduk freed of obligations,
>> [I have] extolled ..., nor did I impugn them!   (10)

Text: Ebeling, KAR 321, rev 2-11.
Edition: None.

C. NARRATIVE AND EXPRESSIVE WORKS

IV.16 ERRA AND ISHUM

Erra and Ishum is one of the most original and challenging compositions in Akkadian. The text is a portrayal of violence: its onset, course, and consequences — how it needs to be recognized and feared as potentially the most powerful of forces. Violence can eliminate even the order ordained by the gods and sweep away in its frenzy all the hopes and accomplishments of civilization. The author, Kabti-ilani-Marduk, who may have lived in the eighth century B.C., must have seen and suffered the consequences of violence and civil strife.[1] He gives witness to a society that had cast off restraints and so ceased to be in balance. If, the text tells, people understand the nature of violence, how it can rage out of control and overwhelm all, they can hope to avoid it. To the modern reader the most salient aspect of this text is its high level of feeling, the willingness of its author to experiment, and the complexity of its thought and structure.

Marduk, as chief Babylonian deity, plays a major role in this poem. He is portrayed as remote and all-wise; he knows Erra's plans even before Erra arrives at his temple. He speaks in sonorous, scholarly diction; there is never any doubt that he is king. Yet the poet is troubled that there could be disorder in his realm that could threaten even Marduk himself.

The form of the text is narrative poetry, most of it direct speech. Ishum, Erra's companion, is invoked near the beginning and plays a crucial role throughout the poem, though he is subordinate to Erra. The device, well known in Western literature, of telling the exploits of a hero from the standpoint of his closest companion, is attested here for the first time. While some narrative is in the third person, in one long passage (see Tablet II Pericope C2, lines 14ff.), Erra narrates his own actions. This represents, in modern critical terms, an attempt to fuse narrative and the narrated, discourse and event. Such an experiment builds on a tradition of self-narrative by a deity in Mesopotamian poetry (see II.6, III.25, IV.27, 54). Perhaps the same tradition is refurbished in a self-praise by Marduk of his own cult statue (Tablet I lines 149ff.), not to mention a description by Marduk himself of destruction done to

---

1. The precise date of the text is disputed; see, for example, Cagni, *Epopea*, 37-45; von Soden, UF 3 (1971), 253-263; AfO 34 (1987), 67-69.

Babylon (Tablet IV lines 40ff.). Some of Erra's actions are also narrated in the second person by Ishum (see Tablet III Pericope C lines 58ff.).

The diction of this text seems strange, or at least idiosyncratic, to some modern readers. Some are inclined to regard this as indicative of an author untutored in the finer points of Akkadian poetics. One might equally consider it a determined effort to refurbish a rich inventory of inherited expressions to lend them greater force, to do such violence, so to speak, to traditional usage as to command attention.

Tablet I

(Narrator invokes Marduk, chief deity of Babylon, and Ishum, vanguard and companion of Erra. Erra is restless and breaks into a soliloquy. He is anxious to fight and campaign, but hesitates through natural inertia. Speaking of himself in the third person, Erra says that what he needs to stir him to action is Ishum's encouragement [i 9].)

> O king of all inhabited lands, creator of the wo[rld], (1)
> O Hendursagga,[1] first-born of Enlil [   ],
> Holder of the "sublime scepter,"[2]
>> herdsman of the black-headed folk, shepherd [of mankind],
> O Ishum, "zealous slaughterer,"[3]
>> whose hands are suited to brandish fierce weapons,
> And to make his sharp spear flash, Erra, warrior of the gods,
>> was restless in his dwelling, (5)
> His heart urged him to do battle!
> Says he to his weapons, "Smear yourselves with deadly venom!"
> To the Seven, warriors unrivalled, "Let your weapons be girded!"
> He even says to you, "I will take to the field!"[4]

1. Another name for Ishum.
2. Translation of Hendursagga (Cagni, *Epopea*, 138–139; Edzard, RLA 4, 325).
3. A learned Sumerian etymologizing of Ishum's name (W. G. Lambert, AfO 18 [1957/58], 400).
4. It is not clear who speaks lines 10–20. Erra may be describing himself, or the narrator may be speaking of Erra. As interpreted here, the narrative statement is that Erra is restless (5–9), while Erra's speech to Ishum, showing both inclination and disinclination to stir, includes the entire passage 10–20. A different reading is offered by Machinist, JAOS 103 (1983), 222–223 (earlier by Hruška, BiOr 30 [1973], 5), whereby Ishum is the subject of I.6–14 and Erra is addressed in 9–14, thus the reverse of the reading adopted here. While in some respects this is an attractive possibility, it seems excluded by 9a, for the "you" there, so far as I can see, must be Ishum (so also Edzard, Cagni and others).

"You are the torch, they will see your light,   (10)
"You are the vanguard, the gods will [   ],
"You are the stanchion, [zealous] slaughterer!
"(So) up, Erra, from laying waste the land
"How cheerful your mood will be and joyful your heart!
"Erra's limbs are slug[gish],
       like those of a mortal lacking sleep,
"He says to himself, 'Shall I get up or go to sleep?'
"He says to his weapons, 'Stay in the corners!'
"To the Seven, warriors unrivalled, 'Go back to your dwellings!'
"Until you rouse him, he will sleep in his bedroom,
"He will dally with Mami his mate."   (20)

(With a second invocation, now of Ishum, the narrator introduces the terrible Seven, who stand ready to massacre the "black-headed folk," or Mesopotamians.)

O Engidudu "who patrols at night," "ever guiding the noble,"[1]
Who ever guides young men and women in safety,
      making light as day,
The Seven, warriors unrivalled, their divine nature is different,
Their origins are strange, they are terrifying,
Whoever sees them is numbed with fear.   (25)
Their breath is death,
People are too frightened to approach it!
Yet Ishum is the door, bolted before [them].[2]
When Anu, king of the gods, sowed his seed in the earth,
She bore him seven gods, he called them the "Seven."
They stood before him, that he ordain their destinies.   (30)
He summoned the first to give his instructions,
"Wherever you go and spread terror, have no equal."
He said to the second, "Burn like fire, scorch like flame."
He c[ommanded] the third, "Look like a lion,
      let him who sees you be paralyzed with fear."

---

1. "Patrols at night" is a literal translation of the Sumerian epithet; "ever guiding" is a learned word play on the same epithet (as shown by Tinney, *Nabu* 1989/3).
  2. Variant: "it."

He said to the fourth, "Let a mountain collapse
    when you present your fierce arms."   (35)

To the fifth he said, "Blast like the wind,
    scan the circumference of the earth."
The sixth he enjoined, "Go out everywhere (like the deluge)
    and spare no one."
The seventh he charged with viperous venom,
    "Slay whatever lives."
After Anu had ordained destinies for all of the Seven,
He gave those very ones to Erra, warrior of the gods,
    (saying), "Let them go beside you.   (40)
"When the clamor of human habitations
    becomes noisome to you,
"And you resolve to wreak destruction,
"To massacre the black-headed folk and fell the livestock,
"Let these be your fierce weaponry, let them go beside you."

(The Seven offer the encouragement that Erra needs. In a rousing call to arms, they extol the heroic excitement of the campaign, the honor, prestige, and gratification it brings. The Seven claim vaguely that they are not respected enough, that others are growing more important than they. They bring up the old charge (see II.39) that men make too much noise for the gods to sleep, although this was not the cause Erra had given for his own lack of sleep. The Seven claim further that there are too many wild animals on the loose. Their final claim, no doubt the most important one, is that they are bored and out of training.)

These are the ones who are in a fury,
    holding their weapons aloft,   (45)
They are saying to Erra, "Up, do your duty!
"Why have you been sitting in the city like a feeble old man,
"Why sitting at home like a helpless child?
"Shall we eat woman food, like non-combatants?
"Have we turned timorous and trembling, as if we can't fight?   (50)
"Going to the field for the young and vigorous
    is like to a very feast,

"(But) the noble who stays in the city can never eat enough.
"His people will hold him in low esteem,
      he will command no respect,
"How could he threaten a campaigner?
"However well developed is the strength of the city dweller,   (55)
"How could he possibly best a campaigner?
"However toothsome city bread,
      it holds nothing to the campfire loaf,
"However sweet fine beer, it holds nothing to water from a skin,
"The terraced palace holds nothing to the [wayside] sleeping spot!
"Be off to the field, warrior Erra, make your weapons clatter,   (60)
"Make loud your battle cry that all around they quake,
"Let the Igigi-gods hear and extol your name,
"Let the Anunna-gods hear and flinch at the mention of you,
"Let (all) the gods hear and bend for your yoke,
"Let sovereigns hear and fall prostrate before you,   (65)
"Let countries hear and bring you their tribute,
"Let the lowly hear and [per]ish of their own accord,
"Let the mighty hear and his strength diminish,
"Let lofty mountains hear and their peaks crumble,
"Let the surging sea hear and convulse,
      wiping out (her) in[crease]!   (70)
"Let the stalk be yanked from the tough thicket,
"Let reeds of the impenetrable morass be shorn off,
"Let men turn cowards and their clamor subside,
"Let beasts tremble and return to clay,
"Let the gods your ancestors see and praise your valor!   (75)
"Warrior Erra, why do you neglect the field for the city?
"The very beasts and creatures hold us in contempt!
"O warrior Erra, we will tell you,
      though what we say be offensive to you!
"Ere the whole land outgrows us,
"You must surely hear our words!   (80)
"Do a kindly deed for the gods of hell,
      who delight in deathly stillness,
"The Anunna-gods cannot fall asleep for the clamor of mankind.
"Beasts are overrunning the meadows, life of the land,

"The farmer sobs bitterly for his [field].
"Lion and wolf are felling the livestock,   (85)
"The shepherd, who cannot sleep day or night
        for the sake of his flocks, is calling upon you.
"We too, who know the mountain passes,
        we have [forgotten] how to go,
"Cobwebs are spun over our field gear,
"Our fine bow resists and is too strong for us,
"The tip of our sharp arrow is bent out of true,   (90)
"Our blade is corroded for want of a slaughter!"

(Erra brightens at this and asks Ishum why he does not proceed at once. Ishum remonstrates, saying that violence and destruction are evil. Erra, thoroughly aroused, launches into a self-praise. He is the bravest. If people do not respect the gods enough, and the others are too pusillanimous to do anything about it, he will remedy matters. Since the supposed lack of respect for him must be contrary to Marduk's wishes, Erra will cause Marduk to forsake his dwelling and thus bring about the punishment mankind deserves.)

The warrior Erra heard them,
What the Seven said pleased him like finest oil.
He made ready to speak and said to [Ish]um,
"Why, having heard, did you sit by silent?   (95)
"Lead the way, let me begin the campaign!
"[   ] the Seven, warriors without rival,
"Make my fierce weapons[1] march at my side,
"But you be the vanguard and rear guard."
When Ishum heard what he said,   (100)
He felt pity and said [to the war]rior Erra,[2]
"O lord Erra, why have you pl[otted evil] against the gods?
"You have remorselessly plotted evil,
        to lay waste the lands and decimate [the people]."
Erra [made ready to sp]eak and said,
To Ishum his vanguard he said [these words],   (105)

1. That is, the Seven.
2. Variant: "He made ready to speak, [say]ing [to the warrior Erra]."

"Keep quiet, Ishum, listen to what I say.

"As concerns the people of the inhabited world,
>   whom you would spare,

"O vanguard of the gods, wise Ishum,
>   whose counsel is always for the best,

"I am the wild bull in heaven, I am the lion on earth,

"I am king in the land, I am the fiercest among the gods,   (110)

"I am warrior among the Igigi-gods,
>   mighty one among the Anunna-gods!

"I am the smiter of wild beasts,
>   battering ram against the mountain,

"[I am] the blaze in the reed thicket,
>   the broad blade against the rushes,

"I am banner for the march,

"I blast like the wind, I thunder like the storm,   (115)

"Like the sun, I scan the circumference of the world.

"I am the wild ram striding forth in the steppe,

"I invade the range and take up my dwelling in the fold.

"All the gods are afraid of a fight,

"So the black-headed folk are contemptuous!   (120)

"As for me, since they did not fear my name,

"And have disregarded Marduk's command,
>   so he may act according to his wishes,[1]

"I will make Marduk angry, stir him from his dwelling,
>   and lay waste the people!"

(Erra repairs to Esagila and asks Marduk why his image is besmirched. In a sonorous speech [see General Introduction, p. 15 note 1] Marduk, having, in his omniscience, seen Erra's intent, recounts what transpired last time he forsook his dwelling: the universe went topsy-turvy, living creatures were nearly wiped out by the ensuing catastrophe. When Marduk found that his cult statue had been sullied, he caused it to be rebuilt by sublime craftsmen who were later dismissed, never to return. Marduk waxes lyrical in praise of his own cult statue and the wonderful tree from which it was fashioned. The present image of Marduk, divinely created, could never be duplicated.)

1. Variant: "they act." As taken here, Erra will motivate Marduk to act as he really wanted to anyway, but had hesitated to for the reasons he gives in lines 132ff.

The warrior Erra set out for Shuanna,[1]
>   city of the king of the gods,
He entered Esagila, palace of heaven and earth,
>   and stood before him.   (125)
He made ready to speak, saying to the king of the gods,
"Why has your precious image,[2] symbol of your lordship,
>   which was full of splendor as the stars of heaven,
>   lost its brilliance?[3]
"Your lordly diadem, which made the inner sanctum shine
>   like the outside tower,[4] (why is it) dimmed?"
The king of the gods made ready to speak, saying
To Erra, warrior of the gods, these words,   (130)
"O warrior Erra, concerning that deed you said you would do,[5]
"Once long ago indeed I grew angry,
>   indeed I left my dwelling, and caused the deluge![6]
"When I left my dwelling,
>   the regulation of heaven and earth disintegrated:
"The shaking of heaven meant:
>   the positions of the heavenly bodies changed,
>   nor did I restore them.
"The quaking of netherworld meant:
>   the yield of the furrow diminished,
>   being thereafter difficult to exploit.[7]   (135)
"The regulation of heaven and earth disintegrating meant:
>   underground water diminished, high water receded.

1. Babylon.

2. The Akkadian word here translated as "precious image" (Bottéro, *Annuaire* 1977/78, 152 note 35 = *Mythes*, 266; cf. W. G. Lambert, AfO 18 [1957/8], 399) can also be understood as "attire" or "fittings."

3. Translation uncertain; perhaps, with Cagni, *Epopea*, 183, "became dirty."

4. Literally, "which made Ehalanki shine like Etemenanki." The meaning is that the inner shrine shone as brightly as if it were outside in open daylight.

5. That is, line 123.

6. "Deluge" may be used here metaphorically for "catastrophe," as the immediate consequence was low, not excessive, water, and no other Mesopotamian tradition associates Marduk with the deluge.

7. Obscure. I take this to mean that the furrow could no longer be reliably "levied" for its "yield," that is, expected to give of its increase to the gatherer.

When I looked again, it was a struggle to get enough.
"Productivity of living offspring declined, nor did I renew it,
"Such that, were I a plowman,
    I (could) hold (all) seed in my hand.
"I built (another) house and settled therein.[1]
"As to my precious image, which had been struck by the deluge
    that its appearance was sullied,   (140)
"I commanded fire to make my features shine
    and cleanse my apparel.
"When it had shined my precious image and completed the task,
"I donned my lordly diadem and returned.
"Haughty were my features, terrifying my glare![2]
"The survivors of the deluge saw what was done.   (145)
"Shall I raise my weapon and destroy the rest?[3]
"I sent those craftsmen[4] down to the depths,
    I ordered them not to come up.
"I removed the wood and gemstone[5] and showed no one where.
"Now then, warrior Erra, as concerns that deed
    you said you would do,
"Where is the wood, flesh of the gods,
    suitable for the lord of the uni[verse],   (150)
"The sacred tree, splendid stripling,[6] perfect for lordship,
"Whose roots thrust down an hundred leagues
    through the waters of the vast ocean to the depths of hell,
"Whose crown brushed [Anu's] heaven on high?
"Where is the clear gemstone that I reserved for [ ]?
"Where is Ninildum, great carpenter of my supreme divinity,   (155)

---

1. Perhaps a reference to (re)construction of Esagila after the catastrophe, or to a special building where his image was refurbished.

2. Difficult. von Soden (AHw, 1383a) suggests "darkened" (though they have just been cleaned); Cagni, *Poem*, 90: "Marduk's countenance expressed haughtiness"; Bottéro, "*altiers*."

3. Variant: "Did you raise your weapon and destroy the re[st]?"

4. The divine craftsmen, or sages, who refurbished Marduk's image after it was damaged in the catastrophe.

5. The original depends upon an untranslatable word play on *mēsu* (a tree) and *elmēšu* (a gemstone). The meaning is that the specific materials used to make the image are no longer to be had. The entire passage implies that the statue of Marduk dated to earliest time and could not be reproduced because it was not made by human hands.

6. A Sumero-Akkadian wordplay on *mēsu* (a tree) and Sumerian mes "young man."

"Wielder of the blinding hatchet, who knows that tool,
"Who makes [it] shine like the day
        and puts it in subjection at my feet?
"Where is Kusig-banda, fashioner of god and man,
        whose hands are sacred?
"Where is Ninagal, wielder of the upper and lower millstone,[1]
"Who grinds up hard copper like hide and who forges to[ols]?   (160)
"Where are the choice stones, created by the vast sea,
        to ornament my diadem?
"Where are the seven [sa]ges of the depths, those sacred fish,
        who, like Ea their lord, are perfect in sublime wisdom,
        the ones who cleansed my person?"

(Erra's reply is lost, but he may offer to produce suitable materials for refurbishing the statue. Marduk then asks who will ward off the forces of evil and chaos while he is being refurbished and is thereby non-combatant. Erra offers to reign in his stead. Marduk assents, forsakes his dwelling for repairs, and the universe is thrown into confusion.)

The warrior Erra [hea]rd him ... [ ],
He made ready to speak, saying to noble Marduk,
"[craftsmen   ],   (165)
"[tree   ],
"Clear gemstone [from] its [pl]ace will I bring up."
When Marduk heard this,
He made ready to speak, saying to the [warrior] Erra,
"(When) I rise [from] my dwelling,
        the regulation [of heaven and earth] will disintegrate, (170)
"The [waters] will rise and sweep over the land,
"Bright [day will turn] to dar[k]ness,
"[Wh]irlwind will rise and the stars of heaven will be [   ],
"Ill winds will blow and the eyesight of living creatures
        [will be darkened?],
"Demons will rise up and seize [   ],   (175)
"[They will ...] the unarmed one who confronts them!
"The gods of hell will rise up and smite down living creatures.

1. Variant: "the perf[ect] ... tool."

"Who will keep them at bay

    till I gird on my weaponry (once more)?"

When Erra heard this,

He made ready to speak, saying to noble Marduk, (180)

"O noble Marduk, while you enter that house,[1]

    fire cleanses your apparel and you return to your place,

"For that time I will govern and keep strong

    the regulation of heaven and earth,

"I will go up to heaven and issue instructions to the Igigi-gods,

"I will go down to the depths and keep the Anunna-gods in order.

"I will despatch the wild demons to the netherworld, (185)

"I will brandish my fierce weaponry against them.

"I will truss the wings of the ill wind like a bird's.

"At that house you shall enter, O noble Marduk,

"I will station Anu and Enlil to the right and left, like bulls."[2]

Noble Marduk heard him, (190)

The words which Erra spoke pleased him.

1. The special building where the cult image is refurbished.
2. The imagery seems to be of great winged bulls, such as stood at the entrances to certain Assyrian palaces.

Tablet II

(Marduk leaves his palace, disaster ensues.)

Pericope A + B

He arose from his dwelling, an inaccessible place,	(1)
He set out for the dwelling of the Anunna-gods.	
He entered that house and sto[od before them].	
Shamash looked upon him and let his protective radiance fall ...,	
Sin looked elsewhere, and did not [leave?] the netherworld.	(5)
Ill winds rose and the bright daylight was turned to gloom.	
The clamor of the peoples throughout the land [was stilled].	
The Igigi-gods were terrified and went up to h[eaven],	
The Anunna-gods were [fright]ened	
and [went down] to the pit [of hell],	
[ ] the entire circumference [ ]	(10)
[ ] in the dust.	
[ ] let us see."	
[ ] its doors.	
[ ] like the stars of heaven,	(15)

(gap)

(The gods convene to discuss the situation. Ea, intent upon restoring Marduk to his place, reasons that, even though the original sublime craftsmen cannot return, Marduk authorized reproductions of them to be made that are endowed with wondrous powers by Ea at Marduk's command. The repairs are proceeding well. Erra, while standing guard at the house where the work is being done lest harm approach, is taking the opportunity to usurp Marduk's power by keeping everyone away from him. So vainglorious is Erra's shouting that Ea resolves to see him humbled.)

"The diadem [   ]
"His heart [   ], let him make it happy.
"The governor's[1] [   ]

---

1. Here possibly Erra, as temporary viceroy for Marduk, as opposed to the human governor who appears later in the poem.

"The awe-inspiring radiance of [his] divine splendor [   ]
     his days [   ],
"[   ] like rain,   (20)
"[Let] Ea in the depths [   ] his springs,
"Let Shamash see ... [   ] and let the people [   ],
"Let Sin behold, and at his sign let him [   ] to the land.
"Concerning that work, Ea [   ] is expert(?)."
"The warrior Erra became very angry,   (25)
"Why, because of foam on the w[aters],[1] the ... of mankind,
"Which I myself created to bring offerings to the Anunna-gods,
"Did noble Marduk give up, not at the appointed time?
"He plotted to lay waste the lands and destroy their people!"
Ea the king considered and said these words,   (30)
"Even now that noble Marduk has arisen (from his dwelling),
     he did not command those craftsmen to c[ome up].
"How can images of them, which I made among mankind,
"Approach his sublime divinity, where no god has access?
"He himself gave those same (human) craftsmen
     great discretion and authority,
‹"He gave them wisdom and perfect dexterity.   (35)
"They have made (his) precious image radiant,
     even finer than before.
"Warrior Erra has stationed himself before him,
     night and day without ceasing,
"Besetting the house for making radiant the precious image
     for the sovereignty of the king, and saying,

    'Don't come near the work!
    '[He who dr]aws near it —
       I will cut short his life and prolong his death agony.'

"[   ] let him hasten at the work,   (40)
"[   ] has no equal.
"[   ] Erra was speaking like a mortal,

---

1. In Tablet IV line 68, foam is used as a metaphor for the human race destroyed by the flood. Here it may refer to something transitory: why did Marduk sacrifice the human race for a passing whim (as it seemed to the speaker), and give the human beings over to Erra, when they were essential for feeding and maintaining the gods?

"[   ] trying to rival the noble one,

"[   ] may he be humbled."

[The images of the craftsmen] made his precious image radiant,   (45)

[   ] ...

[They set the ...] at his door(?)

[   ] king Shamash girds it on,

[   ] he reoccupied his dwelling,

[   ] brilliance was reestablished.   (50)

[All the gods   ] were gathered,

Erra [nob]le Marduk,

"Noble Marduk, [   ]

"Godlike, you [   ]

"Small to great, [   ]   (55)

[   ] Erra ... [   ]

[   ] ... his uproar was terrifying,

"[   ] ... the image,

"[   ] of your [lord]ship are raised up and establi[shed]."   (60)

(The repairs successfully completed, Marduk has returned to his dwelling [line 49]. In a fragmentary passage, Marduk addresses the gods and orders them all to return to their dwellings. The gods are alarmed by astral omens that presage Erra's dominance.)

The king of the gods [made ready] to speak and said,

"[   ] and went up to heaven."

[   ] he commanded, "Return to your dwellings!"

[   ] ... his sign,

"[   ] upon your face,   (65)

"[   ] their peoples.

"[   ] you did not turn back."

[He heard him], ... said [to the k]ing of the gods,

"The word of Marduk [   ] of the day."

He said to him [   ]   (70)

"Come now, [   ]

"To destroy the lands [why did you plot?]."

Erra heard him [   ]

...

He entered [   ].
Anu heard in heaven [   ],   (75)
He bowed his lofty head [   ].
Antu, mother of the gods, was aghast [   ],
She entered [her] cham[ber].
Enlil's [   ]

(gap)

Pericope C1

[   ] father of the gods [   ]   (1′)
[   ] Enlil [   ]
Among the beasts, all of them [   ].
Erra among all the gods [   ].   (5′)
Among the stars of heaven the Fox Star[1] [   ]
Was shining bright and its radiance [   ] for him,
The stars of all the gods were dazzling [   ],
Because they were angry with each other
        and noble Marduk [ ] put [   ],
"The star of Erra is shining bright and is radiant: ... of warfare. (10′)
"His awe-inspiring brilliance will ... and all people will perish(?).
"... the dazzling stars of heaven in his time are [dimmed?].
"... the ant, does it not rise [   ]?
"Among the beasts, the image of their star is the fox,
"Endowed with strength, a raging(?) lion [   ],   (15′)
"Enlil is the father of [   ], he has [   ]."

(Even Ishtar, goddess of war, tries to calm Erra.)

Innina replied in the assembly of the gods [   ],
[   ] her words to Anu and Dagan [   ],
"Keep quiet, all of you, go into your chambers,
"Cover your lips, do not smell the in[cense],   (20′)
"Do not debate noble Marduk's word, do not pl[ead   ]
"Until the days are drawn to a close, the [appointed time] passed,

---

1. For discussion, see al-Rawi and Black, *Iraq* 51 (1989), 112.

"The word Marduk speaks is like a mountain where ...,
    he does not change (it) nor [   ]."

(gap)

Pericope C2

Ishtar went, they entered the ...,
She pled with Erra, but he would not agree.   (30')
Ishum made ready to speak, saying (these) words to Ishtar,
"I have ... that of heaven over what is not of heaven,
"Erra is angry and will heed no one,
"Let him come to rest in the mountains, and I(?) ...
    the seed of the people which you spoke about to [   ],
"The sublime son of Enlil will not go on campaign without
    Ishum the vanguard before [him?]."   (35')

(Erra is furious. All he has done is to perform guard duty, and now has been sent home, his services no longer required, without a campaign. This is because he is the most valiant god — no evil rises to oppose him. This he fails to perceive, but, in his blind rage, he resolves to fight his war anyway, to show Marduk and Ea that he is not to be taken so lightly. Erra's self-praise turns into a self-narrative. This passage is unusual in Akkadian and has been subjected to varying interpretations. In favor of that offered here, note that first person narrative is nearly always past or future, hardly ever renderable as present and in progress. Since, as Cagni has shown [Epopea, 208-209], the passage cannot logically refer to the future, and since the past is difficult for grammatical reasons, we have here a present, first-person narrative, one of Kabti-ilani-Marduk's most interesting experiments.)

He was sitting in the E-meslam,[1] taking up his dwelling.
He thought to himself what had been done,[2]
His heart being stung, it could give him no answer,
But he asked it what it would have him do.[3]
"Lead the way, let me begin the campaign!   (40')
"The days are drawn to a close, the appointed time has passed.

---

1. Temple of Erra at Cutha.
2. That is, the successful completion of Marduk's repairs and his being packed off home again, needed no longer.

"I give the command and despoil the sun
>of his protective radiance,

"By night I muffle the face of the moon.

"I say to the thunderstorm, 'Hold back [your] young bulls!

"'Brush aside the clouds, cut off sn[ow and rain]!'   (45')

"I will make Marduk and Ea mindful!

"[He] who waxed great in days of plenty,
>they bury him on a day of drought,

"He who came by water, [they take him back] on a dusty road.

"I say to the king of the gods, 'Take your place in E[sagila],

>'They must do what you commanded,
>>they must carry out your or[der].   (50')

>'The [black]-headed folk cry out to you,
>>but do not accept their entreaties!'

"I obliterate [the land?] and reckon it for ruins,

"I lay waste cities and turn them into open spaces,

"I wreck mountains and fel[l] their wildlife,

"I convulse the sea and destroy its increase,   (55')

"I bring the stillness of death upon swamp and thicket,
>burning like fire,

"I fell humankind, I leave no living creatures,

"Not one do I retain, [nor any?] for seed to [ ] the land.

"I spare no livestock nor any living creatures,

"I dispatch the soldier from one city against another.   (60')

"Neither son nor father has a care for the other's well-being,

"Mother p[lots ev]il against daughter with a leer.

"I let [yokels into] the abodes of gods,
>where harm must not approach,

"I settle the miscreant in the nobleman's dwelling.

"I let outlandish beasts into the shrines,   (65')

"I block access to any city where they appear,

"I send down beasts of the highlands,

---

3. Obscure. As read here, Erra is furious at what he regards as high-handed treatment, and, consulting only his own wounded feelings, decides to go on a rampage. The lines imply that he debated with his "self," but took guidance from his heart (= emotions) alone. One may also understand (with Bottéro), "He (Ishum) asked him (Erra) his orders."

"Wherever they set foot,
>   they bring the stillness of death to the thoroughfares,
"I cause beasts of the steppe not to stay in the steppe,
>   but to traverse the city street.
"I make omens unfavorable,
>   I turn holy places into foraging grounds,   (70′)
"I let the demon "Upholder-of-Evil"
>   into the dwellings of the gods,
>   where no evil should go,
"I devastate the king's palace [   ] and turn it into a ruin,
"I cu[t o]f the clamor of [mankind] in [dwellings]
>   and rob them of happiness,
"As [I   ] orchards like fire ...
"I let evil enter [   ]   (75′)

Tablet III

*(Erra's speech continues, as he glories in the horrors of war, anarchy,
and privation. There follows a gap in the text.)*

Pericope A

"[   ] heeds no one, (1)
"What he(?) reasoned [   ]
"Lions [   ]
"[   ]
"I make [ ] go towards [ ] (5)
"I confiscate [... their] households and cut short their lives,
"I as[sassinate] the righteous man who intercedes,
"I set the wicked cutthroat in the highest rank.
"I estrange people's hearts so father listens not to son,
"And daughter cavils spitefully to mother. (10)
"I make their utterances evil, they forget their gods,
"They speak gross blasphemy to their goddesses.
"I stir up the [rob]ber and so cut off travel absolutely,
"People rifle one another's belongings in the heart of the city.
"Lion and wolf fell the livestock. (15)
"I aggravate [ ] and she cuts off birth-giving,
"I deprive the nurse of the wail of toddler and infant.
"I banish* the work song of harvest home from the fields,
"Shepherd and herdsman forget their field shelters.
"I cut the clothes from the bodies of men,
      the young man I parade naked through the city street, (20)
"The young man without clothes I send down to hell.[1]
"The ordinary fellow has not so much as a sheep
      to offer up for his life,
"For the nobleman's divination lambs are few and precious.
"The patient yearns for a bit of roast to offer for his recovery,
"It does him no good, so he gets up and walks till he dies. (25)

---

1. Captives in war were sometimes paraded naked. Furthermore, the dead enter the netherworld naked; thus the people in the upper world are little better than dead.

"I incapacitate the nobleman's mount like [   ],
"I cut [   ]

(fragmentary lines, then gap)

(Pericope B too fragmentary for translation)

*(The deed spoken and done, Ishum is remonstrating that Enlil has forsaken his city.
Erra, in a frenzy, cries for more, and, having done enough himself, lets loose the Seven.
Ishum, distressed at Erra's "over-kill," demands the reason for it.)*

Pericope C

(Ishum is speaking, restored from IV 33-39)

"The stro[ng   ]   (1)
"Like the blo[od   ]
"[You homed their weaponry upon?] the people
        under special protection, [sacred to Anu and Dagan],[1]
"You [made] their blood course
        like [ditchwater in the city streets],
"You [opened their] arteries
        [and let the watercourses bear (their) blood away].   (5)
"Enlil [cried], "Woe!" [his heart was hardened],
"[He   ] from his dwelling,
"An irrever[sible curse rose to his lips],
"He swore that [he would not drink from the watercourses],
"He was revol[ted by] their blood [and] would not enter [Ekur]." (10)
Erra said these words to Ishum his vanguard,
"The Seven, warrior[s unrivalled   ]
"For all of them [   ]
"Which no[ble   ]
"O [my] vanguard, [   ]   (15)
"Who can speak [   ]
"Who can [   ] like fire

---

1. Certain Mesopotamian cities were exempt from military service, taxes, or other obligations
to the crown, and Erra has violated their charters. While Cagni and others have interpreted this
passage to mean that Erra armed the citizenry, it could also mean that they were exposed to the
effects of weaponry. In favor of Cagni's view, however, see Tablet IV lines 6-10.

"Who can [   ] before [   ]
"Who can [   ] like [   ]
"Who [   ]   (20)
"Who can [   ] Erra?
"The face of a r[avening] lion [   ]*
"In the rage of [   ] heart [   ]?
"Lead the way, [let me begin the campaign]!
"[Muster?] the Seven, warriors unrivalled,   (25)
"[Make] (them), fierce weaponry, [go at my side],
"And do [you] be [my] vanguard and [rear guard]."
When Ishum heard this [speech] of his,
He felt pity and sa[id to himself?],
"Alas for my people, victims of Erra's fury [   ],   (30)
"Whom the warrior Nergal [overwhelmed]
        like the storm of battle [against] the demons,
"As if to kill that conquered god, his arms lose no tension,
"As if to snare wicked Anzu, [his net] is spread!"[1]
Ishum made ready to speak,
Saying to warrior Erra these words,   (35)
"Why have you plotted evil against god and man?
"And why have you remorselessly plotted evil
        against the black-headed folk?

(Erra replies exultantly that men are too stupid to understand the ways of the gods, so why take their part? Furthermore, Marduk did forsake his dwelling, so the world cannot be as it was before; that would be a denial of Marduk's centrality. Now Ishum narrates Erra's violent course in the second person, a literary experiment building upon the preceding. There follows a gap in the text.)

Erra made ready to speak,
Saying to Ishum his vanguard these words,
"You (who) know the reasoning of the Igigi-gods,
        the counsel of the Anunna-gods,   (40)

---

1. That is, Erra is ready for even the most formidable encounter. Bottéro (*Annuaire* 1977/78, 126 note 16) suggests that the conquered god is Qingu (see Creation Epic, III.17). For Anzu, see III.22.

"Would you give guidance to the black-headed folk
      and try to make them understand?[1]
"Why are you, indeed, talking like a know-nothing?
"You are advising me as if you knew not Marduk's command!
"The king of the gods has risen from his dwelling!
"What of all lands has endured?   (45)
"He removed his lordly diadem:
"King and prince [ ] forget their duties.
"He has undone his girdle:
"The bond of god and man is undone,
      impossible to tighten it again.
"Fierce fire made his precious image glow like the day
      and heightened his protective splendor,   (50)
"His right hand grasped the mace, his enormous weapon.
"Noble Marduk's glare is terrifying!
"As for me, what you said to me [   ],
"O vanguard of the gods, wise [Ishum,
      whose counsels are sound],
"Why, just now, [did you   such a] speech?   (55)
"Marduk's command is not [satisfactory to you]?"
Ishum made ready to speak, saying to [the warrior Erra],
"O warrior Erra ... [   ]
"Mankind ... [   ]
"The livestock [   ]   (60)
"Swamps and reedbanks [   ]
"Now then, what you said, w[arrio]r Erra,
"One stood forth and you [   ] seven,
"You killed seven and did not let go a single one,
"Take away the livestock [   ] ...   (65)
"O Erra, when you strike with your weapons,
"Mountains to[tter], the sea [con]vulses,
"Such a flash of [your] stan[chion], they look east,
      [as if to] see the sun [rise]!
"The palace [   ]

1. That is, why would one privy to the minds of the gods bother with any attempt to make men understand them?

(breaks off)

(gap of unknown length)

(Ishum continues: Erra has taken over the universe, even Marduk's sanctuary. How can he now say that no one respects him?)

Pericope D

Ishum made ready to speak, saying to the warrior Erra,
"O [war]rior Erra, you hold the leadrope of heaven,
"You are master of all the earth, lord in the land!
"You convulse the sea, obliterate mountains, (5)
"You rule over man and herd beasts.
"The primeval sanctuaries[1] are in your hands,
"You control Shuanna and command Esagila.
"You have gathered to yourself all authority,
⠀⠀⠀⠀the gods revere you,
"The Igigi-gods stand in awe of you,
⠀⠀⠀⠀the Anunna-gods are in dread of you. (10)
"When you set forth counsel, even Anu heeds you,
"Even Enlil agrees with you. Aside from you, is there opposition?
"Except for you, is there battle?
"The armor of strife is yours alone!
"But you have said to yourself, 'They hold me in contempt.'" (15)

---

1. Text: Ešarra (Temple of Enlil at Nippur); Eengura (Temple of Ea at Eridu).

Tablet IV

(Ishum's speech continues, one of the longest in Akkadian literature. He narrates the horrors and destruction of civil war, refers to atrocities committed in Babylon by an invading army, and, in lines 36ff. quotes Marduk's moving lament for his city. In 45-49 Ishum goes on to quote Marduk's own description of the appalling conditions there. Ishum then describes events at Sippar, where the city walls are destroyed, and at Uruk, overrun by the barbarous Sutaeans. This fierce nomadic people even went so far as to interfere with the cult devotees of Ishtar, whose practices may have been abhorrent to the poet. In 63-64 Dur-Kurigalzu is referred to, and in 65ff. Ishtaran of Der curses his city. It is not clear where Ishum's speech ends, but the poem continues with a passionate portrayal of indiscriminate violence. In 113ff. Ishum points out that even with decimation of the populace Erra is not satisfied; he must ruin the guidance of the land, its government and sanctuaries, even that of Marduk himself.)

"O warrior Erra, you are the one
    who feared not noble Marduk's name![1]   (1)
"You have undone Dimkurkurra, "the bond of the world,"[2]
    the city of the king of the gods.
"You changed your divine nature
    and made yourself like a mortal,[3]
"You girded on your weaponry and entered Babylon.
"Inside Babylon you spoke like a rabble-rouser(?),
    as if to take over the city,   (5)
"The citizenry of Babylon, like reeds in a thicket,
    had no one in charge, so they rallied around you:
"He who knew nothing of weapons — his sword was drawn,
"He who knew nothing of archery — his bow was taut,[4]
"He who knew nothing of fighting — set to the fray,
"He who knew nothing of wings — flew off like a bird.[5]   (10)

1. That is, granting that Erra is supreme, by virtue of Marduk's command, his continued fighting is tantamount to sin, since it would seem to admit of opposition, an apparent denial of Marduk's supremacy.

2. Babylon.

3. That is, by ravaging sanctuaries?

4. Literally: "He who knew nothing of the *tilpānu*-bow, his bow was nocked."

5. The reference seems to be to precipitous flight in the face of danger (Tsevat, RA 81 [1987], 184).

"The cripple could surpass the fleet of foot,
 the weakling could overpower the strong.
"They give voice to gross insolence against the governor
 who provides for their holy places,
"With their own hands they blockaded the gate of Babylon,
 their lifeline,
"They have torched the sanctuaries of Babylon
 like marauders of the land,
"You, the vanguard, took their lead!   (15)
"You aimed your shaft at the innermost wall,
 "Woe! My heart!" it exclaims,
"You flung the seat of Muhra, its gatekeeper,
 into the blood of young men and girls,
"The inhabitants of Babylon themselves — they the bird,
 you the decoy —
"You snared in a net, caught and killed them, warrior Erra!
"You quit the city and have gone out to the outskirts,   (20)
"You took on a lion's face and have entered the palace.
"When the troops saw you, they girded on their weapons,
"The heart of the governor, avenger of Babylon, turned to fury.
"He issued orders to his army to plunder,
 as if plundering enemies,
"He incited the commander to atrocities,   (25)

 'You, my man, for that city I am sending you to,
 'Fear no god, respect no man!
 'Do young and old alike to death!
 'Spare no one, not even the baby sucking milk!
 'You shall plunder the accumulated wealth of Babylon!'   (30)

"The royal troops drew up and have invaded the city,
"With flashing shafts and outstretched blades,
"You homed their weapons upon those under special protection,
 sacred to Anu and Dagan.
"You made their blood course like ditchwater in the city streets,

"You opened their arteries
          and let the watercourses bear their blood away.   (35)
"When the great lord Marduk saw that, he cried 'Woe!'
          and his heart was hardened,
"An irreversible curse rose to his lips.
"He swore that he would not drink from the watercourses,
"He was revolted by their blood and would not enter Esagila,

          'Alas for Babylon,
                    whose crown I fashioned luxuriant as a palm's,
                    but which the wind has scorched!   (40)
          'Alas for Babylon,
                    that I had laden with seed, like an evergreen,
                    but of whose delights I could not have what I hoped for!
          'Alas for Babylon,
                    that I tended like a thriving orchard,
                    but whose fruit I could not taste!
          'Alas for Babylon,
                    that I suspended like a gemstone seal
                    on the neck of the sky!
          'Alas for Babylon,
                    that I clasped in my hand like the tablet of destinies,
                    not handing it over to anyone else!'

"[And this too has] noble Marduk said,   (45)

          '[   ] from former days [   ]
          'Let one quit the wharf: he shall cross
                    at two cubit's depth of water on foot,[1]*
          'Let one go down sixty fathoms in a well,
                    not one man shall keep himself alive (on the water),
          'Let them (still have to) punt the fishing boat
                    a hundred leagues out in the open sea!'

"As for Sippar, the primeval city,
          through which the lord of the world did not allow

---

1. The sense may be that there will be so little water at the city docks that one can walk across the riverbed, starting at the pier, and the water will scarcely reach to one's waist (von Soden *apud* Cagni, *Epopea*, 229). Cutting off of water could also be a military maneuver; see B. Meissner, *Babylonien und Assyrien* (Heidelberg, 1920), 1: 108–109.

the deluge to pass, because it was precious to him, (50)
"You destroyed her ramparts against the will of Shamash,
     and threw down her fortifications.
"As for Uruk, the dwelling of Anu and Ishtar,
     the city of courtesans, harlots, and prostitutes (for the cult),
"Whom Ishtar deprived of husbands
     and reckoned as her own(?),[1]
"There Sutaean nomads, men and women, bandy war whoops![2]
"They turned out the actors and singers (of) Eanna, (55)
"Whose manhood Ishtar changed to womanhood
     to strike awe into the people,
"The wielders of daggers and razors,
     vintner's shears and flint knives,
"Who take part in abominable acts for the entertainment of Ishtar,[3]
"A haughty, remorseless governor you placed over them,
"He harassed them and interfered with their rites. (60)
"Ishtar was angered, she flew into a rage against Uruk,
"She stirred up the enemy and swept clean the country,
     like granules on the water's face.
"The dweller in Parsa had no respite
     from lamenting the destroyed Eugal-sanctuary.[4]
"The enemy you roused has no desire to stop.
"Ishtaran responded thus, (65)

    'You turned the city Der[5] into a wasteland,
    'You fractured her populace like reeds,
    'You extinguished their clamor
         like the (dying hiss of) foam on the water's face!
    'And as for me, you did not spare me
         but gave me over to the Sutaean nomads!

1. With Bottéro; otherwise, "left to their own authority" (Diakonoff *apud* Cagni, *Poem*, 52-53).

2. The Sutaeans, from the point of view of the Mesopotamian city dweller, were marauding nomadic people; see M. Heltzer, *The Sutaeans* (Naples, 1981).

3. The cult of Ishtar was associated with prostitution, both male and female (lines 52, 56), and, perhaps, self-mutilation (57). See also IV.2b.

4. Parsa (see Nashef, RA 77 [1983], 169-174) is to be identified with Dur-Kurigalzu, a large city northwest of Babylon.

5. Important Mesopotamian city near present-day Badra, near the Iranian frontier.

'For the sake of my city Der,   (70)
'I will judge no disputed truth,
       nor make any ruling for the land,
'I will give no guidance nor aid in understanding.
'Men forsook truth and took up violence,
'They abandoned justice and were plotting wickedness.
'Against (but) one country I raised up seven winds.   (75)
'He who did not die in battle will die in the epidemic,
'He who did not die in the epidemic,
       the enemy will plunder him,
'He whom the enemy has not pl[undered],
       the bandit will murder him,
'He whom the bandit did not murder,
       the king's weapon will vanquish him,
'He whom the king's weapon did not vanquish,
       the prince will slay him,   (80)
'He whom the prince did not slay,
       a thunderstorm will wash him away,
'He whom the thunderstorm did not wash away,
       the sun will parch him,*
'He who has gone out in the world,
       the wind will sweep him away,
'He who has gone into his home,
       a demon will strike him,
'He who has gone up to a high place
       will perish of thirst,   (85)
'He who has gone down to a low place
       will perish in the waters!
'You have obliterated high and low place alike.
'The man in charge of the city says to his mother,[1]

       "If only I had stuck in your womb the day you bore me,
       "If only our lives had come to an end,   (90)
       "If only we had died together,
       "For you gave me a city whose walls are destroyed!

---

1. As the text stands, it is difficult to decide who speaks what lines; the reading offered here is only a suggestion.

"Its people are the beasts,
>their god is he who hunts them down.
"He it is whose net is tight-meshed: those engaged
>cannot slip through but die a violent death."
'He who begot a son, saying,

"This is my son, (95)
"When I have reared him he will requite my pains,"

'I will put that son to death, his father must bury him,
'Afterwards I will put that father to death,
>but he will have none to bury him.
'He who built a house, saying

"This is my home,
"I built it for myself, I shall spend my leisure in it, (100)
"On the day fate claims me, I shall fall asleep inside,"

'I will put him to death and wreck his home,
'Afterwards, though it be wreckage(?), I will give it to another.'
"O warrior Erra, you have put the righteous man to death,
"You have put the unrighteous man to death, (105)
"He who sinned against you, you put him to death,
"He who did not sin against you, you put him to death,
"The high priest, assiduous with divine offerings,
>you put to death,
"The functionary who served the king you put to death,
"The old man on the doorstep you put to death, (110)
"The young girls in their bedrooms you put to death,
"Even then you found no appeasement whatsoever!
"Even then you told yourself, 'They hold me in contempt!'
"Even then you said to yourself, O warrior Erra,

'I will strike down the mighty, I will terrorize the weak, (115)
'I will kill the commander, I will scatter the troops,
'I will wreck the temple's sacred chamber, the rampart's
>battlement, the pride of the city I will destroy!
'I will tear out the mooring pole so the ship drifts away,
'I will smash the rudder so she cannot reach the shore,
'I will pluck out the mast, I will rip out the rigging. (120)

'I will make breasts go dry so babies cannot thrive,
'I will block up springs so that even little channels
    can bring no life-sustaining water.
'I will make hell shake and heaven tremble,
'I will make the planets shed their splendor,
    I will wrench out the stars from the sky,
'I will hack the tree's roots so its branches cannot burgeon,   (125)
'I will wreck the wall's foundation so its top tumbles,
'I will approach the dwelling of the king of the gods,
    that no direction be forthcoming!'"

(Erra is gratified that the extent of his power is recognized; he has at last won his respect. He decrees that the rabble of the world should fight on; at length Babylon shall rule what is left. Erra then allows Ishum to campaign against a mountain that is apparently the homeland of the Sutaeans, the human arch-villains of the narrative. Erra has destroyed most of the world, but Ishum now puts violence to useful purpose.)

The warrior Erra heard him,
The speech that Ishum made pleased him like finest oil.
Thus spoke the warrior Erra,   (130)
"The Sealand the Sealand,[1] Subartu Subartu, Assyrian Assyrian,
"Elamite Elamite, Kassite Kassite,
"Sutaean Sutaean, Gutian Gutian,
"Lullubaean Lullubaean, land land, city city,
"House house, man man, brother brother must not spare
    (one another), let them kill each other!   (135)
"Then, afterwards, let the Akkadian arise to slay them all,
    to rule them,[2] every one."
The warrior Erra said these words to Ishum his vanguard,
"Go, Ishum, the matter you spoke of,[3] do as you wish."

1. This and the following list the countries surrounding Babylonia to the south, north, east, and west, partly in contemporaneous, partly in archaizing terms. "Akkadian" in 136 refers to an unnamed Babylonian king whose victories are here "prophesied."

2. Variant: "let him cast them."

3. If there was a referent for this speech, it is now missing in one of the gaps in the poem.

Ishum set out for the mountain Hehe,[1]
The Seven, warriors unrivalled, fell in behind him.   (140)
When the warriors reached the mountain Hehe,
He raised his hand, he destroyed the mountain,
He reckoned the mountain Hehe as level ground.
He cut away the trunks of the cedar forest,
The thicket looked as if the deluge[2] had passed over,   (145)
He laid waste cities and turned them into open spaces,
He obliterated mountains and slew their wild life,
He convulsed the sea and destroyed its increase,
He brought the stillness of death upon swamp and thicket,
    burning like fire,
He cursed the wildlife and returned it to clay.   (150)

1. Known only here, but plausibly argued by Cagni, *Epopea*, 33-34 and 242-243 to be a reference to the homeland of the Sutaeans.
2. Text: Hanish. (For the reading of the line I follow Cagni, *Epopea*, 244-245).

Tablet V

(Erra, in a last boast, addresses the gods. He praises Ishum and points out, not without pride, that in his rage and valor he, Erra, had made the blunder of attacking the leadership of the universe as well as its subjects. Were it not for Ishum's timely intervention, who knows where Erra's terrible strength might have led him? Ishum rejoins that this is all very well, but would Erra please calm himself now that his point has been made?)

After Erra was calmed and took up his own abode,   (1)
All the gods were gazing at his face,
All the Igigi-gods and Anunna-gods stood in awe.
Erra made ready to speak, saying to all the gods,
"Quiet, all of you, learn what I have to say.   (5)
"No doubt I intended evil in the bygone lapse,
"I was angry and wanted to lay waste the people.
"Like a hireling, I took the lead ram from the flock,
"Like one who did not plant an orchard,
      I was quick to cut it down,
"Like a scorcher of the earth,
      I slew indiscriminately good and evil.   (10)
"One would not snatch a carcass
      from the jaws of a ravening lion,
"So too no one can reason where one is in a frenzy.
"Were it not for Ishum my vanguard,
      what might have happened?
"Where would your provider be, where your high priest?
"Where your food offering? You would smell no incense."   (15)
Ishum made ready to speak,
      saying to the warrior Erra these words,
"Quiet, warrior, hear what I have to say,
"No doubt this is true, now, calm down, let us serve you!
"At a time you are angry, where is he who can face you?"

(Erra returns to his home and pronounces a blessing upon Babylon, that she will at last prevail over her enemies and wax rich on the tribute of her foes throughout the world.)

When Erra heard this, his face beamed,   (20)
Like radiant daylight his features glowed.
He entered E-meslam and took up his abode,
He called Ishum to tell him the sign,
To give him instructions concerning the scattered peoples of Akkad,
"Let the people of the country, who had dwindled,
      become numerous again,   (25)
"Let short and tall alike traverse its paths,
"Let weak Akkadian fell mighty Sutaean,
"Let one drive off seven like sheep.
"You shall make his cities into ruins
      and his highlands into open ground,
"You shall take massive booty from them
      (and put it) in Shuanna,   (30)
"You shall reconcile the angry gods with their own abodes,
"You shall make gods of livestock
      and grain descend (once more) to the land,
"You shall make mountain deliver its yield, sea its produce,
"You shall make the ruined fields deliver produce.
"Let the governors of all cities haul their massive tribute
      into Shuanna,   (35)
"Let the [ru]ined temples lift their heads like rays of the sun,
"Let Tigris and Euphrates bring abundant water,
"Let the governors of all cities make the provider for Esagila
      and Babylon their lord."*

Erra's speech melds into that of the narrator. The poet introduces himself by name, and explains that the text, or "sign" of the god, was approved by Erra himself after it was revealed to the author in a half-waking state. Having become a sign, the text acquires prophylactic powers.)

Praise to the great lord Nergal and warrior Ishum
      for years without number!
How it came to pass that Erra grew angry
      and set out to lay waste the lands and destroy their peoples, (40)
But Ishum his counsellor calmed him and left a remnant,

The composer of its text was Kabti-ilani-Marduk,
     of the family Dabibi.
He revealed it at night, and, just as he (the god?)
        had discoursed it while he (K.) was coming awake,*
        he (K.) omitted nothing at all,
Nor one line did he add.
When Erra heard it he approved,   (45)
What pertained to Ishum his vanguard satisfied him.
All the gods praised his sign.[1]
Then the warrior Erra spoke thus,
"In the sanctuary of the god who honors this poem,
     may abundance accumulate,
"But let the one who neglects it never smell incense.   (50)
"Let the king who extols my name rule the world,
"Let the prince who discourses the praise of my valor have no rival,
"Let the singer who chants (it) not die from pestilence,
"But his performance be pleasing to king and prince.
"The scribe who masters it shall be spared in the enemy country
     and honored in his own land,   (55)
"In the sanctum of the learned, where they shall constantly
     invoke my name, I shall grant them understanding.
"The house in which this tablet is placed, though Erra be angry
     and the Seven be murderous,
"The sword of pestilence shall not approach it,
     safety abides upon it.
"Let this poem stand forever, let it endure till eternity,
"Let all lands hear it and praise my valor,   (60)
"Let all inhabitants witness and extol my name."

1. The text. See above, General Introduction, D.1.

Text: L. Cagni, *Das Erra-Epos, Keilschrifttext, Studia Pohl* 5 (Rome, 1970); W. G. Lambert, AfO 27 (1980), 76-81; H. W. F. Saggs, AfO 33 (1986), 29; F. al-Rawi, J. Black, *Iraq* 51 (1989), 112-113, pl. XX.

Edition: L. Cagni, *L'Epopea di Erra, Studi Semitici* 34 (Naples, 1969). This contains a detailed commentary that is essential for close study of the text. Tablet II has been edited by al-Rawi and Black, *Iraq* 51 (1989), 111-122.

Translation: L. Cagni, *The Poem of Erra*, SANE 1/3 (1977), with additions and modifications to his former commentary; J. Bottéro, *Annuaire* 1977/78, 107-164 = *Mythes*, 221-278; *Mythologie*, 680-727; Dalley, *Myths*, 282-315.

Literature: In addition to the works cited in Cagni, 1977, and the essay by Bottéro, there is a discussion by Edzard, "Irra (Erra)-Epos," RLA 5, 166-170. with bibliography through 1977, and P. Machinist, "Rest and Violence in the Poem of Erra," JAOS 103 (1983), 221-226.

★Notes to Text: (III A.17) Reading *naŝû* Š (with Bottéro). (III C.22) Schramm, OrNS 40 (1971), 271. (IV 47) For lines 47-49 see Vanstiphout, *Nabu* 1987/69. (IV 82) Text *ittabbal* "be carried off," though one expects a form of *'bl* "dry out." (V 38) For discussion of this difficult line, see Cagni, *Epopea*, 253. The interpretation of *libīlu* (variant: *ŝubēl*) as derived from *bēlu*, used here, was suggested by Brinkman, AnOr 43, 285 note 1852. (V 43) Deller-Meyer, OrNS 53 (1984), 121-122.

IV.17 THE BABYLONIAN THEODICY

The Theodicy takes the form of a debate between two friends on divine justice. The sufferer, a younger son without means, sees everywhere around him strength and wealth being equated with right and justice, while poverty is considered a crime. The gods take no notice of strict obedience to their rites and concede nothing to the serious seeker after understanding. Even injustice is of divine origin. As the debate proceeds, always with great courtesy and eloquence, the sufferer craves his friend's indulgence by acknowledging that his doubts about divine justice were merely fruits of his personal circumstances (compare Literary Prayer to Ishtar [III.28]), and were themselves faults of the kind he has normally tried to avoid. He concludes by voicing, in effect, a challenge to his gods to take better care of him in the future — at least, mercy and a greater sense of divine responsibility are his only hope. The reader is left to judge whether or not he concludes with a vote of no confidence.

The poem is a technical *tour de force*. Within a constrictive rhythmic scheme of four units to the line, the author begins each ten-line stanza with the same syllable. The beginnings of each stanza, read vertically, form an acrostic which reads, "I, Saggilkinamubbib, am adorant of god and king." The text contains numerous rare and dialectal words, partly because of its severe formal restrictions, and was the subject of an ancient philological commentary that is only partly preserved.

I. Sufferer

O sage, [   ], come, [let] me speak to you,   (1)

[   ], let me recount to you,

[   ] ...

[I ...], who have suffered greatly, let me always praise you,

Where is one whose reflective capacity is as great as yours?   (5)

Who is he whose knowledge could rival yours?

Wh[ere] is the counsellor to whom I can tell of woe?

I am without recourse, heartache has come upon me.

I was the youngest child when fate claimed (my) father,

My mother who bore me departed to the land of no return,   (10)

My father and mother left me, and with no one my guardian!

II. Friend

Considerate friend, what you tell is a sorrowful tale,
My dear friend, you have let your mind harbor ill.
You make your estimable discretion feeble-minded,
You alter your bright expression to a scowl.   (15)
Of course our fathers pay passage to go death's way,
I too will cross the river of the dead,[1]
    as is commanded from of old.
When you survey teeming mankind all together,
The poor man's son advanced, someone helped him get rich,★
Who did favors for the sleek and wealthy?   (20)
He who looks to his god has a protector,
The humble man who reveres his goddess will garner wealth.

III. Sufferer

My friend, your mind is a wellspring of depth unplumbed,
The upsurging swell of the ocean that brooks no inadequacy.
To you, then, let me pose a question, learn [what I would say].   (25)
Hearken to me but for a moment, hear my declaration.
My body is shrouded, craving wears me do[wn],★
My assets have vanished, my res[ources?] dwindled.
My energies have turned feeble, my prosperity is at a standstill,
Moaning and woe have clouded [my] features.   (30)
The grain of my mead is nowhere near satisfying [me],
Beer, the sustenance of mankind, is far from being enough.
Can a happy life be a certainty?
    I wish I knew how that might come about!

IV. Friend

My well-thought-out speech is the ulti[mate] in good advice,★
But you [make?] your well-ordered insight [sound] like babble.   (35)
You force [your ...] to be [sca]tter-brained, irrational,
You render your choicest offerings★ without conviction.

---

1. Hubur, here the Mesopotamian equivalent of the Styx or the "River Jordan." The line may also refer to the forefathers rather than the speaker, "They say from of old 'I must cross the river of death.'"

As to your [ever]lasting, unremitting desire [ ],
The [fore]most protection [lies] in prayer:
The reconciled goddess returns to [   ],   (40)
The re[conciled gods] will take pity on the fool(?),
    the wrong-doer.
Seek constantly after the [rites?] of justice.
Your mighty [   ] will surely show kindness,
[   ] ... will surely grant mercy.

V. Sufferer

I bow down before you, my [comrade],
    I apprehend your w[isdom],   (45)
[   ] what you say.
Come, let me [tell you],
The on[ager], the wild ass, that had its fill of [wild grass?],
Did it carefully ca[rry out?] a god's intentions?
The savage lion that devoured the choicest meat,   (50)
Did it bring its offerings to appease a goddess' anger?
The parvenu who multiplies his wealth,
Did he weigh out precious gold to the mother goddess
    for a family?*
[Have I] withheld my offerings? I prayed to my god,
[I] said the blessing over the regular sacrifice
    to my goddess, my speech [ ].   (55)

VI. Friend

O date palm, wealth-giving tree, my precious brother,
Perfect in all wisdom, O gem of wis[dom],
You are a mere child,
    the purpose of the gods is remote as the netherworld.
Consider that magnificent wild ass on the [plain],
An arrow will gash that headstrong trampler of the leas!   (60)
Come, look at that lion you called to mind,
    the enemy of livestock,
For the atrocity that lion committed, a pit yawns for him.
The well-heeled parvenu who treasured up possessions,

A king will put him to the flames before his time.
Would you wish to go the way these have gone?   (65)
Seek after the lasting reward of (your) god.

VII. Sufferer

Your reasoning is a cool breeze,
     a breath of fresh air for mankind,
Most particular friend, your advice is e[xcellent].
Let me [put] but one matter before you:
Those who seek not after a god can go the road of favor,   (70)
Those who pray to a goddess have grown poor and destitute.
Indeed, in my youth I tried to find out the will of (my) god,
With prayer and supplication I besought my goddess.
I bore a yoke of profitless servitude:
(My) god decreed (for me) poverty instead of wealth.   (75)
A cripple rises above me, a fool is ahead of me,
Rogues are in the ascendant, I am demoted.

VIII. Friend

O just, knowledgeable one, your logic is perverse,
You have cast off justice, you have scorned divine design.
In your emotional state you have an urge
     to disregard divine ordinances,   (80)
[   ] the sound rules of your goddess.
The strategy of a god is [as remote as] innermost heaven,
The command of a goddess cannot be dr[awn out].*
Teeming humanity well understands trouble,*

(fragmentary lines, then large gap)

XIII. Sufferer

I will forsake home [   ]
I will crave no property [   ]
I will ignore (my) god's regulations, [I will] trample on his rites.   (135)
I will slaughter a calf, I will [ ] the food,
I will go on the road, I will learn my way around distant places.
I will open a well, I will let loose a fl[ood?],

I will roam about the far outdoors like a bandit.
I will stave off hunger by forcing entry
    into one house after another,   (140)
I will prowl the streets, casting about, ravenous.
Like a beggar I will [   ] inside [ ],
Good fortune lies afar off [   ].

XIV. Friend

My friend, [you have] resolved [upon]
The transactions of mankind,
    which you had no urge to [   ],   (145)
[   ] are in your mind,
Your discretion has forsaken [you   ]

(fragmentary lines)

XV. Sufferer

(four lines lost)

Daughter says [unjust words] to her mother.
The fowler who casts [his net] is fallen (into it),   (160)
All in all, which one [will find] profit?
Many are the wild creatures that [   ],
Which among them has gotten [   ]?
Shall I seek son and daughter [   ]?
Shall I not leave behind what I find [ ]?   (165)

XVI. Friend

O modest, submissive one, who [ ] all [   ],
Your mind is always receptive, most precious one [ ],

(fragmentary lines, then gap)

XVII. Sufferer

The son of a king is clad [in rags?],
The son of the destitute and naked is dressed in [fine raiment?].
The maltster [can pay in] finest gold,

While he who counted red gold shoulders a [debt?].
He who made do with vegetables [sates himself]
    at a princely banquet, (185)
While the son of the eminent and wealthy
    (has only) carob to eat.
The man of substance is fallen, [his income] is removed.

(fragmentary lines, gap)

XX. Friend

You have let your subtle mind wander,
[   ] you have overthrown wisdom.
You have spurned propriety, you have besmirched (every) code.
Far will be the workman's basket from him who ... (215)
[   ] is established as a person of importance,
[   ] he is called a scholar,
He is well served, he gets what he wants.
Follow in the way of a god, observe his rites,
[   ] be ready for good fortune! (220)

(gap)

XXII. Friend

As for the rascal whose good will you wanted, (235)
The ... of his feet will soon disappear.
The godless swindler who acquires wealth,
A deadly weapon is in pursuit of him.
Unless you serve the will of a god, what will be your profit?
He who bears a god's yoke shall never want for food,
    though it may be meager. (240)
Seek after the favorable breeze of the gods,
What you lost for a year you will recoup in a moment.

XXIII. Sufferer

I have looked around in society, indications are the contrary:
God does not block the progress of a demon.
A father hauls a boat up a channel, (245)

While his firstborn sprawls in bed.
The eldest son makes his way like a lion,
The second son is content to drive a donkey.
The heir struts the street like a peddler,
The younger son makes provision for the destitute.[1]   (250)
What has it profited me that I knelt before my god?
It is I who must (now) bow before my inferior!
The riff-raff despise me as much as the rich and proud.

XXIV. Friend

Adept scholar, master of erudition,
You blaspheme in the anguish of your thoughts.   (255)
Divine purpose is as remote as innermost heaven,
It is too difficult to understand, people cannot understand it.
Among all creatures the birth goddess formed,
Why should offspring be completely unmatched(?)?
The cow's first calf is inferior,   (260)
Her subsequent offspring is twice as big.
The first child is born a weakling,
The second is called a capable warrior.
Even if one (tries to) apprehend divine intention,
        people cannot understand it.

XXV. Sufferer

Pay attention, my friend, learn my (next) parry,   (265)
Consider the well-chosen diction of my speech.
They extol the words of an important man
        who is accomplished in murder,
They denigrate the powerless who has committed no crime.
They esteem truthful the wicked to whom tr[uth] is abhorrent,
They reject the truthful man who he[eds] the will of god.   (270)
They fill the oppressor's st[rongroom] with refined gold,
They empty the beggar's larder of [his] provisions.
They shore up the tyrant whose all is crime,

---

1. The meaning may be that the elder expects the world to provide him a living, while the younger provides for others as well as himself.

They ruin the weak, they oppress the powerless.

And as for me, without means, a parvenu harasses me. (275)

XXVI. Friend

Enlil,[1] king of the gods, who created teeming mankind,

Majestic Ea,[2] who pinched off their clay,

The queen who fashioned them, mistress Mami,

Gave twisted words to the human race,

They endowed them in perpetuity with lies and falsehood. (280)

Solemnly they speak well of a rich man,

"He's the king," they say, "he has much wealth."

They malign a poor man as a thief,

They lavish mischief upon him, they conspire to kill him.

They make him suffer every evil

      because he has no wherewithal(?). (285)

They bring him to a horrible end,

      they snuff him out like an ember.[3]

XXVII. Sufferer

You are sympathetic, my friend, be considerate of (my) misfortune.

Help me, see (my) distress, you should be cognizant of it.[4]

Though I am humble, learned, suppliant,

I have not seen help or succor for an instant. (290)

I would pass unobtrusively through the streets of my city,

My voice was not raised, I kept my speaking low.

I did not hold my head high, I would look at the ground.

I was not given to servile praise among my associates.

May the god who has cast me off grant help, (295)

May the goddess who has [forsaken me] take pity,

The shepherd Shamash will past[ure] people as a god should.[5]

---

1. Text: Narru.

2. Text: Zulummar.

3. One would expect this speech from the sufferer rather than the friend. Is the text in disorder, or is he swayed by the sufferer?

4. That is, in judging his interlocutor's state of mind, the friend should weigh his dire circumstances and not condemn him too harshly. Compare III.28 lines 174-175.

5. That is, a just god takes proper care of his subjects.

Text: W. G. Lambert, BWL, Plates 19-26.

Edition: W. G. Lambert, BWL, 63-89.

Translation: Biggs, ANET³, 601-604; Labat, *Religions*, 320-327; von Soden, TUAT III/1, 143-157, whence readings used here.

Literature: J. Bottéro, "La 'Theodicee'," *Annuaire* 1966/67, 100-116; G. Buccellati, "La Teodicea: Condanna dell'abulia politica," OrAn 11 (1972), 101-178; von Soden, MDOG 96 (1965), 51-55; Finkel, *Studies Sachs*, 144-145.

★Notes to Text: (19) von Soden, TUAT III/1, 147. (27) So von Soden, AHw, 336b; the text, as read by Lambert, means something like "darkens me." The latter is the better parallel, though the former reading is here adopted. (34) von Soden, TUAT III/1, 148. (37) So dictionaries, but obscure. "Offering" may be intended, as taken here, as a metaphor for "proposal" or the like, though the expression would be unparalleled. (53) von Soden, TUAT III/1, 149. (83) von Soden, TUAT III/1, 151. (84) Unpublished ms. quoted by CAD A/2, 168b; S, 27a.

IV.18 THE DIALOGUE OF PESSIMISM

This satirical dialogue sets a master proposing various undertakings, for which his servant offers facile encouragements. When the master changes his mind and asserts the opposite, the servant is equally ready with facile discouragements. The master lapses into despair at the futility of life, and, when he finally asks what the best course for him to follow might be, the slave suggests suicide.

Whether one reads the mood of this text as somber or light-hearted, it has a clear, universal appeal and is an original and effective composition.

I

(1) "[Servant, listen to me]." "Yes, master, yes." "[Quickly, get me the chari]ot and hitch it up for me so I can drive to the palace." "[Drive, master, drive, it will bri]ng you where you want to go; the (others) will be outclassed, [the prince] will pay attention to you." (5) "[No, servant], I will certainly not drive to the palace." "[Do not drive, mas]ter, do not drive. [The pr]ince will send you off on a mission, he will send you on a [journey that] you do not know. He will expose you to discomfort [day and ni]ght."

II

(10) "Ser[vant, list]en to me." "Yes, master, yes." "Quic[kly br]ing me water (to wash) my hands, give it to me so I can dine." "Di[ne], master, dine. Regular dining expands the inner self, [he who eats well]* is his own god. Shamash goes with him whose hands are washed." "No, [ser]vant, I will certainly not dine." (15) "Do not dine, master, do not dine. Hunger, (then) eating, thirst, (then) drinking — this is what agrees with a man."

III

"Servant, listen to me." "Yes, master, yes." "Quickly get me the chariot and hitch it up so I can drive to the open country." "Drive, master, drive. The roaming man has a full stomach, (20) the roving dog cracks open the bone, the roaming [bi]rd will find a nesting place, the wandering wild ram has all the [gra]ss he wants."* "No, servant, I will certainly not d[rive to the open country]." "Do not drive, master, do n[ot dri]ve. (25) The roaming man loses his reason, the roving dog breaks his [te]eth(?), the roaming bird [puts] his home in the [   ] of a wall, and the wandering wild ass has to live in the open."

IVa

"Servant, listen to me." "Yes, master, yes." (30) "I am going to make a [household and have] children." "Do it, master, do it. [The man who makes] a household [   ] ...* "No, I will certainly <not> make a household." "Do not make a household. The one who follows such a course has broken up his father's household, [he has gone in] a door called 'the trap'. [The man with a wife and child is one third] robust and two thirds a weakling."

V

"Servant, listen to me." "Yes, master, yes." (40) "I will do something dishonest." "So, do it, master, do it. Unless you do something dishonest, what will [you] have to wear? Who will give you anything so you can fill [your] stomach?" "No, servant, I will certainly not do something dishonest." "<Do not do it, master, do not do it>. The man who does something dishonest is executed or skinned alive or (45) blinded or apprehended or jailed."

VI

"Servant, listen to me." "Yes, master, yes." "I will fall in love with a woman." "[So], fall in love, master, fall in love. The man who falls in love with a woman forgets sorrow and care." "No, servant, I will certainly not fall in love with a woman." "[Do not] fall in love, master, do not fall in love. A woman is a pitfall, a pitfall, a hole, a ditch, a woman is a sharp iron dagger that slashes a man's throat."

VII

"Servant, listen to me." "Yes, master, yes." "Quickly bring me water (to wash) my hands, give it to me (55) so I can sacrifice to my god." "Sacrifice, master, sacrifice. The man who sacrifices to his god makes a satisfying transaction, he makes loan upon loan." "No, servant, I will certainly not sacrifice to my god." "Do not sacrifice, master, do not sacrifice. (60) You will train your god to follow you around like a dog. He will require of you rites or a magic figurine* or what have you."

VIII

"Servant, listen to me." "Yes, master, yes." "I will make loans." "So make them, master, [make them]. The man who makes loans, his grain is (still) his grain while his interest is profit." "No, servant, I will certainly not make loans." "Do not make them, master, do not make them. Loaning is [swee]t(?) as falling in love, getting back as pain[ful] as giving birth. They will consume your grain, be always abusing you, and finally they will swindle you out of the interest on your grain."

IX

(70) "Servant, listen to me." "Yes, master, yes." "I will do a good deed for my country." "So do it, master, do it. The man who does a good deed for his country, his good deed rests in Marduk's basket."[1] "No, servant, I will certainly not do a good deed for my country." (75) "Do not do it, master, do not do it. Go up on the ancient ruin heaps and walk around, look at the skulls of the lowly and great. Which was the doer of evil, and which was the doer of good deeds?"

X

"Servant, listen to me." "Yes, master, yes." "What, then, is good?" "To break my neck and your neck and throw (us) in the river is good.[2] Who is so tall as to reach to heaven? Who is so broad as to encompass the netherworld?" "No, servant, I will kill you and let you go first." "Then my master will certainly not outlive me even three days!"[3]

---

1. The meaning of this expression is unclear. The idea may be that if one distributes largesse, the recipient is god himself, so good will thereby accrue to the giver.

2. Possibly a word play on *ṭābu* "good" and *ṭebû* "sink in water" is intended; see Kinnier Wilson, *Etana*, 177.

3. Examples of this motif have been collected by Sir Walter Scott, *Quentin Durward*, Chapter xxix (Louis XI and his astrologer).

Text: W. G. Lambert, BWL, Plates 37-38.

Edition: W. G. Lambert, BWL, 139-149.

Translation: Biggs, ANET[3], 600-601; J. Bottéro, "Le 'dialogue pessimiste' et la transcendance," *Revue de théologie et de philosophie* 1966, 7-24; Labat, *Religions*, 342-346; von Soden, TUAT III/1, 157-163 (dates to seventh century).

Literature: G. Buccellati, "Dialogo del Pessimismo: La scienza degli oppositi come idea sapienzale," OrAn 11 (1972), 81-100.

★Notes to Text: (13) von Soden, TUAT III/1, 160. (24) CAD M/2, 308a; von Soden, TUAT III/1, 160. (31) Text corrupt here, and inserts part of a section dealing with litigation. The latter is too fragmentary to be intelligible. I insert lines 32-33 at the end of line 38; see BWL, 325. (61) von Soden, TUAT III/1, 162.

IV.19 THE BIRTH LEGEND OF SARGON OF AKKAD

This fragment of a pseudonymous text of uncertain character purports to tell the story of the birth and early life of Sargon of Akkad, and how he became king of the Mesopotamians ("black-headed folk"). Language and content point to a first millennium date for this composition, which may have its origins in the court of Sargon II of Assyria, who named himself after Sargon (see IV.2). The point of this narrative may not be that Sargon was of humble origins but rather, as offspring of a high priestess, he was noble by birth, as confirmed by his subsequent success.

I am Sargon the great king, king of Agade. (1)

My mother was a high priestess, I did not know my father.

My father's brothers dwell in the uplands.

My city is Azupiranu, which lies on Euphrates bank.

My mother, the high priestess, conceived me,

she bore me in secret. (5)

She placed me in a reed basket, she sealed my hatch with pitch.

She left me to the river, whence I could not come up.

The river carried me off, it brought me to Aqqi, drawer of water.

Aqqi, drawer of water, brought me up as he dipped his bucket.

Aqqi, drawer of water, raised me as his adopted son. (10)

Aqqi, drawer of water, set (me) to his orchard work.

During my orchard work, Ishtar loved me,

Fifty-five years I ruled as king.

I became lord over and ruled the black-headed folk,

I ... [   ] hard mountains with picks of copper, (15)

I was wont to ascend high mountains,

I was wont to cross over low mountains.

The [la]nd of the sea I sieged three times, I conquered Dilmun.

I went up to great Der, I [   ], (20)

I destroyed [Ka]zallu and [   ].

Whatsoever king who shall arise after me,

[Let him rule as king fifty-five years],

Let him become lo[rd over and rule] the black-headed folk.

Let him [   ] hard mountains with picks [of copper], (25)

Let him be wont to ascend high mountains,

[Let him be wont to cross over low mountains].
Let him siege the [la]nd of the sea three times,
[Let him conquer Dilmun].
Let him go up [to] great Der and [   ].
... from my city Agade   (30)

(breaks off)

Text: King, CT 13 42 (K 3401 + Sm 2118), 43 (K 4770, BM 47449).

Edition: Brian Lewis, *The Sargon Legend: A Study of the Akkadian Text and the Tale of the Hero who was Exposed at Birth*, ASOR Dissertation Series 4 (Cambridge, MA, 1980).

Translation: Lewis, *Sargon Legend* (with extensive literature); Speiser, ANET[3], 119; Labat, *Religions*, 307-308.

Literature: J. -J. Glassner, "Le récit autobiographique de Sargon," RA 82 (1988), 1-11; H. Limet, "Aspect mythique de la royauté en Mésopotamie, Sargon l'Ancien et Cyrus le Grand," in F. Jouan and A. Motte, eds., *Mythe et Politique* (Paris, 1990), 167-169.

IV.20 THE GILGAMESH LETTER

Assyrian school exercises from Sultantepe preserve three copies of a fictional letter from Gilgamesh to a foreign king, in which he makes gargantuan demands for goods and services. While there are obvious allusions to the epic of Gilgamesh here, one may wonder if a parody on the Assyrian royal style is intended (compare, for example, the penultimate paragraph to the Hunter [III.6]).

Whereas the "Sargon Letter" (II.12b) is the closest literary parallel, other texts with presumably fantastic figures and commodities may be compared to this one; see Foster, ArOr 50 (1982), 238-241; Wiseman, BSOAS 30 (1967), 495-504.

> Say to Ti[ ], king of [ ]ranunna, thus says [Gilgamesh, k]ing of Ur, the Kullabian, created by Anu, [Enlil], and Ea, favorite of Shamash, beloved of Marduk, who rules all lands from the horizon to the zenith like a cord [ ], whose feet daised monarchs kiss, the king who draws in(?) all lands, from sunrise to sunset, like a cord, this [according to the com]mand* of Enlil-of-Victory:
>
> [   ] I wrote to you and sent 600 work-troops ... I wrote to you concerning the great [   ] of obsidian and lapis, overlaid with finest gold, to attach to the [   ] of my friend, Enkidu, but you said, "There are none."
>
> Now I write to once again! As soon as you see this letter, [make re]ady* and go to the land of ..., take with you a caravan* of horses, send ahead of you [   ] vicious(?) dogs that attack like lions, [   ] white horses with black stripes, 70,000 black horses with white stripes, 100,000 mares whose bodies have markings like wild tree roots, 40,000 continually gamboling miniature calves, 50,000 teams of dappled mules, 50,000 fine calves with well-turned hooves and horns intact, 20,000 jars of ..., 30,000 jars of ghee, 80,000 jugs of wine, 80,000 bundles of crocuses, 90,000 great tabletops of dark applewood, 100,000 donkeys laden with ... and juniper, and then come yourself.
>
> I want to fashion one nugget of gold, its ... should weigh 30 minas, to the chest of my friend Enkidu. I want to fashion [   ] thousand ...-stones, jasper(?)-stones, lapis, every sort of exotic stone

into a necklace for it.

40,000 ... of white tin for the treasury* of the great lord Marduk, (25) 90,000 talents of iron: pure, excellent, choice, select, scrutinized, precious, ... beaten, that has no ..., the smith will make(?) a stag(?) ...

120,000 talents of good ..., the smith will do work for the temple with it.

Something novel,* anything precious, exotic, which I have never seen, look for [   ] troops [to bri]ng them,* ready or not(?),[1] and gather them together. Fill big new barges(?)* with silver and gold and float them down to the Euphrates with the silver and gold. You should send(?) them to the port of Babylon so I can see for myself and be struck dumb with awe.

If I don't meet you in the gate of my city Ur on the fifteenth day of the month Tashritu, then I swear by the great gods, whose oath cannot be done away with, and I swear by my gods Lugalbanda, Sin, Shamash, Palil, Lugalgirra, Meslamtaea, Zababa, and (my personal?) god that I will send my lord "Attacker-in-My-Vanguard"(?), whose fame you always hear about, and he will wreck your cities, loot your palaces, [cut down] your orchards, and put wickets(?) in your canal mouths. I(?) will enter the ... of your fortified cities, who ... and speak of its ..., and I, Gilgamesh, will occupy them, they must not entrust their(?) ... to me.

[I will   ] your [   ], your gener[al], your craftsmen(?), your children, your belongings, and your offspring [   ] (40) at the gate of Ur. I will bring you and your family(?) into the [   ]-house and ... talents of copper ... I will inscribe. I will set you up with the (statues of) protective spirits in the thoroughfare,* [the citizens] of Ur will lord it over (you) as they go by.

Quickly send me an[swer to my letter]* and come, you will not have to bear anything from me.

Letter of Gilgamesh, the mighty king, who has no rival.

---

1. Unknown expression: "full or empty," here taken to refer to the preparedness of the addressee (having eaten or not).

Text: Gurney, STT 40-42.

Edition: Gurney, AnSt 7 (1957), 127-135; AnSt 8 (1958), 245.

Literature: F. R. Kraus, "Der Brief des Gilgameš," AnSt 30 (1980), 109-121; B. R. Foster, "A Postscript to the Gilgamesh Letter," AnSt 32 (1982), 43-44.

*Notes to Text: (7) Kraus, "Brief," 110 note 10. (12) Kraus, "Brief," 110 notes 15, 16. (24) Kraus, "Brief," 111 note 30. (28) Kraus, "Brief," 112 note 33. (29) Kraus, "Brief," 112 note 35. (30) Kraus, "Brief," 112 note 36. (42) Kraus, "Brief," 113 note 48. (44) Kraus, "Brief," 113 note 50.

IV.21 THE JESTER

This text may record the routine of a buffoon or jester. The performer cracks a variety of jokes, some of them presumably of double entendre. In a satire of professions, the jester acts the exorcist by burning down a house to rid it of its haunt. Next an unappetizing religious diet is set forth in prescriptive form. Other, fragmentary, portions of the text dealt with a heroic quest and bizarre omens, but these are too fragmentary for connected translation.

(a)

The lion can terrify,
I can make a roar too!
The lion can switch his tail,
I can wag my tail too!
I'm as trustworthy as a sieve,
I hold on to my followers like a net.
I sing like a she-ass.
I can't stand a thief: whatever I see doesn't stay where it was.
I've gotten large from starvation, enormous from eating,
I breakfast on ten quarts, I dine on thirty,
I don't leave off till I've filled the "bushel"[1] to the brim.
The long, the short of them,
    there's none like me among the girls!
My limbs are elephantine, my face a hyena's,
I tower like a tortoise, I have no rival.
I'm frisky, I'm a lively one:
So much would my lover be loving me,
He keeps turning over, front and back, like a snared crab.
He wouldn't herd his ewes within a league[2]
    of the city gate because of me,
I've used up all the plants for my [ ]!
I'm frisky, I'm a lively one!

(fragmentary lines, then gap)

1. His stomach?
2. Text: "400 acres."

(b)

"Jester, what can you do?"
[I can ...] and sing laments,
I can squeeze out apple juice and brew beer.

"Jester, what can you do?"
I can snatch on the run pod-weeds from turnips,
      groats from stink-wort.

"Jester, what can you do?"
Of the whole exorcist's craft, nothing's beyond me.

"Jester, how do you exorcise?"
Here's how: I take over the haunted house,
     I set up the holy water,
I tie up the scape goat,
I skin a donkey and stuff it with straw.
I tie a bundle of reeds, set it on fire, and toss it inside.
I spared the boundaries of the house and its surroundings,
But the haunt of the house, the serpent, the scorpion,
     are not spared.

(gap)

(c)

"In October what is your diet?"
Thou shalt dine on spoiled oil in onions,
     and goose pluckings in porridge.

"In November what is your diet?"
Thou shalt dine on pod-weed in turnips,
     and "cleanser-plant" in crowfoot(?)"[1]

---

1. Or: "asafoetida powder."

"In December what is your diet?"
Thou shalt dine on wild donkey dung in bitter garlic,
And emmer chaff in sour milk.

"In January what is your diet?"
Thou shalt dine on goose eggs and dung(?) embedded in sand,
And cumin infused with Euphrates water in ghee.

"In February what is your diet?"
Thou shalt dine on hot bread and donkey's ass,
Stuffed with dog turds and fly dirt.

(fragmentary lines, then gap)

Text: K 4334 = Norris, II R 60 no. 1; K 9886 = Pinches *apud* Weidner, AfO 16 (1952/3), 320 with pl. xiv; K 6392 = Virolleaud, *Revue Semitique* 9 (1901), 257 = Langdon, *Babyloniaca* 7 (1913/23), pl. xvi; K 9287 = Boissier, *Revue Semitique* 9 (1901), 159-160; K 8321 = Meissner, BA 3 (1898), 51; all mss. collated.
Edition: Ebeling, TuL, 9-19.
Literature: B. R. Foster, "Humor and Cuneiform Literature," JANES 6 (1974), 74-79; W. Römer, "Der Spassmacher im alten Zweistromland, zum 'Sitz im Leben' altmesopotamischer Texte," *Persica* 7 (1975/6), 43-68.

IV.22 LOVE LYRICS OF ISHTAR OF BABYLON

Fragmentary collections of enigmatic songs and rituals involving Ishtar of Babylon seem to a modern reader scurrilous, abusive, and bizarre. Scattered excerpts from this collection follow.

(a)

Into your vulva, where you put your trust,
I'll bring in a dog and fasten the door,
Into your vulva, where you put your trust,
As if it were(?) your precious jewel in front of you.
O my girl friend's vulva, why do you keep acting like this?
O my girl friend's vulva, Babylon-town is looking for a rag!
O vulva of two fingers, why do you keep making trouble?

★ ★ ★

(b)

By night there's no prudish housewife,
By night there's no prudish housewife,
By night no man's wife makes objection!

★ ★ ★

(c)

Before her was a fieldmouse,
Behind her was a rat.
He girded(?) his hems,
He's a shrew, son of a fieldmouse.
I sent [you?], my girl friend, to Kar-bel-matati,[1]
Why did you break wind and feel mortified?
Why did you stink up her boyfriend's wagon like a wi[ld ox]?
At Kar-bel-matati's crossing point,

1. Name of a wharf at Babylon.

I saw my girl friend and was stunned:
You are chalky like a gecko,
Your hide is swart like a cook[ing pot].
You are in full bloom, brought to [bliss].

★ ★ ★

(d)

O my girl friend's [genitals], Babylon-town is looking for a rag,
To swab your vulva, to swab your vagina.
[So] let him say to the women of Babylon,
"Won't they give her a rag,
"To swab her vulva, to swab her vagina?"

Into your vulva, where you put your trust,
I'll bring in a dog and fasten the door,
I'll bring in a watchbird so it can nest.
Whenever I go out or come in,
I'll instruct my little watchbirds,
"Please, my little watchbirds,
"Don't go near the fungus!
"Please, my little watchbird,
"Don't go near the stench of (her) armpits!"

You are mother, O Ishtar of Babylon,
You are mother, O queen of the Babylonians,
You are mother, O palm tree, O carnelian!
The beautiful one, oh so beautiful!
Whose figure is oh so lustrous, oh so beautiful!

Text: W. G. Lambert, in *Unity and Diversity*, (Baltimore, 1975), 127-135.
Edition: W. G. Lambert, in *Unity and Diversity*, 98-126.
Literature: D. O. Edzard, "Zur Ritualtafel der sog. 'Love Lyrics,'" *Studies Reiner*, 57-69.

IV.23 THE POOR MAN OF NIPPUR

This is a unique example of a Babylonian folktale, in which a poor man takes revenge on a mayor who wronged him.

There once was a man of Nippur, poor and needy, (1)
His name was Gimil-Ninurta, a wretched man.
He dwelt in his city Nippur in abject misery:
He had no silver, as befits his people,
He had no gold, as befits mankind, (5)
His larder wanted for pure grain.
His insides burned, craving for bread,
His face was wretched, craving meat and good drink,
Every day, for want of a meal, he went to sleep hungry.
He wore a garment for which there was none to change. (10)
He took counsel with his wretched heart,
"I'll strip off my garment, for which there is none to change,
"I'll buy a ram in the market of my city, Nippur."
He stripped off his garment, for which there was none to change,
He bought a three-year old[1] nanny goat in the market
    of his city Nippur. (15)
He took counsel with his wretched heart,
"What if I slaughter the nanny-goat in my yard,
"There won't be a meal, where will be the beer?
"My friends in my neighborhood will hear of it and be angry,
"My kith and kin will be furious with me. (20)
"I'll take the nanny goat and bring it to the mayor's house,
"I'll work up something good and fine for his pleasure."[2]
Gimil-Ninurta took [his] nanny-goat by the neck,
[He went off] to the gate of the mayor of Nippur.
To Tukulti-Enlil, who minded the gate,
    he sa[id] (these) words, (25)
"Say that I wish to enter to see the ma[yor]."
The doorman said (these) words to his master,

---

1. Variant omits. Note the change of sex and species of the animal.
2. Wordplay on "his stomach" and "his mood" in original.

"My lord, a citizen of Nippur is waiting at your gate,
"And as a [   ] present he has brought you a nanny-goat."
The mayor was ang[ry with Tuk]ulti-Enlil,
"Why is a citizen of Nippur [(kept) waiting] at the gate?"   (30)
The doorman [   ] to [   ] ...,
Gimil-Ninurta [came] happily [be]fore the mayor.
When Gimil-Ninurta came before the mayor,
He held his nanny-goat by the neck wi[th] his left hand,   (35)
With his right hand he greeted the mayor,
"May Enlil and Nippur bless the mayor,
"May Ninurta and Nusku prosper [him] greatly!"
The mayor said (these) words to the citizen of Nippur,
"What is your trouble, that you bring me a gift?"   (40)
[Gimil]-Ninurta related his errand to the mayor of Nippur,
"Every [day], for want of a meal, I go to sleep hungry,
"[I stripped off] my garment, for which there is none to change,
"I bought a three-year old nanny-goat [in the market]
        of my city Nippur,
"I said to myself [on account] of my wretched heart,   (45)

        '[What if] I slaughter the nanny-goat in my yard,
        '[There won't be] a meal, where will be the beer?
        'My friends in my neighborhood [will hear of it] and be angry,
        '[My kith and k]in will be furious with me.
        'I'll bring the nanny goat [to the may]or's [house],'   (50)

"[That's what I s]aid in the wretchedness(?) of my heart."

                (fragmentary lines, then gap)

        (The mayor has the goat slaughtered and the meal prepared.)

"Give him, the citizen of Nippur, a bone and gristle,
"Give him third-rate [beer] to drink from your flask,
"Expel him, throw him out the gate!"   (60)
He gave him, the citizen of Nippur, a [bone] and gristle,
He gave him [thi]rd-rate [beer] to drink from h[is] flask,
He expelled him, threw [him out] the gate.

As Gimil-Ninurta went out the gate,
He said to the doorman, who minded the gate, (these) words,   (65)
"Joy of the gods to your master! Tell him thus,

    'For one disgrace you [laid] upon me,*
    'For that one I will requite you three!'"

When the mayor heard that, he laughed all day.
Gimil-Ninurta set out for the king's palace,   (70)
"By order of the king! Prince and governors give just verdicts."

Gimil-Ninurta came before the king,
He prostrated and did homage before him,
"O noble one, prince of the people,
    king whom a guardian spirit makes glorious,   (75)
"Let them give me, at your command, one chariot,
"That, for one day, I can do whatever I wish.
"For my one day my payment shall be a mina of red gold."
The king did not ask him, "What is your desire,
"That you [will parade about] all day in one chariot?"   (80)
They gave him a new chariot, f[it for] a nobleman,
They wrapped him in a sash, [   ] his [   ].
He mo[unted] the new chariot, fit for a nobleman,
He set out for [   ] Duranki.[1]
Gimil-Ninurta caught two birds,   (85)
He stuffed them in a box and sealed it with a seal,
He we[nt off] to the gate of the mayor of Nippur.
The mayor came o[utside] to meet him,
"Who are you, my lord, who have traveled so la[te in the day]?"*
"The king, your lord, sent me, to [   ],   (90)
"I have brought gold for Ekur, temple of Enlil."
The mayor slaughtered a fine sheep to make
    a generous meal for him.
While in his presence the mayor said "Ho-hum, I'm tired!"
(But) Gimil-Ninurta sat up with the mayor
    one (whole) watch of the night.
From fatigue the mayor was overcome with sleep.   (95)

---

1. Nippur.

Gimil-Ninurta got up stealthily in the night,
He opened the box lid, [the birds flew] up into the sky.
"Wake up, mayor! The gold has been taken
    and the box opened!
"The box lid is open, the gold has been taken!"
Gimil-Ninurta rent his clothes in anguish(?),   (100)
He set upon the mayor, made him beg for mercy.
He thrashed him from head to toe,
He inflicted pain upon him.
The mayor at his feet cried out, ... pleading,
"My lord, do not destroy a citizen of Nippur!   (105)
"The blood of a protected person, sacred to Enlil,
    must not stain your hands!"
They gave him for his present two minas of red gold,
For the clothes he had rent, he gave him others.
As Gimil-Ninurta went out the gate,
He said (these) words to Tukulti-Enlil, who minded the gate, (110)
"Joy of the gods to your master! Say thus to him,

    'For one disgrace you [laid upon me],
    'I've requited you one, [two remain].'"

When the mayor heard (that), he [ ] all day.
Gimil-Ninurta [went] to the b[arb]er,   (115)
He shaved off all his hair on the le[ft],[1]
He filled a fire-scorched pot [with water?].
He [went off] to the gate of the mayor of Nippur,
He said to the doorman, who minded the gate,
"Say that I want to come in to see [the mayor]."   (120)
"Who are you, that you should see [him]?"
"[I am] a physician, a native of Isin, who examines [ ],
"Where there are disease and emaciation [ ] in the body [   ]."
When Gimil-[Ninur]ta came before the mayor,
He showed him his bruises where he had thrashed his body. (125)
The may[or] said [to] his servants, "This physician is skillful!"
"My lord, my remedies are carried out in the dark,
"In a private place, out of the way."

---

1. Reading doubtful; a shaved head was perhaps sign of being a physician.

He brought him into an inaccessible chamber,
Where no friend or companion could take pity on him.   (130)
He threw the pot into the fire,[1]
He drove five pegs into the hard-packed floor,
He tied his head, hands, and feet (to them),
Then he thrashed him from head to toe,
     he inflicted pain upon him.
Gimil-Ninurta, as he went out the gate,   (135)
Said (these) words to Tukulti-Enlil, who minded the gate,
"Joy of the gods to your lord!" Say thus to him,

    'For one disgrace you laid upon me,
    'I've requited you two, one remains.'"

Gimil-Ninurta was anxious, pricking up his ears like a dog,   (140)
He looked carefully at the folk (around him),
    he scrutinized all of the people.
He sent(?) a certain man, having recouped his losses(?),
He gave him a nanny goat(?)* for [his] present,
"Go to the gate of the mayor [of Nippur?], start shouting,
So all the numerous [people] will crowd around
    at your shouting,   (145)

    'I'm knocking(?) at the mayor's gate,
      I'm the man with the nanny goat!'"*

[Gimil-Ninurta] crouched [under] a bridge like a dog.
The mayor came out at the man's shouting,
He brought out the people of his household, male and female,
They rushed off, all of them, in pursuit of the man.   (150)
While they, all of them, were in pursuit of the man,
[They left] the mayor outside alone.
Gimil-Ninurta s[prang] out from under the bridge
    and seized the [mayo]r,
He set upon the mayor, made him beg for mercy.
He thrashed him from head to toe,   (155)
He inflicted pain upon him.
"[For one disgrace you la]id upon me,

---

1. To extinguish the fire and thus proceed in darkness?

"I've requited you [three]!"
He [left him] and went out in the open country,
The mayor, crawling, went into the city.

Text: Gurney, STT 38, 39; K 3478 = Gurney, AnSt 6 (1956), 148; Ellis, JCS 26 (1974), 89.
Edition: Gurney, AnSt 6 (1956), 145-162; AnSt 7 (1957), 135-136.
Translation: von Soden, TUAT III/1, 174-180.
Literature: J. S. Cooper, "Structure, Humor, and Satire in the Poor Man of Nippur," JCS 27 (1975), 163-174; O. R. Gurney, "The Tale of the Poor Man of Nippur and its Folktale Parallels," AnSt 22 (1972), 149-158; H. Jason, "The Poor Man of Nippur: An Ethnopoetic Analysis," JCS 31 (1979), 189-215; Leichty, *Studies Finkelstein*, 145-146.
*Notes to Text: (67) Moran, *Studies Tadmor*, 327f. (86) Reiner, JNES 26 (1967), 183 note 7. (89) von Soden, TUAT III/1, 177. (104) Compare von Soden, TUAT III/1, 178. (140) Leichty, *Studies Finkelstein*, 145. (142) von Soden, TUAT III/1, 179. (143) Leichty, *Studies Finkelstein*, 145. (146) Cooper, JCS 27 (1975), 174 note 36.

IV.24 WHY DO YOU CURSE ME?

This humorous tale involves an ignorant physician who goes to the city Nippur to collect a fee. As he asks directions, he is answered in Sumerian, which, as a scholar, he is supposed to have mastered. Failing to recognize the academic language of the land, he assumes that his interlocutor is abusing him. The text ends with a remark that school children should run such a man out of their city.

Ninurta-sagentarbi-zaemen, [brother of N]inurta-mizidesh-kiaggani, [nephew] of Enlil-Nibru-kibigi, having been bitten by a dog, went to Isin, city of the Lady of Health. Amel-Ba'u, a citizen of Isin, priest to Gula, examined him, recited an incantation for him, and cured him.

"For your cure of me on this wise, may Enlil, lord of Nippur, bless (you)! If you will come to Nippur, I will put a bib(?) on you, I will feast you with choice viands, and I will give you two massy(?) jugs of fine beer to drink."

"Where should I go in Nippur your city?"

"When you come to Nippur my [city], you should enter by the principal gate and leave a street, a boulevard, a square, [Til]lazida Street, and the ways of Nusku and Nininema to your left. You should ask [Nin-lugal]-absu, daughter of Ki'agga-Enbilulu, a woman of the qu[arter of street-priests] of Ana-Ea-Takla, a gardening woman of the garden Henun-Enlil, sitting on the ground of Tillazida pulling up reeds ..., and she will show you."

Amel-[Ba'u], citizen of Isin, priest of Gula, arriving at Nippur, entered by the principal gate and left a street, a boulevard, a square, Tillazida Street, [the way of Nusku and] Ninimena to his left. He s[aw Nin-lu]gal-apsu, daughter of Ki'agga-Enbilulu, [a woman of the quarter] of the street priests of Ana-Ea-Takla, a gardening woman of the garden Henun-Enlil, [who was sitting on the gr]ound of Tillazida pulling up reeds.

"Ni[n-lu]gal-apsu?"

"*anni lugalmu.*"

"Why do you curse me?"

"Why would I curse you? I said, 'Yes sir.'"

"May I ask you to show me the way to the house of Nin[urtasag]entarbi-zaemen, son of Mizidesh-ki'aggani, nephew of Enlil-Nibru-kibigi?"

"*namtushmen.*"

"Why do you curse me?"

"Why would I curse you? I said, 'He is not at home.'"

"Where did he go?"

"*Edingirbi shuzianna sizkur gabari munbala.*"

"Why do you curse me?"

"Why would I curse you? I said,

> 'He is making an offering in the temple
> of his personal god Shuzianna.'"

Thereupon he [   ].

The students ought to get together, and, on account of these ...,
    they should throw him out of the main gate!

Text: Cavigneaux, BaM 10 (1979), 112-113.
Edition: Cavigneaux, BaM 10 (1979), 114-117.
Translation: E. Reiner, "Why Do You Cuss Me?" PAPS 130/1 (1986), 1-6.

IV.25 THE DOG'S BOAST

This excerpt is taken from a large but fragmentary composition dealing with a contest among a wolf, fox, and dog. In this passage, the dog praises his own prowess.

> I am mighty in strength, the talon of Anzu,
>> the fury(?) of a lion,
> My legs run faster than birds on the wing,
> At my loud outcry mountains and rivers dry up(?).
> I take my onerous place before the sheep,
> Their lives are entrusted to me,
>> instead of to shepherds or herdsmen, (20)
> I am sent off on my regular path in the open country
>> and the watering place, I go around the fold.
> At the clash of my fearsome weapons I flush out ...,
> At my baying, panther, tiger, lion, wildcat take to flight,
> The bird can[not] fly away nor go on course.
> No rustler thieves [from] my pens!

Text: W. G. Lambert, BWL, plate 50, 16-25.
Edition: W. G. Lambert, BWL, 192-193.
Literature: H. Vanstiphout, "The Importance of 'The Tale of the Fox'," ASJ 10 (1988), 191-227.

IV.26 LAMENT FOR TAMMUZ

This lament, known from a tablet of the Hellenistic period, is cast in an antique Sumerian style, in the manner of a lament for Tammuz, lover of Ishtar, patron deity of Uruk. The text deals primarily with the devastation of war and the cries of women deprived of their husbands. Like Erra and Ishum (IV.16), it may refer to some specific warfare of the first millennium B.C. In its tone and content it may be compared to various passages in Erra and Ishum, for example Tablet IV lines 40ff.

> "O grieving (women) of Uruk, O grieving (women) of Akkad,
> > I am prostrate!"* (1)
> The goddess of Uruk wept, whose attendant was gone,
> The goddess of Uruk wept, whose loincloth was snatched away.
> The daughter of Uruk wept,
> > the daughter of Akkad was crying aloud.
> The face of the daughter of Larak was shrouded
> > with the fringe of her garment.
> The goddess of Hursagkalamma wept,
> > who was deprived of her husband. (5)
> The goddess of ... wept, whose seven brothers were killed,
> > whose eight brothers-in-law were prostrate.
> The goddess of Akkad wept, whose sandals were torn,*
> > whose lord, in whom she delighted, was killed.
> The goddess of Kesh wept, sitting in the alleyway,
> > the lord of her house slain by a lynx(?).*
> The goddess of Dunnu wept,
> > "For whom the couch, for whom the coverlet?
> > For whom do I treasure the coverlet, (now) deathly still?" (10)
> The daughter of Nippur wept,
> > "Finishing the task was for Gutians!"[1]
> Her cheeks were sore (from weeping),
> > she was deprived of her husband, in whom she delighted.
> The goddess of Der <wept>, "Finishing the task was for Gutians!"

---

1. The Gutians were a by-word for hateful barbarian invaders; see III.17b (3), p. 265 note 4.

<Her> cheeks were sore (from weeping),
>   she was deprived of her husband, in whom she delighted.
She whose city was wrecked, whose ancestral home
>   was broken into and desecrated, (cried)   (15)
"(O women), weep for Uruk, (my) headband caught in thorns,
"As for me, I do not know where I stepped in the tempest.
"(O women), weep for Larak, [ ],* I am deprived of my cloak,
"My eyes cannot look upon ..., slashing of mother's wombs,
"(O women), weep for Nippur, silence dwells upon me.   (20)
"The heavens have shrouded me,
"My chair that supported me has been overturned upon me.
"The lord has deprived me of my spouse,
>   the husband in whom I delighted!"

Text: Pinches, PSBA 23 (1901), after p. 192.

Edition: W. G. Lambert, JAOS 103 (1983), 211–215 (with many improved readings and proposals adopted here).

Notes to Text: (1) As taken here, the goddess and women of Uruk are the referents of *marṣātu*. (7) With Lambert, JAOS 103 (1983), 213 note 8. (9) Doubtful, reading *a-za-ri!?*; differently Groneberg, JAOS 107 (1987), 323. (18) For proposed restorations, see CAD E, 66b; Lambert, *ad loc.*

D. INCANTATIONS

IV.27 MARDUK AND THE DEMONS

This incantation-like composition is, in part at least, a first-person address by Marduk, setting forth his qualities that can counteract evil. The composition was once of considerable length (well over 200 lines?), and was evidently popular in learned circles, as numerous manuscripts have survived and a hermeneutic commentary was prepared on it in antiquity. The application of this text is unknown; W. G. Lambert has tentatively proposed that it was part of the Babylonian New Year's festival when the Marduk statue was taken in procession and hence was for a time more than usually vulnerable to attack. The last preserved line of the text seems intended for a human speaker. The repetitiveness and inclusiveness of this piece are typical of later Mesopotamian magical tradition.

Fragment A

[I am Asalluhi, by whose ri]tual [   ]
[I am Asalluhi, who in] combat and bat[tle   ]
[I am Asalluhi ...] furious [   ]   (5)
[I am Asalluhi, who] was formed in E-unir[1] and [ ],
[I am Asalluhi], radiant, furious, the princely sage of the gods,
[I am Asalluhi], who surveys the heights of the distant heavens,
[I am Asalluhi], who knows the bottom
    of the wide river of the dead,[2]
[I am Asalluhi], to whom ... call in the seas above,   (10)
[I am Asalluhi], whom Laguda glorifies in the seas below.[3]
[I am Asalluhi], indeed the bond of everything,
    firstborn of Mami,
[I am Asalluhi], who overthrows the one who harbors evil,
[I am Asalluhi], who ... the gods of distant heaven,

1. Temple in Eridu. This means that Marduk is son of Ea.
2. Text: Hubur. See p. 807 note 1.
3. That is, in Babylonian cosmology, the waters above the sky and below the earth. Laguda is a little-known deity, cited here perhaps to associate Asalluhi=Marduk with primeval gods; compare Marduk Prophecy (III.13), opening lines.

[I am Asalluhi ...] life to the numerous peoples,   (15)
[I am Asalluhi, w]ho overthrows the evil one,

Fragment B

[I am Asalluhi, com]mander of the Heavenly Abode,[1]   (5)
[I am Asalluhi], who is clad in fiery brilliance, full of terrors,
I am Asalluhi, wearing a tiara,
    whose divine splendor is laden with awe,
[I am Asalluhi, who feeds?] the hungry, who rescues the weak,
[I am Asalluhi, ...] watercourses, who sustains the life of the land,
I am Asalluhi, who perceives decisions (to be made),
    who decides ...,   (10)
I am Asalluhi, explainer of wedges,[2]
    destroyer of wicked and evil,
I am Asalluhi, who daily keeps watch on what people say,
I am Asalluhi, whose brilliance illumines the lands,
I am Asalluhi, whose effulgence destroys walls of stone,
I am Asalluhi, wise, experienced, who excels in understanding,   (15)
I am Asalluhi, whose weapon is a raging deluge,
[I am Asalluhi, who bu]rns up foe and wicked,

Fragment C

I am Asalluhi, at whose words mountains [   ],
I am Asalluhi, who, like the sun, surveys the lands,   (5)
I am Asalluhi, who turns back calumnies, who helps the [   ],
I am Asalluhi, who purges good and evil in the river ordeal,
I am Asalluhi, powerful and fierce lord of the land,
I am Asalluhi, eminent, glorious, archetype of lordship,
I am Asalluhi, in the face of whose awesomeness
    every evil returns to its lair,   (10)
I am Asalluhi, who scans the hidden subterranean waters,
    who devises designs,

---

1. Andurna, a cosmic locality; see Creation Epic (III.17) Tablet I line 24.
2. Reference to cuneiform writing; compare Gula Hymn of Bullutsa-rabi (III.25) line 184.

I am Asalluhi, who bestows pasture and drinking place,
    who showers down abundance,
I am Asalluhi, at whose command the assault
    of plague is driven back,
I am Asalluhi, whose divinity is supreme everywhere,
I am Asalluhi, who ever guides [his] peoples
    like father and mother,   (15)
[I] am Asalluhi, the response of whose heart
    the g[reat] gods do not know,
[I am Asallu]hi, who plucks out disease,
    who destroys demons [   ],
[I am Asalluhi], a fierce, onrush[ing] storm [   ],

Fragment D¹

Or you (demons) [   ] who always glow,
Or you [   ] who are always in shadow,
Or you [   ] who always charge like a bull,   (5)
Or you [   ] who are always spying,
Or you who are ever intruding into houses,
Or you who loiter on thresholds,
Or you who pace about foundations,
Or you who are wont to squat in storage pits,   (10)
Or you who are always stalking attractive young men,
    attractive young women, in the street,
Or you who go peeking at naptime,
Or you who eavesdrop,
Or you who stand at the sufferer's head,
Or you who sit at the sufferer's head,   (15)
Or you who pace at the sufferer's head,
Or you who eat with him when he eats,
Or you who drink with him when he drinks,
Or you who haunt such-and-such a sufferer,
Or you who terrify such-and-such a sufferer,   (20)
Or you who startle such-and-such a sufferer,

---

1. Variant manuscript has lines 14-16 followed by 26-33.

Or you who scare such-and-such a sufferer,
Or you who snuffle at such-and-such a sufferer,
Or you who bare your fangs at such-and-such a sufferer,
Or you who lie in wait for such-and-such a sufferer,   (25)
Or you who gnash your teeth at such-and-such a sufferer,
Or you who stick out your tongues at such-and-such a sufferer,
Or you who open your mouths at such-and-such a sufferer,
Or you who ... [   ] at such-and-such a sufferer,
Or you who charge like an ox [   ] at such-and-such a sufferer,   (30)
Or you who [butt?] like a goat at such-and-such a sufferer,
Or you who [grunt?] like a pig at such-and-such a sufferer,
Or you who slither around like little snakes
    at such-and-such a sufferer,*   (a′)
Or you who slithering around like chameleon(s)
    at such-and-such a sufferer,
Or you who slither around like worms
    at such-and-such a sufferer,
Or you who slither around like geckoes
    at such-and-such a sufferer,

Fragment E

[Or you] who have no [father or mother],
Or you who h[ave no] brother [or sister],
Or you who h[ave no] kith [or kin],
Or you who h[ave no] son or [daughter],
Or you who h[ave no] be[loved?] heir,   (10)
Or you who [   ] in [   ]

[May   ] uproot you,
[May   ] uproot you,
[May   ] calm you,
[May   ] you   (15)
        (two lines lost)

A[salluhi] exorcises you [by   ],
Asalluhi exorcises you by Nin-[   ],

Asalluhi exorcises you by Shamash, creator of [   ],   (20)

Asalluhi exorcises you by Hendursagga who traverses [   ],[1]

Asalluhi exorcises you by Sharur and Shargaz[2]

[who   ] enemies!

May Meslamtaea give you over <to> the netherworld,

May he commit you to the seven doorkeepers [of] Ereshkigal,

May he commit you to Namtar, courier of the netherworld,

who keeps the door of the p[risoners],   (25)

May he bring you through the ga[te of] the great [netherworld],

May he deliver you into the hands of the great devils,

May Nedu, the chief doorkeeper of the netherworld,

hold the door against you (inside),

May he give you over to Ningizzida,

prefe[ct] of the vast [nether]world,

May the great gods of the netherworld burn you up!   (30)

I exorcise you by the great prefect of Allati:[3]

May the netherworld river hold you back!

[You shall not] ... me, you shall not keep on hounding me,

you shall not [   ] me, so-and-so, son of so-and-so!

(fragmentary lines, then breaks off)

Text: W. G. Lambert, AfO 17 (1954/6), pl. XIII-XVI; AfO 19 (1959/60), pl. XXIV-XXVII; various unpublished duplicates and joins noted by Borger, HKL 2, 156 could not be utilized here.
Edition: W. G. Lambert, AfO 17 (1954/6), 310-320; AfO 19 (1959/60), 114-119.
Notes to Text: (7) Lines a-d, placement not clear, are from an unpublished manuscript quoted CAD N/2, 56a (etc.).

1. For Hendursagga as another name for Erra, see Erra and Ishum (IV.16), Tablet I line 2.
2. Personified divine weapons, usually of Ninurta.
3. Netherworld deity, see IV.5 line 30.

IV.28 AGAINST AN ADVERSARY IN A LAWSUIT

To be said "when entering the palace." Blocking of the mouth and anus in connection with a lawsuit is referred to in an Assyrian curse formula, "He who talks too much in the Step Gate (= law court), the [demon] of ruins will seize his mouth and anus ..." (Grayson, ARI 1, 13). Compare also III.16d line 6.

Listen [ye] of heaven,	(1)
Hear my speech, ye of the netherworld!	
So-and-so, son of so-and-so, my adversary,	
Until I slap his cheek,	
Until I rip out his tongue,	(5)
Until I send his words back into his mouth,	
I will not allow his mouth to speak,	
I will not allow his bottom to break wind.*	

Text: Ebeling, KAR 71, rev 1-8.
Edition: Ebeling, MAOG 5/3 (1931), 32-33.
Notes to Text: (8) With CAD A/2, 305a against CAD N/1, 54b.

IV.29 AGAINST AN ANGRY MAN

(a) I WILL DISSOLVE YOUR ANGER

Why are you angry, seized (by rage),	(1)
Your eyes bloodshot,	
Your gums spattered with gall,	
The hair of your chest bristling?	
Your (own) son,[1] taking my part,	
is angry at you and seized (by rage),	(5)
My eyes (too) are bloodshot,	
My gums are spattered with gall,	
The hairs of my chest bristle.	
Be it a door, I will open your mouth,	
Be it a bar, I will put a stop to your lips,	(10)
Be it bonding of a wall, I will dissolve your anger!	

Text: Ebeling, KAR 43, rev 7-17; KAR 63, rev 4-15.
Edition: Ebeling, MAOG 5/3 (1931), 17, 19.

(b) ANGER

Spittle was considered to be endowed with magical properties; see Ebeling, MAOG 5/3 (1931), 14-15.

I have escaped the spittle of your mouth,
I have given the word of your father,
    the word of your mother, the word of your sister,
(As if it were) the word of a trouper, a city whore,
To the covering earth,
That does not make ready to speak,
That does not wag its tongue.

Text: Ebeling, KAR 43, obv 1-6; KAR 63, obv 1-6.
Edition: Ebeling, MAOG 5/3 (1931), 16, 18.

1. Variant adds: "son of so-and-so."

IV.30 AGAINST BILE

Biliousness is here symbolized by a greenish goat browsing in a green world.

The she-goat is green, its offspring is green, (1)
Its shepherd is green, its herdsman is green,
It feeds on green grass in a green plot,
It drinks green water from a green canal.
He threw a stick at it, it did not turn around, (5)
He threw a clod at it, it did not raise its head,
He threw a wad(?) of thyme and salt at it:
Bile beset the wasted man like a fog.

(The spell is not mine, it is a spell of Ea, Asalluhi, Damu, and Gula.)

Text: Köcher, BAM 578, ii 45-49.
Edition: None.

IV.31 AGAINST THE EVIL EYE

For evil caused by gazing at a person, see A. Dundes, *The Evil Eye* (Madison, 1991); M.-L. Thomsen, "The Evil Eye in Mesopotamia," JNES 51 (1992), 19-32. See also I.3.

> ... Eye, eye! It is hostile,[1]   (1)
> It is eye of a woman, it is eye of a m[an],
>   it is [ey]e of an enemy, it is anyone's(?) eye,
> It is eye of a neighbor, it is eye of a neighbor (woman),[2]
>   eye of a child minder(?), it is the eye!
> O eye, in evil purpose, you have called at the door,   (5)
> The threshold shook, the beams quaked.
> When you enter(ed)[3] a house, O eye, [   ].
> You smashed the potter's kiln, you scuttled the boatman's boat,
> You broke the yoke of the mighty ox,
> You broke the shin of the striding donkey,   (10)
> You broke the loom of the expert weaver,[4]
> You deprived the striding horse of its foal(?)
>   and the ox of its food(?),[5]
> You have scattered the ... of the ignited stove,
> You have left the livestock(?) to the maw of the murderous storm,
> You have cast discord among harmonious brothers.   (15)
> Smash the eye! Send the eye away!
> Make the eye cross seven rivers,
> Make the eye cross seven canals,
> Make the eye cross seven mountains!
> Take the eye and tie its feet to an isolated r[ee]d stalk,   (20)
> Take the eye and smash it in its owner's face like a potter's vessel!

(fragmentary lines, then breaks off)

Text: Ebeling, ArOr 17/1 (1949), 203-204 VAT 10018 (transliteration only); VAT 14226 cited p. 204.
Edition: Ebeling, ArOr 17/1 (1949), 204-206; Thomsen, JNES 51 (1992), 24.

1. Variant omits three lines.
2. Text repeats "neighbor" without change of gender.
3. Variant has third person here and following.
4. Variant omits two lines.
5. Or, perhaps, "companion."

IV.32 AGAINST EVIL SPIRITS

(a) THE SEVEN

They are seven, they the seven, (1)
They are seven in the springs of the depths,
They are seven, adorned in heaven.
They grew up in the springs of the depths, in the cella.
They are not male, they are not female, (5)
They are drifting phantoms,
They take no wife, they beget no son.
They know neither sparing of life nor mercy,
They heed no prayers nor entreaties.
They are steeds that grew up in the mountains, (10)
They are the evil ones of Ea,
They are the prefects of the gods.
They loiter in the side streets to make trouble on the highway.
They are evil, they are evil!
They are seven, they are seven, they are twice seven! (15)
Be conjured by heaven, be conjured by the netherworld!

Text: Campbell Thompson, CT 16 15, v 29-59 (bilingual).
Edition: Campbell Thompson, *Devils* 1, 76-79.

(b) BLACK TRAGACANTH

A black tragacanth grew up in Eridu,
    it was created in a pure place.   (1)
Its appearance was pure blue, stretching out to the depths.
The way of Ea in Eridu is full of plenty,
His dwelling is at the netherworld,
His sleeping place is the watery deep.
In the pure house, the shade of which stretches like a forest's,
    where none may enter,   (5)
Therein are Shamash and Tammuz,
Between the mouths of the two rivers.
The gods Kahegal, Igihegal,
    and [Lahama-absu] of Eridu [took] that tragacanth,*
They set it near the patient (to cure him).
Let a favorable spirit,
    a favorable genius always be at the side of (this) man,
      son of his (personal) god ...

(remainder of text too fragmentary for translation)

Text: Campbell Thompson, CT 16 46, 183-203 (bilingual).
Edition: Langdon, JRAS 1928, 846-848.
Literature: see Borger, HKL 2, 288.
Notes to Text: (8) CAD K, 453b.

(c) MYSTERIOUS DEMONS

Evil phantom, evil demon, evil wraith,
    evil sprite have come forth from the netherworld, (1)
[They] have come forth from the infernal regions into the land.
They are not known in heaven,
They are not understood in the netherworld.
They do not know how to stand up, (5)
They do not know how to sit down.
They eat no food,
They drink no water!

Text: Campbell Thompson, CT 17 41, K 2873, 1-10 (bilingual).
Edition: Campbell Thompson, *Devils* 2, 134-135.

IV.33 AGAINST EYE DISEASE

Eye disease was a common problem in Babylonia, so numerous incantations try to cure it.

(a) DAUGHTERS TO THE WIND

This incantation is known from a manuscript discovered at Ugarit on the Syrian coast.

> Blurred eyes, troubled eyes!   (1)
> Eyes, daughters to the wind,
> Eyes, porous blood vessels!
> You have brought upon me a rainfall [of blood?] and fire!*
> Let it be extinguished as if with water,   (5)
> Let it cease (running) as if with algae.[1]
>
> (This incantation is not mine,
>   it is an incantation of Damu and Ninkarrak.
> O Ninkarrak, heal, that the specialist receive (his) fee.*
> Let it not go out above, let it go out below.[2])

Text: Nougayrol, *Ugaritica* 5 19 (p. 379).
Edition: Nougayrol, *Ugaritica* 5, 64-65.
Notes to Text: (4) So Nougayrol, reading and translation doubtful. (8) So here, though in parallel texts reference is made to a gift for the goddess of healing.

1. If correctly understood, may refer to clotting of blood or stanching a flow of fluid from the eye.
2. The disease is supposed to be excreted.

(b) BLOODSHOT EYES

Cloudy eyes, blurred eyes, bloodshot eyes! (1)
Why do you cloud over, why do you blur?
Why do sand of river, pollen of date palm,
Pollen of fig tree, straw of winnower sting you?
If I called you, come, (5)
If I did not call you, you must not come!
(Be off), before north, south, east, and west wind
       have risen against you!

Text: Köcher, BAM 514, iii 13′-18′.
Edition: Landsberger, JNES 17 (1958), 57 (partial).

(c) THEY ARE TWO

They are two, the daughters of Anu, (1)
Between them bars a barrier,
Never goes sister to her sister!
Whom shall I send to the daughter(s) of Anu of heaven?
Let them bring their pots of chalcedony,
  their pots of pure bright lapis, (5)
Let them draw water and quench the clouded eyes,
  the blurred and troubled eyes.

Text: Köcher, BAM 514, iii 22′-26′.
Edition: Landsberger-Jacobsen, JNES 14 (1955), 16.

(d) MOTE

In the beginning, before creation,
      the work song came down to the land,   (1)
Seeder plow bore furrow, furrow bore sprout,
Sprout root, root node, node ear, ear mote.
Shamash reaped, Sin gleaned.
While Shamash was reaping and Sin was gleaning,   (5)
Mote entered the young man's eye.
Shamash and Sin stand by, so the mote will come out!

Text: Köcher, BAM 510, iv 41-45.
Edition: Landsberger, JNES 17 (1958), 56.
Literature: See II.16.

(e) WIND BLEW DOWN

Wind blew down from heaven and has set a sore in the man's eye,   (1)
It has set a sore in the diseased eyes,
This man's eyes are distressed, his eyes are troubled,
This man is weeping bitterly for himself.
Nabu saw this man's disease,   (5)
"Take crushed cassia,
"Cast the spell of the Deep,
"Bind the man's eye,
"When the Mother of the gods touches the man's eye
      with her pure hands,
"Let the wind which blew in the man's eye go out of his eye!"   (10)

Text: Köcher, BAM 510, iv 5-21 (bilingual).
Translation: Campbell Thompson, *Proceedings of the Royal Society of Medicine* 17 (1923/4), *Historical Section*, 32.

(f) VESSELS OF BLOOD

O eyes, porous vessels of blood!   (1)
Why do you carry away chaff, thorns, berries, riverweed?
Clods from the streets, litter from the ...,
          why do you carry them away?
Rain down like stars, soar down like sky-fire,
Before flint knife and scalpel of(?) Gula ... get to you!*   (5)

(A spell of Asalluhi and Marduk,
A spell of Ningirimma, lord of spells, and Gula,
The lord of the physician's art cast it, I bore it up.)

Text: Köcher, BAM 510, iv 34-39.
Edition: Landsberger, JNES 17 (1958), 58.
Notes to Text: (5f.) Syntax of final lines not clear.

IV.34 AGAINST FEVER

(a) FIRE, FIRE!

This incantation alludes to the spread of contagious disease.

Fire, fire!   (1)
Fire seized a lone man.
It seized (his) insides, (his) temple,
It spread (to others) the consumption of (his) insides,
The stock of the human race was diminished.   (5)
Belet-ili went before Ea the king,
"O Ea, mankind was created by your spell,
"Second, you pinched off their clay
        from the sky of the depths.[1]
"By your great command, you determined their capacities.
"I cast a spell on the ...-disease, fever, boils,   (10)
"Leprosy(?), jaundice!
"Rain down like dew,
"Flow down like tears,
"Go down to the netherworld!"*

(This incantation is an incantation of Belet-ili, the great queen.)

Text: W. G. Lambert, AfO 23 (1970), pl. IV, V, IX.
Edition: W. G. Lambert, AfO 23 (1970), 42-43 lines 20-33.
Notes to Text: (14) Lambert, AfO 23 (1970), 43 note to III, 32.

---

1. That is, from the ground (Lambert, AfO 23 [1970], 43 note to III, 25-27).

(b) HAS YOUR SMOKE NO SMELL?

Fire, fire! (1)
Fire of storm, fire of battle,
Fire of death, fire of pestilence, consuming fire!
Has your smoke no smell?
Has your fire no warmth? (5)
May Asalluhi drive you away
      and send you across the Tigris river.[1]
I conjure you by Anu your father,
I conjure you by Antu your mother,
Go out, like a snake from you(r hole in) the foundations,
Like a partridge(?) from your hiding place! (10)
Do not go back towards your prey,*
Disperse like mist, rise like dew,
Go up, like smoke, to the heaven of Anu!

Text: W. G. Lambert, AfO 23 (1970), pl. I, III, VI, X.
Edition: W. G. Lambert, AfO 23 (1970), 40 lines 5-15.
Notes to Text: (11) Lambert, AfO 23 (1970), 40 note to II,13.

1. Variant: Tigris and Euph[rates].

IV.35 AGAINST FLATULENCE

This may be one of the few apotheoses of flatulence in world literature.

> Wind, O wind!
> Wind, you are the fire of the gods.
> You are the wind between turd and urine.
> You have come out and taken your place
> Among the gods, your brethren.

Text: Köcher, BAM 574, iii 56-64.
Edition: Küchler, *Assyriologische Bibliothek* 18 (Berlin, 1909), No. 1.
Translation: Ritter, AS 16 (1965), 312; Farber, TUAT II/2, 272.

IV.36 AGAINST HEADACHE

(a) EPIDEMIC

[He]adache has come forth from the Ekur,	(1)
It has come forth [fr]om the house of Enlil.	
A Lamashtu,[1] who wipes out (names),	
It grants no rest, makes sleep unpleasant,	
It is the sickness of night and day.	(5)
Its head is a demon, its body a deluge,	
Its appearance is a darkened sky,	
Its [fa]ce is the thick(?) shadow of a forest,	
Its [ha]nd is a snare, its foot a noose(?),	
... it makes the sinews smart ...,	(10)
It makes the limbs smart,	
It makes the [b]elly(?) tremble, it wastes the body,	
It makes [the stomach] rumble like a porous pot,	
It contorts the tendons, it twists the sinews,*	
It twists the sinews like a heavy rope,	
It contorts [the mus]cles,	(15)
It chokes the mouth and nostrils as with pitch,*	
It crushes the armpit like malt,	
It snaps off the [ha]nd like a thread in a tempest,	
It destroys the shoulder like an embankment,	
It slits open the breast like a (flimsy) basket,	(20)
It staves in the ribs like an old boat,	
It gets a grip on the colon as if it were intestines,	
It flattens the tall like a reed,	
It slaughters the great one like an ox.	
It struck the ox, it did not pity the ox,	(25)
It struck the wild ox, it did not relent to the wild ox,	
It struck the ibex, it could not grow its horns full size,	
It struck the wild ram, the mountain ram,	
it did not spare their young,	

---

1. A she-demon; see II.31, IV.37. For erasing of family names by killing offspring, see p. 183 note 1.

It struck the beasts of the steppe so they butted one another
    like an orchard whose branches are being torn away,[1]
It punctures everything like a ... throw stick.   (30)
Asalluhi saw it,

(cure follows)

Text: Campbell Thompson, CT 17 25, 1-48; cf. Ebeling, KAR 368 (bilingual).
Edition: Campbell Thompson, Devils 2, 86-87.
Literature: See Borger, HKL 2, 289.
*Notes to Text: (14) Landsberger, MSL 9, 23-24. (16) With CAD I/J, 310 etc., against Borger, BiOr 14 (1957), 194 note 7.

(b) AFFLICTION

Headache, applied[2] in heaven, removed in the netherworld,   (1)
Which brought to an end the strength of the strong young man,
Which has not returned her energy to the beautiful young woman,
Which has set upon the sick man.
Ishtar, without whom no one has relaxation or delight,
    made (it) come down from the mountain.   (5)
It drew near the limbs of the afflicted man,
The man stands (saying), "Alas!"
Who will remove it, who will cast it out?
Ishtar, daughter of Sin,
Enkum,[3] son of Enlil,   (10)
Asalluhi, son of Eridu,
Let them cast it out from the body of the afflicted man!

(cure follows)

Text: Campbell Thompson, CT 17 19, 147-166; von Weiher, SBTU III 65 (bilingual).
Edition: Campbell Thompson, Devils 2, 76-79; von Weiher, SBTU III, 43-44.
Literature: Borger, HKL 2, 289.

1. The comparison may be between the thrashing of branches and the clashing of horns.
2. Literally: "bound on."
3. A servant god to Enki; see Geller, FAOS 12 (1985), 90; Borger, JCS 21 (1967), 11 (26+a).

(c) MISERY

Head disease charges about the steppe, blowing like the wind, (1)
It flashes on and off like lightning, it is poured out,
 above and below.
It cut off, like a reed, the man who did not revere his god,
It slashed his sinews like a (flimsy) basket,
It wastes the flesh of him who has no protective goddess. (5)
It flashes like stars of the sky, it runs like water at night,
It has confronted the afflicted man and paralyzed him,
 as if it were a storm.
It killed that man!
That man writhes like one with intestinal disease,
Like one disemboweled he tosses about. (10)
He burns like one cast in a fire.
(He is) like an onager,[1] whose shrunken eyes are clouded,
He is fed up with his life, he is bound over for death.
Headache, whose course, like a thick fog's, no one knows,
Whose full sign, whose means of restraint no one knows! (15)

(cure follows)

Text: Campbell Thompson, CT 17 19, 1-30; von Weiher, SBTU II 2, 1-27 (bilingual).
Edition: Campbell Thompson, *Devils* 2, 64-67; von Weiher, SBTU II, 22, lines 1-51.
Literature: See Borger, HKL 2, 289.

---

1. Sumerian adds: "fleet."

(d) DO NOT ENTER THE HOUSE I ENTER

Pazuzu son of Hanbu was one of the rare Mesopotamian demons with a personal name and patronymic. This demon appears only in first millennium sources. In the following spell, which has many variant versions, Pazuzu is associated with headache.

O mighty one, who comes over high mountains,
 who withstands all winds   (1)
Raging wind, whose rising is terrible, furious, raging,
 who comes on furiously,
Murderer of the world regions, wrecker of high mountains,
Who parches the marshland, who parches its reeds:

It beat on the forest, dropped its trees,
It passed into the garden, dropped down its fruit,   (5)
It passed down the river, dropped down ice,
It went up into the desert, dropped down frost,
It peered down the well, dropped down ice,[1]
It went up into the desert, dropped down frost!   (10)

O headache of humanity, head pain of humanity,
 disease of humanity,
Do not enter the house I enter,
Do not come near the house I come near,
Do not approach the house I approach!

Be conjured by Anu and Antu, Enlil and Ninlil,
 Ea and Damkina, heaven and netherworld!   (15)

Text: See Borger, *Studies Reiner*, 16.
Edition: Borger, *Studies Reiner*, 19-22 lines 31-47.

---

1. Variant adds: "It struck the young man, hunched him over / It knocked against the young girl, deformed(?) her hips / When you blow, the world regions heave."

(e) I AM PAZUZU

Amulets and collections of spells preserve a short self-predication by Pazuzu. Although the original text is in Sumerian, it was probably composed at a late date, long after Sumerian was a dead language.[1] Several variant Akkadian translations are found. The mythological reference to climbing a mountain and overcoming a wind (see also IV.36d) is not known elsewhere in more detail.

I am Pazuzu, son of Hanbu, king of the evil phantoms.
I ascended the mighty mountain that quaked.
The winds that I went against were headed towards the west.
One by one I broke their wings.

Text: See Borger, *Studies Reiner*, 24-27.
Edition: W. G. Lambert, *Forschungen und Berichte* 12 (1970), 41-47.

1. W. G. Lambert, *Forschungen und Berichte* 12 (1970), 45.

IV.37 AGAINST LAMASHTU

For the Lamashtu-demon, see above, I.6 and II.26. Here the magician sends her on a long journey, away from her victim.

(a) "BRING ME YOUR SONS!"

She is furious, she is fierce, she is uncanny,
    she has an awful glamor, and she is a she-wolf,
        the daughter of Anu!   (1)
Her feet are those of Anzu, her hands are unclean,
    the face of a ravening lion is her face.
She came up from the reed bed, her hair askew,
    her loincloth torn away.[1]
She stalks the cattle's tracks, she dogs the sheep's tracks,
    her hands are gory with flesh and blood.
She comes in the window, slithering like a serpent,   (5)
She enters a house, she leaves a house (at will).
"Bring me your sons, that I may suckle (them),
    and your daughters, that I may nurse (them),
"Let me put my breast in your daughters' mouths!"
Ea his father heard her,
"O daughter of Anu, instead of trying to be the nursemaid
    of mankind,   (10)
"Instead of your hands being gory with flesh and blood,
"Instead of entering a house, leaving a house (at will),
"Accept from the traveling merchant a cloak and provisions,
"Accept from the smith bracelets as befit your hands and feet,
"Accept from the jeweler an earring as befits your ears,   (15)
"Accept from the gem cutter a carnelian as befits your neck,
"Accept from the wood worker a comb, a distaff,
    and your pectoral."
I conjure you by Anu your father, Antu your mother,
I conjure you by Ea, who created your name!

---

1. Compare I.6 line 7, a description of her wild state expanded here by having her come from a swamp.

Text: Thureau-Dangin, RA 18 (1921), 163; von Weiher, SBTU III 84, 63-78.
Edition: Thureau-Dangin, RA 18 (1921), 166-167, 170-171; von Weiher, SBTU III, 118, 121f.

(b) SHE TORTURES BABIES

Great is the daughter of Anu, who tortures babies, (1)
Her hand is a net, her embrace is dea[th].
She is cruel, raging, wrathful, rapacious,
A runner, an abductor is the daughter of Anu.
She touches the bellies of women in labor, (5)
She yanks out the pregnant woman's baby.
She suckles it, she stands it up and it goes about.
Her breasts(?), her belly(?), her muscles are large.
The daughter of Anu is the one of the gods, her brethren,
    with no child of her own.
Her head is the head of a lion, (10)
Her form is the form of a donkey,
Her lips are a rushing wind, they pour out [ ].
She came down from the peaks(?) of the mountains,
She roars like a lion,
She keeps up the howling of a demonic dog. (15)

Text: Pinches, IV R² 58, iii 29-48; Lutz, PBS 1/2 113, iii 15-35.
Edition: Myhrman, ZA 16 (1902), 180-181.
Literature: See Borger, HKL 2, 230.

(c) "I AM THE DAUGHTER OF ANU"

"I am the daughter of Anu, the sky,   (1)
"I am a Sutaean,[1] [I have] an awful glamor.
"I enter a house, I leave a house (at will),

'Bring me your sons that I may suckle (them),
'Let me put my breast in your daughters' mouths!'"   (5)

Anu heard and began to weep,
Aruru, mistress of the gods, shed her tears,
"Why shall we destroy what we have created?
"Shall she carry off what we brought to be?
"Take her and throw her into the ocean ...,   (10)
"Tie her to a mountain tamarisk or a solitary reed stalk!
"Like a dead person who has no burial,
"Or a stillborn child who suckles not a mother's milk,
"May the daughter of Anu, like smoke,
          not return to (this) house!"

Text: Pinches, IV R² 58, iii 13–27; Lutz, PBS 1/2 113, iii 2–14.
Edition: Myhrman, ZA 16 (1902), 178–179.
Literature: See Borger, HKL 2, 230.

1. A bandit folk who were a byword for violence and marauding; see Erra and Ishum (IV.16), p. 797 note 2.

(d) SHE SEIZED

[She is furious, she is uncanny, she has an awful glamor],   (1)

[   ]

She crossed a watercourse and made its water muddy,

She leaned against a wall and smeared it with filth.

She seized an old man, they call her "wipe-out."   (5)

She seized a young man, they call her "sunstroke."

She seized a girl, they call her "Lamashtu."

She seized a boy, they call her "Lamashtu."

Because you have come, you will seize the form of his features,

You seize the limbs, you destroy the members,   (10)

You consume(?) the sinews, you twist the muscles,

You make the face pale, you change the countenance around,

You cause depression, you burn the body like fire!

To remove you, to drive you out so you cannot return,
        so you cannot approach,   (15)

So you cannot come near the body of so-and-so,
        son of so-and-so,

I conjure you by Anu, father of the great gods,

I conjure you by Enlil, the great mountain,

I conjure you by Ea, king of the depths, creator of everything,
        lord of all,

I conjure you by Belet-ili, great queen,
        who formed created things,   (20)

I conjure you by Sin, lord of the tiara, who renders decisions,
        who discloses signs,

I conjure you by Shamash, light of above and below,
        creator of the universe,

I conjure you by Asalluhi, lord of exorcism,

I conjure you by Ninurta, foremost of the gods his brethren,

I conjure you by Ningirimma, mistress of incantations,   (25)

I conjure you by Ninkarrak, housekeeper of Ekur,

I conjure you by Ishtar, mistress of the lands!

Be conjured by Assembly Place of the Gods,[1]
        abode of counsel of the great gods in Ekur,

You will not return to so-and-so, son of so-and-so
    nor draw near him.

(This incantation is not mine,
    it is an incantation of Ea and Asalluhi,
It is an incantation of Damu and Ninkarrak,   (30)
It is an incantation of Ningirimma, mistress of incantations.)

Text: Pinches, IV R² 56, [i 30] - ii 21; Lutz, PBS 1/2 113, i 23-41.
Edition: Myhrman, ZA 16 (1902), 156-160.
Literature: See Borger, HKL 2, 230.

---

1. Ubshu-ukkenna, a cosmic locality; see Creation Epic (III.17) Tablet II line 160.

IV.38 AGAINST NURSES HARMFUL TO CHILDREN

O wetnurse!	(1)
Wetnurse, whose breast is (too) sweet,	
Wetnurse, whose breast is (too) bitter,	
Wetnurse, whose breast is infected,	
Wetnurse, who died from an infected breast,	(5)
Nursemaid, whose armclasp is relaxed,	
Nursemaid, whose armclasp is loose,	
Nursemaid, whose armclasp is limp,	
Nursemaid, whose armclasp is wrong,	
Be conjured by heaven!	(10)
Be conjured by the netherworld!	

Text: Haupt, ASKT 11, 35-44 (bilingual).
Edition: Borger, AOAT 1 (1969), 5 VII.

IV.39 AGAINST PHANTOMS

(a) LIFE PASSED THEM BY

Mesopotamian demonology recognized a wraith in the form of a young man or woman (Ardat-lili) that had never known a full or normal life. The excerpts translated below show the nature of this demon and the sometimes fervid descriptions lavished on it by the scribes.

(a, = Lackenbacher, Group 1 col i)

[A young man who] sits stock still in the street, [all al]one,   (1)
A young man who groans bitterly in the grip of his fate,
A young man who, on account of his destiny, is aghast,
A young man whose mother, sobbing, bore him in the street,
A young man whose body is seared by woe,   (5)
A young man whose (personal) god bound him out of hostility,
A young man whose (personal) goddess forsook him,
A young man who took no wife, raised no child,
A young man who felt no pleasure in his wife's loins,
A young man who did not strip the garment from his wife's loins, (10)
A young man expelled from his wedding ...

(b, = Lackenbacher, Group 1 col ii, variant = Group 3 col ii 1′-14′)

They (the demons) confront the man who has no god,   (1)
They s[et] their hands on his hand,[1]
[They set their] feet on his feet,
[They set their] neck with his neck,
They traded his self [for theirs].   (5)
"I am the son of a prince," he said to her,
"I will fill your lap with silver and gold,
"You be the wife,
"I will be your husband," he said to her,
He made himself as alluring to her as the fruit of an orchard.   (10)

---

1. Variant: "He (the demon) touched his hand and made it his own hand ..." (etc.).

(c, = SBTU II 6, 36-45, variant =Lackenbacher, Group 2 obv i, rev i 9'-26')

Ardat-lili wafts through a man's window: (1)
The girl who has no (natural) destiny(?),
The girl who was never impregnated like a woman,
The girl who never lost her virginity like a woman,
The girl who felt no pleasure in her husband's loins,   (5)
The girl who never removed her garment at her husband's loins,
The girl whose garment pin no handsome young man released,
The girl who had no milk in her breasts,
     but only bitter fluid came out,
The girl who felt no pleasure in her husband's loins,
     whose desire was never fulfilled,
The girl without a bedroom, who did not call for her mother.   (10)

(d, continues directly in one version, = SBTU II 7, 4-13)

Who made her cheek ugly through unhappiness,   (1)
Who did not enjoy herself with (other) girls,[1]
Who never appeared at her city's festival,
Who never wanted anything,
Who was taken away from her husband in the bedchamber,   (5)
Who had no husband, bore no son,
Who had no husband, produced no son,
Whose husband was taken away, whose son was taken away,
Who was expelled from her wedding,
Ardat-lili, who was expelled from the window like air,   (10)
Ardat-lili, whose spirit was not in her breathing(?),
Ardat-lili, whose misery took her to the grave.

---

1. Variant: "go about the roads and streets."

(e, = Lackenbacher, Group 1 rev ii 3'-17', variant K 5443)

So long as you have not left (this) house,   (1)
So long as you have not left (this) city,
You shall eat no food, you shall drink no water,
You shall taste no sea water, fresh water, brackish water,
     Tigris water, Euphrates water, well water, canal water!   (5)
If you would fly towards heaven, you shall have no wings,
If you would stay on earth, you shall have no place to sit!

Text: Lackenbacher, RA 65 (1971), 119ff., figs. 1-14; von Weiher, SBTU II 6, 7; Geller, AfO 35 (1988), 8, 10, 13, 16.
Edition: Lackenbacher, RA 65 (1971), 119-154; von Weiher, SBTU II, 22-30, 41-47; Geller, AfO 35 (1988), 7-21.
Literature: Farber, ZA 79 (1989), 14-35.

(b) AGAINST A GHOST THAT HAS APPEARED

Mesopotamian magic included spells and rituals against ghosts and the dead. For a detailed study of this material, see J. Bottéro, "Les morts et l'au-delà dans rituels en accadien contre l'action des 'revenants'," ZA 73 (1983), 153-203; compare III.39.

> The ghost which has set upon me, keeps harassing me,
>   and [does not quit me] day or [nig]ht,   (1)
> Be it a stranger ghost,
> Be it a forgotten ghost,
> Be it a ghost without a name,
> Be it a ghost which has no one to provide for it,   (5)
> Be it a ghost of someone who [has no one to invoke his name],
> Be it a ghost of someone killed by a weapon,
> Be it a ghost of someone who died for a sin against a god
>   or for a crime against a king,
> [Place] it [in the care of the ghosts of his family],
> May it accept this and let me go free!

Text: Campbell Thompson, CT 23 15, 6-9.
Edition: Castellino, OrNS 24 (1955), 244-245.
Literature: Borger, HKL 2 292; Bottéro, ZA 73 (1983), 157.

(c) WHY DO YOU KEEP APPEARING TO ME?

O dead people, why do you keep appearing to me,   (1)
People whose cities are ruin heaps,
Who themselves are just bones?
I don't go to Cutha,[1] where ghosts congregate,
Why do you keep coming after me?   (5)
Be conjured by Abatu[2] the queen and Ereshkigal,
By Ningeshtinanna, scribe of the gods,
Whose stylus is lapis and carnelian!

Text: Campbell Thompson, CT 23 15, 13-15.
Edition: Castellino, OrNS 24 (1955), 246-247.
Literature: Borger, HKL 2, 292; Bottéro, ZA 73 (1983), 157.

1. Cult city of Nergal, king of the netherworld.
2. "Destruction"(?), otherwise unknown. Ereshkigal is queen of the netherworld (see III.19).

IV.40 AGAINST "REDNESS"

This spell may refer to a disease affecting the head and scalp.

Cloud, cloud!	(1)
Red cloud arose, covering red cloud,	
Red rain arose, flooded* red earth,	
Red flood(?) arose, filled red watercourse!	
Let(?) a red plowman bring a red [spa]de(?) and a red carrier,	(5)
Let him dam up the red water.	
Red door, red bolt, whose aperture is pitch(?),*	
Who will open you?	
Irishmara, irishmara![1]	

Text: Köcher, BAM 480, iii 65-68.
Translation: Campbell Thompson, AJSL 53 (1937), 235.
Literature: Nougayrol, ArOr 17/2 (1949), 225.
Notes to Text: (3) Reading ir-ḫu-<ṣa> A.ZI.GA (7) If correctly read, meaning "blocked up"?

1. Abracadabra words.

IV.41 AGAINST SCORPIONS

(a) IT IS GREEN

This brief spell, mid-second millennium or earlier in date, is accompanied by an abracadabra and brief instructions as to how to treat the affected flesh.

> It is green in the thornbush(?),
> It is silent in the sand,
> It is venomous in the brickmold!

Text: Nougayrol, RA 66 (1972), 141.
Edition: Nougayrol, RA 66 (1972), 142.

(b) WOLF OF THE STOREROOM

The god Enlil encounters a scorpion as he builds a house, and brushes it away with his little finger.

> Wolf of the storeroom, lion of the larder,   (1)
> Its pincers stick out, like a wild bull's horns,
> Its tail is curved up, like a mighty lion's.
> Enlil built the house.
> When he mortars the brick stack,   (5)
> When he turns over the lapis-blue brick,
> Let Enlil's little finger take (it) away!
> O waters, ... let the libation bear (it) off!
> Let gentle sleep fall upon (this) man.

>   (Incantation to relieve a scorpion's sting)

Text: Gadd, CT 38 38, 59-66; Caplice, OrNS 34 (1965), pl. xvi K 5944.
Edition: Caplice, OrNS 34 (1965), 121-122.

IV.42 AGAINST SICKNESS AND PAIN

The magical work *Shurpu*, "Incineration," deals primarily with ways to avert the consequences of a wide range of evils, especially in cases where the source of the trouble is not known with certainty or comes from within the sufferer (see further Introduction to Chapter IV, p. 695). This excerpt is from a group of short spells that use incineration of garlic, dates, matting, various wools, goat's hair, and flour as a means of symbolically burning the evil besetting a person.

As this garlic is peeled off and thrown into the fire,	(1)
(And) Girra burns it up with fire,	
Which will not be cultivated in a garden patch,	
Which will not be hard by a ditch or canal,	
Whose roots will not take hold in the ground,	(5)
Whose sprout will not come forth nor see the sun,	
Which will not be used for the repast of god or king,	
(So) may the curse, something evil, revenge, interrogation,	
The sickness of my suffering, wrong-doing, crime, misdeed, sin,	
The sickness which is in my body, flesh, and sinews	(10)
Be peeled off like this garlic,	
May Girra burn it with fire this day,	
May the wicked thing go forth, that I may see light.	

Text: Pinches, IV R² 7-8 i 51 - ii 7.
Edition: Reiner, *Šurpu*, 31, lines 60-72.
Translation: Farber, TUAT II/2, 265-267.

IV.43 AGAINST TOOTHACHE

This incantation tells how toothache found its place in the world.

After Anu created [heaven],	(1)
Heaven created [earth],	
Earth created rivers,	
Rivers created watercourses,	
Watercourses created marshes,	(5)
Marshes created the worm.	
The worm came crying before Shamash,	
Before Ea his tears flowed down,	
"What will you give me, that I may eat?	
"What will you give me, that I may suck?"	(10)
"I will give you a ripe fig and an apple."	
"What are a ripe fig and an apple to me?	
"Set me to dwell between teeth and jaw,	
"That I may suck the blood of the jaw,	
"That I may chew on the bits (of food) stuck in the jaw."	(15)
...	
Because you said this, worm,	
May Ea strike you with the might of his hand!	

Text: Campbell Thompson, CT 17 50; cf. AMT 25/1 1-7; 25/2 15-28.
Edition: Campbell Thompson, *Devils* 2, 160-161.
Translation: Campbell Thompson, *Proceedings of the Royal Society of Medicine* 19 (1925/6), Historical Section, 59-60; Speiser, ANET³, 100-101; Heidel, *Babylonian Genesis²*, 72-73; Thureau-Dangin, RA 36 (1939), 3-4.
Literature: See Borger, HKL 1, 547.

IV.44 AGAINST WITCHCRAFT

The magical work *Maqlû*, "Burning," consists of nine large tablets of
incantations, prayers, and rituals, mostly to be used against witchcraft (see
further Introduction to Chapter IV, p. 695).

(a) MY MAGIC WORKS

The magician's magic is legitimate because it is controlled; the opponent's not.

> Netherworld, Netherworld, O Netherworld! (1)
> Gilgamesh[1] is master of your curse,
> Whatever you have worked, I know it,
> Whatever I shall work, you know it not,
> Whatever my sorceresses shall work (against me) is confusion, (5)
> With none to sort it out or solve it!

Text: Pinches, IV R² 49, 37-40; Tallqvist, *Maqlû* I, 37-41; Finkelstein, STT 78, 37-42.
Edition: Meier, *Maqlû*, 8, lines 37-41.

---

1. Here a god of the netherworld.

(b) BLOCKADING

The magician cuts off all alien magic to ensure the efficacy of his alone.

I blocked the ford, I have blocked the quay,	(1)
I blocked the machination of all lands.	
Anu and Antu send me,	
Whom shall I send to Belet-seri (saying),	
"Put muzzles on the mouth of my sorcerer and sorceress,	(5)
"Cast the incantation of Marduk, sage of the gods!"	
Let them call to you — you, (Belet-seri), shall not answer them.	
Let them speak to you, you shall not listen to them.	
Let me call upon you, answer me!	
Let me speak to you, listen to me!	(10)
(This is) according to the command spoken by Anu,	
Antu, and Belet-seri.	

Text: Pinches, IV R² 49, 48-58 = Tallqvist, Maqlû I, 50-60; Finkelstein, STT 78, 50-60.
Edition: Meier, Maqlû, 9, lines 50-60.
Literature: Farber, JNES 49 (1990), 320-321.

(c) THEY ARE WORKING AGAINST ME

They worked and keep on working against me,   (1)
To roll me up like a mat,
To clamp down on me like a bird trap,
To wreck me like an embankment,
To close over me like a net,
To cord me like cordage,   (5)
To climb over me like a rampart,
To fill a foundation ditch with me,
      as if (I were) ditchwater,
To pitch me out at the door like sweepings!
I, by command of Marduk, lord of the evening (rites),
And Asalluhi, lord of exorcism,   (10)
Roll up my sorcerer and my sorceress like a mat,
Clamp down on them like a bird trap,
Wreck them like an embankment,
Close over them like a net,
Cord them like cordage,   (15)
Fill a foundation ditch with them,
      as if (they were) ditch water,
Pitch them out at the door like sweepings.
[May] the figurines of my sorcerer
      and my sorceress tu[rn into ashes?]!

Text: Tallqvist, *Maqlû* II, 148-168.
Edition: Meier, *Maqlû*, 19, lines 160-180.

(d) THE FOOTPAD

The sorceress, she who walks about the streets,   (1)
Who intrudes in houses,
Who prowls in alleys,
Who lurks in the square,
She keeps turning around in front and behind,   (5)
She stands in the street and turns foot(ways) around,
She has blocked passage on the square.
She robbed the fine young man of his vigor,
She took away the attractiveness of the fine young woman,
With her malignant stare she took away her charms,   (10)
She looked at the young man and took away his vigor,
She looked at the young woman and took away her attractiveness!
The sorceress saw me, she came up behind me,
She has blocked passage with her poison,
She cut off progress with her spell.   (15)
She drove away my (personal) god and my (personal) goddess
        from my person!
I have pinched off my sorceress's clay from potter's clay,
I have fashioned a figurine of the woman who bewitched me.
I put tallow in your insides, it harms you!
I implant an ashwood stick in the small of your back
        to burn you!   (20)
The ashwood which burns you, may it cut off your poison![1]
I have kindled a fire above the city,
I have thrown ashes(?) below the city,
I have cast fire towards the house you enter!
(For) what you have done, may Fire[2] consume you,   (25)
(For) what you worked, may Fire overcome you,
(For) what you plotted, may Fire kill you,
(For) what you conspired, may Fire burn you up!
May Fire, who harms you, send you on the road of no return,
May furious Girra burn your body!   (30)

1. Variant: "speech."
2. Girra, the fire god; see III.40.

Text: Tallqvist, *Maqlû* III, 1-30; Finkelstein, STT 82, 15-30; von Weiher, SBTU III 74A, i 1-32; 74B, i 1-11.
Edition: Meier, *Maqlû*, 22-23, lines 1-30; von Weiher, SBTU III, 76.
Literature: Meier, AfO 21 (1966), 74.

IV.45 LOVE CHARMS

For other love charms, see I.4 and II.33.

(a) THE HARPSTRING

Wind blow, orchard shake,	(1)
Clouds gather, droplets fall!	
Let my potency be (steady as) running river water,	
Let my penis be a (taut) harpstring,	
Let it not slip out of her!	(5)

Text: Ebeling-Köcher-Rost, LKA 95, rev 6-11; 101, rev(!) 12-15; Gurney, STT 280, iv 37-41.
Edition: Biggs, ŠÀ.ZI.GA, 35.

(b) GET UP!

The magician takes control of the woman. Her clothes are to turn into an impromptu bower, her bed a covered spot for a tryst, and, if she is asleep when the spell is wrought, her own couch will unceremoniously awaken her to send her off to the embrace of her admirer.

I have seized you, I have seized you, I will not let you free!	(1)
As pitch holds fast to boat,	
As Sin to Ur, as Shamash to Larsa,	
As Ishtar to Ekur hold fast,[1]	
I have seized you and I will not let you free!	(5)
May the clothes you are wearing be your bower(?),	
May the bed you sleep on be a tent(?),	
May the bed dump you on the ground!	
May the [grou]nd say to you "Get up!"	
[At the com]mand spoken by the Capable Lady, Ishtar.	

Text: Ebeling, KAR 69, rev 10-22.
Edition: Biggs, ŠÀ.ZI.GA, 77-78.

1. Ur was the sacred city of Sin, the Moongod, and Larsa the sacred city of Shamash, the sungod, but the connection of Ishtar with a temple called Ekur is unknown.

(c) I HAVE MADE A BED

Potency, potency! I(?) have made a bed for potency!   (1)
What Ishtar does for Dumuzi,
What Nanay d[oes] for her lover,
What Ishara d[oes] for her mate(?),[1]
Let me do for my lover![2]   (5)
Let the flesh of so-and-so, son of so-and-so, tingle,
[Let his penis stand erect]!
May his ardor[3] not flag, night or day!
By command of the Capable Lady, Ishtar, Nanay,
    G[azbaba, Is]hara.[4]

Text: Gurney, STT 280, ii 10-17.
Edition: Biggs, ŠÀ.ZI.GA, 44-45.

1. Variant: "Almanu" (name of a god?).
2. Variant omits.
3. Variant: "May his penis not relax."
4. Love goddesses. See II.1, 2, and p. 168 note 3.

(d) MAY I NOT MISS MY PREY!

Wind come, mountains [quak]e,   (1)
Clouds gather, droplets fall!
Let the (penis of the) ass become stiff, let him mount the jenny,
Let the he-goat have an erection,
    let him mount the she-goat ... time after time.
At the head of my bed a he-goat is tied,[1]   (5)
At the foot of my bed a ram is tied.
You at the head of my bed, have an erection, make love to me!
You at the foot of my bed, have an erection, caress me!
My vagina is a bitch's vagina, his penis is a dog's penis.
As the bitch's vagina holds tight the dog's penis,   (10)
(So may my vagina hold tight his penis)!
May your penis grow long as a warclub!
I'm sitting in a web of seduction,
May I not miss my prey!

Text: Ebeling, KAR 70, rev 10-21; 236, obv 1-13; 243, obv! 1-10.
Edition: Biggs, ŠÀ.ZI.GA, 32-35.
Translation: Farber, TUAT II/2, 273-274.

---

1. Variant has here and in following lines "I have tied ..."

IV.46 FOR ABSOLUTION

Disease and suffering were often treated as consequences of sin or wrong-doing. These spells belong to a collection that seeks release or absolution from illness or other affliction.

(a) THE BRAZIER

I am the master exorcist, I have lit a fire,	(1)
I have set up a brazier, I have burned the absolving materials.	
I am washed and pure, the clean (agent) of Ea,	
messenger of Asalluhi.	
May all the gods I invoked bring about absolution,	
By command of Ea and Asalluhi,	
may no god nor goddess be angry.	(5)

I have damped [the brazier] I lit,
    I have put out the fire I kindled,
I have smothered the grain I poured (into the fire).
May Sirish, who absolves god and man,
    loose his (the patient's) bond.
Just as I damped the brazier I lit,
Just as I put out the fire I kindled, (10)
Just as I smothered the grain I poured (into the fire),
May Sirish, who absolves god and man, loose his bond,
May the disease, the accursed thing, of so-and-so,
    son of so-and-so, be released
    and absolution brought about!

Text: Norris, II R 51 no. 1 (+), improved copy by Jensen in *Zeitschrift für Keilschriftforschung* 2 (1885), 320-321.
Edition: Reiner, JNES 15 (1956), 138-139, lines 109-121.

(b) MAY MY SIN RISE UP TO THE SKY!

May my sin [rise up to the sky like smoke],   (1)
May my sin [run off from my body like water],
May my sin, l[ike a drifting cloud, make rain in another field],
May my sin [burn out like a flame],
May my sin [flicker out like a flickering flame],   (5)
May my sin [be peeled off like an onion(skin)],
[May my sin be stripped off like a date(skin)],
[May my sin be unraveled like a mat],
[May my sin, like a shattered potter's vessel,
    never return where it was],
May my sin [be shattered like a potsherd],   (10)
May my sin, like silver and gold brought from [its] mine,
    [never return where it was],
May my sin, like ... iron,[1] [never return where it was],
May my sin, like sweet waters of a river,
    [never return where it was],
May my sin, like an uprooted tamarisk,
    [never return where it was],[2]
May a bird take my sin up to the sky,   (15)
[May] a fish [take] my sin [down] to the de[pths]!

Text: Reiner, JNES 16 (1956), 140 K 3059+ (transliteration only); Ebeling, KAR 295 "2.Seite" +408+409; Ebeling-Köcher-Rost, LKA 29 i "Rs.", 148 obv (= "2.S."); 149 obv (= "2.S.").
Edition: Reiner, JNES 16 (1956), 140-141, lines 7' - 22'.

   1. Reiner suggests "meteoric(?)"; J. Bjorkman, *Meteoritics* 1973/8 = Center for Meteoritic Studies, Arizona State University, *Publication* 12, 113 suggests "smelted iron."
   2. See III.37d line 32.

IV.47 FOR A RULER'S FAVOR

(a) I AM PROUD

Various spells and rituals were compiled for the use of people about to go to the lawcourt or government buildings. These call for strength, dignity, and protection. IV.29a, b also belong to this group. Others hope to make a person in authority glad to see the speaker.

> I rub on oil for dignity, (1)
> My hands are full of oil for control.*
> I am proud before god, king, lord, prince, great men,
> My lord's face will show (enough) favor for seven maidens!

Text: Ebeling, KAR 237, 13-15.
Edition: Ebeling, MAOG 5/3 (1931), 37, 40.
Notes to Text: (2) Variant unclear.

(b) I'VE PUT ON MY SHOES

This spell is to be said three times over a person's shoes when he puts them on, so that, wherever he goes, people will be glad to see him.

> I've put my shoes on my feet. (1)
> I've taken my place before you.
> My laughter is the flowering of my features,
> The winsome charm of my eyes.
> I'm a treat,[1] whatever I say to you will be amusing.*

Text: von Weiher, SBTU II 24, 36-40.
Edition: von Weiher, SBTU II, 127f., lines 36-40.
Notes to Text: (5) Variant unclear.

1. Text: "I am a festival," meaning a delight for the person who encounters the speaker.

IV.48 FOR A WOMAN IN LABOR

Numerous Sumerian and Akkadian incantations and rituals were intended for help in pregnancy and delivery. See also II.30.

(a) THE BABY IS STUCK!

The woman in labor is having a difficult labor,	(1)
Her labor is difficult, the baby is stuck,	
The baby is stuck!	
The doorbolt is locked, about to end life,	
The door is fastened against the suckling kid, ...	(5)
The woman giving birth is covered with death's dust,	
She is covered with the dust of battle, like a chariot,	
She is covered with the dust of tuffets, like a plow.	
She sprawls in her own blood, like a struggling warrior,	
Her eyesight is waning, she cannot see,	(10)
Her lips are coated, she cannot open them ...,	
Her eyesight is dim, ... she is alarmed, her ears cannot hear!	
Her breast is not held in, her headbands are askew,	
She is not veiled with ..., she has no shame.	
Stand by me and keep calling out(?), O merciful Marduk,	(15)
"Here is the confusion, I'm surrounded, get to me!"[1]	
Bring out the one sealed up, created by the gods,	
Created by mankind, let him come out and see the light!	

Text: W. G. Lambert, *Iraq* 31 (1969), pl. VI.
Edition: W. G. Lambert, *Iraq* 31 (1969), 31 lines 33-50.

---

1. This line is evidently spoken by the baby; see W. G. Lambert, *Iraq* 31 (1969), 36; Finkel, AfO 27 (1980), 45.

(b) SIN AND THE COW

The story of Sin, the Moongod, and the cow, exists in several widely varying versions from the mid-second millennium on. Only the most important variants have been noted here; for a full study, see Röllig's edition listed below. Compare also II.30a.

There was once a moon-cow named Geme-Sin, (1)
Perfect in form, beautiful in limb.
When Sin saw her he fell in love with her,
He set the glory of moonlight ... upon her,[1]
He set her at the front of the herd, (5)
The cattle came after her.
He pastured her in moist grass,
He would let her drink in a meadow
    wherein was a watering place.
Out of sight of the cowherd, the herdsman not seeing,
A fierce young bull mounted her, raised her tail(?).* (10)
When her days were ended, her months fulfilled,
The cow knelt down, the cow went into labor.
Her cowherd's face was downcast,
All the herd boys with him felt distress for her.
The herd boys comforted her. (15)
Sin heard her shrieks of anguish, her cries in labor,
The radiance of the moon in heaven heard her cries, ...
He raised his head, he responded,
He sent down two daughters of Anu[2] from heaven.
One brought a jar of oil,
The other brought water of labor. (20)
She rubbed oil from the jar on her brow,
She sprinkled her whole body with water of labor.
A second time she rubbed oil from the jar on her brow,
She sprinkled her whole body with water of labor.
A third time, as she rubbed oil from the jar on her brow, (25)

1. Line corrupt.
2. Variant: "Two protective spirits."

As she sprinkled the front of her body,
The calf fell like a (running) gazelle to the ground.
She called the calf's name "Suckling Calf."
Just as Geme-Sin, the moon-cow, gave birth successfully,
(So) let th(is) young woman who is having difficult labor
    give birth,   (30)
Let th(is) woman with child give birth successfully.[1]

Text: Köcher, BAM 248, iii 10-35; Campbell Thompson, AMT 67/1, iii 1-25; W. G. Lambert, AS 16 (1965), 287-288 obv 20-36; *Iraq* 31 (1969), pl. VI, 51-62.
Edition: Röllig, OrNS 54 (1985), 260-273.
Translation: Farber, TUAT II/2, 274-276 (whence readings used here).
Notes to Text: (10) Farber, TUAT II/2, 275.

(c) RUN HITHER TO ME!

This little spell addresses the baby about to be born.

Run hither to me like a gazelle,
Slip out to me like a little snake!
I, Asalluhi, am the midwife,
I will receive you!

Text: Köcher, BAM 248, iv 2-3.
Edition: Ebeling, *Archiv für Geschichte der Medizin* 14 (1923), 72-73.

1. Variant adds: "May her midwife not be hindered."

(d) THE BOAT

The mother having a difficult birth tosses like a ship in a storm.

(beginning fragmentary)

May her taut mooring rope be slackened,   (1′)
And her battened amidships be opened,
The mooring rope of the boat for the quay of well-being,
The mooring rope of the barge for the quay of health.
May the limbs be relaxed, the sinews loosen,   (5′)
May the sealed womb ease, may the creature come forth,
The separate framework, the human form,
May it come forth soon and see the sunlight!
Like rainfall, may it not turn back,
Like one fallen from a wall, may it not return,   (10′)
Like a leaky trough, may its waters not stay behind.

(Asalluhi carries out the spell)

Text: Köcher, BAM 248, ii 49-59.
Edition: Ebeling, *Archiv für Geschichte der Medizin* 14 (1923), 68-69.

IV.49 TO CALM A BABY

Those plagued by the crying of babies had various magic speeches to deal with the problem; compare also above, II.36 and the study by W. Farber, "Magic and the Cradle, Babylonian and Assyrian Lullabies," *Anthropos* 8 (1990), 139-148.

(a) BE PLACID AS A POND

For the simile, compare III.27b, line 96.

> [Baby, who has aggravated his father], (1)
> [Who has brought tears to his mother's eyes],
> [At whose uproar, at the clamor of whose crying],
> The hairy hero-men were frightened,
> Ishtar got no sleep in her bedchamber,
> May sweet sleep bring you to rest!
> May sleep, life, and release (from care) befall you! (5)
> Burp like a drunkard, wheeze(?) like a barmaid's boy![1]
> Till your mother comes, touches you, and takes you up,
> Be placid as a pond,
> Be still as a pool!
> May sleep befall you, like an oxherd in repose. (10)
> Listen to me, child, you infant,
> You should be asleep, he who sleeps is released (from care).
>
> (The spell is not mine, it is a spell of Ningir[imma, mistress of spells],
> A spell of Gula, mistress of healing,
> A spell of Ea and Asalluhi, may it work for you!)

Text: Craig, ABRT 2, 8 rev 1-13 = Farber, *Baby-Beschwörungen*, pl. 7; Campbell Thompson, CT 51 193.
Edition: Farber, *Baby-Beschwörungen*, 84-89.

1. See II.31, p. 137 note 2.

(b) BE STILL AS SWAMP WATER

Dwel[ler] in darkness, who had not seen the sunrise,
You've come out, [you've seen the sunlight].
Be still as swamp[water],
Sleep like a ba[by gazelle].[1]
Like a boundary stone (protected by) the gods,
May there be no one to disturb you!

Text: Hussey-van Dijk, YOS 11 96, 19-22.
Edition: Farber, *Baby-Beschwörungen*, 96 section 30.

1. Perhaps proverbial, like Italian *come un ghiro*, or perhaps a misunderstanding of *sabītu* "barmaid" (see II.36). Babies coming speedily from the womb are also compared to gazelles; see IV.48c.

(c) LET MOTHER GET HER CHORES DONE

This spell was to be recited three times with a piece of bread set by the baby's head. Then the child was to be rubbed all over with the bread and the bread thrown to a dog. After this, the child was supposed to fall silent.

> The one who dwelt in darkness, where no light shone,   (1)
> He has come out and has seen sunlight.
> Why does he scream till his mother sobs,
> Till, in heaven, Antu herself's in tears?

> "Who is this, that makes such a racket on earth?   (5)
> "If it's a dog, someone give it some food!
> "If it's a bird, someone fling a clod at it!
> "If it's a human child that's angry,
> "Someone cast the spell of Anu and Antu over him!
> "Let his father lie down, to get the rest of his sleep,   (10)
> "Let his mother, who has her chores to do, get her chores done."

> (The spell is not mine, it is a spell of Ea and Asalluhi,
> A spell of Damu and Gula, a spell of Ningirimma, master [of spells].
> They said it to me, I repeated it.)

Text: Ebeling, KAR 114, 1-15; Ebeling-Köcher-Rost, LKA 143, 1-15 = Farber, *Baby-Beschwörungen*, pl. 11.
Edition: Farber, *Baby-Beschwörungen*, 98-100.

IV.50 TO RECAPTURE A RUNAWAY SLAVE

O door of the bedroom, you who are so firm,
I have firmed up your support with oil and wine.
Just as you swing out from your position,
But tu[rn back] the other way to where you were,
(So) may so-and-so, a runaway slave, swing out
But turn back the other way to his master's house.

Text: Ebeling-Köcher-Rost, LKA 135, obv 11-17.
Edition: Ebeling, OrNS 23 (1954), 52-56.

IV.51 TO SECURE BRISK TRADE AT A TAVERN

Taverns, besides providing strong drink, could evidently serve as brothels as well. This incantation is part of a ritual designed to enliven traffic in such an establishment. For Ishtar and strong drink, compare III.26 iv 66.

> O Ishtar of the lands, most valorous of goddesses,
> > this is your bower, rejoice and be glad!   (1)
> Come, enter our house!
> Let your sweet bedmate enter with you,
> May your lover and boyfriend [enter] with you.
> May my lips be white honey, may my hands be charm,
> May the lips, my labia(?), be lips of honey!   (5)
> As birds flutter around a serpent coming out of his hole,
> > so may these people fight over me!
> Seize him, bring him here, make him feel at home,
> > in the bower of Ishtar, the chamber of Ninlil,
> > the herds(?) of Ningizzida.
> May the far-off come around, may the angry come back,
> > may his heart come back to me as if (to) gold.[1]
> Just as when rain has fecundated the earth, plants become plentiful,
> So too may there be many a basket of (sprouting) malt[2] for me!

Text: Ebeling, KAR 144, rev 1-8; F. Lenormant, *Choix de Textes Cunéiformes* ... (Paris, 1873), no. 99 = Boissier, PSBA 23 (1901), 120-121 obv 16 - rev 12.
Edition: Ebeling, RA 49 (1955), 182-183; Zimmern, ZA 32 (1918), 174-175.
Translation: Caplice, SANE 1/1 (1974), 23-24; Farber, TUAT II/2, 280.
Literature: W. Farber, "Associative Magic: Some Rituals, Word Plays, and Philology," JAOS 106 (1986), 447-449.

1. Caplice (SANE 1/1, 24 note 6) suggests "like smoke."
2. This may refer to a "bumper crop" of excited customers; differently Farber (JAOS 106 [1986], 449), who proposes that a double entendre suggesting "proposition" is meant.

E. MISCELLANEOUS

IV.52 WHEN OLD MEN DANCE

Adad-shuma-usur was a prominent scholar of the time of Esarhaddon and Assurbanipal. His letters to his royal patrons are remarkable for their elaborate rhetoric. In this letter, addressed to Assurbanipal, he pleads that a post be given to his son, Urad-Gula. This petition was unsuccessful, for Urad-Gula had offended Assurbanipal as crown prince. No plea could move him, so Urad-Gula languished in poverty and unemployment after Assurbanipal's accession. For the possibility that this family had some connection with the composition of the "Netherworld Vision," see IV.5. For the life of Urad-Gula, see the study by Parpola cited IV.5.

To the king [my] lord, (from) your servant Adad-shuma-[usur]: May it be well with the king [my lord], may Nabu and Marduk bestow ever so many blessings upon the king [my lord]. Assu[r, king of the gods], nominated the [king] my lord for the kingship of the land of Assyria. Adad and Shamash have confirmed to the king my lord, through their truthful extispicy, the kingship of all lands.

The reign is propitious, truthful the days, the years are of justice. Rainfall is plentiful, spring floods surging, the economy is excellent. The gods are well disposed, there is much reverence for the divine, temples are prosperous, the great gods of heaven and netherworld have been prayed to in the time of the king my lord. Old men dance, young men sing, women and girls are happy and joyful, women are being married and rings set upon them, they bear boys and girls, the newborn thrive.

The king my lord has given a new life to the malefactor (and) the man condemned to death, you have released the man imprisoned [for year]s, the man sick for many days has revived. The hungry are filled, the parched anointed, the naked clothed in a garment.

Why should I and Urad-Gula, in the midst of them, be glum and downcast? Now the king my lord has displayed his love for Nineveh to the people, (saying) to the principal citizens, "Bring me your sons, let them be in my service." Urad-Gula is my son; he too should be with them in the service of the king my lord. We too should be joyful and dance along with the people (and) bless the king, my lord.

My eyes dwell upon the king my lord. Of all those who serve in the palace, no one cares about me, there is no one of good will to me to whom I could give a present, (who) would accept it (and) take my part.

May the king my lord take pity upon his servant! Among all (those) people, may I not per[ish]. May my ill-wishers not have what they wish for!

Text: Harper, ABL 2.

Edition: Parpola, LAS 121.

Literature: K. Deller, "Die Briefe des Adad-šuma-uṣur," AOAT 1 (1969), 45-64; F. M. Fales, "L''Ideologico' Adad-šuma-uṣur," *Rendiconti della Classe di Scienze morali, storiche e filologiche, Accademia Nazionale dei Lincei*, ser viii vol xxix, 453-490.

IV.53 SELF-PRAISE OF ISHTAR

These excerpts from a lengthy but badly damaged self-predication of Ishtar may be compared to the earlier fragment II.4. The passages chosen here illustrate Ishtar's prowess in battle, concern for the king, and her love of opposites and reversal (compare also IV.16 Tablet IV line 56 and III.43).

Hurrah for me, hurrah for me,
    the foremost one who [has no] rival, (1)
[I am] Ishtar, who sets kings to fighting, who causes c[onfusion],
[I am she who] gives the brevet, who casts down [   ],
[   ] bow, quiver, and combat.
Anu is my father, Shamash [my] twin, (5)
At my appearance my glow is like the sun's.
All the great gods stand in attendance upon me.
The Igigi-gods p[ress] their lips to the ground.
I hold the staff of the gods,
    [I] grasp the leadrope[1] of heaven in my hands,
[I am she who ca]uses confusion, sets enemies to fighting! (10)

★ ★ ★

I watch over the king in his combat,
[I] cre[ate] good will where there is discord,
[I] cau[se] discord where there is good will.
[I am she who] le[vels] the lands by strife,
I am the charging wild ox that gores.
[I am she wh]o slays the king's enemies! (15)

Text: Ebeling, KAR 331+306.
Edition: C. Frank, *Kultlieder aus der Ischtar-Tamuz-Kreis* (Leipzig, 1939), 36–42.

1. For this concept, see p. 113 note 1.

IV.54 LOVE LYRICS OF NABU AND TASHMETU

These lines are lover's talk between Nabu and Tashmetu on the occasion of their marriage rite. The manuscript dates to the eighth century B.C. Indications of speakers are supplied by the translator; compare II.11.

(singers)

Let whom will trust where he trusts,   (1)
As for us, our trust is in Nabu,
We give ourselves over to Tashmetu.
What is ours is ours: Nabu is our lord,
Tashmetu is the mountain we trust in.   (5)

(singers, to Tashmetu)

Say to her, to her of the wall, to her of the wall, to Tashmetu,
..., take your place in the sanctuary,
May the scent of holy juniper fill the dais.

(Tashmetu?)

Shade of cedar, shade of cedar, shade of cedar
        (is) come for the king's shelter,
Shade of cypress is (for) his great ones,   (10)
The shade of a juniper branch is shelter for my Nabu,
        for my play.

(singers)

Tashmetu dangles a gold ornament in my Nabu's lap,
'My lord, put an earring on me,
'That I may give you pleasure in the garden,
'Nabu, my darling,[1] put an earring on me,   (15)
'That I may make you happy in the [   ].'

---

1. Literally: "my lord," a term of endearment; compare II.9 line 12.

(Nabu)

My [Tashmetu], I put on you bracelets of carnelian,
[   ] you bracelets of carnelian,
I will open [   ]

(gap)

(O Tashmetu), [whose] thighs are a gazelle in the steppe,   (1')
(O Tashmetu), [whose] ankles are a springtime apple,
(O Tashmetu), whose heels are obsidian stone,
(O Tashmetu), whose whole self is a tablet of lapis!

(singers)

Tashmetu, looking voluptuous, entered the bedroom,   (5')
She locked her door, sending home the lapis bolt.
She washes herself, she climbs into bed.
From (one) lapis cup, from (the other) lapis cup, her tears flow,[1]
He wipes away her tears with a tuft of red wool,
There, ask (her), ask (her), find out, find out!   (10')

'Why, why are you so adorned, [my] Tashmetu?'

'So I can [go] to the garden with you, my Nabu.'
'Let me go to the garden, to the garden and [   ]
'Let me go again to the exquisite garden,*
'They would not have me take my place among the wise folk!'[2] (15')

(singers)

I would see with my own eyes the plucking of your fruit,
I would hear with my own ears your birdsong.

---

1. Her eyes; for the metaphor, compare IV.33f.
2. Literally: "counsellors." This activity is to be private, not for the audience in her throne room.

(Nabu)

There, bind fast, hitch up,
Bind your days to the garden and to the Lord,
Bind your nights to the exquisite garden,   (20')
Let my Tashmetu come with me to the garden,
(Though) among wise folk her place be foremost.

(gap)

May she see with her own eyes the plucking of my fruit,
May she hear with her own ears my birdsong,
May she see with her own eyes,
    may she hear with her own ears!   (25')

Text: van Dijk, TIM 9 54.
Edition: Matsushima, ASJ 9 (1987), 143-149, 164-175; Livingstone, *Court Poetry*, 35-37.
Literature: E. Matsushima, "Le rituel hiérogamique de Nabu," ASJ 9 (1987), 131-175.
Notes to Text: (rev 14') von Soden, WdO 22 (1991), 191.

IV.55 ELEGY FOR A WOMAN DEAD IN CHILDBIRTH

This poem tells the story of a woman's death in childbirth as if she were narrating it herself. Her pleas and those of her husband fail to move Belet-ili, goddess of birth.

Why are you cast adrift, like a boat in midstream,
Your planking stoven, your mooring rope cut?
With shrouded face, you cross the river of the City.[1]

How could I not be cast adrift,
     how could my mooring rope not be cut?
The day I carried the fruit, how happy I was,
Happy was I, happy my husband.
The day I went into labor, my face grew overcast,
The day I gave birth, my eyes grew cloudy.

I prayed to Belet-ili with my hands opened out,
'You are mother of those who give birth, save my life!'
Hearing this, Belet-ili shrouded her face,
'You [ ], why do you keep praying to me?'

[My husband, who lov]ed me, uttered a cry,
'[ ] me, the wife I adore!'

(gap)

[All ...] those days I was with my husband,
While I lived with him who was my lover,
Death was creeping stealthily into my bedroom,
It forced me from my house,
It cut me off from my lover,
It set my foot toward the land from which I shall not return.

Text: Strong, BA 2 (1894), 634; photo in R. Albertz, *Persönliche Frommigkeit und offizielle Religion* (Stuttgart, 1978), plate after p. 54.
Edition: Reiner, *Poetry*, 86-89; Livingstone, *Court Poetry*, 37-39.
Translation: Hecker, TUAT II/5, 780-781.
Literature: Reiner, "An Assyrian Elegy," in *Poetry*, 85-93.

1. Assur is meant.

Glossary of Proper Names

In general, readers seeking more information on the items in this glossary are referred to the appropriate articles in the RLA or WdM.

Adad: God of thunderstorms and rainfall, see III.34, 51; IV.2a(1).

Addu: Another form of Adad.

Agade: Capital city of the Sargonic empire, located in northern Babylonia. It was noted for its wealth and magnificence during the Sargonic period, but was of little importance thereafter.

Agushaya: Form or attribute of Ishtar, referring to a whirling dance, as if in battle, see II.6.

Akkad: Originally northern Babylonia; in later literary texts used anachronistically to refer to Babylonia as a whole.

Amurru: God of the western nomads whose home was in the region of Jebel Bishri.

Annunitum: See Ishtar-Annunitum.

Anshar: Primeval deity, father of Anu the sky god. In late Assyrian texts artificially equated with Assur in order to afford Assur primacy over the Babylonian Marduk, see III.17, IV.4b.

Antu: Wife of Anu the sky god.

Anu: Sky god, head of pantheon. Father of Adad, Enlil, Ishtar (in some traditions), and Nisaba, among others. His principal sanctuary was at Uruk.

Anunna-gods: A grouping of the gods, originally the great Sumerian gods. In some texts, such as II.40, they may be superior to another group of gods called the Igigi-gods; in other texts the terms are used in parallelism. In some texts it refers to gods of the netherworld, see III.17 Tablet VI.

Anzu: A monstrous bird, subject of various mythological stories, see III.22.

Apsu: A zone of fresh water found under the earth, domain of Ea/Enki, god of wisdom. Personified as husband of Tiamat in the Creation Epic, III.17.

Arbela: Modern Irbil, important Assyrian city and cult center of Ishtar, see IV.6.

Ardat-lili: A spirit or demon that haunted and tempted at night, see IV.39a.

Asalluhi: Son of Ea/Enki, god of incantations, often synonymous with Marduk, see IV.27, III.17 Tablet VI line 147.

Ashgi: A little-known Sumerian deity.

Assur: God of the city Assur and of the land of Assyria, after the late second millennium a warlike figure. In some texts referred to as "Assyrian Enlil," that is, chief deity of Assyria, see III.1, IV.2a(2), 4b.

Atrahasis: "Super-wise," Mesopotamian flood hero, see II.39.

Aya: Goddess of dawn; wife of Shamash, the sun god.

Baltil: Name for a district of the city Assur sometimes used *pars pro toto* for the city itself, see p. 227 note 4.

Bel: "Lord," often a name for Marduk.

Belet-ili: "Mistress of the Gods," name for the birth goddess.

Belet-seri: "Mistress of the Steppe," wife of Amurru and scribe of the netherworld.

Black-headed folk: A general term for Mesopotamians, as opposed to inhabitants of other lands.

Borsippa: Important city south of Babylon, cult center of Nabu.

Bunene: Courier and chariot driver of Shamash the sun god.

Calah: Ancient name for the Assyrian capital city Nimrud.

Cutha: City in Babylonia, cult center of Nergal.

Dagan: God at home on the Middle and Upper Euphrates.

Damgalnunna: Another name for Damkina, wife of Ea/Enki.

Damkina: Wife of Ea/Enki, mother of Marduk.

Damu: God of healing and healing magic.

Der: City on the eastern edge of Mesopotamia, cult center of Ishtaran.

Dilmun: Ancient name for Bahrein, important commercial entrepôt sometimes portrayed in Sumerian tradition as a paradisiacal place.

Dumuzi: Akkadian Tammuz, shepherd god, lover of Inanna, netherworld deity whose death was annually mourned, vegetation deity, specifically of the spring grass, see III.35, IV.26.

Dunnu: A small city in Babylonia.

Dur-Kurigalzu: Important Babylonian city of the Kassite period.

Ea: Sumerian Enki, god of wisdom, father of Marduk, noted in Mesopotamian tradition for his tricks and clever solutions to problems, as well as for his knowledge of magical lore, see III.36, IV.2a(3). The "daughters of Ea" (see I.7) were beings who assisted in magical cleansing.

Ebabbar: Temple of Shamash at Sippar.

E-engurra: Temple of Enki at Eridu.

Egalmah: Temple of Gula at Isin.

Ekishnugal: Temple of Sin at Ur.

Ekur: Temple of Enlil at Nippur, sometimes used as a general term for "temple."

Elam: Land in southwestern Iran, usually portrayed in Akkadian literary texts as hostile and threatening to Babylonia.

Emashmash: Temple of Ishtar at Nineveh.

Emeslam: Temple of Nergal at Cutha.

Enbilulu: Sumerian god of irrigation, used as a name of Marduk in Creation Epic, (III.17) Tablet VII.

Enki: See Ea.

Enlil: Chief god of Sumerian pantheon, whose domain was the earth and whose major cult center was at Nippur, lord of destinies and responsibilities of other gods, see III.38.

Enmeduranki: Antediluvian king of Sippar, a city in Babylonia.

Ennugi: Netherworld deity.

Ereshkigal: Goddess and queen of the netherworld, see III.19.

Eridu: City in Sumer, cult center for Ea/Enki, sometimes portrayed as the primeval city of Mesopotamia.

Erra: God of scorched earth, of battle, violence, and destruction, see IV.16.

Errakal: A name for Nergal.

Esagila: Sanctuary of Marduk in Babylon.

Esharra: (1) Region in heaven, see III.17 Tablet VI; (2) Temple of Assur in the city Assur; (3) Name for the temple of Enlil in Nippur.

Etemenanki: Part of Marduk temple complex at Babylon.

Eunir: Temple of Enki at Eridu.

Ezida: Temple of Nabu at Borsippa.

Gilgamesh: Sumerian king of Uruk, subject of epic poem wherein he tries to escape death, see IV.20.

Girra: God of fire, see III.40.

Gula: Goddess of healing, see III.25, 42.

Gutium/Gutian: In Akkadian literature, a name used anachronistically for barbarian peoples, especially to the north and east of Mesopotamia.

Hana: City and country on the middle Euphrates.

Hanish: Divine servant of Adad the storm god.

Hendursagga: Sumerian deity equated with Ishum, a fire god, in IV.16 Tablet I.

Hubur: River in the netherworld, personified in the Creation Epic (III.17).

Hursagkalamma: Temple of Ishtar at Kish.

Igigi-gods: Generally a group of great gods of heaven; in II.39 used of a group of gods inferior to the Anunna-gods.

Inanna: See Ishtar.

Innin(i):   Name for Inanna/Ishtar.

Irnina: Name for Ishtar.

Ishara: Name for Ishtar.

Ishtar: Sumerian Inanna, goddess of war, sex, and fertility; astral deity (Venus), see II.1; III.4, 18, 26–28, 43; IV.3, 4c, 10a, 22, 54.

Ishtar-Annunitum: Militant aspect of Ishtar.

Ishtaran: Healing deity, with cult center at Der.

Ishum: Herald and counsellor god, especially to Nergal, fire god, protective of mankind, see IV.5, 16.

Kalkal: Servant god to Enlil.

Kassites: A non-Mesopotamian people who took power in Babylonia and ruled there during the second half of the second millennium B.C.

Kesh: Sanctuary of the birth goddess in Sumer, see II.3.

Kish:	Important city in northern Babylonia, in Mesopotamian tradition seat of the world's first kings.
Kullab:	City in Sumer, close to or part of Uruk.
Lamashtu:	Demon specializing in the harming of children, see I.6, II.31.
Larak:	A city in Sumer.
Lugalbanda:	King of Uruk, father or ancestor of Gilgamesh, subject of several Sumerian epic poems.
Lugalgirra:	Warrior and netherworld god.
Mama, Mami:	Names for the birth goddess.
Marduk:	National god of Babylon, credited in the Babylonian Creation Epic (III.17) with reorganization of the universe with Babylon at the center of the world, see III.13, 29-30, 37, 44, 45f(1); IV.4d, 7, 8a-e, g, 9, 10b, c, 27.
Meslamtaea:	Name for Nergal.
Muati:	Husband of Nanay, goddess of love, see II.10.
Mummu:	Creative power or intelligence, personified in Creation Epic (III.17) as an advisor to Apsu.
Nabu:	Son of Marduk, a scholar god, patron of scribal arts, see III.31, 45; IV.2a(4), 4f, 8f, g, k, 11, 54.
Namrasit:	"Brightly-Rising-God," epithet of Sin, the moon god.
Namtar:	Netherworld deity, god of death by plague.
Nanay:	Goddess of love, see II.2, 10; IV.2b.
Nanna:	See Sin.
Nanshe:	Sumerian goddess, daughter of Enki.
Nergal:	Netherworld deity, king of the netherworld, see III.19, 46; IV.5.
Nineveh:	Assyrian capital city, near present-day Mosul.
Ningal:	Wife of Sin, mother of Shamash, see IV.2f(5).
Ningirimma:	Goddess of exorcism.
Ningirsu:	Patron deity of Lagash, a vegetation and warrior god later equated with Ninurta.
Ningizzida:	In Adapa story, a door-keeper in heaven.
Ninhursag:	Mother goddess.
Ninkarrak:	Healing goddess.

Ninlil: Wife of Enlil, see IV.1b.

Ninmah: Mother goddess, see IV.8h.

Ninpanigingarra: Name for Ninurta.

Ninshiku: Epithet of Enki of uncertain meaning, here translated "leader."

Ninshubur: Courier deity.

Nintinugga: Healing deity, see III.25.

Nintu: Birth goddess.

Ninurta: Warrior and vegetation deity, subject of Sumerian narrative poems dealing with his exploits, most celebrated of which was his defeat of the monstrous bird, Anzu, see III.47; IV.2a(6).

Nippur: Sumerian city sacred to the god Enlil, important cultural and religious center.

Nisaba: Grain goddess and patron of scribal arts.

Nudimmud: Name for Ea/Enki.

Nunamnir: Name for Enlil.

Nusku: Courier deity, see III.48.

Palil: Protective deity.

Pabilsag: Son of Enlil, equated with Ninurta.

Purushhanda: City in Anatolia famous for its wealth and commerce.

Qingu: Deity elevated by Tiamat to kingship in the Creation Epic (III.17) and slain by Marduk.

Saltu: "Discord," a monster created by Enki to discomfit the warlike Ishtar, see II.6.

Sarpanitu: Wife of Marduk.

Sealand: Ancient name for marshy regions in the south of Mesopotamia, sometimes seat of a royal dynasty.

Shakkan: God of cattle.

Shala: Wife of Adad or Dagan, mother of Girra.

Shamash: Sun god, patron of truth, justice, and divination, see III.32, 50, 53; IV.4e, 8i, j, 10d, e.

Shazu: "He-who-knows-the-inside (of things)," a name of Marduk in III.17 Tablet VII lines 35ff., but also applied to Nabu in III.45e line 8.

Sherua: Goddess of dawn.

Shi-laba: "She-is-a-lioness," perhaps a form of the warlike Ishtar.

Shullat: Servant god of Adad.

Shuzianna: Little-known Sumerian deity.

Sin: Moon god, see III.52; IV.2a(7), 10f, 48b.

Sippar: City in Babylonia, cult center of Shamash.

Sirish: Goddess of fermentation.

Subartu: Third-millennium term for northern Mesopotamia; in later texts used anachronistically for Assyria.

Sumer: Southern Babylonia.

Sutaeans: Nomadic people portrayed as destructive and barbaric in Akkadian literature, see IV.16 Tablet IV line 54.

Tammuz: See Dumuzi.

Tashmetu: Wife of Nabu, see IV.54.

Tiamat: Ocean goddess, see III.17.

Tutu: In Akkadian literature, used as a name for Marduk, see III.17 Tablet VII line 9.

Umshu: Deified day in Old Akkadian period.

Ur: Sumerian city, cult center of Sin.

Uruk: Sumerian city, cult center of Anu and Ishtar.

Index of Texts Translated

This index is keyed to Borger, HKL where possible. For abbreviations used here not found in the List of Abbreviations, see Borger, HKL 2, xiff.

Select Bibliography

ANTHOLOGIES OF TRANSLATIONS

Bottéro, J., and Kramer, S. N., *Lorsque les dieux faisaient l'homme, Mythologie mésopotamienne* (Paris, 1989). Translations of Sumerian and Akkadian myths, with substantial introductions and commentaries, *nonpareil*.

Dalley, S., *Mesopotamian Myths* (Oxford, 1989).
Translations of Nos. II.39, III.17-20a, 21, 22, and IV.19 of this anthology, with brief introductions and notes. Includes Gilgamesh Epic and one short cosmological text not treated here.

Kaiser, O., ed., *Texte aus der Umwelt des alten Testaments* (Gütersloh, 1982-). Authoritative translations of Sumerian and Akkadian texts; introductions and notes mostly of a bibliographical and philological nature.

Kovacs, M., *The Epic of Gilgamesh* (Stanford, 1989). Translation of the Gilgamesh Epic with introduction and notes for the general reader.

Pritchard, J., ed., *Ancient Near Eastern Texts Relating to the Old Testament*[3]. (Princeton, 1969).
Collection of translations from various ancient Near Eastern literatures. Akkadian literary works found there, Part I, 60-119, retranslated for this work are as follows: "Creation Epic" = III.17, "Creation of Man by the Mother Goddess" is now known to belong to Atrahasis = II.39; "Worm and the Toothache" = IV.43; "Adapa" = III.20a; "Nergal and Ereshkigal" = III.19; "Atrahasis" = II.39; "Descent of Ishtar" = III.18; "A Vision of the Nether World" = IV.5; "Myth of Zu" = III.22; "Etana" = III.21; "Legend of Sargon" = IV.19. In addition, "Naram-Sin in the Cedar Mountain" (p. 268) is treated here as I.1.

Seux, M.-J., *Hymnes et prières aux dieux de babylone et d'assyrie* (Paris, 1976).
Translations, with philological notes, of 247 hymns and prayers, 129 of which are included in this anthology.

STUDIES IN ASSYRIAN AND BABYLONIAN LITERATURE

Bottéro, J., *Mythes et rites de babylone* (Paris, 1985).
Collection of essays primarily concerned with Mesopotamian religious literature.

_____, "Symptomes, signes, écritures" in J. P. Vernant, ed., *Divination et Rationalité* (Paris, 1974), 70-197.
Authoritative survey of Mesopotamian divination.

Buccellati, G., "Towards a Formal Typology of Akkadian Similes," AOAT 25 (1976), 59-70.

Cooper, J., "Gilgamesh Dreams of Enkidu: The Expansion and Dilution of Narrative," *Studies Finkelstein*, 139-144.
Together with the following, study of how Akkadian narrative texts were altered in succeeding periods.

_____, "Symmetry and Repetition in Akkadian Narrative," JAOS 97 (1977), 508-512.

Finkelstein, J. J., "Mesopotamian Historiography," PAPS 107/6 (1963), 461-472.

Foster, B. R., "On Authorship in Akkadian Literature," *Annuario del Istituto Orientale di Napoli* 51/1 (1990), 17-32.
_____, "Humor and Cuneiform Literature," JANES 4 (1974), 69-85.

Hallo, W. W., "New Viewpoints on Cuneiform Literature," IEJ 12 (1962), 13-26.
Survey, with bibliography, of various issues in the study of cuneiform literature.

_____, "Akkadian Apocalypses," IEJ 16 (1966), 231-242.
Discussion of prophecy and apocalyptic in Akkadian.

Hecker, K., *Untersuchungen zur akkadischen Epik* AOATS 8 (1974).
Authoritative study of Akkadian poetics, intended for the specialist.

_____, "Tradition und Originalität in der altorientalischen Literatur," ArOr 45 (1977), 245-258.

_____, and Sommerfeld, W., eds., *Keilschriftliteraturen, xxxii rencontre assyriologique internationale* (1985), *Berliner Beiträge zum Vorderen Orient* 6 (Berlin, 1986). Collection of papers on Akkadian literary topics.

Jacobsen, T., *The Treasures of Darkness* (New Haven, 1976). Contains studies of Creation and Gilgamesh Epics.

Komoróczy, G., "Akkadian Epic Poetry and Its Sumerian Sources," AASH 23 (1975), 41-63.

Lambert, W. G., "Ancestors, Authors, and Canonicity," JCS 11 (1957), 1-14, 112.

_____, *Babylonian Wisdom Literature* (Oxford, 1960). Edition of seventeen extended Akkadian literary works and numerous proverbs and short compositions, most of which are found in this anthology. The principal omission here is the fragmentary group of fables (BWL, Chapter 7), from which IV.25 has been excerpted.

_____, "A Catalogue of Texts and Authors," JCS 16 (1962), 59-77.

"Literary Style in First Millennium Mesopotamia," JAOS 88 (1968), 123-132. Edition and study of Late period texts, two of which are included here as III.45f.

_____, "The Cosmology of Sumer and Babylon," in C. Blacker and M. Loewe, eds., *Ancient Cosmologies* (London, 1975).

_____, "Zum Forschungsstand der sumerisch-babylonischen Literaturgeschichte," ZDMG Supplement III,1 (1977), 64-73.

Liverani, M., "La concezione dell'universo" in S. Moscati, ed., *L'Alba della Civiltà* (Torino, 1976), 3: 439-521. Includes discussion of Egypt, Syria/Palestine, Anatolia. Deals with concepts of space, time, cosmology, the past, causality, and classification, with illustratory excerpts from Akkadian literature.

Livingstone, A., *Court Poetry and Literary Miscellanea*, State Archives of Assyria 3 (Helsinki, 1989).
Edition of fifty-two texts, twelve of which appear in this anthology.

Longman, T., *Fictional Akkadian Autobiography* (Winona Lake, IN, 1991).
Literary study of fifteen Akkadian texts, including III.7b, 8-10, 12b, 13, and IV.19, recommend to general reader.

M. Mindlin, *et al.*, eds., *Figurative Language in the Ancient Near East* (London, 1987).

Oppenheim, A. L., *Ancient Mesopotamia: Portrait of a Dead Civilization*[2] (Chicago, 1977).
Survey of Mesopotamian civilization, intended for the general reader, but of more interest to a specialist.

Reiner, E., "La Magie babylonienne," in *Le Monde du sorcier* (Paris, 1966), 69-98.
Essay on Mesopotamian magic and exorcism.

_____, "Die akkadische Literatur," in W. Röllig, ed., *Neues Handbuch der Literaturwissenschaft, Altorientalische Literaturen* (Wiesbaden, 1978), 151-210.
Concise survey, with excerpts and bibliography.

_____, *Your Thwarts in Pieces, Your Mooring Rope Cut, Poetry from Babylonia and Assyria* (Ann Arbor, MI, 1985).
Essays on selected Akkadian literary works (see nos. III.14, 18, 19, 32; IV.55), with attention to poetics, recommend to general reader.

_____, "First-Millennium Akkadian Literature," CAH[3] 3/2 293-321.
Excellent survey, with bibliography, recommend to general reader.

Röllig, W., "Volksliteratur in mesopotamischer Überlieferung," CRRAI 32 (1985), 81-87.

_____, "Literatur, Akkadisch," RLA 6, 48-66.
General survey, with bibliography.

Tigay, J., *The Evolution of the Gilgamesh Epic* (Philadelphia, 1982).
Close study of the text history of a major Akkadian narrative poem, showing how the text changed and evolved over time.

von Soden, W., "Das Problem der zeitlichen Einordnung akkadischer Literaturwerke," MDOG 85 (1953), 14-26.

_____, "Zweisprachigkeit in der geistigen Kultur Babyloniens," *Sitzungsberichte der österreichischen Akademie der Wissenschaften, Philologisch-Historische Klasse* 235/1 (1960).

_____, "Das Fragen nach der Gerechtigkeit Gottes im alten Orient," MDOG 96 (1965), 41-59.

_____, "Untersuchungen zur babylonischen Metrik," ZA 71 (1982), 161-204.
Study of metrics of Akkadian poetry, with proposed scansion of selected passages, for the specialist.

Wilcke, W., "Die Anfänge der akkadischen Epen," ZA 67 (1977), 153-216.
Study of how selected Akkadian narrative poems begin, for the specialist.